Assessment with Projective Techniques

A. I. Rabin, Ph.D., is professor of psychology and former director of the Psychological Clinic at Michigan State University. He also served as professor of psychology at the City University of New York and visiting professor at Aarhus University (Denmark) and the Hebrew and Bar-Ilan universities in Israel. He has been guest lecturer and colloquium speaker at a number of other universities in the United States and abroad. In addition to many contributions to the professional periodical literature, he published several books, including *Projective Techniques with Children* (co-editor), *Projective Techniques in Personality Assessment, Growing up in the Kibbutz,* (Springer) *Clinical Psychology: Issues of the Seventies* and most recently—*Further Explorations in Personality* (co-editor). From 1965 to 1973 he served as a member of the board of consulting editors of the *Journal of Consulting and Clinical Psychology,* and since 1969 has been serving as a consulting editor of the *Journal of Personality Assessment.* Professor Rabin was the recipient of the Distinguished Contribution Award of the Society for Personality Assessment in 1977.

Assessment with Projective Techniques

A Concise Introduction

A. I. Rabin, Ph.D.
Editor

Springer Publishing Company
New York

Springer Publishing Company, Inc.
536 Broadway
New York, NY 10012

89 90 / 10 9 8 7 6

Library of Congress Cataloging in Publication Data
Main entry under title:

Assessment with projective techniques.

Edition for 1968 published under title: Projective techniques in personality assessment.
Bibliography: p.
Includes index.
1. Projective techniques—Addresses, essays,
lectures. I. Rabin, Albert I. II. Rabin,
Albert I. Projective techniques in personality
assessment. [DNLM: 1. Personality assessment.
2. Projective technics. WM 145A 844]
BF698.7.R3 1981   155.2'84   80-26229
ISBN 0-8261-3550-1

Printed in the United States of America

Contents

Preface

In 1968, Springer Publishing Company published a sizable volume, which I edited—*Projective Techniques in Personality Assessment*. The 19 chapters, authored by many outstanding authorities in the field, and the 638 pages covered the area of "projectives" intensively as well as extensively. The book has been the standard work for over a decade. It served as the main source for specialized courses on projective methods. In many instances it served as the sole text for such courses.

In recent years, more general and global courses in assessment have taken over and, in many instances, replaced the specialized ones. There seems to be a need for a briefer survey of projective techniques that would cover a more circumscribed area of specifics, yet present a broad general introduction. It is in response to this need that the present volume was prepared.

Two important features characterize this book: (1) it is a more *concise* introduction—about half of the length of the earlier book, (2) it contains updated material and takes into account recent developments. Thus, the first introductory chapter is an expanded and updated version of the introduction to the field. Another chapter was entirely rewritten. Two new chapters were especially written for this briefer introduction, while two more chapters were updated. All in all, eight of the chapters were retained in one form or another. Some theoretical and statistical material was eliminated because it was not crucial to an introduction to projective techniques. Also deleted were chapters concerned with rather specialized techniques which are either spinoffs of the major methods (Rorschach, TAT) or have lost their popularity and fallen into disuse.

Hence, the present book is a practical introducton to projective methods. It will whet the students' appetite for further exploration in more encyclopedic volumes of the kind represented by the earlier *Projective Techniques in Personality Assessment*.

A. I. Rabin, Ph.D.

Contributors

Joel Allison

Lecturer
Yale University

Samuel J. Beck

Professorial Lecturer (retired)
University of Chicago

Sidney J. Blatt

Professor of Psychology
Yale University

Emanuel F. Hammer

Adjunct Associate Professor of
Psychology
New York University

Wayne H. Holtzman

Professor of Psychology & Education
University of Texas
President, Hogg Foundation

Bertram P. Karon

Professor of Psychology
Michigan State University

Walter G. Klopfer

Professor of Psychology
Portland State University
Executive Editor, *Journal of
Personality Assessment*

David Levine

Late Professor of Psychology
University of Nebraska

A. I. Rabin

Professor of Psychology
Michigan State University

Jerome L. Singer

Professor of Psychology
Yale University

Zoli Zlotogorski

Ph.D. candidate in Clinical
Psychology
Michigan State University

1

Projective Methods:
A Historical Introduction

A. I. Rabin

Methods of personality assessment that were to become known as projective techniques developed gradually over a long period of time. It is even tempting to paraphrase Ebbinghaus' remark about psychology (Boring, 1929), that projective techniques have a "long past but a short history." The penchant of man for imposing his own ideas and interpretations upon unstructured stimuli was noted, and occasionally recorded, centuries ago. For example, Leonardo da Vinci reports in his *Introduction to the Painter* concerning the associative experiences possible as a result of viewing a blot made by a sponge upon the wall: ". . . various experiences can be seen in such a blot, provided one wants to find them in it—human heads, various animals, battles, cliffs, seas, clouds or forests and other things . . ." (quoted in Zubin, et al., 1965, p. 167). Also mentioned by Leonardo is the possibility of "hearing" words when a bell is ringing. The stimuli are, therefore, not restricted to any one sensory modality as to their potential to evoke the associative experiences.

Some centuries later, in 1857, Justinus Kerner published a volume entitled *Die Klecksographie*. In it the author reproduced a series of blots accompanied by rhymes expounding their meaning. Many of the blots were described "as scenes of Hades" (Tulchin, 1940; Zubin, et al., 1965).

These are instances from the pre-scientific or pre-experimental era which exemplify the potential of unstructured stimuli to induce a wide array of associations and responses once the subject gives himself free rein and permits his imagination to range untrammeled by reality considerations. Towards the end of the 19th century, and at the beginning of the 20th, psychologists attempted to exploit visual stimuli, inkblots, and pictures, in a more systematic and experimental fashion. These efforts were briefly described by Tulchin (1940) early in the era of the projective techniques.

EXPERIMENTAL EFFORTS

In 1895 Binet and Henri suggested the use of a series of inkblots in the investigation of visual imagination. About the same time, in 1897, Dearborn at Harvard proposed the use of inkblots in experimental psychology. "Content of consciousness," "memory," "qualitative and quantitative imagination," etc., were some of the areas to be investigated by means of the inkblots. In a paper the following year, he actually reports detailed findings accompanied by some interesting observations concerning the problem of inhibition in producing responses and the important effects of early experience upon the imaginative productions.

A number of other studies using inkblots followed during the subsequent two decades into the 20th century. Stella Sharp (in 1899) used inkblots as a test of imagination. She evolved a typology on the basis of the responses obtained. The "constructive or imaginative type" organized details into wholes, whereas the "matter-of-fact or scientific type" exhibited primarily analytic activity. Kirkpatrick (in 1900) noted age differences in the performance of children responding to inkblots. Pyle's (1913–1915) studies of several groups of children centered on the concept of association. He employed 20 inkblots which he felt tested the same kind of ability as the association test (which will be mentioned later in this section). He also reported differences due to age, sex, brightness, and race. In 1917 Parsons studied the range of associations in boys and girls, classified the content of the associations to a standard series of inkblots, and reported some detailed age and sex differences. The standard series of inkblots she employed was contained in Whipple's *Manual of Mental and Physical Tests,* published in 1914–15. Other early experimenters with inkblots were F. C. Bartlett in England, F. L. Wells in the United States, and Rybakow in Russia.

From the above we may note that considerable research interest was focused on the medium of inkblots prior to the time when Hermann Rorschach first published his test results in the *Psychodiagnostik* (1921).

The early concern with imaginative productions, such as stories told to pictures, which heralded the arrival of what was to be called later the Thematic Apperception Test (TAT), was much more limited and circumscribed (Zubin, et al., 1965). In 1905 Binet and Simon used pictures to stimulate verbal responses from which intellectual development was assessed. In 1906 Brittain studied differences in stories told by boys and girls; he noted systematic differences in content and related them to the differences in the living conditions of the sexes at that time, especially to restrictions of the social environment. Libby studied, in 1908, the imagination of adolescents via their responses to a picture, dealing primarily with objectiveness and subjectiveness in the stories as a function of age. Schwartz (1932) used pictures as an aid in interviewing delinquent boys. This is, perhaps, the first "clinical" employment of pictures: they were used to gain rapport and facilitate the acquisition of more extensive information about the subjects. A possible additional precursor of the TAT is Van Lennep's Four Picture Test (1951), which is traced by its originator to the year 1930.

Another method which is frequently included among the projective techniques is the Word Association Test. This method has a distinguished experimental and clinical history—beginning with Galton, then in Wundt's laboratory, Kraepelin's clinic, and Jung's consultation room. In this method, the stimulus is a word, not a picture or an inkblot. Moreover, the presentation is usually auditory, not visual. The subject is asked to respond with the first word that comes to his mind. Here the associative processes (and their inhibitions) are studied. This method is thought to have had considerable influence on the subsequent development and theoretical rationale of a number of projective methods.

It is not the purpose of this section to trace the earliest origins of *all* of the methods which have become known as projective but to sample some of the trends, especially the ones that have anticipated the development of the two major techniques—the Rorschach and the TAT. We are now ready for an account of the development of some of the major projective methods proper—the dominant techniques of the present time, which are described in greater detail in other parts of the book and in the chapters that bear their names.

METHOD AND PERSONALITY THEORY

Hitherto, our brief overview of experiments with inkblots, pictures, and words has indicated that the findings were limited in scope. They dealt with such concepts as mental content, imagination, individual differences, and so on. No attempts were made to describe *personality*. This is due, in part, to the status of personality as a concept and a theory during that period. No encompassing concept or psychological theory of personality was yet available. Personality was not part of the psychology of that period. It was at the advent of psychoanalysis and its crystallization as a full-fledged personality theory that the various methods found a conceptual home. The data obtained, and their interrelationships, assumed greater meaning and significance. It is in the beginning of this new era in psychology and psychiatry, in the 1920s, that we see the true roots of development in the field of projective techniques.

RORSCHACH'S INKBLOTS

The relationship of the earlier work with inkblots to Rorschach's test is not at all clear. It is actually not known whether Hermann Rorschach was at all acquainted with the work of his predecessors. After experimenting for some time with various geometrical forms of different colors, he was led to prefer the less structured inkblots and finally selected a series of ten. The results of his experiments are reported in his monograph *Psychodiagnostik* (1921), which is subtitled "Methodology and results of a perceptual-diagnostic experiment (interpretation of accidental forms)."

Whereas previous experiments with inkblots were primarily concerned with imagination and associational content, Rorschach stressed the formal characteristics and determinants of the responses, the modes of perception, and their relationship to personality and psychopathology. He was quite modest in presenting his findings, with normals and with several neuropsychiatric groups, as "provisional" and as an "experiment"; also, he introduced the work by pointing out its primarily empirical nature and its incomplete theoretical foundation. Yet he points out the value of the method, both as a test and as a research tool.

It is not the purpose of this presentation to discuss the details of Rorschach's empirical hypotheses. This will be done elsewhere in this volume. Suffice it to say, however, that the influence of Freud in the interpretive process and the more direct reliance upon Jungian psychology are evident in the *Psychodiagnostik*. The psychoanalytic influence is even more clearly discerned in Rorschach's posthumous paper (1924) published by Oberholzer. In it the congruence between the personality description based on the test (blind analysis) and the one based on psychoanalytic material, obtained by Oberholzer, is illustrated in detail.

Interest in the Rorschach technique was far from immediate. During the first ten years following the publication of Rorschach's work, only 38 studies dealing with the method appeared in the professional literature. However, in the 1930s there was a marked increase of work with the method; by 1940 Rorschach publications numbered 251 (Krugman, 1940). The small trickle burst into a veritable flood. By 1945 there was a bibliography of 786 Rorschach items, and the years 1945–1955 produced nearly 1900 additional items (Klopfer, et al., 1956). This phenomenal escalation in research activity stimulated by Rorschach's test shows few signs of abatement (Rabin & Hurley, 1964). In 1972 the number of Rorschach items reached beyond 4200 and is much higher in 1980 (Buros, 1972). It may also be mentioned, parenthetically, that the bulk of the Rorschach publications appeared in the United States.

David M. Levy imported the Rorschach from Switzerland around 1925 and introduced it to Samuel J. Beck, whose lifelong career since his first publication on the method in 1930 has been intimately connected with it. Beck's primary efforts include the first Rorschach manual in English (Beck, 1937)—an *Introduction to the Rorschach Method*. Around the same period, in the early and middle 1930s, Marguerite Hertz, Bruno Klopfer, and others began to teach the Rorschach and write extensively concerning it. Under the leadership of Klopfer, a periodical devoted exclusively to Rorschach work, *The Rorschach Research Exchange*, was founded. The Research Exchange was eventually transformed into the *Journal of Personality Assessment*, which is vigorously continuing publication as the organ of the Society for Personality Assessment—the heir of the Rorschach Institute—with a membership of over 800 at the time of this writing.

Thus, the Rorschach was not only the first major clinical and research instrument to be classified later as a projective technique, but it was also most important in spearheading the projective techniques movement. Since the Rorschach method was not readily acceptable to university psychology departments, most of the instruction in the administration and interpretation of the test proceeded in special workshops and institutes. This trend prompted the projective movement to be viewed as a movement of dissent, a deviant from psychology's "establishment." Hence, a separate and autonomous organization, concerned with the new methods, was established.

MURRAY'S TAT

In 1935 the Rorschach was joined by a native son—the Thematic Apperception Test (Morgan & Murray, 1935). This method, according to the authors, "is based upon the well-recognized fact that when a person interprets an ambiguous social situation he is apt to expose his own personality. . . ." Unlike the Rorschach, the first publication was more modest in its dimensions, and the pictures themselves, portraying the "ambiguous social situations," were revised several times before the final series, as we know it today, was established.

In the context of the epoch-making *Explorations in Personality* (Murray, et al., 1938) the TAT, although only one of many methods described in the volume, gained its stature, significance, and subsequent popularity. The "Explorations," which was the culmination of the efforts of a number of psychologists under the leadership of Henry Murray, set out to construct a *theory* of personality as well as *techniques* for its assessment. Thus, the TAT, unlike the mainly empirical Rorschach, was from the start embedded in a theoretical framework which was markedly influenced by the dynamic principles of psychoanalysis. With the orientation that "personalities constitute the subject matter of psychology," Murray and his associates rejected the exclusive positivism, peripheralism, and elementarism which dominated the psychology of that period. They advocated a more dynamic approach to personality, one that is concerned with "drives, urges, needs, or instincts." This revolt against the traditional, academic, and arid psychology of that period started a new era in American psychology. Of the numerous techniques pressed into the service of new theory construction expressing the disaffection with the extant psychology, the TAT became the main survivor and the most durable instrument.

The TAT did not remain exclusively wedded to the conceptual matrix from which it arose. The standard manual (Murray, 1943) served as a starting point. Furthermore, the instrument proved to be most flexible, and a host of scoring methods, representing different orientations, have been spawned (Murstein, 1963). Discussion of these developments would lead us far afield and is beyond the scope of the present introductory chapter.

The flexibility of the TAT not only engendered a variety of approaches to scoring and interpretation, but also facilitated its ready adaptation to the clinic as well as to the research laboratory. A tremendous research and clinical literature has accumulated in which the TAT is the prime instrument. Moreover, numerous derivative methods, based on the design of the TAT, have been created and fruitfully applied and investigated.

THE ADVENT OF "PROJECTIVE TECHNIQUES"

As noted earlier, actual experimental application of various unstructured stimuli for the purposes of personality assessment by psychologists is traceable to the end of the 19th century. However, the term *projective techniques* or *methods* and the placement of a number of extant modes of personality diagnosis under one umbrella did not take place until the late 1930s and the early 1940s.

It was in the groundbreaking volume *Explorations in Personality* (1938) that Murray first introduced the term *projection tests*. He described these methods as follows: "In an attempt to discover the covert (inhibited) and unconscious (partially repressed) tendencies of normal persons, a number of procedures were devised. These procedures are simply different methods of stimulating imaginative processes and facilitating their expression in words or in action."

The section in the "Explorations" that deals with the projection tests lists, in addition to the Thematic Apperception Test (TAT), which had been introduced three years earlier (Morgan & Murray, 1935), several other techniques, such as the Rorschach, a "musical reverie test," and a "Dramatic Production Test." It is also well to note that Murray concluded the volume by pointing out that "of all our technical procedures, the series that were termed projection tests, which were designed to evoke imagery and fantasy, brought to light the most significant data" (1938, p. 728).

During the same year—1938—when the "Explorations" was published, Lawrence Frank, in a "privately circulated memorandum," first used the term *projective methods*. The following year he published the first theoretical paper on "Projective methods for the study of personality" (Frank, 1939), which was subsequently expanded into the well-known monograph entitled *Projective Methods* (Frank,

1948). In this monograph the author presents a detailed theoretical discussion of personality against the background of recent developments in science and philosophy of science. He also lists and describes a series of procedures which he terms *projective techniques*. Essentially Frank describes a projective technique as "a method of studying the personality by confronting the subject with a situation to which he will respond according to what the situation means to him and how he feels when so responding" (p. 46).

A more complete and up-to-date characterization of projective techniques and their distinctive features will appear in a later section of this chapter, following the discussion of the concept of projection which is basic to them.

Concerning Projection

Before we attempt a complete definition of projective methods, it is imperative that we deal with the fundamental concept of projection.

Originally, the term *projection*, introduced by Freud, involved only psychopathological connotations. It was considered the main mechanism underlying paranoia and paranoid disorders. The tendency on the part of the patient to externalize unacceptable inner drives and other undesirable internal proclivities to the outer world was described as projection. To date, projection is widely viewed as a defense mechanism, similar to many others, the purpose of which is to avoid the experience of guilt or anxiety.

This usage of the term in psychopathology is well established and undisputed. However, it is too limited an application. In later years Freud and some of his followers extended the meaning of the term. The extended and broader meaning of projection is a most significant ingredient in the understanding and definition of projective methods.

Some time after the introduction of the term, Freud (1911) wrote concerning projection that

> . . . it makes its appearance not only in paranoia but under other psychological conditions as well, in fact it has a regular share assigned to it in our attitude to the external world. For when we refer the causes of certain sensations to the external world, instead of looking for them (as we do in the case of others) inside ourselves this normal proceeding, too, deserves to be called projection [p. 452].

Consonant with the broader definition of projection is Rapaport's (1952) statement covering

. . . a graduated continuum which becomes more general extending from the externalization of a specific type of tension in paranoid projections to that of any kind of tension in infantile projection, to that of a whole system of attitudes and tensions in transference phenomena, to where it imperceptibly shades into the externalization in the form of a "private world" defined by the organizing principles of one's personality [pp. 270–271].

In their review of the concept of projection, Murstein and Pryer (1959) set aside the theoretical discussions and examined the research literature in which the term was employed. They evolved four categories of the concept of projection: *classical, attributive, autistic,* and *rationalized.* The *classical* view of projection is the one originally suggested by Freud—that of attribution of one's characteristics to the outside world because of their unacceptability to ego and their anxiety-evoking nature. *Attributive projection* refers to the process of "ascribing one's own motivations, feelings and behavior to other persons." This usage is broader than the classical one; it contains it, and is consonant with Freud's later and more encompassing definition of projection referred to above. *Autistic projection* is most closely related to perception; it is the process by which the needs of the perceiver influence what he perceives. Finally, *rationalized projection* describes the process whereby the individual uses unconscious, classical projection but "attempts to justify it by inventing a rationale."

Projection, as used in projective techniques, is most consonant with the broad attributive definition as well as with the elements of autistic projection. This broader definition of the term is illustrated in an early statement by Freud in *Totem and Taboo* (1919):

> But projection is not especially created for the purpose of defense, it also comes into being where there are no conflicts. The projection of inner perception to the outside is a primitive mechanism which, for instance, also influences our sense perceptions, so that it normally has the greatest share in shaping our outer world. Under conditions that have not yet been sufficiently determined even inner perceptions of ideational and emotional processes are projected outwardly, like sense perceptions, and are used to shape the outer world, whereas they ought to remain in the inner world [pp. 107–108].

Thus, as I have pointed out previously (Rabin, 1960), "perhaps the broader term 'externalization' is more appropriate in the case of projective techniques. It avoids the constricting misconception of projection as a mere defense mechanism. . . ." (p. 4). This is the sense in which the originator of the term *projective techniques* and subsequent authors in the field have understood and employed the term *projection*. Viewing it in the broader context made it possible for workers with these methods to ferret out trends of the whole range of defense mechanisms from projective test data, including the defense mechanism of projection itself.

DEFINING PROJECTIVE TECHNIQUES

Although the process of projection is a prerequisite for projective techniques, it is by no means sufficient for a definition of these methods. In the broader sense of projection a person is "projecting" all the time when he perceives and responds to the environment as an individual with personal needs, motivations, and unique tendencies. There are actually two basic aspects to any projective technique. First, the particular situation or stimulus with which the subject is confronted; and, second, the responses of the subject in terms of the meaning the particular stimulus or situation has for him. Thus, as Frank has pointed out, any situation may evoke the "idiomatic way" of responding in the individual which gives a basis for inference concerning his personality process. Frank (1948) further characterizes projective techniques as follows:

"The essential feature of a projective technique is that it evokes from the subject what is in various ways expressive of his private world and personality process" (p. 47, Frank's italics).

The "private world" referred to by Frank is one which is created by the individual himself as a result of his special experiences under the influences of the geographical, cultural, and social environments throughout his development. Personality, to which projective techniques are the key, is viewed as "a dynamic process, the conformal activity of the individual who is engaged in creating, maintaining and defending that 'private world.' . . ."(Frank, 1948).

Earlier definitions of projective techniques have stressed the response and its interpretation, but not the stimulus or "situation." More recent attempts include an awareness of the nature and characteristics of the stimulus, its objective features which may evoke common responses, as well as its "unstructured" nature which allows for uniqueness and "private world" responsiveness.

More recently, after an analysis of several definitions of projective techniques and of the criteria on which they are based, Lindzey (1961) proposed the following definition:

> a projective technique is an instrument that is considered especially sensitive to covert or unconscious aspects of behavior, it permits or encourages a wide variety of subject responses, is highly multi-dimensional, and it evokes unusually rich and profuse response data with a minimum of subject awareness concerning the purpose of the test.

He adds further that

> the stimulus material presented by the projective test is ambiguous, interpreters of the test depend upon holistic analysis, the test evokes fantasy responses, and there are no correct or incorrect responses to the test [p. 45, Lindzey's italics].

Thus, the ingredients of any thoroughgoing and complete definition of projective techniques are threefold. In the first place, the nature of the stimulus is characterized mainly by its ambiguity or, more appropriately, by the freedom it allows the respondent, due to the fact that it is not overly limited to conventional form requiring conventional response. Secondly, the response, the task of the subject, involves quantity, variety, and richness with little awareness of the purpose to which the material may be put and the implications that may be drawn from it. Third, the task of the examiner-interpreter is complex, for his analysis is holistic-ideographic, and he attributes to the responses that he obtains a multidimensionality necessary for such analysis.

VARIETIES OF TECHNIQUES

Not only did Frank attempt to define and provide a rationale for the projective methods, but he also suggested a classification for the wide array of techniques which he felt are to be encompassed by the general term projective (Frank, 1948). The criterion for the categorization centered upon "what they require or seek to evoke from the subject." His five-fold grouping of methods is as follows: Constitutive methods involve the imposition of structure upon relatively unstructured material. The Rorschach is the most obvious candidate for this category. Constructive methods require arrangement of materials into certain patterns, as in the mosaics test. Interpretive methods, such as

the TAT, involve the subject in "an interpretation of some experience
. . . in which he finds a personal meaning or affective significance."
Cathartic methods, for example, doll play, are expressive—they
stimulate emotional reaction. *Refractive* methods are those in which
conventional modes of communication are altered idiosyncratically.
Handwriting analysis qualifies under this rubric.

After surveying a number of previous attempts to classify projective techniques, including Frank's, Lindzey (1961) proposed still
another classification. He recognized that different criteria adopted
may dictate different classifications. The criteria he noted are: the
attributes of the test material; origins of method, whether from theory
or empirical findings; manner of test interpretation (formal vs. content analysis); the target or purpose of the test—whether directed to
the assessment of motives, conflicts, or some form of psychopathology; mode of administration of the test; and, finally, the kind of *response* the technique elicits from the subject. This last criterion is the
one considered by Lindzey as most significant as a basis for the
classification of projective techniques. The five-fold classification
that emerges from this analysis is not too unlike the one offered by
Frank 13 years earlier. Some important differences, however, may be
discerned in the following list:

    1. Association techniques (word association, Rorschach, etc.)
    2. Construction techniques (TAT, Blacky)
    3. Completion techniques (sentence completion, Picture-
Frustration Study)
    4. Choice or ordering techniques (Szondi, Picture Arrangement
Test)
    5. Expressive techniques (psychodrama, painting)

The preceding, all-too-brief discussion illustrates not only the
wide range of projective methods but the complexity involved in
finding the common elements that characterize them. Furthermore,
the implications of these difficulties for "projective theory" should
not escape us.

THE HOSPITABLE ZEITGEIST

In the preceding few sections of the chapter we made a brief excursion
of a theoretical nature, into the field of projection and projective
techniques. We shall now pick up the historical thread at the point

when the term projective techniques as well as the techniques themselves began to gain currency and much popularity. The late 1930s and the subsequent 15 years or so mark a period of hospitality and burgeoning development in this field.

The hospitable atmosphere for the projective techniques, in the 1940s and later, was due to certain fundamental changes in American psychology itself and to certain events and social forces in our society around mid-century. Some of the causes of the new trend, the new *zeitgeist* which provided the hospitality, will be discussed in the paragraphs that follow.

First we must consider the budding discipline of clinical psychology in the 1920s and '30s. Traditional academic psychology supplied it with few concepts and even fewer means by which it could attain the status of a full-fledged profession. Aside from being limited to the diagnostic function, the clinical psychologist had very few tools even for this circumscribed area of activity. He was a tester and had precious few tests at that. His kit contained the Stanford-Binet and some personality inventories of limited range. His diagnostic contribution was primarily in terms of numerical indices—IQs, percentiles on introversion or dominance scales, and similar bits of nomothetic information. The new projective techniques, which he so avidly embraced, gave him a tremendous boost and an opportunity to communicate something meaningful to his professional colleagues about the personality structure, dynamics, and diagnosis of his patients. They also facilitated contribution to the planning of the therapeutic process.

Another facilitating circumstance in the adoption and popularity of projective techniques was the advances and dissemination of dynamic theories of personality. Psychoanalytic theories and methods gained great influence in American psychiatry and, eventually, in psychology. The concepts of the unconscious, of repression, defenses, etc., have become central in the mental health field. As a result, they have also favored the development of special methods, such as projective techniques, which were by their very nature and definition suitable in the assessment of these dynamic processes.

Last, but not least, were the pressures and needs created by World War II for a variety of assessments—including personnel selection and screening as well as clinical assessment. The Binet and the Bernreuter were no longer sufficient. Projective techniques became a major part of the psychologist's armamentarium in the fulfillment of the service demands placed upon him. These experiences, and the postwar crystallization of a full-fledged profession of clinical psychology provided increasing receptiveness to the penetrating instruments for personality assessment and clinical diagnosis.

The popularity of projective methods among clinicians, and the involvement of the universities in the formal training of clinical psychologists immediately after the war, gained entrance for these methods to the curricula of the training programs in clinical psychology. It was during this period that several significant and influential books were published. Among these may be mentioned the report of the Menninger group on the Word Association Test, Rorschach, and TAT (Rapaport, 1946). In reporting the detailed test findings for a number of diagnostic groups with the three projective methods and by relating the empirical results to psychodynamic theory of pathology, Rapaport and his colleagues noticeably extended the horizons of clinicians and advanced the development of projective techniques in their *Diagnostic Psychological Testing*. Bell's *Projective Techniques* ("a dynamic approach to the study of personality") offfered a useful survey of a wide range of methods (1948). The extended theoretical presentation of the methods by Frank (1948), mentioned earlier, and the publication of several introductory textbooks, such as *Projective Psychology* (Abt & Bellak, 1950) and *An Introduction to Projective Techniques* (Anderson & Anderson, 1951), supplied many a budding clinician in the university training programs with the fundamentals of the projective methods. In addition to the more general presentation of projective techniques, a number of specialized technical manuals for the application of specific methods also appeared during the '40s and '50s. The work of Beck, Klopfer, and Piotrowsky with the Rorschach, of Tomkins, Stein, and Henry with the TAT are some of the more prominent examples. Moreover, the inventiveness of clinicians and researchers extended to the creation of new methods. The new methods introduced by Blum, Sargent, Shneidman, and many others (to be described in subsequent chapters of this book) further exemplify the stimulation of projective techniques and of the "projective hypothesis" to American psychology and personology.

Finally, this period was also marked by burgeoning research activity. As mentioned earlier, work with the Rorschach alone is represented by nearly 2000 titles during the decade following World War II. Much of the research dealt with the investigation of the projective techniques themselves. However, a great deal of work employed projective techniques as a method of investigation of personality processes, psychopathology, culture-personality relationships, and other theoretical issues as well as clinical and applied problems.

Some of the methods were also "adopted" by less holistically oriented psychologists for the purpose of studying more isolated personality variables instead of "total" personalities.

THE PROLIFERATION OF METHODS

The sudden freedom from the shackles of the psychometric tradition that was experienced by some psychologists led to rather spurious trends in the field of projective techniques. Since projection and projective techniques were so broadly defined, any type of situation that was conducive to the elicitation of individual differences and "uniqueness" or idiosyncracy in response could be nominated to membership in the new assessment armamentarium. Many issues of journals published "still another projective technique," mainly on the basis of novel stimuli of different modalities and some differentiation between normals and some psychopathological classifications. Little attention was paid to the theoretical underpinnings of these new methods or to the conceptualization of the response patterns within some theoretical framework of personality theory. Many of them were mere suggestions, prematurely published and lacking in sufficient data of a validating nature, especially construct validity. Some author likened this state of affairs to the opening of a Pandora's box.

In reaction to this "rampant empiricism" this author (Rabin, 1963) raised the question, "Do we need another projective technique?" The response to this question was conditional: "New projective techniques are needed, but the novelty is not to consist solely of new stimulus materials. The new methods should be genuinely new in conception, and should validly tap significant personality variables, buttressed by sound psychological theory" (p. 76).

CURRENT STATUS

During the 1960s there has developed a new "spirit" in American psychology and a more sober and balanced view of projective techniques. A number of factors have contributed to this trend.

First to be considered is the change that has taken place in clinical psychology as a profession. It is quite clear that the *practice* of clinical psychologists has been steadily shifting from assessment and diagnosis to psychotherapy and behavior modification. There are many reasons for this trend. At any rate, as Shakow (1965) pointed out, diagnosis has become "infra dig" and treatment is the clinician's activity of prestige. Thus, along with other diagnostic devices, projective techniques no longer enjoy the status they once had. Shakow bemoans this state of affairs, for aside from the whole issue of "therapy without diagnosis," psychological workers miss the opportunity for the development and the sharpening of their assessment tools.

Another source of the change in the atmosphere may be found in the projective methods themselves. Numerous studies reporting negative or equivocal findings with the several methods have had a sobering effect upon the original unqualified enthusiasm of workers in the field. Psychometrically oriented psychologists who have been more interested in precision of measurement than in the substance and significance of what is measured have never accepted projective techniques, which they considered methodologically unmanageable and "sloppy." Psychologists who have been interested in the study of "persons" and their problems remain convinced of the significant contribution projective techniques can continue to make to the understanding of personality dynamics and in the study of human problems.

Finally, it must be pointed out that the recent trend is that of "reentrenchment of the academe." Academic psychology has been moving back into its ivory tower, to study behavior of infrahumans or isolated and trivial behavior variables extirpated from the living and functioning person. This led Sanford to raise the very pertinent question: "Will psychologists study human problems?" (1965). Projective techniques remain an important method and an important source of information in the study of human problems. The criterion problem is still a most thorny issue in the validation of personality assessment methods. Continued research in assessment will proceed with constant research in personality and behavioral criteria, for their mutual benefit.

As we enter into the 1980s it is incumbent upon us to take stock and review the current status of projective techniques. Some writers have relegated the entire projective movement to the oblivion to which many trends and fads in psychology have been doomed. However, the evidence is that projective techniques are very much alive and well as we enter the new decade.

To be sure, changes in the *zeitgeist* during the '60s and '70s have brought about a somewhat reduced activity in the field of projectives. With the shift away from diagnosis and to psychotherapy in clinical psychology there was a marked reduction in the use of diagnostic tests and other assessment instruments in general. This trend applied to the projective methods as well.

In addition, numerous studies with projectives, reporting negative findings, have had a sobering effect and even an inhibiting influence upon the employment of projective methods in research as well as in clinical settings. Considerable research, however, with more improved and sophisticated designs is proceeding apace, as indicated in the last three reviews of projective methods published in the *Annual Review of Psychology* (Fisher, 1967; Molish, 1972; Klopfer & Taulbee, 1976).

In comparing two surveys concerned with the employment of tests in clinical settings, in 1961 and 1971, Weiner (1972) reports some interesting findings. The Rorschach and TAT were being used in 91 percent of the clinical settings in 1971 as compared with 93 and 88 percent for the two tests respectively in 1961. The WAIS has acquired the preeminent position of first place (93 percent of the settings in 1971)—a shift from sixth place in 1961 (72 percent). Thus, in terms of representation in clinical settings, projective techniques have not changed much and certainly have not disappeared from the diagnostic scene. When the tests are classified under the rubric "Using test frequently or in the majority of cases," the Rorschach has dropped to third place—after the WAIS and Bender-Gestalt. Whereas in 1961 the Rorschach was used "frequently, or in the majority of cases" with 80 percent of the clients, the figure was 60 percent in 1971. The TAT showed a similar drop—from 60 to 43 percent. Thus, the major projectives remain a part of the standard armamentarium of the clinic, although the frequency of their employment in day-by-day operation has somewhat declined. This is very much related to a trend in psychology in general, as well as in clinical psychology, which involves the concern with behavior primarily. There is a reduction of interest in intrapsychic processes. This trend represents ignoring what is referred to as the "inferred psychological structure." For a full evaluation of mental health, we need, according to Strupp & Hadley (1977)

> Clinical judgment, aided by behavioral observations and psychological tests of such variables as self-concept, sense of identity, balance of psychic forces, unified outlook on life, resistance to stress, self-regulation, ability to cope with reality, absence of mental and behavioral symptoms, adequacy in love, work and play, adequacy in interpersonal relations [p. 190].

Consonant with the above, a full evaluation of a person's mental health status cannot rely solely on behavioral observations, but needs to include many of the other, more subtle variables which are more customarily assessed by our psychological tests of personality, espe-cially the projective ones. The figures quoted above seem to indicate that the vast majority of clinical settings continue to utilize the projec-tive methods in the assessment of the mental health of their clientele.

Research activity involving projective methods remains quite considerable in the 1970s and will probably continue into the '80s as well. Klopfer and Taulbee (1976), in the last *Annual Review* pub-lished at this writing, report that more than 500 journal articles pertaining to projective techniques "were published during their review period of 1971–74." This number did not include "a number of books that have been published as new volumes or revised editions." The considerable employment of projective techniques in cross-cultural research is well-documented in Abel's (1973) extensive re-view.

Many of the research publications are critical of psychological tests in general and of projectives in particular. Yet "while a sizable proportion of clinicians were cognizant of the poor reliability of many tests, such awareness was apparently not important in their decisions to use them" (Wade & Baker, 1977). Furthermore,

> They feel that the relevant research is inadequate; they do not view behavioral prediction or accurate diagnostic assignment (common criterion measures in testing research) as the most important goals of test usage; they adhere to therapeutic models that value intrapsychic asessment over other assessment with greater face validity (e.g., be-havioral observations); they believe testing is too subjective or com-plex to objectify and examine in analytic fashion; they depend upon personal experience with tests to determine the utility of testing [Wade & Baker, 1977, p. 881].

This critical comment is, in many respects, quite in agreement with the more positively toned statement by Strupp and Hadley (1977) quoted above. As we commented elsewhere (Rabin & Hayes, 1978), "With the possible exception of the criticism regarding the failure of clinicians to analytically examine their instruments, the foregoing statement fairly accurately portrays the present attitudes and state of affairs in diagnostic testing."

In recent years important publications on projective methods in the areas of clinical diagnosis and research have appeared. The *Ror-schach Handbook of Clinical and Research Applications* (Goldfried, et al., 1971) summarizes in a useful way, for clinicians as well as researchers, the most reliable information on the application of the Rorschach in the diagnosis of schizophrenia, organicity, neurosis, prediction of suicide, etc. A similar effort is represented by Lerner's volume entitled *Handbook of Rorschach Scales* (1975). Exner's attempt to develop a "comprehensive" scoring system for the Rorschach (1974) unifies several systems which have introduced and perpetuated a good deal of confusion in the clinical and research application of the method. Most distressing was the effect of the multiplicity of systems upon the generalization of research findings and communication among workers in the field. The "comprehensive system" may well have the potential for producing more uniform and comparable data, utilizing the Rorschach, in different settings.

Exner's second volume (1978) reports a considerable amount of research with the comprehensive scoring system which strengthens the position of the Rorschach as a reliable instrument and gives it a "new lease on life" (Rabin, 1980). The volume contains normative data on nearly 1000 adult subjects (325 nonpatients, and the others— depressive, schizophrenics, etc.) for 42 Rorschach variables. Similarly impressive are the normative data on more than 2500 children, ages 5 to 16 years. These are placed into three broad categories of nonpatients, "behavior problems," and "withdrawn." Most important, however, is the establishment of test–retest reliability at different intervening time periods. One is inclined to agree with the author that "The matrix of these studies offers substantial support for the contention that the majority of Rorschach variables underpinning interpretation are stable over time." A number of experiments that bear on the validity of a number of Rorschach interpretations (of variables) are also included.

While the "comprehensive system" and the results based upon it are reviving the use of structural variables, which was Rorschach's original contribution to the inkblot method, the earlier trend stressing content primarily still persists. Many workers with the method abandoned the structural variables and have employed the Rorschach as a "standard interview," based on content only. This position has received extensive support in a recent publication by Aronow and Reznikoff (1976) and will apparently remain tenable for a number of diagnosticians in the future. Perhaps the conclusions of my earlier review of the Rorschach (Buros, 1972) still hold: "Although research activity in the area has abated and concern with diagnosis among clinicians is lessened, Rorschach's ten inkblots persist in providing important stimulation to psychologists in producing increasingly challenging and useful research and applications." This comment concerning the Rorschach method may be extended to apply to the field of projective techniques in general.

REFERENCES

Abel, T. M. *Psychological Testing in Cultural Contexts.* New Haven: College & University Press, 1973.

Abt, L., & Bellak, L. (Eds.). *Projective Psychology.* New York: Knopf, 1950.

Anderson, H. H., & Anderson, Gladys, L. (Eds.). *An Introduction to Projective Techniques.* New York: Prentice-Hall, 1951.

Aronow, E., & Reznikoff, M. *Rorschach Content Interpretation.* New York: Grune & Stratton, 1976.

Beck, S. J. Introduction to the Rorschach method: A manual of personality study. *Am. Orthopsychiatr. Assoc. Monogr.*, 1937, 1.

Bell, J. E. *Projective Techniques.* New York: Longmans, Green, 1948.

Boring, E. G. *A History of Experimental Psychology.* New York: The Century Company, 1929.

Buros, O. K. (Ed.). *The Seventh Mental Measurements Yearbook.* Highland Park, N.J.: The Gryphon Press, 1972.

Exner, J. *The Rorschach: A Comprehensive System.* New York: John Wiley & Sons, Vol. 1, 1974; Vol. 2, 1978.

Fisher, S. Projective methodologies. *Annu. Rev. Psychology*, 1967, *18*, 165–190.

Frank, L. K. Projective methods for the study of personality. *J. Psychology*, 1939, *8*, 389–413.

Frank, L. K. *Projective Methods.* Springfield, Ill.: Charles C. Thomas, 1948.

Frank, L. K. Toward a projective psychology. *J. Proj. Tech.*, 1960, *24*, 246–253.

Freud, S. *Totem and Taboo.* New York: Moffatt, Yard & Co., 1919.

Freud, S. Psycho-analytic notes upon an autobiographical account of a case of paranoia (dementia paranoides). *Collected Papers*, Vol. III. London: The Hogarth Press, 1949 (originally published in 1911).

Goldfried, M., Stricker, G., & Weiner, I. E. *Rorschach Handbook of Clinical and Research Applications.* Engelwood Cliffs, N.J.: Prentice-Hall, 1971.

Klopfer, B., et al. *Development in the Rorschach Technique*, Vol. II. Yonkers-on-Hudson, N.Y.: World Book Co., 1956.

Klopfer, W. G., & Taulbee, E. S. Proj. Tests *Annu. Rev. Psychology*, 1976, *27*, 543–567.

Krugman, M. Out of the inkwell: the Rorschach method. *Character & Pers.*, 1940, *9*, 91–110.

Lennep, Van D. I. The four-picture test. In H. H. Anderson & Gladys L. Anderson (Eds.). *An Introduction to Projective Techniques.* New York: Prentice-Hall, 1951.

Lerner, P. M. (Ed.). *Handbook of Rorschach Scales.* New York: International Universities Press, 1975.

Lindzey, G. *Projective Techniques and Cross-cultural Research.* New York: Appleton-Century-Crofts, 1961.

Molish, H. B. Projective methodologies. *Annual Review of Psychology*, 1972, *23*, 577–614.

Morgan, Christiana D., & Murray, H. A. A method for investigating fantasies. *Arch. Neurol. Psychiatry*, 1935, *34*, 289–306.

Murray, H. A., et al. *Explorations in Personality*. New York: Oxford University Press, 1938.

Murray, H. A. *Thematic Apperception Test Manual*. Cambridge, Mass.: Harvard University Press, 1943.

Murstein, B. I. *Theory and Research in Projective Techniques*. New York: Wiley, 1963.

Murstein, B. I., & Pryer, R. S. The concept of projection: a review. *Psychol. Bull.*, 1959, *56*, 353–374.

Rabin, A. I. Projective methods and projection in children. In A. I. Rabin & Mary R. Haworth (Eds.). *Projective Techniques with Children*. New York: Grune & Stratton, 1960.

Rabin, A. I. Do we need another projective technique? *Merrill-Palmer Quart.*, 1963, *9*, 73–77.

Rabin, A. I. The Rorschach - a new lease on life (Review of Exner's Vol. 2). *Contemporary Psychology*, 1980, *25*(1), 52–53.

Rabin, A. I., & Hayes, D. L. The rationale of diagnostic testing. In B. Wolman (Ed.). *Clinical diagnosis of mental disorder*. New York: Plenum Press, 1978.

Rabin, A. I., & Hurley, J. R. Projective techniques. In L. Abt & E. Reiss (Eds.). *Progress in Clinical Psychology*, Vol. VI. New York: Grune & Stratton, 1964.

Rapaport, D. *Diagnostic Psychological Testing*, Vol. II. Chicago: Year Book Publishers, 1946.

Rapaport, D. Projective techniques and the theory of thinking. *J. Proj. Technol.*, 1952, *16*, 269–275.

Rorschach, H. *Psychodiagnostik*. Bern and Leipzig: Ernst Bircher Verlag, 1921.

Rorschach, H., & Oberholser, E. The application of the interpretation of form to psychoanalysis. *J. Nerv. Ment. Dis.*, 1924, *60*, 225–379.

Sanford, N. Will psychologists study human problems? *Am. Psychologist*, 1965, *20*(3), 192–202.

Schwartz, L. A. Social-situation pictures in the psychiatric interview. *Am. J. Orthopsychiatry*, 1932, *2*, 124–133.

Shakow, D. Seventeen years later: clinical psychology in the light of the 1947 committee on training in clinical psychology report. *Am. Psychologist*, 1965, *20*, 353–362.

Strupp, H. H., & Hadley, S. W. A tripartite model of mental health and therapeutic outcomes. *Am. Psychologist*, 1977, *32*(3), 187–196.

Tulchin, S. H. The pre-Rorschach use of ink blot tests. *Rorch. Res. Exsch.*, 1940, *4*, 1–6.

Wade, T. C., & Baker, T. B. Opinions and use of psychological tests: A survey of clinical psychologists. *Am. Psychologist*, 1977, *32*(10), 874–882.

Weiner, I. E. Does psychodiagnosis have a future? *J. Personality Assessment*, 1972, *36*, 534–546.

Zubin, J., Eron, L. D., & Schumer, Florence. *An Experimental Approach to Projective Techniques.* New York: Wiley, 1965.

2

Reality, Rorschach, and Perceptual Theory

Samuel J. Beck

I.

The psychologist setting out to study the human personality faces a dilemma. The knowledge he seeks is about men, women, children, as we know them in their real lives—their thinking, emotions, anxieties, moods, their daydreams, purposes, gratifications—all that fusion of mental experience which, at any particular moment, is a total human being. This is the psychologist's objective. His disciplined habits of research follow the precept that Descartes formulated as the second of his four guidelines which, from the age of 23 on, he used in directing and criticizing his own thinking. It is, he writes, "to divide each of the difficulties that I shall be examining into as many parts as possible and as will be requisite the better to resolve them" (Descartes, 1943, p. 88).*

The dilemma is compounded by the circumstance that any total human being is divisible into so many parts. The psychological vari-

The reasoning in this article grew in part out of research carried out under grant no. 17156, Department of Mental Health, State of Illinois.

*My published translation does not seem to me to render Descartes' meaning adequately for this passage. The French reads: "Le second, de diviser chacune des difficultés que j'examinerais en autant de parcelles qu'il se pourrait et qu'il serait requis pour les mieux résoudre."

23

ables manifest in overt behavior seem endless. Just as no two persons are the same in physical features, neither are they similar in their psychological features—the way they walk, talk, eat breakfast, dress, and all the habits that make up one's way of life. This variegation is stock in trade for the psychopathologist. The patient in the mental hospital may be reacting with symptoms which to the observer are quite different from those of the patient in the next bed. Yet the diagnosis of the two may be the same.

Dissimilar though the manifest symptoms are, the psychological forces of which they are the expression are similar or the same. The problem for the psychologist is to ascertain these psychological forces. They are the unseen realities that become the seen realities or the symptoms. This reasoning extends from the various clinical pictures to the population generally. The visible behaviors of any two or more persons will differ in the eyes of those about him. Yet of anyone whom we know, we know generally how he will act, given certain circumstances. We take for granted certain constancies in each person. In everyday language, these are his character traits, the sources of the style of life which we take for granted in our friends, our wives or husbands, our children, the associates in our vocations; and, insofar as their public images are delineated, those of our national leaders.

The task before a psychology of personality is to delineate the forces, the constancies (hypothetical constructs, to be sure), that are the sources of the observables. A corollary from the hypotheses of the constancies is that they enable us to predict the behavior of others. This inheres in the sheer fact that they are constants. In our transactions with one another we are, in fact, always predicting. We are pretty sure regarding what a person is likely to do, sure that what he does today he will do tomorrow, and on another morrow. These are the judgments of everyday life and its wisdoms.

Yet we do not normally break the person down into his component character traits, i.e., into his several psychological processes. The psychologist, on the other hand, is on a search. He asks now, "Can the hypothetical constructs, the processes, be verified? What is the connection between the processes and the person as we see him with his everyday behaviors and his lifetime character patterns?" Is there any method whereby these questions can be answered?

The Rorschach test, as its exponents claim, cuts across intellectual and emotional variables. Its critics question or reject this claim. In this chapter, I propose to examine Rorschach test theory in the light of some perception theory. Let it first be noted here that Rorschach did not discover new mental processes. The separate psychological areas to which the concepts of the test are referred are familiar to psychology. The intellect and the emotions have long been the provinces of the laboratory and the former a large enterprise of the clinic. Imaginative activity has been more elusive, but ventures into it have been undertaken. Those very human devices, the defenses, have grown out of psychodynamic insights of Anna Freud and of Fenichel. Rorschach did not discover any of these, though they are the foundations of his test. He did discover ways of searching for and recognizing these psychological activities or experiences. Nevertheless, emphasis needs to be placed on the penetration of his test to fantasy activity. This was a discovery original with him, and a most important one from a viewpoint of whole personality research.

The great advance in the exploration of personality that Rorschach achieved is in enabling us to judge the effects of the intellectual and the emotional processes on one another. A set of objective stimuli mirrors the individual's use of his mental resources and their fusion into that unit which is the person that we see, the individual striving to adapt to his circumstances, as he, at that point in his life, perceives them. This is what Rorschach did that was new.

II.

The psychological field in which a Rorschach test concept can most definitely be observed is that of perception. In the subtitle to his *Psychodiagnostik* he uses the expression: "a perception-diagnostic experiment" *(Ergebnisse eines Wahrnehmungsdiagnostischen Experiments)*. Visual phenomena are stressed by von Fieandt as the principal source by which we know external objects. In a paper, "Toward a Unitary Theory of Perception" (1958) he says, "The conditions of object perception can consequently be reduced by operations not exceeding the optical sphere." He points to the dependence of other modalities on the visual. Regarding tactual experience he writes, "Only men with normal visual images (not the born blind) are able to objectivize their exclusively tactual impressions." He adds a similar observation concerning the sense of hearing; it " . . . can mediate thing impressions only if the auditory stimulation comes combined with optic or haptic stimuli simultaneously and is localized in the same direction." At still another point he comments, "For man, undoubtedly the world of sight is the most important, but," he adds, "surely a purely visual world would be an abstraction. Such a thing is never found in empirical reality."

Rorschach's inkblots are, of course, visual stimuli. The associations that they elicit point to memory images held by the subject, and as such, they report a former visual experience on the part of the subject. He must have seen the "man," "butterfly," "tree" at some time in order to extract these forms from the Rorschach test figures. His associations then report a reality with which he has once interacted. This is to say that the Rorschach inkblots yield information regarding the subject's realities. These are the phenomenal realities, or "experienced reality," using von Fieandt's pertinent language.

The clinical observer cannot, however, be content with his patient's phenomena. The things which the patient says he sees are the measure of his ability to know reality. Here we must be crystal clear about what we mean by "reality." The patient's phenomena may be unmistakably vivid to him, sharp in outline. As a clinical example, the animals, elves, and other creatures of delirium tremens are terribly real to the patient. Yet doctor, nurse, ward attendants go their merry way unaffected by these horrors: the patient's reality is private and his own. In our everyday comings and goings we deal with numerous objects to which most people react in about the same way. These are the realities of our external world.

Rorschach did his perception experiment within this modality by which we take in most of our information. He invented, in fact, a totally new visual world. It is a simple experiment in what each person sees, and it uncovers "the experienced reality of the individual." But Rorschach's invention went a giant step further. The test contains a technique for judging the subject's experienced reality using as a frame of reference the reality experienced by his society generally. In processing the Rorschach form associations—and by far the greatest number of the associations are wholly or partially determined by form—we mark some F+ for good form, and some F− for poor form. Although the terms "good" and "poor" have social significance as behavior acceptable or undesirable, the scoring does not make social value its criterion.

The criterion for F+ is the empirical, objective one: do people of average or higher intelligence, normally behaving in their environments, see this "man," "alligator," "lake," and the rest when looking at this inkblot? These are the people that establish a community's realities. They usually make the correct decisions in their affairs with those about them; they know how to protect and care for themselves, whether in physical hazards or social ones. What they do brings them through the vicissitudes of life with the success that is the lot of the majority of us. So the way they see things, physical objects as well as social values, is the measure of everyday pragmatic reality. I return to this point below.

It follows that anyone who behaves as these "normally behaving" people do, in the major matters of life and in a large enough proportion of his activities, knows reality. Important implications concerning ego follow, therefore, from the F+ concept. It was by the associations of these people that we established the Rorschach realities, i.e., what is F+ and what is F−. When a person perceives in the test a large enough number of forms that agree with these criterion percepts, we can predict of him that he will be a realist in a world external to himself.

The Rorschach perceptions are explicable from phenomenological theory if we simply inspect any one response taken by itself. The F+ concept as societal reality points up the inadequacy of phenomenology for purposes of judging the person in the context of a social setting. Phenomenology does not provide a frame of reference whereby one can evaluate one's ability to know the realities outside oneself, those hard and sometime terribly uncomfortable realities with which the world confronts us. Whatever a person's inner experience may be when he says "two clowns" (fig. II) or "a bear climbing on some rocks" (fig. VIII), it is his private experience.* It cannot, as Mandler and Kessin point out, be subjected to public tests (1959, p. 38). They say on a later page, "It should be obvious by now that private events, mental operations or not, cannot be adequately named in the language of science. Our discussion of phenomenology is directly relevant to this point . . ." (Mandler & Kessen, 1959, p. 113).

However truly a subject's percept reports the phenomenal appearance to him of a thing, i.e., his experienced reality, we have no way of knowing whether what he sees is what healthy people see in that object. We cannot say whether within certain conditions he will behave as the healthy do in regard to whatever social values will be involved; whether he will come through a peril unhurt, or will survive. From the fact that most healthy individuals do see in fig. II of the Rorschach test "two clowns" or the "two animals" (above), and many

---

*Numbers in parentheses refer to card numbers on a standard set of Rorschach figures.

other associations in any accumulated F+ lists (see Beizmann, 1966), we can make plausible predictions concerning our subject under scrutiny and can do so within a pragmatic range of accuracy. This reasoning is of critical significance to the clinical psychologist. An experiment in perception, Rorschach or other, that cannot reveal to what degree the person's experienced reality conforms to the realities with which he will collide is of only academic value to the clinical investigator. It may be added here that the "practical man" in industry or in politics would not expect to survive long if he rested only on his own, private, phenomenal realities. His is a reality which is being constantly put to the grim test of a competitive world. Thus it is that Rorschach perceptions correct for the inadequacy of phenomenology. The test has a technique for appraising the perceiver's realities as public events.

Let us say that a certain number of the S's responses are designated F−. Where most persons see a human form (e.g., in the central detail of fig. I) he sees "a scorpion." This is phobic thinking. As a clinical symptom it is likely to be evidence that the patient carries a fearful attitude about some particular person. Concerning no one else does he react with the idea, "a scorpion." The subject's transactions with this particular person are thus likely to cause that person some disagreeable moments. The percept is, however, reality only to the subject, his private reality. As F− it has not stood the test of reality when subjected to public scrutiny. To no one else is any person a scorpion. Thus the F+ procedure assays the public quality of a private reality.

The decision on any Rorschach association as F+, F− should be a simple enough undertaking. Two steps are necessary. First, the test is administered to other S's, a criterion population sample. Their responses are listed. A statistical gauge is worked out, and the new response is checked against the list so constructed. Second is clinical validation. The patient's overall reality perception is estimated from his Rorschach pattern. This is scrutinized from a perspective of the clinical investigation. How nearly do they conform to each other?

III.

A most illuminating paper on perception theory, and one which I see as fitting the F+, F− concept, is Bruner's "On Perceptual Readiness" (1957). To the Rorschach student, it is exciting to recognize so much of Rorschach's explicit principle in Bruner's thinking. Here is one theory of perception within which Rorschach's psychology fits comfortably.

Rorschach sets up four criteria for an F+ percept. In the second of these he refers to the memory impression, *Engramme*, which a person must possess. The third reads, "The ability to evoke these memory images, to awaken them, to bring them to consciousness" (Rorschach, 1932, p. 61). Bruner's point of departure concerning perceptual readiness is each person's "differential use of cues in identity categorizing [an object]" (p. 124). His description and detailed discussion of the cues constantly awaken recognition in anyone familiar with the associational activity that goes on in responding to the test.

Bruner's "cues" are Rorschach's *Engramme*. The subject is using the cues that emerge from the inkblot figure in order to identify and categorize the object that come to his mind. In the act of categorizing, i.e., in the associational content, he states a meaning that the percept has for him. The "bat," "animal skin," "women, girls" have the potential in them for a certain experience on his part because of the general class or category in which these objects belong. So these percepts demonstrate one of Bruner's postulates, " . . . that all perception is generic in the sense that whatever is perceived is placed in and achieves its 'meaning' from a class of percepts with which it is grouped" (p. 124). Implicit always in the "meaning" of the class is the effect which the object seen may have on the subject. Some objects are, by reason of the general properties of the class, known to be benign, gratifying; some are noxious. Whatever the meaning is, the subject reacts adaptively. When Bruner, in the paragraph preceding, makes the "bold assumption" that " . . . all perceptual experience is necessarily the end-product of a categorizing process," he is stating implicitly a dynamic principle: perception serves the adaptive urge. One's percepts have meaning to him insofar as the object in the percept is something good or bad for him.

However, Bruner is, in this article, interested in perception theoretically—what it is as a cognition process. But the clinical psychologist wants to know whether his patient judges the object before him using the same frame of reference as his society generally. Does the patient use the presented cues as others do? Does he categorize accurately? Is his experienced reality that of his fellow citizens?

The empirical facts are that some persons using these same cues perceive objects deviating in form, hence in category, and hence in meaning from those of the norm population. The cues, i.e., the stimuli, are the same but in Rorschach language the percept is F–. The cognition of the subject is deviant. This is the important differential which the test achieves for us in the F+, F– concept. Call his cognition good–bad, accurate–erratic, realistic–dereistic. Whatever one calls it, the clinical investigator has a clue as to how this patient is likely to react in the universe outside the test: in bad social form, making poor judgments, being unrealistic. At the dynamic level he has a clue to ego functioning.

The diagnostic information that is being unearthed is what principally interests the clinical thinker. Recall that Rorschach called his test one of both perception and diagnosis. The obvious indications are that either the persons did not attend to and use the portions in the inkblot figures, the cues, that the norm population uses, or he did attend to these but his own *Engramme*, the cues which the blot figure awakened in him, differed from those in the population generally. This is still reasoning within cognition, not clinical, theory. The clinician's questions from the F– alone (and disregarding for the moment the other information in the particular Rorschach pattern) spread out in the following directions:

(1) The subject does not possess the cues for the "bat" or the other F+ percepts. If so, it is because (2) he has not learned them; which could be because (3) he is too young, has not been exposed to the objects in the class "bat" or "skin" and others. Or again (4) he does not have the brain tissue with which to fix the memory cues, and never did have it. He is one of those unfortunates who was born mentally defective. Still again (5) he did at one time possess the brain tissue necessary for such cognitive processes, but he suffered the misfortune of an illness or an accident, either of which impaired the functioning of the brain. He lost his intellectual ability, his memory, and the other cognitive processes. These deficits may also be due to senility.

All the foregoing inadequacies are related to brain pathology. But in the majority of patients no such pathology can be established. The person may well be grown up in years and intellect, an adult or an adolescent, and with an IQ of 130 or even more. He has learned the cues to the object "butterfly" and "animal skin" and the others. That is, he has always had, and he still has, adequate brain tissue with which to categorize the objects that life presents before him. He can do so for the Rorschach test figures. One presents these stimuli to him and he sees a "spider" (fig. I) or a "snowflake" (fig. VI) or a "mask" (fig. X). What has happened to his cognitive cues for the "good" or "correct" percept? The answer: he still possesses these and he also possesses the cues for spiders and the other F–. Something in his psychological makeup activates more valence on his part for these deviant associations. The clinical student recognizes here the psychodynamic factor, i.e., the factor of personality—or if you prefer, the concept of need (Murray).

A person's perception, his cognitive functioning, is in instances erratic because he distorts the object. He sees it not as it is, meaning not in accordance with the experienced reality of a normative segment of the population. That is, he sees it not as *it* is, but as *he*, the patient, is. Here we enter on the problem of the whole personality as a psychological determinant.

Theorists, as cited by Bruner (1957), are aware of perceptual experience as something dynamic. Thus:

> Gibson like Titchener before him, urges a distinction between the visual field and the visual world, the former the world of attributive sense impressions, the latter of objects and things and events. Pratt urges that motivation and set and past experience may affect the things of the visual world but not the stuff of the visual field [p. 125].

Von Fieandt in his article (1958) also focuses on this distinction: " 'Pure sensation' is never found in natural surroundings. It can only be experienced in laboratories as a result of artificial refinements." We may recall his comment that a purely visual world is never found in reality. He puts his finger on the psychodynamic factor in stating essentially a Rorschach thesis: "The psychological side of the process implies that the organism reacts as a whole to a relational system of stimulus effects."

Von Fieandt is saying that it is the person as such who does the perceiving. This view corresponds with those of the writers above cited from Bruner. In the Rorschach test the F– percepts are the person mirrored in his unique, at times idiosyncratic, percepts. Some of his F– responses result from inadequate size of, or damage to, the brain; some from foggy mental state (drug influence); some from flighty attention caused by undirected spontaneity. In some it is the psychological person: his self distorted, he distorts his percepts.

Bruner, too, when he discusses perception as varyingly veridical, expresses a Rorschach proposition. He is formulating what the generic meaning of F+ is, as it can be empirically demonstrated in clinical findings. "What we generally mean when we speak of representation or veridicality is that perception is predicted in varying degrees," and,

" . . . the categorical placement of the object leads to appropriate consequences in terms of later behavior directed towards the perceived object; it appears as an apple and indeed it keeps the doctor away if consumed once a day" (p. 126).

This reasoning is validated in F+ experience as follow: (1) From my rationale concerning the adaptive significance of F+, it follows that in the associations of the subject so scored, he is categorizing the object correctly for the consequence to be expected later. (2) Experience with the test in the several personality pictures in the normal population is that individuals in differentiated groups respond with varying percentages of F+. Their perception is varyingly veridical. (3) In the clinical groups, the F+, F− variances consistently follow clinical logic. The more disturbed a patient, the lower his F+ percent; the more integrated, the higher his finding. An overview of these differentials is presented in the accompanying table (see Table 2.1).

The general statement from findings in normal and in clinical groups is: F+ varies directly with veridical perception. The persons who manage their affairs successfully in life, those who accurately perceive the meanings of objects and accurately predict consequences to follow from confrontation with these objects, are those (assuming always certain other Rorschach data in their total patterns) whose F+ percentages range between 75 and 90. Quoting this generalization in Bruner's language: "In fine, adequate perceptual representation involves the learning of appropriate categories, the learning of cues useful in placing objects appropriately in such systems of categories" (p. 127).

Empirical F+ findings for the persons in the healthy population samples are consistent with another detail of Bruner's theorizing. He speaks, at several points, of learning that goes on in perceptual categorizing: "Learning how to isolate, weigh, and use criterial attribute values . . . In learning to perceive we are . . . *learning to predict and to check what goes with what* . . . " (p. 126, Bruner's italics). He reasons: "The most appropriate pattern of readiness at any given moment would be that one which would lead on the average to the most 'veridical' guess about the nature of the world around one" (p. 130). These excerpts, and also the one below concerning "the most ready perceiver, otc.," exactly describe the persons with F+ percentages in the 75–95 percent levels. Using my results (Table 2.1) as point of reference and assuming the validity of the F+ concept, I may put it that the Rorschach data support Bruner's theorizing.

A word is in order here concerning the way I constructed my normative F+ lists. In my early years with the test I tried it out on many persons with whom I had professional contact. Principally, there were psychologists, psychiatrists, social workers, people in academic positions, others in business or in public affairs. All were of mature but not advanced age. These persons (51 in all; their responses collected in the years 1929–32), all necessarily of superior intelligence, were my original criterion population. I always felt a pressing need for an average population with which to test out this list

Table 2.1. F+ Trends in Various Personality Groups

Personality Groups	F+ Percentage
Normal adults	
Superior intelligence	85 to 95*
Average intelligence	75 to 90
Inferior intelligence	60 to 75
Children	
Ages 10 and up	60 to 85
Ages 6 to 9	58 to 70
Ages 5 and below	55 and lower
Simple feeble-minded	
Medium deficiency	45 to 70
Severest deficiency	40 and lower
Affective psychoses	
Manic depression	
manic	40 to 70
depressed	up to 100
In two patterns of schizophrenia	
Very disordered	
paranoid	below 60; varying with degree of disorder
In one pattern of schizophrenia	
Intellectually cramped,	
rigid; emotionally bland	65 to 85
In transition schizophrenics	50 to 75
Organic psychoses	varies downward with degree of deterioration

For healthy adults, all intelligence levels, mean percent is 83.91; SD 8.12. Critical minimum for healthy is 60.
*All ranges are approximate.

obtained from a group at the upper end of the intelligence curve. The opportunity came in 1948–49 on an NIH grant. Rorschach response records were collected individually from 157 persons. This is the Spiegel sample composed of employees in a large mail-order house from the lowest work classification to a subexecutive group. In the report for this research (Beck, et al., 1950) we describe the method whereby I set up the original F+ list (the superior group) and the corrections that were indicated by the findings in the 157 men and women representative of the mid-range of the population in Chicago.

The F+ list that I have been using in recent years rests on two foundations. One is the percepts of my superior persons intellectually, persons functioning effectively in their respective fields and presumably healthy. Among them were a university professor who later became president of a university and is now directing a leading scientific institution; a woman professor in another university; a woman filling an important governmental post when she took the Rorschach and who continued to serve in that post for more than 30 years—these individuals and their full test records I have reported (Beck, 1967).

My theory is that brighter individuals of a society are the first to perceive the realities of that society's universe. They "know the properties of objects and events we encounter," to use Bruner's language. They invent the complex tools and they grasp the social values. They are "the brains" in the literal as well as the figurative sense. On their growth and thinking depends their society's survival. The principle is as old as biblical wisdom: except the leaders have vision, the people perisheth. However, the visions of its leaders are not yet the people's realities. The percepts must also become the experienced realities of the greater portion of the people, in the middle range—in statistical jargon, those within two sigma on each side of the mean. The intellectual discovers the realities. The middle two-thirds are the final authority regarding what are to be the current realities. What they accept as of now, goes, is true, is real.

Therefore, we subjected our original F+ list (as obtained from the superior adults) to the scrutiny of the authority. We gave the test to the sample out of the middle two-thirds of the population. This is the second foundation for the F+ norms which I presently use. By the associations so gathered we corrected and enlarged the original list. It is of interest that Beizmann's manual, which I received only in June of 1966, from Paris, is a compilation of the F+, F– scorings as published by Rorschach, Loosli-Usteri, and myself (1966). The Beizmann manual is likely to become an international standard reference source.

The corollary of all the foregoing is that F+ is a major index to the ego's functioning. A person responding within the healthy F+ range (75–95 percent) knows the realities of his society. He knows the "criterial attribute values required of an instance to be coded in a given class . . . " (p. 131, Bruner's italics). That is, he knows what to do in most exigencies presented by daily life. It may be only that he can fix a minor defect in one of the numerous electrical appliances that now make up a household; it may be that he pays his bills with reasonable promptness; or it may be that in his interpersonal transactions he has due regard for the rights and dignity of the other. He has acquired both the pragmatic know-how available to most persons in the middle two-thirds of the population, and he is sensitive to the values of his group culture. To the extent that he carries on practically and lives by those values—again, it takes variables in addition to F+ to indicate that he does so—he has the esteem of those about him. His awareness that he has that esteem is the psychodynamic source of his own self-esteem. And the measure of one's self-esteem is the measure of one's ego. One's F+ percent, as a principal measure of self-esteem, is a principal dimension in measuring one's ego.

Some other of Bruner's attributes of the perception process are recognizable in the Rorschach concept. Bruner writes, "Where the fit to accessible categories is not precise, or when the linkage between cue and category is low in probability in the past experience of the organism, the conscious experience of cue searching occurs. 'What is that thing?' Here, one is scanning the environment for data in order to find cues that permit a more precise placement of the object" (p. 131). He is here stating the fourth of Rorschach's four criteria for F+, that is, critical discrimination. Rorschach puts it this way: "Fourth is the ability to select out the most similar among the memory images that present themselves. This is in the main a many sided associational process which again itself depends on the attention. This must be directed now not only to the external stimulus but also on the mobilizing memory images, in order to enable one to control the perception activity and to criticize his perception" (Rorschach, 1932, p. 61). (The German word is Deutung, literally "interpretation"; in this context better rendered as "perception").

Bruner writes, "The most ready perceiver would then have the best chances of estimating situations most adequately and planning accordingly" (p. 130). In taking the Rorschach test, the persons in the high-average to superior intelligence ranges speedily associate with the usual F+ percepts, as indicated in the measured time per first response and average time for all responses. They disclose their planning and foresight abilities in the high level at which they grasp relationships between their percepts (the organization activity, z), an ability that varies directly with levels of intelligence in integrated individuals.

The accessibility of categories is another feature of perceptual readiness in Bruner's theorizing, and he adds, "The more frequently in a given context instances of a given category occur, the greater the accessibility of the category" (p. 132). The category most accessible in the Rorschach test stimuli is the animal forms. This is universal experience with the test. Human forms are next in frequency, i.e., they are next in accessibility. The empirical fact is that the higher the intelligence of the person, the smaller the animal percentage in his associational content, and the greater the number of his human forms. Cues are available for both animal and human percepts. The test, as it taps these two most accessible categories, differentiates those of higher intelligence insofar as they utilize the less common cues. By associating more about humans, they disclose a broader interest in their fellows.

The identification of things realistically, important as it is toward getting on in one's world, is not the first step in the perception process. Before one categorizes the object, one must attend to it. The Rorschach test technique for any S's attention pattern is the proportion in which he selects wholes, major details, and minor details of the inkblot figures (respectively designated as W, D, Dd). Regarding this variable I had for many years been perplexed by my readily obtaining data that conflicted with Rorschach's formulated theory. It took a paper by Roger Brown, "How Shall a Thing Be Called" (1958), to help clear what was a theoretical roadblock.

Rorschach writes: " . . . the number of W is before all index to the energy available for the drive to associate. Often it is also an index to the conscious or unconscious wish for complex achievement, of abstracting or synthesizing. Large number of good, primary W responses are frequently found in the philosophically disposed while larger number of good, synthesized W responses are frequently produced by those with imaginative talent. These abilities when optimally found are additional components of high intelligence" (1932, pp. 63–64). While, to be sure, Rorschach also describes various kinds of W, some of which would be inconsistent with high intelligence, my own empiric data stubbornly insisted that some persons responded with many W who could not be of high intelligence. The very young child consistently associates to the whole test figure. The feeble-minded do so and, what is even more perplexing, the lower the intelligence rating, the more W's I have been finding in some; occasionally a feeble-minded subject in the lowest range would produce 10 W, one for each blot figure. Differentiating features, to be sure, emerged in the framework of the response record in its entirety and valid diagnostic pictures could be drawn. This was pragmatic method, based on empiric results. Theory remained obscure.

Brown's article (1958) provided the clarifying leads. Citing an older study (M. E. Smith, 1926) on the topic of children's vocabulary, he writes,

> Fish is likely to be learned before perch and bass. House before bungalow and mansion; car before Chevrolet and Plymouth. The more concrete vocabulary waits for the child to reach an age where his purposes differentiate kinds of fish and makes of cars [p. 18].

Thus the child first learns the name of the class as a whole. He reacts to a category of objects before he discriminates the particulars that enter them. "The child over-generalizes the use of a conventional word," wrote Brown. "The word dog may, at first, be applied to every kind of four-legged animal. It sometimes happens that every man who comes into the house is called daddy" (p. 19).

The child in his earlier learning phases reacts to whole classes. It is what he does with his Rorschach test stimuli. He responds to them holistically. At the older ages, the attention distributes to details; perception is now more discriminating. This shift in the W-D selection can be traced also in the feeble-minded but later in the chronological ages and varying directly with the degree of mental deficiency. Some patients with brain pathology also associate excessively to wholes, and an occasional depressed person does so. The ability to discriminate the salient elements of one's environment, like the ability to recognize the particular individuals in it, develops thus with chronological growth, and depends on a healthy brain in an individual psychologically liberated.

Brown's observation about naming the class is exemplified also in Rorschach test experience. Younger children more frequently associate "an animal," "a bird," "a man," than they do "an elephant," "a clown," "a dancer." "The best generalization," comments Brown, with regard to vocabulary growth, "seems to be that each thing is first given its most common name. This name seems to categorize on the level of usual utility . . . " (p. 19). Once again, then, a Rorschach test procedure is comfortable in a theoretical bed made for a particular component in perception, namely, the attention process.

This support can be found also in the position which Brown takes relative to cognitive development. "The primitive state in cognition is one of comparative lack of differentiation. Probably certain distinctions are inescapable; the difference between a loud noise and mere silence; between a bright contour and a dark ground, etc. These inevitable discriminations divide the perceived world into a smaller number of very large (abstract) categories. Cognitive development is increasing differentiation. The more distinctions we make, the more categories we have and the smaller (more concrete) these are" (Brown, 1958, p. 19).

In the Rorschach test experience, the order of W findings is: (1) the young child's wholes, a monolithic, nondiscriminating percept; (2) attention to component details, and in some responses a reorganizing of them into wholes—the themes are not likely to be unusual; rather, they are in categories frequently produced; (3) much distribution of the attention both to wholes and details, including fine details—after the blot figure is thus broken down, it may be energetically resynthesized into a meaningful unit, usually of original content. The university president (Beck, 1967) is the exemplar, but similar responses form the associational products of many men and women at leadership levels in their professions.

These persons are the abstract thinkers in the sense that Rorschach uses the term. They are the ones who detect the commonalities in varied events and penetrate to the general force or principle inherent in the many instances. Thus are hypotheses created in science. Newton grasped that the falling apple and the planets revolving around the sun exemplified the same law; in a similar manner did Darwin hypothesize in his observations about the habits of giant turtles and wingless locusts; and so did Freud concerning a young woman's aphonia and a young man's hostility to his fiancée. Gravity, evolution, and unconscious were their respective abstractions.

Brown erroneously construes the vocabulary of the very young child as abstraction. When the child says "fish," "house," "car" he is not abstracting in the sense of penetrating and understanding the properties that make them the one class that they are. What the child is reacting to is what he can see, eat, touch. This is so when all dogs are just "dog" and all men are "daddy." This is not abstract but decidedly concretistic cognition. Brown is only partly right when he says:

"Cognitive development is increasing differentiation" (p. 19). It is that and in another, later developmental stage, and more rarely achieved, it is a resynthesizing of the differentiated and an abstracting out of general significance.

The Rorschach test offers important evidence concerning the development of the thinking process. The course of W as an index to undifferentiated holistic perception, then to discrimination of parts and wholes, and then to abstraction at the highest level, parallels the chronological growth of the child. And as Brown notes, "The school boy who learns the word quadruped has abstracted from differentiated and named subordinates . . . " (p. 20).

IV.

Now about an opportunity that is being missed by academic, experimental psychologists, that is, the opportunity to be both psychologists and scientists. I assume that we psychologists are engaged in our particular work because of our interest in human nature. I assume this for all psychologists, whether in the laboratory or in the clinic, whether watching the rat in his maze, the human being in his neurosis, the dog responding to a bell, or the man to a red light on the street corner; the bee or the ant societies toiling and swarming in their nests and their hives, or Homo sapiens wasting himself and striving in his conglomerate, competitive society. On whichever of these areas we concentrate, our interests as psychologists ultimatley root back to one source: What makes the most intelligent of all animals behave as he does? What are the mainsprings and what are the inner works of human behavior?

One of our difficulties is that we feel the Socratic doubt: What can we really know? Which is to say, what is the truth? And an even more difficult question, what is the truth about human nature? The laboratory psychologist rigorously controls all variables but one. But how much does he see? The clinical psychologist "feels" himself into his fellow human being. But how clearly—or rather, how dimly—does he see that being? It is the dilemma of the psychologist: he can be either rigidly accurate and know less, or he can venture farther and lose his way. On the other hand, each one of us, whatever our interest area, is making some real advance in psychological knowledge even though none of us can apprehend truth in its entirety. This is aside from the circumstance that "all our truths are only relative truths, truths but relative to man and to all other aspects of truth, and yet the nearest thing to absolute truth that man can obtain; that absolute truth is, in

fact, at least insofar as man is concerned, a semantic confusion"
(Huskins, 1951, p. 688). Truth to its pursuer is, in fact, what in Keats'
"Ode on a Grecian Urn" the maiden is to the lover:

> Bold Lover, never, never canst thou kiss,
> Though winning near the goal—yet do not grieve;
> She cannot fade, though thou hast not thy bliss,
> For ever wilt thou love, and she be fair!

The pursuit goes on then. On the stage of personality research,
prior to the time that the Rorschach test made its bow, a number of
actors had made their entrances and their exits. There were the
Kent-Rosanoff list, sundry questionnaires and personality inventories, the eidetic imagery of the Jaensches, the constitutional types out
of Marburg, Jung's extrovert hypothesis out of Zurich.

Yet we in clinical psychology and the people in our sister disciplines—psychiatry, social work, or the specialized ones, such as
delinquency—were not happy with our results. Something was
amiss. Findings were fragmentary. They turned up information about
part functions of the individual which remained static descriptions.
The investigators did not dare reason, or even speculate, about how
the individual uses these functions in his overall adaptive stuggle.
Rorschach and his test turned a corner in the history of the exploration of personality. It is an instrument that comes near to being one
that can trace out a behavior pattern both in breadth and in depth.
With its entry on the stage of personality exploring, let us say that Act
One closed.

The curtain rises on Act Two, and some new characters enter on
the scene. The statisticians have sharpened their daggers. Let us not
call them the villains of the piece—we need them. I prefer to look on
them as the Loyal Opposition. Their methodology and logic are ever
essential for the inspection of our data. They worm their way through
our errors and provide the compass with which we set the new
directions of our research. The trouble with so many statisticians is
that they want to put the statistical cart before the psychological
horse. They criticize results on the ground that they do not fit the cut
prescribed by this or that statistical rule.

There is a hazard in the tight constraint effected by the reins of
statistics. The result can be to snaffle scientific venture and freedom.
We bend the knee before the authority of the coefficient of correlation,
of chi square, of the t-test, and then there is the statistical test with two
tails. Research reports close with an affirmation of faith: "The results
are significant at the .01 or the .001 or the .05 degree of confidence."

Critically essential as statistics are as correctives in any scientific endeavor, the question is in order whether the statistician always remembers that his rationales are *aids* to science, but not science, in the sense of observing events in nature. Statisticians may in fact be vulnerable to an occupational hazard. In becoming so enamored of their own brain child, they lost sight of its relationship to the data which it helps to illuminate. It may be their escape from reality.

Authoritarianism in science is of course nothing new. Where the danger lies, again citing the Huskins paper, is in "the desire to accept authority." That is, the younger recruits in the field, in their yearning for security, cling to the rules and the formulae for dear life. Becoming compulsively bound, the loss which they take in terms of scientific imagination may be irreparable. The freedom to err is the price of creativity.

But freedom can loosen into license and license degenerate into anarchy. The Rorschach scene is at present a chaos of sights and a cacophony of sounds, with very little sign of real order. With few exceptions, so far as I can judge from published reports of Rorschach test material, everyone using the test does that which is right in his own eyes. Examiners ignore rules of administration. In evaluating responses they disregard such statistical norms as have been worked out. Many use the test simply for the thematic content which it evokes. Since there are no established guidelines to semantics of theme, what these examiners are doing is no more than free associating to the patient's free associations. They thus evade the task of identifying the formal variables and of doing the structural analysis. Such method of analysis is the most important contribution the Rorschach has made toward the objective exploration of a personality. It is a demanding task but psychologists bypass it. The Rorschach scene can thus be described in the words of another writer in the *American Scientist* (Stern, 1956) and I use his Latin: *Quot capita tot sensus.* Freely rendered, "The number of heads is equal to the number of Rorschach methods."

For relief from this turbid scene we turn to the statisticians. The questions they have been opening up concerning the principles of the test, its assumptions, its claims, are welcome ones to serious workers with it. They are challenges which, when met, must lead to discarding what is not valid, confirming what is. Accepting these challenges, we ask them to meet our request: to devise a statistical method that will aid us in solving our problem. As statisticians progress toward that end they will be advancing their own science toward a new, creative phase. As they progress they will aid the clinician in eschewing his own occupational hazard: the basis which enters into any psychological judgment. In point here is the caution in the Huskins (1951) paper:

> The biologist, beyond all other scientists, has to recognize that all his data, all his conclusions, are part of a web of which he himself is a component, his experience strands therein; he is never on the outside looking in, but always a part of the problem he is seeking to solve [p. 691].

If this is so about a presumably objective science such as biology, how much more true is it in the field of psychology, and more especially in the field of personality!

V.

What are the research opportunities in general psychology arising out of Rorschach test concepts? I list here, in condensation, some suggestions to be undertaken by laboratory—not Rorschach—experimental techniques set up *ad hoc*. Rorschach test principles and insights are certain to profit as these are carried out and general psychological knowledge is thereby extended.

DW, DdW, DdD.   These are the responses in which S attends only to a detail (DW) and refers the meaning (categories) to the entire blot figure. Or S does so although attending only to a rare detail (DdW). In instances he attends to a rare detail and refers the meanings to a larger detail of which it is a part (DdD). Some questions for general psychology are: What are the variances in the amount of cue used by S's in categorizing an object? What variances in accuracy of the percept go with variances in the amount of cue used? Among relevant theoretic questions in perception are: Do some persons perceive the part as a whole? Do some persons reason regarding the whole from the part? What is the relation of speed in categorizing to accuracy?

W.   The ability to comprehend objects as units. The experimental stimuli will need to be constructed so that S may be free to attend to parts or the wholes. The stimuli are to vary in difficulty. The population sample is to consist of children ranging in age from earliest years into adolescence. This experiment is especially applicable to Brown's theorizing.

Z.   The ability to relate percepts meaningfully. Two or more percepts are organized into a new form. The new categorizing obtains in none of the parts alone, only in the new unit. While W is one form of Z, the mental process involved in Z is more complex. It frequently consists first in breaking down the whole stimulus and then organizing—an analytic-synthesis activity. Gestalt principles are demonstrated in Z, as I have shown(Beck,1933).The population sample for Z is to be principally adults; if tried in children psychometric ratings should be available. The results are to be studied for their variance with generalizing and abstracting abilities in the respective persons.

The personal F–.   Erratic perceptions that can be shown as mirroring interests or needs of serious personal importance to the subject. The individual distorts what he sees under pressure of intense emotions. Gombrich, in his *Art and Illusion*, asserts the primacy of the person in what one sees. Quoting from a review of Gombrich's book by Wollheim,

> Perception, he [Gombrich] argues, is conditioned by the attitude and expectations, by the "mental set" of the observer: and what the observer sees cannot be dissociated from the *schemata* or patterns he imposes upon experience [1960].

The psychologist's experimental technique may well be tachistoscopic and should be a simple one to set up. The difficulty will lie in the validating source. Could a word-association list be set up—one in which the content of the responses suspected of being personal F– would be interspersed with the neutral words?

The white space(s).   The valence for attending to empty, rather than filled, space in the stimulus figure. Gestalt psychology has of course provided a considerable background pertinent to this phenomenon: the figure-and-ground experiments. The psychodynamic interest in the preference for these white spaces has to do with their projecting self-will, obstinacy, negativism. As in the case of the personal F–, the important question is that of a validating criterion.

The textural determinant (T).   This variable, first reported by Klopfer (1956), is more important than the research attention it has received in Rorschach test investigations. There are reasons for this scanty effort. One is the fact that the responses thus scored are rare. Second is the more than usual uncertainty in identifying this determinant. It derives from the shading quality in the stimulus with which the person associates as if with a tactual experience. When S so associates it may be dynamically important when interpreted as stemming out of erotic hunger. Harlow's researchers on the maternal behavior in monkeys come to mind (1958); also Liddel's on sheep (1956). The skin, it has been observed, is probably the largest organ in humans. It is the agent most involved in personal interaction from earliest infancy on. In respect to texture, then, the opportunity is an exceptionally inviting one all the more so because the area has been so little explored. Validating information will of course be a major task.

The fantasy association (M).   Much has been written about this very important Rorschach concept. On the basis of his theory concerning its significance it would seem untestable by experimental method. For M is a window into the unconscious and *ex hypothesis* the unconscious cannot, in working life (when psychological experiment would be carried on), be brought to consciousness. Bruner (1957), to be sure, uses the term *unconscious* in connection with the "silent process in perception as once identified by Helmholtz." However, the unconscious which Bruner describes is not the unconscious of Freud or of psychoanalytic theory. It is the preconscious.

When that world of our dreams, from which we are so hermetically sealed in our waking hours, can be investigated by non-Rorschach sources, we will be in a position to validate or refute the claims for M. The assertions concerning the significance of M are so far-reaching, its dynamic potential for exploring the deeper motivations of human behavior so large, that the psychologist who devises the method may himself be turning a corner in personality study.

Defensive blocking.   The Rorschach test evokes this in a number of its variables: low productivity (R), heightened perceptual accuracy (F+), increased attention to details (D), increased perception of animal forms (A), reduction of the organizing ability (Z). The individual is reducing influx of stimuli and so staves off excitation. An experiment which in varying degrees cuts down the influx of stimuli should be a simple one for the psychology laboratory. This could directly test out the varying incidence of the Rorschach test variables which I here note.

Color shock and shading shock.   The novel stimulus evokes the maximum response. This too is defensive, shuts out more stimuli, and reduces excitement. Are there learning experiments or even sensory (pupillary, auditory) methods of research that educe measurable variation in response with variation in novelty of the stimulus? And does the measure return to normal as the novelty wears off? As the subject becomes acclimated to the novel stimulus first presented, does he then react within his normal measure to any other new stimuli? This kind of research would be a direct experimental check on Rorschach theory concerning color shock and shading shock.

Such are some of the opportunities for psychological investigation that the Rorschach test sphere presents, with promise of fruitfulness for general psychology. To the Rorschach test student they will provide critical information at both the practical and the theoretic levels. The suggested experiments do not exhaust the list of opportunities. There are also the color phenomena, the several shading variables, the experience balance (EB), and the experience actual (EA); the total personality pattern conceived as a functional proposition (Beck, 1966; Rapoport, 1952). It is up to the younger generation of psychologists to push back the horizon.

In closing one can but remember how brief was the life of Hermann Rorschach. Had he lived, it is certain that he would himself have undertaken some laboratory testing of his ideas. He in fact outlines some experiments: the stimulus is a cat painted in the color of a frog; a frog in the color of a finch. He also discusses control series for the present original blot figures (see Rorschach, 1932, pp. 57–58). For the clinical psychologist, Rorschach's great contribution is that he closed the gap between psychometrics and depth personality testing. More important, he made it possible to bridge the gulf between two minds, those of the examiner and of his patient, to bring out into the open regions of the mind otherwise stored away, veiled from the patient and the therapist. One can only speculate how much further Rorschach's fertile mind would have carried this task, had he lived longer.

REFERENCES

Beck, S. J. Configurational tendencies in Rorschach responses. *Am. J. Psychol.*, 1933, 45, 433–443.

Beck, S. J. Emotions and understanding. In *International Psychiatry Clinics.* Vol. 3, No. 1. Boston: Little, Brown, 1966, pp. 93–114.

Beck, S. J. *Rorschach's Test, Vol. II, A Variety of Personality Pictures.* New York: Grune and Stratton, revised edition, with H. B. Molish, 1967.

Beck, S. J., Rabin, A. I., Thiesen, W. G., Molish, H. B., & Thetford, W. N. The normal personality as projected in the Rorschach test. *J. Psychol.*, 1950, 30, 241–298.

Beizmann, C. *Livret de Cotation des Formes dans le Rorschach.* Paris: Centre de Psychologie Appliquée, 1966.

Brown, R. How shall a thing be called? *Psychol. Rev.*, 1958, 65, 14–21.

Bruner, J. S. On perceptual readiness. *Psychol. Rev.*, 1957, 64, 123–152.

Descartes, R. *Discours de la Méthode.* Paris: Editions de Cluny, 1943.

Fieandt, K. von. Toward a unitary theory of perception. *Psychol. Rev.*, 1958, 65, 315–320.

Harlow, H. F. The nature of love. *Am. Psychologist*, 1958, *13*, 673–685.

Huskins, C. L. Science, cytology and society. *Am. Scientist*, 1951, *39*, 688–699, 716.

Klopfer, B., et al. *Developments in the Rorschach Technique*, Vols. I and II. World Book, 1956.

Liddell, H. S. *Emotional Hazards in Animals and Man*. Springfield, Ill.: Charles C. Thomas, 1956, pp. x–97.

Mandler, G., & Kessen, W. *The Language of Psychology*. New York: Wiley, 1959.

Rapoport, A. What is semantics? *Am. Scientist*, 1952, *41*, 123–135.

Rorschach, H. *Psychodiagnostik: Methodik und Ergebnisse eines Wahrnehmungsdiagnostischen Experiments* (ed. 2). Bern: Huber, 1932.

Smith, M. E. An investigation of the development of the sentence and the extent of vocabulary in young children. *Univ. Iowa Stud. Child Welfare*, 1926, *3*(5).

Stern, A. Science and the philosopher. *Am. Scientist*, 1956, *44*, 281–295.

Wollheim, R. Visions of the truth. (Review of E. H. Gombrich, *Art and Illusion*). In The London *Observer*, April 3. 1960.

3

Holtzman Inkblot Technique (HIT)

Wayne H. Holtzman

Drawing heavily upon studies with the Rorschach, the Holtzman
Inkblot Technique (HIT) was designed to overcome psychometric
limitations in the Rorschach by constructing completely new sets of
inkblots. Unlike the Rorschach, which has only ten inkblots in a
single form, the HIT consists of two parallel forms, A and B, each of
which contains 45 inkblots constituting the test series and two practice blots, X and Y, that are identical in both forms. Thus, standardized responses can be obtained from a total of 92 different inkblots
rather than just ten.

The HIT differs from the Rorschach in several important respects
other than merely the number of inkblots. (1) The characteristics of
the HIT stimuli are richer and more varied in color, form, and shading. (2) The blots vary considerably in degree of symmetry or balance,
providing a new stimulus dimension for analysis. (3) The subject is
encouraged to give only one response per card rather than as many as
he wishes, thereby holding more constant the number of responses
given. (4) A brief, simple inquiry follows immediately after each
response. (5) Carefully matched, parallel forms of the HIT are available, permitting the use of test–retest designs and the study of change
within the individual. (6) Standardized percentile norms are provided for 22 inkblot scores on a variety of populations, facilitating
interpretation and analysis. And (7) group methods of administration
and computer scoring make it possible to use the HIT for rapid,
large-scale screening as well as individual diagnosis and assessment.

Development of the HIT was prompted by the growing number of experimental studies following World War II which were critical of the Rorschach. The vigorous postwar growth of psychodiagnostic testing and the resulting fusion of academic and clinical psychology produced a flood of dissertations and related studies evaluating the Rorschach. Although much of this research was irrelevant or too poorly conceived to provide an appropriate evaluation of the Rorschach method, an impressive number of carefully designed validity studies yielded negative results. In the wake of these experimental studies came the growing realization that the Rorschach had inherent psychometric weaknesses, which cast considerable doubt on the interpretation of its quantitative scores.

Such critics as Cronbach (1949), Zubin (1954), and Hertz (1959) have pointed to major difficulties in the Rorschach arising from the examiner–subject interaction and variations in style of inquiry, from lack of satisfactory internal consistency or test–retest reliability for many scores, from lack of agreement as to scoring criteria for different variables, and from the widely varying number of responses often obtained for the ten Rorschach cards. The complex, curvilinear relationship between number of responses and most other scores on the Rorschach makes it impossible to establish adequate norms for most Rorschach scores, forcing the clinician to fall back upon rough rules of thumb for interpretation.

Once one abandons the basic idea of using only ten inkblots, of permitting the subject as few or as many responses as he cares to give, and of conducting a highly variable inquiry for purposes of illuminating the scoring categories, most of the weaknesses inherent in the standard Rorschach can be overcome. The fundamental issue is how to alter the task and develop psychometrically sound scoring procedures for responses to inkblots while still preserving the rich projective material for which the Rorschach has been quite rightly recognized.

The development of the HIT can be thought of in terms of six stages taking place over a period of five years prior to any large-scale reliability or validity studies. First, techniques for producing inkblots were perfected to take advantage of modern inks, papers, and artistic approaches. Second, many hundreds of inkblots were screened by actual administration to subjects and evaluation of the outcome. Third, a conceptual framework and objective scoring procedures were developed by which the inkblots (test "items") could be selected. Fourth, matched pairs of inkblots were established on the basis of item analyses and randomly assignd to Form A or Form B to assure the exact psychometric equivalence of the parallel forms. Fifth, preliminary studies were made using the original inkblots to perfect the scoring system and to produce the evidence needed to justify the great expense of mass production for general use. And sixth, the final engraving and printing of the 92 inkblots was carried out with high precision to assure the fidelity of the copies released for experimental use and eventual clinical application. Only after these major developmental stages were completed was it feasible to undertake large-scale, systematic studies of possible variance due to examiners, inter- and intrascorer agreement, the internal consistency of scores, test–retest reliability using parallel forms, the correlates of inkblot variables, the similarities and differences between the Rorschach and the HIT, group differences for diagnostic purposes, and experimental or clinical applications. Much of this early research is presented in the extensive monograph by Holtzman, Thorpe, Swartz, and Herron (1961) describing the HIT and its development and in the more recent account of the early studies leading up to its publication (Holtzman, 1976).

DESCRIPTION OF THE TEST MATERIALS

Standard materials for the HIT consist of the two parallel series, Form A and Form B, the accompanying printed Record Forms and Summary Sheets, and the *Guide for Administration and Scoring*.[1] Sets of 35-mm slides are also available for use with the group method of administration. A handbook (Hill, 1972) for clinical application of the HIT and a workbook (Hill & Peixotto, 1973) have been published as guides for clinicians. A programmed text and other HIT materials are available in a three-volume series (Hartmann & Rosenstiel, 1977).

The inkblots are printed on thin but tough white cardboard 5½ by 8½ inches in size. Cards X and Y contain practice blots that are usually not scored. These two cards appear at the beginning of both Forms A and B. Card X is a massive achromatic blot which looks like a bat or butterfly to most people. Very few individuals reject this card although some prefer to use a smaller area rather than the whole blot.

---

[1] Materials for the Holtzman Inkblot Technique can be obtained from the Psychological Corporation, 757 Third Avenue, New York, N.Y., 10017.

Card Y is suggestive of a person's torso to most people. Red spots of ink introduce the subject to color and often evoke responses such as "spots of blood," either given alone or integrated with the torso.

Cards 1 and 2 in both A and B are achromatic and sufficiently broken up to make a whole response difficult unless there is integration of detail, or unless the subject gives a very vague concept or one in which the form of the concept fails to fit the form of the inkblot. Both cards have popular responses in smaller areas of the blot, helping to break up a response set to give only wholes. Card 3 is irregular in form and has a large red "sunburst" splotch overlaid on an amorphous black inkblot. It is very difficult to give a form-definite, form-appropriate whole response to Card 3 because of the chaotic, unstructured nature of this inkblot. Card 4 is just the opposite, containing several finely detailed popular concepts that can be interrelated, together with color and shading that produces a vistalike effect. A "battle scene" or "cowboy watching a sunset" are typical of Card 4A, and "knight carrying a spear and shield" is typical of Card 4B.

Cards 5A and 5B are asymmetrical, grayish-colored blots unlike any in the Rorschach. By penetrating the charcoal-like quality of these blots, one can distinguish a number of detailed objects. Together with several similar, rather wispy, amorphous, asymmetrical blots later in the series, these cards are difficult, particularly for the individual who is searching for definite concepts having good form or who wishes to use the entire blot.

The remaining inkblots cover a wide range of stimulus variation, giving the individual ample opportunity to reveal certain aspects of his mental processes and personality by projecting his thoughts onto otherwise meaningless inkblots. Twelve of the inkblots in Form A are black or gray, two are monochromatic, 11 are black with a bright color also present, and the remaining 20 are multicolored. Most of the blots have rich shading variations which help to elicit texture responses. A similar distribution of color, shading, and form qualities is present in Form B.

PROCEDURES OF ADMINISTRATION

Standard procedures have been developed for administering the HIT so that published normative data may be used as an aid to interpretation. Instructions to the subject have been designed to make the task as simple as possible while eliciting sufficient information to score major variables reliably. The basic problem is one of encouraging the subject to respond fully without at the same time revealing to him the specific nature of the variables to be scored. The standard instructions differ from those for the Rorschach inkblots in several ways. First, the examiner instructs the subject to give only one response to each card. Second, the brief inquiry is given immediately after each response. And third, the permissible questions by the examiner during inquiry are limited in scope and are asked rather regularly to avoid inadvertent verbal conditioning of certain determinants or content.

A Record Form and a Summary Sheet are available for the examiner to use in recording responses and scoring. Space is provided on the front page of the Record Form for the subject's name, age, sex, and other identifying data. To facilitate the recording of location, schematic diagrams for the inkblots are included. As each response is given, the examiner outlines the specific area used. Adjacent to the diagram is a blank space for recording the verbatim response or a shortened version of it.

After making appropriate introductions and establishing rapport, the examiner picks up the cards one at a time, handing each one in upright position to the subject. The instructions given the subject should be informal and should stress the following points: (1) these inkblots were not made to look like anything in particular; (2) different people see different things in each inkblot; and (3) only one response for each card is desired.

Immediately following each response, a brief inquiry is made by the examiner to check on certain aspects of the response and to obtain additional information helpful in scoring. Three kinds of questions are permissible in the standard administration: a question to clarify location (Q_L), a question regarding characteristics of the percept (Q_C), and a general question encouraging elaboration (Q_E). The actual wording used can vary a great deal so that the inquiry becomes a natural part of the conversation between examiner and subject. Typical phrasing would be as follows:

Q_L —"Where in the blot do you see a _____?"
Q_C —"What is there about the blot that makes it look like a _____?"
Q_E —"Is there anything else you care to tell me about it?"

Usually the subject comprehends the nature of the task very

quickly and the actual inquiry can be kept to a minimum. A skilled examiner, sensitive to subtle nuances in the examiner–subject interaction, can control the flow of conversation by stimulating a reticent individual and slowing down a verbose person.

In spite of the many interesting variations in test administration that can be attempted, there is much to be said for adhering closely to the standard method of administration. This method has proved highly practical and yields objective, reliable scores on a number of important variables. Currently published normative data and statistical studies of value in the interpretation of the protocols assume close adherence to the standard method of administration.

SCORING

In the course of standardization, an attempt was made to develop quantitative variables which it was believed would cover nearly all of the important scoring categories and dimensions commonly employed with the Rorschach. After an exhaustive review of previous systems for the Rorschach and preliminary studies to determine interscorer agreement, 22 variables were finally carried forward for standardization and analysis. Two variables, Location and Space, deal with the particular parts of the inkblot used by the person in organizing his response and the figure-ground relations of these parts. Form Definiteness, Form Appropriateness, Color, Shading, and Movement are closely related to the stimulus qualities often referred to as the determinants of the response. The more important kinds of content are çoded into Human, Animal, Anatomy, Sex, and Abstract. The quality of the response content is captured in part by such scores as Anxiety, Hostility, Barrier, Penetration, and Pathognomic Verbalization. Integration, Balance, Popular, Reaction Time, and Rejection complete the set of 22 variables for which standardization data have been compiled. A twenty-third variable, Affect Arousal, was included in many of the earlier studies although it proved to be too sensitive to examiner differences for normative purposes. A very brief definition of each variable is given below:

Reaction Time (RT)—the time, in seconds, from presentation of the inkblot to the beginning of the primary response.

Rejection (R)—score 1 when the subject returns the inkblot to the examiner without giving a scorable response.

Location (L)—tendency to break down the inkblot into smaller fragments; score 0 for use of whole blot, 1 for use of a large area of the blot, 2 for use of smaller areas of the blot.

Space (S)—score 1 for response involving a figure-ground reversal where white space constitutes the figure and the inkblot is the ground.

Form Definiteness (FD)—a five-point scale ranging from a score of 0 for a concept having completely indefinite form ("squashed bug") to a score of 4 for highly specific form ("man on horse").

Form Appropriateness (FA)—goodness of fit of the form of the concept to the form of the inkblot; score 0 for poor, 1 for fair, and 2 for good form.

Color (C)—importance of both chromatic and achromatic color as a determinant; score 0 when not used, 1 when used only in a secondary manner (like FC in the Rorschach), 2 when color is a primary determinant but some indefinite form is present or implied (as in the Rorschach CF), and 3 when color is primary and no form is present (like C in the Rorschach).

Shading (Sh)—importance of shading or texture as a determinant; score 0 when not used, 1 when used only in a secondary manner, and 2 when shading is a primary determinant.

Movement (M)—a five-point scale for measuring the degree of movement, tension, or dynamic energy projected into the percept by the subject, regardless of content; score 0 for none, 1 for static potential (sitting, looking, resting), 2 for casual movement (walking, talking), 3 for dynamic movement (dancing, weeping), and 4 for violent movement (whirling, exploding).

Pathognomic Verbalization (V)—a five-point scale ranging from 0 (no pathology present) to 4 (very bizarre verbalizations) for measuring the degree of disordered thinking represented by fabulations, fabulized combinations, queer responses, incoherence, autistic logic, contaminations, self-references, deteriorated color responses, and absurd responses.

Integration (I)—score 1 when two or more adequately perceived blot elements are organized into a larger whole.

Human (H)—score 0 for no human content present, 1 for parts of human beings, featureless wholes or cartoon characters, 2 for differentiated humans or the human face if elaborated.

Animal (A)—score 0 for no animal content, 1 for animal parts, and 2 for whole animals.

Anatomy (At)—score 0 for no penetration of the body wall, 1 for X-rays, medical drawings, or bone structures, and 2 for viscera or soft internal organs.

Abstract (Ab)—score 0 if no abstract concept is present, 1 if abstract elements are secondary, and 2 if the response is wholly abstract, e.g., "Reminds me of happiness."

Anxiety (Ax)—a three-point scale for rating the degree of anxiety apparent in the content of the response as reflected in feelings or attitudes ("frightening animal"), expressive behavior ("girl escaping"), symbolic responses ("dead person"), or cultural stereotypes of fear ("witch"); score 1 when debatable or indirect and score 2 when clearly evident.

Hostility (Hs)—a four-point scale for rating degree of hostility apparent in the content of the response, with increasing score as hostility moves from vague or symbolic expressions to more direct, violent ones in which human beings are involved.

Barrier (Br)—score 1 for reference to any protective covering, membrane, shell, or skin that might be symbolically related to the perception of body-image boundaries.

Penetration (Pn)—score 1 for concepts symbolic of body penetration.

Balance (B)—score 1 where the subject expresses concern for the symmetry–asymmetry dimension of the inkblot.

Popular (P)—score 1 if a popular response is given, popular responses being defined statistically for specific areas of the inkblots in earlier normative studies of the HIT.

The total score for each of the 22 variables is obtained by summing across the 45 cards, using the Summary Sheet as a convenient form for this purpose. In addition to the total scores, it is a simple matter to derive a number of other special scores from the basic elements coded for each blot. For example, the number of W, D, or Dd responses in Rorschach terms can be determined by counting the number of cards coded 0, 1, or 2, respectively, on Location. If the number of human movement responses is desired, one need only count the cards in which Movement is coded 2 or higher and Human is coded 1 or 2. The number of FC, CF, or C responses in the Klopfer system for the Rorschach can be readily derived by merely counting the number of chromatic cards coded 1, 2, or 3, respectively, for Color. Such configural scoring is easy to do directly from the Summary Sheet and opens up a large number of special-purpose scores, some entirely new and others highly similar to scores in the several Rorschach systems.

Detailed scoring instructions and examples are provided in the *Guide* as well as elsewhere (Holtzman, et al., 1961; Hill, 1972; Hill & Peixotta, 1973). The brief definitions given above serve only to introduce the reader to the kinds of inkblot variables scored. It is important to study carefully the detailed scoring guide before attempting to score the HIT.

Nearly all of the scores developed for the HIT are based upon earlier studies with the Rorschach. Because of the greatly increased number of cards in the HIT, most of the scores have higher reliability than is attainable with only the ten cards in the Rorschach. Rejection, in particular, becomes a variable of some significance in its own right. The total score on Color is rather similar to the weighted Sum C score on the Rorschach. Movement is similar to the dynamic energy level scores proposed by Sells, Frese, and Lancaster (1952) and Zubin and Eron (1953) for the Rorschach. Pathognomic Verbalization is a refinement of the system developed by Rapaport, Schafer, and Gill (1946) for interpretation of deviant verbalizations. Integration is taken directly from the work by Beck (1949) and Phillips, Kaden, and Waldman (1959). The five content variables are rather similar to some of Zubin and Eron's (1953) special content rating scales. Anxiety and Hostility are adapted from the studies by Elizur (1949) and Murstein (1956). The two body-image scores, Barrier and Penetration, are taken directly from the extensive studies of body image and personality by Fisher and Cleveland (1958). Balance is a completely new variable made possible by the varying degrees of asymmetry in the HIT blots. And Popular is defined conventionally as responses which occur with a frequency of at least one in seven over a large normal population. Using a sample of 304 cases for Form A and a sample of 309 cases for form B, this statistical definition yielded 25 inkblots in each form with popular percepts, testifying further to the precise equivalence of the parallel forms.

No doubt there are other variables which can be scored for standard HIT protocols. Indeed, several investigators have already developed new scores for special purposes. The standardized set of 22 variables, however, covers most contemporary systems for measuring dimensions present in inkblot perception and includes several new variables of interest.

A useful procedure for mastering the subtleties of the HIT scoring system is to practice administering the inkblots to several individuals after a careful reading of the *Guide*. These protocols can then be scored, one or two variables at a time, to gain familiarity with the system. Samples of difficult responses already scored are given in the monograph, providing additional practice for the beginner. While the first several protocols will take hours for the novice to score, it is common experience that after ten or twelve protocols an individual can score a protocol in 20 to 30 minutes with reasonably high reliability.

RELIABILITY OF INKBLOT SCORES

The original standardization studies for the HIT were carried out on 15 different samples totaling 1334 individuals and 1642 protocols. Among normal populations, the samples ranged from five-year-olds through elementary and secondary schools to college students, housewives, and working-class men. Among the abnormal populations were samples drawn from chronic paranoid schizophrenics, general schizophrenic patients, mentally retarded individuals, and mentally depressed adult patients. Studies of both intrascorer and interscorer consistency were carried out for several of these samples. Determinations of test–retest reliability or intrasubject stability over time intervals ranging from one week to one year were made for four of the normal samples. And estimates of internal consistency or immediate intrasubject stability were routinely obtained by the split-half method for each variable in each one of the 15 samples.

Highly trained scorers agree to a high degree on nearly all the 22 variables, according to one study of interscorer consistency on a sample of 40 schizophrenic protocols. The interscorer correlations ranged from .89 to .995, with a median value of .98. But what about the average person who may be scoring HIT records? What kind of accuracy can he hope to achieve? One study aimed at answering this question involved four examiners, nine inkblot variables, and 96 protocols. Each examiner collected 24 protocols assigned randomly from the pool of subjects. He scored his own protocols immediately and once again three months later. In addition, each examiner scored 24 protocols drawn in a balanced manner from those collected by the other three examiners. The examiners varied in experience from one highly trained person to two moderately trained persons to an intelligent secretary who read the *Guide*, learned the system as best she could by herself, and then served as an examiner in the experiment. The average interscorer consistency of these four examiners across the nine most difficult variables to score ranged from a low of .73 for Form Appropriateness to a high of .89 for Color, with a median of .84 (Holtzman, et al., 1961). Similar correlations for intrascorer consistency ranged from .89 for Penetration to .97 for Color, with a median of .93.

While the interscorer agreement is appreciably less than that obtained when only highly trained scorers are used, in most cases it is sufficiently high to indicate that moderately trained scorers can agree very well. The untrained scorer did almost as well as the moderately trained ones, demonstrating that a neophyte can master most of the system fairly well entirely on his own. At the time the study was conducted, the scoring manual was incomplete and only the highly experienced examiner had sufficient experience to incorporate all of the subtle but important scoring criteria which are now explicitly outlined in the *Guide*. Others have obtained interscorer correlations at least this high on various populations and under varying conditions. Whitaker (1965) reported interscorer agreement of .81 for Pathognomic Verbalization, and Megargee (1965a) obtained agreement coefficients ranging from .73 to 1.00, with a median value of .96, in scoring all 22 variables.

Another important concern is the extent to which the examiner may be a factor influencing the performance of the subject. Two of the examiners in the original methodological study on administration and scoring reliability were men and two were women; each differed greatly from the others in personality and appearance; and, of course, they varied considerably in experience. Since the subjects were randomly assigned to examiners, and since every protocol was scored three times in a balanced design, any significant sources of variance due to examiners or due to scoring could be isoalted and interpreted. Only two variables—Color and Pathognomic Verbalization—showed significant examiner bias for the rescored records. In each case the source of bias was the untrained examiner, the secretary who tried to learn the system on her own.

In a study by Megargee, Lockwood, Cato, and Jones (1966), three inexperienced female examiners each gave the HIT to 30 college students, half women and half men, a total of 90 cases. For one-half of the cases each examiner assumed a positive, pleasant, reassuring role, while for the other half she tried to be negative and foreboding. Unlike Lord's (1950) study with the Rorschach where both the examiner and the tone of administration proved to be major factors influencing responses, the HIT was quite free of situational influences with two minor exceptions—small examiner differences in Rejection and Shading. Together with the earlier studies, these results indicate that the examiner is not an important source of variance in the HIT.

By using the parallel forms of the HIT in a test–retest design, the amount of intrasubject stability over time can be determined. This design was employed in four of the standardization samples: 139 college students with an interval of one week between testing sessions, 72 eleventh-grade high school students with a three-month interval, 42 elementary school pupils with an interval of one year, and 48 college students with a one-year interval. This same design was also employed in a longitudinal study of school children who were tested annually for a period of six years, alternating Forms A and B from year to year (Holtzman, Diaz-Guerrero, & Swartz, 1975). Test–retest coefficients for the first three years of this study, based on 691 cases ranging in age from six to 14 years, are very similar to those obtained in the standardization studies reported by Holtzman and associates (1961).

The most stable scores over time are Reaction Time, Location, Movement, and Human. Test–retest correlations between Forms A and B for these scores run in the 60s and 70s even after a one-year interval. The most unstable scores for normals over a period of one year are Popular, Anatomy, Space, Sex, Abstract, Balance, and Pathognomic Verbalization, usually with coefficients in the 20s or 30s. The remaining 11 scores are moderately stable over a year's time, generally yielding test–retest coefficients in the 40s or 50s. As indicated in Table 3.1, test–retest coefficients are slightly higher for an interval of only one week. In general, it can be concluded that the stability of most scores is sufficiently high to justify use of the HIT to study changes in perception and personality over a period of many months.

In all of these studies using both Forms A and B with the same subjects, statistical tests were also made to determine the equivalence of the parallel forms. In every instance, neither means, standard deviations, nor intercorrelations of any inkblot scores differed significantly from Form A to Form B, testifying further to the precise equivalence of the two forms.

Another approach to reliability is the computation of split-half reliability coefficients as measures of internal consistency or immediate intrasubject stability. Six of the variables—Reaction Time, Location, Form Definiteness, Form Appropriateness, Animal, and Popular—have good, reasonably normal distributions in all of the standardization samples. For these variables, the reliability estimates should be generally accurate. Color, Movement, Human, Hostility, Anxiety, and Barrier have good distributions in all the normal samples but are sharply skewed in one or more of the abnormal samples. Shading, Integration, and Penetration have good distributions only in the samples of college students. The remaining eight variables are sharply skewed or truncated in every sample, making somewhat questionable the accuracy of the reliability estimates using the split-half method. The range and median reliability values for the 15 samples and 18 of the variables are given in Table 3.1.

Reaction Time, Rejection, Location, Form Definiteness, and Color have consistently high reliability, a large number of coefficients

Table 3.1.   Split-Half Reliability and Test–Retest Stability of Inkblot Variables

Inkblot Variable	Split-Half r's for 15 Samples		Test–Retest r with Interval of 1 Week (139 College Students)
	Range	Median	
Reaction Time	.95–.98	.97	.77
Rejection	.79–.98	.93	.76
Location	.86–.94	.91	.82
Form Definiteness	.81–.96	.88	.68
Form Appropriateness	.44–.91	.85	.55
Color	.70–.94	.88	.59
Shading	.62–.94	.78	.70
Movement	.71–.93	.81	.70
Pathognomic Verbalization	.49–.96	.87	.68
Integration	.59–.84	.79	.70
Human	.66–.93	.79	.67
Animal	.53–.95	.70	.38
Anatomy	.54–.94	.71	.53
Anxiety	.31–.91	.66	.54
Hostility	.54–.89	.71	.61
Barrier	.47–.85	.70	.45
Penetration	.41–.92	.62	.54
Popular	.00–.77	.51	.39

above .90. Most of the remainder are also highly satisfactory, only Popular proving to be generally low. Complete tables are given in the monograph by Holtzman and co-workers (1961), including standard errors of measurement as well as means, standard deviations, and reliability coefficients for each variable and population studied. Normative statistical data for other populations have been compiled by Hill (1972) and by Holtzman, et al. (1975). These data are useful in establishing a confidence interval for an individual score prior to interpretation.

DIMENSIONS PRESENT IN INKBLOT SCORES

What can be said about the psychological meaning of inkblot variables, granted that they can be reliably measured? How do such variables relate to each other and to independent measures of personality? Are they of value in the differential diagnosis of mental or emotional disorders? What do they tell us about developmental processes? Before examining the validity of inkblot variables for various purposes, it may be instructive to look at the intercorrelations among the 22 HIT variables and the major dimensions they have in common.

Complete intercorrelation matrices of all inkblot scores were computed routinely for each of the samples in the standardization program. While correlations between any two inkblot scores may be of some interest when replicated over many samples, a more efficient way of examining the relationships among inkblot variables is to employ factor analysis and factor matching across samples. In nearly every case, six factors account for all the significant common variance present among the 22 variables. The first three of these have appeared in a number of factor-analytic studies of HIT variables, including some on samples from other countries. The last three tend to be less stable, shifting somewhat in composition according to the kind of population studied. The major patterns that have clearly emerged are as follows:

Factor I. Perceptual Maturity and Integrated Ideational Activity

Invariably defined by Movement, Integration, Human, Barrier, and Popular, Factor I usually accounts for more variance than any other. Anxiety and Hostility may also have moderately high loadings on

Factor I, particularly among children or mentally retarded adults. A high amount of this factor would be indicative of well-organized ideational activity, good imaginative capacity, well-differentiated ego boundaries, and awareness of conventional concepts.

Factor II. Perceptual Sensitivity

Defined primarily by Color and Shading, and to a lesser extent by Form Definiteness (reversed), this bipolar factor involves sensitivity to the stimulus qualities of the blots. Balance also shows significant loadings in some populations, most notably adult schizophrenics. The positive pole of this factor would indicate overreactivity to the color, shading, or symmetrical balance of the inkblot, while the negative pole would indicate primary concern for form alone as a determinant.

Factor III. Psychopathology of Thought

Pathognomic Verbalization is the best single variable for defining this factor, although Anxiety and Hostility frequently have high loadings. Among children, Penetration is often a significant contributor to this underlying dimension, and in many abnormal populations Form Appropriateness (reversed) has appreciable loadings. A high amount of this factor would be indicative of disordered thought processes coupled with an active, though disturbed fantasy life.

Factor IV. Perceptual Differentiation

Although not as well defined because of the overshadowing influence of the first three factors, in most samples, particularly among children, Form Appropriateness and Location serve as defining variables. The factor is bipolar, the positive pole tending to indicate perceptual differentiation coupled with a critical sense of good form.

Factor V.

Reaction Time, Rejection, and Animal (reversed) are the primary variables defining this factor. While Reaction Time and Rejection tend to go together in nearly every population, other scores vary in their contribution to this pattern, making it difficult to generalize from one sample to the next. A high score on this factor may reflect either strong inhibition or inability to perceive concepts in the blots, depending on other factors present.

Factor VI.

In about half of the populations studied, this residual factor takes the form of a minor pathological dimension defined by Penetration, Anatomy, and, where present, Sex. This particular pattern signifies a dimension indicative of bodily preoccupations independent of pathological components noted in Factor III.

Among children, Factors I and III often tend to be correlated. A moderately high amount of Pathognomic Verbalization, Anxiety, and Hostility in children may not be indicative of psychopathology. The turmoils of early adolescence often result in a welling up of primary affective processes that break loose from ego control in an active fantasy life, thus accounting for the convergence of Factors I and III.

After accounting for most of the common variance across the 22 variables by these six underlying dimensions, there still remains sufficient unique, reliable variance in many of the scores to justify their individual consideration. Most notably, Reaction Time, Location, Form Definiteness, Form Appropriateness, Color, Shading, and Pathognomic Verbalization show consistently significant residual variance. Only Popular, Penetration, and Integration are sufficiently well represented by one of the major factors to leave little or no residual unique variance. Consequently, it is recommended that, for most purposes, the individual scores be used for interpretation and analysis rather than only factor scores representing these six dimensions. Where it is desirable to have only two or three broadly based dimensions for analysis, factor scores for the first three factors—Perceptual Maturity, Perceptual Sensitivity, and Psychopathology of Thought—can be crudely computed by simple, weighted combinations of the defining inkblot variables. Factor loading tables for each population are presented in the HIT monograph for those who wish to develop factor scores.

COMPARISON OF THE HIT AND THE RORSCHACH

Any new technique such as the HIT is likely to be viewed rather critically by clinicians or research psychologists who have built up a wealth of experience in the use of an established projective method such as the Rorschach. Quite rightly, they wish to know what advantages are to be gained by adopting the HIT, what information may be lost by substituting it for the Rorschach, and how similar the two methods are with respect to the projective, qualitative material elicited as well as the more quantitative, psychometric variables. Quite aside from the similarities and differences noted earlier, several studies have been reported which throw considerable light on these questions.

The first systematic comparison of the HIT and the Rorschach was conducted in a cooperative study involving Beck, Haggard, Bock, and Holtzman (Holtzman, et al., 1961). Both Rorschach and Holtzman inkblots were administered twice to 72 high school students by Mrs. Samuel Beck—a total of four protocols per subject. The Rorschach always preceded the Holtzman by about three weeks, with an interval of approximately three months between original and retest sessions. The Rorschach protocols were scored by Mrs. Beck, using Beck's system of analysis, and the HIT protocols were scored by Holtzman's research staff.

Eight scores within the two systems were sufficiently comparable in a priori definition to justify computing correlations between them. Variability in number of responses on the Rorschach was partially controlled by converting raw scores on other variables into average values per response. Since the true relationships between the Rorschach and Holtzman systems are attenuated by several sources of error, most notably the unreliability of scores, corrections for unreliability were applied to each validity coefficient, using the Spearman-Brown formula and split-half reliability estimates from the HIT. Corrected correlations across the two methods ranged from lows of .51, .57, and .66 for Shading, Human Movement, and Color, respectively, to values greater than 1 for Human and Animal, the two content scores. Whitaker (1965) obtained a correlation of .76 (uncorrected for unreliability) for Pathognomic Verbalization when scored on Rorschach and HIT protocols.

The stimulus qualities of the Rorschach and Holtzman inkblots with respect to associative value have been studied systematically by Otten and Van de Castle (1963). The ten Rorschach cards and 45 HIT cards in Form A were mixed into one series which was rated using 14 semantic differential scales consisting of bipolar adjectives like clean–dirty, heavy–light, and active–passive. The connotations of the Holtzman cards were more varied, while at the same time covering all the "meanings" associated with the Rorschach cards. It was also discovered that some Holtzman cards tap patterns of meaning not found in the Rorschach cards, although the reverse was not true.

Rigorous comparisons between the Rorschach and Holtzman systems dealing with the subtle, qualitative aspects of the methods are more difficult to make. To the extent that one leans heavily upon sequential analysis of multiple responses to a single inkblot, the one-response-per-card format of the standard HIT is unsuitable. Intensive analysis of single responses is also less satisfactory on the HIT than on the Rorschach. Of course one can select a subset of HIT inkblots and administer them in a manner similar to the Rorschach; but such a procedure is not generally recommended since all the advantages of the HIT method are lost. When there is considerable interest in multiple responses and depth analysis of single responses, it would be better to administer a subset of inkblots from either the same or parallel form of the HIT in a second testing session using the Rorschach method following the standard HIT. In this way one would have the advantages of both methods, plus the flexibility of specially derived subsets for intensive analysis.

Most clinicians who use the HIT, however, find that it yields ample qualitative material of a projective nature for depth analysis. Numerous illustrations of case analyses involving the integration of both qualitative and psychometric approaches are given in the HIT monograph and by Hill (1972).

In general, the studies to date indicate quite conclusively that the Rorschach and Holtzman systems have a great deal in common as far as the underlying meaning of their respective variables is concerned. The important difference between the two methods is the psychometric advantage of the HIT with respect to standardization, reliability, clearer interpretability of quantitative scores, and the availability of truly parallel forms.

EXTERNAL CORRELATES OF INKBLOT SCORES

A considerable amount of information has accrued bearing upon the relationships between inkblot scores from the HIT and independently obtained behavioral, personality, cognitive, perceptual, developmental, sociocultural, and psychodiagnostic measures. Extensive reviews have been provided by Gamble (1972), Hill (1972), Holtzman, et al., (1975), Hartmann and Rosenstiel (1977), and Swartz, Witzker, Holtzman, and Bishop (1978). Only representative findings from these many studies can be summarized here. First, correlations of HIT variables with measures of cognition and perception are cited. Then correlations with personality tests are discussed, followed by a presentation of evidence bearing upon behavioral correlates. Developmental trends in children and major intergroup differences related to differential diagnosis and sociocultural factors complete the discussion.

Correlations with Cognitive and Perceptual Measures

Correlations between HIT scores and standard measures of intelligence, scholastic achievement, and convergent thinking are low though statistically significant. In a sample of 197 seventh-grade children collected as part of the standardization study for the HIT, a large number of significant correlations ranging from .20 to .31 were obtained between Rejection (reversed), Location, Form Appropriateness, Shading, Movement, Integration, Anxiety, Hostility, and Barrier, on the one hand, and ten mental ability tests on the other. Measures of intelligence and social status were found by Thorpe and Swartz (1963) to be related to Rejection, the number of rejections dropping from an average of 12 to an average of six per protocol in going from low to high IQ groupings of seventh-grade chidren. Holtzman, Gorham, and Moran (1964) found similar significant but low correlations between Wechsler-Bellevue Vocabulary and Integration, Movement, and Form Appropriateness in a sample of 99 chronic paranoid schizophrenic men. Results from the Austin-Mexico City longitudinal project based upon testing of 860 school children of three ages in two cultures (Holtzman, et al., 1975) yielded correlations between WISC Vocabulary and Movement ranging from .14 to .42 with a mean value of .25. A similar low positive relationship exists between WISC scores and Location, Form Definiteness, Form Appropriateness, Integration, Human, Barrier, and Popular. Clearly, inkblot scores, particularly those defining the Perceptual Maturity Factor, do relate significantly to general intelligence, though at a low level.

Tests of divergent thinking, creativity, and other forms of cognitive functioning also correlate with inkblot scores in a meaningful manner. Using Guilford's tests of divergent thinking, Clark, Veldman, and Thorpe (1965) found that junior high school students who were high in divergent thinking ability gave more whole responses and got higher scores on Movement, Anxiety, Hostility, Color, and Penetration than did students who were low in this ability. They concluded that divergent thinkers give freer rein to imaginative production, have higher verbal facility, and are more responsive to the stimulus characteristics of inkblots. In a study of attitudes toward the imaginary,

Codkind (1964) found that individuals with a high degree of fantasy acceptance have more complex cognitive organization and a greater openness to experience as shown by significantly higher scores on Integration, Abstract, Popular, Form Appropriateness, Color, Movement, Anxiety, Hostility, and Fabulation, and significantly lower scores on Location and Rejection.

In a factor-analytic study of schizophrenic thought processes, Holtzman and associates (1964) obtained eight orthogonal dimensions, five of which had high loadings from HIT variables as well as cognitive measures: Verbal Ability, Integrated Ideation, Stimulus Sensitivity, Pathological Verbalization, and Conceptual Autism. Gardner and Moriarty (1968) report several significant correlations between cognitive style dimensions and HIT factor scores. High Conceptual Differentiation (number of groups in the Object Sorting Test) is related to low Psychopathology of Thought (Factor III) in the HIT, a finding that has since been replicated for adolescents in the Austin-Mexico City longitudinal study (Holtzman, et al., 1975). Other correlations between HIT and cognitive style variables are more tentative, varying inconsistently across different samples.

Correlations with Personality Tests

Various paper-and-pencil approaches to the study of personality by self-inventory have been studied for possible HIT correlates but without much success. Among the variables included in the extended correlation matrix for the 197 seventh-grade children in the HIT standardization study were 12 scores from Cattell's Junior Personality Quiz. Only one of the correlations between inkblot scores and the personality scales proved highly significant statistically—a correlation of $-.25$ between Human and Neuroticism, a relationship that is at least in the expected direction. High scores on Factor III variables— Pathognomic Verbalization, Anxiety, and Hostility—tend to be associated with high scores on Neuroticism from the Maudsley Personality Inventory (Megargee & Swartz, 1968), with Rigidity on the Sanford-Gough Test (Kidd & Kidd, 1971), and with the Guilt scale on the MMPI given to depressed patients (Moseley, Duffey, & Sherman, 1963).

The more limited area of anxiety and hostility has been studied by Ruebush (1960), Barger and Sechrest (1961), Swartz (1965), Rosenstiel (1973), Cook, Iacino, Murray, and Auerbach (1973), Iacino and

Cook (1974), and Fehr (1976), using such measures as the Manifest Hostility Scale of the MMPI, Taylor's Manifest Anxiety Scale, Sarason's Test Anxiety Scale for Children, Spielberger's State-Trait Anxiety Inventory, or the Buss-Durkee Inventory. Low positive relationships have been found between self-inventory scores and inkblot scores of Anxiety and Hostility in about one-half of the studies, the remainder reporting negative results. While there are some notable exceptions in several of the above studies, HIT content scales are generally unrelated to self-inventory measures, an expected outcome in view of the fact that Anxiety and Hostility in the HIT are strictly ratings at the fantasy level.

The most extensive study involving correlations between inkblot variables and self-report inventories is the cross-cultural longitudinal investigation involving children in Mexico and the United States (Holtzman, et al., 1975). While Anxiety and Hostility from the HIT failed to show any relationship to personality traits from the self-report inventories, interestingly, several other inkblot scores did prove to be significantly associated with certain scales in Jackson's Personality Research Form. High Color scores were significantly correlated with high scores on Exhibitionism, Impulsiveness, and Nurturance, all in the expected direction based on Rorschach theory concerning the meaning of Color. Integration proved to be positively correlated with the Understanding scale from the Personality Research Form, a finding also in the expected direction.

Correlations with Behavioral Measures

Investigations involving specific behavioral measures of personality as they relate to HIT variables are uncommon, although a number of studies have been reported demonstrating the effectiveness of the HIT in classification of groups or in differential diagnosis, studies in which behavioral ratings or manifestations often play a determining role in the criterion classification. These latter findings will be reported in later sections dealing with differential diagnosis and cross-cultural differences.

High Barrier appears to be related to more effective communication in small group settings, according to Cleveland and Morton (1962), who studied 70 psychiatric patients in a group therapy program. Increased Barrier scores were found by Darby (1970) to result from body awareness training in schizophrenics. Decreased Penetration scores were discovered after body awareness training (Chasey, Swartz, & Chasey, 1974). Megargee (1965b) found a significant, though low, relationship (.23) between Barrier and ratings of aggressiveness in 75 detained juvenile delinquents, indicating that the most seriously delinquent adolescents had lower Barrier scores. An extensive review of empirical work on both Barrier and Penetration has been made by Fisher (1970), who reports a number of interesting behavioral correlates.

Sociometric peer ratings within normal groups usually fail to show any relationship to inkblot scores (Barger & Sechrest, 1961; Holtzman, et al., 1966). A notable exception is the significant correlation found by Holtzman, et al. (1975) between sociometric rejection by peers of children in the first and fourth grades and high scores for Anxiety and Hostility on the HIT for these same children six years later. School counselors rated the emotional adjustment of 46 of these first-graders nine years later. Four inkblot scores from first-grade HIT protocols proved to be effective precursors of later teenage maladjustment: Pathognomic Verbalization, Anxiety, Hostility, and Form Appropriateness (Currie, Holtzman, & Swartz, 1974).

Other studies using ratings by skilled observers or field performance ratings also show significant, meaningful correlations with inkblot variables. Barrier and Color scores, combined with scales from the Edwards Personal Preference Schedule, effectively predicted the rated performance of Peace Corps volunteers in villages of Brazil 15 months after psychological testing (Holtzman, et al., 1966). Mueller and Abeles (1964) found a correlation of .44 between Movement and judged degree of empathy.

Megargee (1966) reported that extremely assaultive adolescents give significantly fewer pure color responses (those coded C 3) than do moderately assaultive boys, a finding consistent with his theory that the infrequent violent act results from high control coupled with high aggression which finally reaches the breaking point. Megargee and Cook (1967) found low but significant correlations between Hostility and behavioral criteria of aggression for 76 juvenile delinquents. In addition, they found correlations of about .40 between several similar scales of Hostility in the HIT and in the Thematic Apperception Test, providing further evidence of the consistency of fantasy productions and symbolic hostile content from both apperception and inkblot methods.

Developmental Trends in Children

Following the lead of earlier Rorschach studies, several major investigations have been reported which demonstrate a strong relationship between HIT scores and developmental level. Thorpe and Swartz (1965) derived new pattern scores using elements in the Holtzman scoring system drawn primarily from Location, Form Definiteness, Integration, Movement, Color, Shading, Human, Animal, and Pathognomic Verbalization. Highly significant age trends were found in a large sample of 586 normal subjects ranging in age from five to 20 years. Integration, Movement, Human, and Shading showed a regular increase with increasing age throughout the age span studied. Color and Pathognomic Verbalization generally decreased with age. Form Appropriateness and Form Definiteness rose fairly rapidly in preadolescent years, leveling off thereafter. Location increased steadily until the college years, when it dropped to a new low. All of these trends are highly consistent with developmental theory.

Largely because of the striking and provocative findings in these basic studies of developmental trends across different age groups, a major longitudinal study was undertaken in Austin, Texas, involving 133 first-graders, 142 fourth-graders, and 142 seventh-graders who were tested initially in the 1962–63 school year. Consisting of a variety of perceptual, cognitive, and personality measures in addition to the HIT, the test battery was administered to each child in each of the three groups at precisely the same age—initially 6 years 8 months, 9 years 8 months, and 13 years 8 months. Annual testing took place on the anniversary date of initial testing until six years of repeated measurement had been completed. Other data from parental interviews, school records, and sociometric ratings were gathered periodically to shed light on the environmental and sociocultural factors that interplay with psychological development.

A complete replication of the Austin longitudinal project was begun in 1964 in Mexico City under the direction of Rogelio Diaz-Guerrero and his associates. Numerous technical reports of this work have been published as well as a definitive analysis after completion of the study (Holtzman, Diaz-Guerrero, & Swartz, 1975). Cross-age analysis of HIT scores from the first year of testing in both Austin and Mexico City yielded results very similar to those reported by Thorpe and Swartz (1966).

Differential Diagnosis

One of the primary uses of the HIT is to provide information of value in the differential diagnosis of various kinds of psychiatric patients or behavior disorders. Because of the qualitative nature of nosological systems, the external correlates of inkblot scores are represented by intergroup differences rather than correlation coefficients. The most extensive information bearing upon differential diagnosis is given in the monograph by Holtzman, et al. (1961), which contains standardization data on 15 different populations. Percentile norms are presented for eight major reference groups, five of which are different developmental levels ranging from five-year-olds to superior adults and three of which deal with psychiatric classes: chronic paranoid schizophrenics, depressed neurotics and psychotics, and mentally retarded individuals. The reference groups of average adults and elementary school children provide excellent control groups for comparison with the three abnormal populations.

Chronic schizophrenics differ significatly from normal controls of similar age and social background in a number of inkblot variables. Schizophrenics get higher scores on Rejection, Pathognomic Verbalization, Penetration, Anatomy, and Sex, and lower scores on Location, Form Definiteness, Form Appropriateness, Shading, Movement, Integration, Human, Barrier, and Popular. While the means for Color, Anxiety, Hostility, and Animal are about the same in schizophrenics and normals, the variances are much greater for schizophrenics, who tend to show either a lot of uncontrolled color and symbolic or animal content or none at all. Only Reaction Time, Space, Abstract, and Balance fail to discriminate between normals and schizophrenic patients. Using 100 schizophrenics and 100 normals from the HIT standardization samples, Moseley (1963) applied linear-discriminant-function analysis to develop weights for use in separating schizophrenic from normal protocols. All 16 of the HIT scores that he used, except Reaction Time, contributed significantly to the analysis, resulting in a classification by formula that was 88 percent correct. The procedure held up completely when cross-validated on a second sample of schizophrenic and normal cases, indicating that it can be used with some confidence in the diagnosis of schizophrenia.

Differentiating schizophrenics from depressed patients is a much more difficult task than separating schizophrenics from normals. When Moseley applied discriminant-function analysis to develop procedures for the differential diagnosis of schizophrenics and depressives, the results were almost as good as in the case of schizophrenics and normals; the percent correctly classified was 78. Depressives differ most markedly from schizophrenics by getting higher scores on Reaction Time, Location, Form Definiteness, Form Appropriateness, Movement, Human, Integration, Hostility, Barrier, and Popular and lower scores on Rejection, Color, and Pathognomic Verbalization. Depressives can also be distinguished from normals using Moseley's discriminant-function weights, though the accuracy of classification is somewhat less, 71 percent. The chief differences here are due to higher scores by depressives on Reaction Time, Pathognomic Verbalization, Sex, and Penetration and lower scores on Rejection, Color, and Movement.

Use of the HIT for differential diagnosis of other disorders has been tried by other investigators with equally good success. Barnes (1963) was able to discriminate between brain-damaged individuals and normal controls with about 80 percent accuracy. Megargee (1965a) published norms for male juvenile delinquents tested while in custody. He obtained a number of significant differences on HIT scores when compared with several normal control groups. And Connors (1965) reported a number of highly significant differences between emotionally disturbed children seen in an outpatient clinic and normal controls of the same age and background. In Connors' study, disturbed children got higher scores on Rejection and Anatomy and lower scores on all other variables except Pathognomic Verbalization, Sex, Abstract, Hostility, Penetration, and Balance. Using HIT factor scores, Connors found that neurotic children appeared to be more differentiated in response (Factor IV) and more inhibited (Factor V) than did hyperkinetic children. Cleveland and Fisher (1960) differentiated sharply between arthritic patients and those with ulcers, using only the Barrier score; the arthritics got much higher scores, confirming their hypothesis concerning the meaning of Barrier. Cleveland and Sikes (1966) discriminated between alcoholics and nonalcoholic patients using Penetration and two new inkblot variables, Decadence (all responses involving decay) and Water (all references to water), all of which are higher in alcoholics.

The HIT appears to be well suited for improving differential diagnosis and psychiatric screening, particularly when appropriately combined with other valid techniques. While most of the studies cited have not been concerned with the problem of controlling base rates, it is obvious that inkblot scores provide a powerful tool for diagnostic purposes. A more extensive discussion of differential diagnosis using the HIT together with other clinical instruments is given by Hill (1972) in her handbook on the clinical application of the HIT.

Cross-cultural Correlates

Because of the nonverbal, "meaningless" nature of inkblots and the standard, simple instructions to give only one response per card, the HIT is ideally suited for cross-cultural studies ranging from industrialized societies to primitive, nonliterate tribes. The method has been used successfully in many countries under widely varying conditions.

One of the most extensive cross-cultural studies involving the HIT is the Austin-Mexico City project referred to earlier. The project involved careful matching of Mexican and Texas children on sex, age, and father's education and occupation. In general, the American child produced faster reaction times, used larger portions of the inkblots in giving his responses, gave more definite form to his responses, and was still able to integrate more parts of the inkblot while doing so. He used more color and ascribed more movement to his percepts than did the Mexican child. At the same time his active fantasy life and attempts to deal with all aspects of the inkblots in an active manner produced a higher amount of deviant thinking and anxious and hostile content.

Almost identical results were obtained by Tamm (1967), who studied 90 children in the first, fourth, and seventh grades of the American School in Mexico City. Although every child could speak both English and Spanish, half came from well-educated Mexican families and half from American. The HIT and WISC were given to each child by a bilingual examiner in either Spanish or English, whichever language happened to be the dominant one. In spite of the common school system and similar general environment, Mexicans were higher on Location and lower on Color, Movement, and Pathognomic Verbalization at all ages. Several age-by-culture interactions were found, but the Mexicans and Americans were still as distinctly separate in the seventh grade as in the first, suggesting that the cultural difference is fairly fundamental, being relatively unaffected by formal schooling. In contrast to the HIT, no cross-cultural differences were found for the WISC in Tamm's study.

A somewhat different approach to cross-cultural research using the HIT was taken by Gorham, Moseley, and Holtzman (1968). Over 2200 group-administered protocols were collected from college samples in 16 foreign countries throughout the world. A special computer-based scoring system for simulating hand-scoring of 17 of the 22 HIT variables (Gorham, 1967) was employed to assure comparability of results. Moseley (1967) applied the Holtzman Inkblot Technique in a multivariate comparison of seven cultures: Argentina, Mexico, Panama, Venezuela, the United States, and two subcultures of Colombia—Bogota and Cartagena. Using the 17 inkblot scores in a multiple discriminant analysis, Moseley applied his formula in predicting the cultural identity of 714 college students, about 100 from each of the seven cultures. He then compared the actual cultural identity with that predicted solely from inkblot responses. The resulting classification matrix for selected North, Central, and South American cultures is most interesting.

On the basis of patterns of inkblot scores alone, not a single college student from Argentina, Colombia, or Venezuela (the three South American countries) was misclassified as a Mexican, a Panamanian, or a North American. Nor were any of the Mexicans or Panamanians misclassified as Argentines. Only two Mexicans and five Panamanians were misclassified as Colombians, while only one Mexican and no Panamanians were misidentified as from Venezuela.

It is interesting to note which countries seem closest to others in their patterns of responses. Among the six Latin American cultures, only Mexico appeared close to the United States; 21 percent of the Americans were misclassified as Mexican compared to less than one percent of Americans misclassified in any other culture. Of the Mexicans, 17 percent were misclassified as Americans while 24 percent were misclassified as Panamanians.

While this type of global analysis across major cultures of the Americas is difficult to interpret in any depth, it is clear from Moseley's study that the degree of cultural exchange and diffusion between two countries is strikingly parallel to the degree of similarity in personality patterns as measured by inkblot scores.

The HIT has also been used in a search for transcultural universals rather than differences. Knudsen, Gorham, and Moseley (1966) derived popular concepts using the same statistical methods and criteria employed in the derivation of Popular for the standard HIT. The majority of Populars appeared universally in all five countries that were studied: Denmark, Germany, Hong Kong, Mexico, and the

United States. While interesting idiosyncracies were noted in each culture, only one of the 25 original Populars failed to appear in at least two of the samples.

CLINICAL APPLICATIONS

Compared to the Rorschach on which a great deal of clinical material has been amassed, the HIT is a relatively new projective technique. And yet it draws so heavily upon the Rorschach for its basic method and rationale that many clinicians find it valuable to combine the quantitative approaches stressed in the previous discussion with qualitative content analysis frequently employed with the Rorschach. Certainly there is sufficient continuity between the extensive work on the Rorschach and the recent studies employing the HIT to justify considerable generalization from one to the other. Quite understandably, most of the published material on the HIT deals with reliability, validity, basic experimental investigations, and other exploratory or evaluative work rather than clinical applications per se. Widespread application of a method should await thorough evaluation. The current review of recent work strongly suggests that a sufficient mass of promising evidence has now accrued to justify use of the HIT in practical, everyday assessment situations of a clinical nature.

Percentile norms for each of the 22 variables are presented in the standardization monograph as well as the Guide, making it possible to develop an individual profile of scores for assessment purposes. The norms are given separately for eight reference groups: five normal ones, ranging from five-year-olds to superior adults, and three abnormal ones—schizophrenics, depressives, and mental retardates. Norms have also been published for male juvenile delinquents (Megargee, 1965a), emotionally disturbed adolescents, adult neurotics, and adult alcoholics (Hill, 1972). When dealing with the assessment of a particular individual, comparisons can be made with any of the reference groups, selecting first that group which is most similar to the reference population to which the individual belongs. A detailed illustration of the use of percentile norms in combination with Moseley's multivariate statistical approach to psychodiagnosis is given in a case analysis by Holtzman and co-workers (1961).

As computers become more routinely accessible to clinicians, the multivariate approach possible with the HIT will become sufficiently efficient as an assessment tool to find extensive application in practical situations. A computer-based system for clinical diagnosis and personality interpretation of HIT scores has been developed on a preliminary basis to demonstrate the value of such automated aids for the clinician (Holtzman, et al.,1975). Several hundred rules for coding complex patterns of scores and assigning phrases for personality interpretation to the patterns were constructed. Panels of experienced clinical psychologists refined these rules, reducing them to 60 carefully defined patterns with their accompanying interpretative statements, which were then coded and stored in a specially constructed computer program. An exploratory study of their validity was undertaken using 58 normal men (Naval enlistees), 78 neurotics, and 100 depressed patients as criterion samples. A large reference group of normals provided percentile norms for decision points on each score in a given pattern. Whenever the specific conditions for a given rule were met, the computer printed out the accompanying interpretive statement. A set of such statements constituted a "personality description" for a given individual.

Analysis of the frequency of occurrence of each rule among individuals in the three samples revealed highly significant differentiation for 28 of the rules. These 28 rules can be arranged in three clusters according to whether the statement is diagnostic of normality, neurotic trends, or depression. Diagnosing normality in a positive sense is the most difficult of the three tasks, as evidenced by the fact that only two statements were significant. For example, the decision rule coupling the statement, "An integrative approach to life situations is revealed," with its configural score pattern (Location less than 21 percent, Form Definiteness greater than 79 percent, and Integration greater than 79 percent) appeared in 10 percent of the normals and in none of the neurotics or depressed patients. The largest set of significant rules was differentially diagnostic of neurotics when compared with normals and depressed individuals.

This preliminary computer-based interpretive system is not ready for practical application. The number of significant patterns and accompanying statements must be enlarged and cross-validated in clinical settings. But the results thus far are encouraging. The striking differential diagnostic accuracy of some configural patterns and their associated statements can be considered further validation of the HIT.

Of course there is still a wealth of information in inkblot responses that remains uncoded in the 22 standard variables. At least for the immediate future there is no good substitute for a skillful, experienced clinical analysis which can incorporate both the quantitative and qualitaive aspects of HIT protocols.

VARIATIONS IN THE STANDARD METHOD

Unlike the Rorschach, the HIT is particularly well suited for group administration because of the simple format involving only one response. The group method is more economical since almost any number of individuals can be tested at once, using colored slides projected on a screen and having each individual write out his responses on the Record Form. There is a slight restriction imposed by presenting inkblots only in an upright position, but most individuals fail to give inverted responses even in the standard individual method where they can turn the card. There is also some loss of information which can be gained only through the personalized, verbal interaction of the examiner and subject, thereby increasing the difficulty of scoring some variables. For use in large-scale psychiatric screening or research projects, however, the advantages of the group method outweigh the disadvantages.

Details concerning the standard method for group administration are given by Swartz and Holtzman (1963). Based on a series of studies aimed at developing a procedure to insure scores comparable to those obtained with the individual method, the group method involves reading special instructions to the subjects, using trial inkblots X and Y to illustrate the technique, and projecting colored slides at exposure times of 75 seconds per blot after slightly longer exposures for the first nine cards. With the exception of Reaction Time and Balance, which are lost in the group method, all of the inkblot variables are scored in the usual manner.

Split-half reliability and test–retest stability using parallel forms with a one-week interval are essentially as high for the group method as for the individual. Using a latin-square design involving Forms A and B given to large numbers of students by both the individual and group methods one week apart, Holtzman, Moseley, Reinehr, and Abbott (1963) made a systematic comparison of the group and individual methods of administration. Only five of 18 inkblot scores studied showed any significant mean differences attributable to method of administration. Location, Space, and Color scores were higher for the group method, and Barrier and Popular scores were higher for the individual method. Standard deviations of scores were the same for all variables except Anxiety, which had a higher variance in the group method. Comparing the cross-method correlations in a multitrait-multimethod matrix revealed a striking degree of similarity across the two methods. From these studies it was concluded that the group method could be safely substituted for the individual method when one is dealing with subjects who can write out their own responses to the inkblots.

While the group method of administration is a far more economical way of collecting inkblot responses than is the individual method, there still remains the problem of scoring by hand each record, a task that takes at least 20 minutes per protocol. Gorham, Moseley, and their associates (Moseley, Gorham, & Hill, 1963; Gorham, 1964; Gorham, 1967) have successfully developed a method for scoring 17 HIT variables by high-speed computer. A dictionary-building program was written for the IBM 7090 computer which alphabetizes words and counts their frequency of occurrence for any sample of protocols where the responses have first been properly key-punched. An empirically derived dictionary containing about 7000 words has been compiled in several languages to facilitate cross-cultural studies. Each word in the dictionary is assigned multiple scoring weights by an individual experienced in scoring HIT variables. These weights are checked and refined by independent expert review before the dictionary is ready for use. Stored in the computer as a large table of scoring weights, the dictionary provides an automatic scoring system in any language for which words and weights have been compiled. Thus far, most applications have been restricted to English or Spanish. Some of the problems of translating Spanish HIT protocols into English have been outlined by Cook de Leonard (1964).

The amount of agreement between hand and computer scoring of the same protocols is surprisingly high in spite of the fact that syntax is taken into account by the computer program in only a rudimentary way. Intercorrelations between the two methods of scoring are high (above .80) for seven variables: Rejection, Location, Movement, Human, Color, Form Definiteness, and Animal. Cross-method correlations for Hostility, Popular, Anxiety, Anatomy, Shading, Penetration, Abstract, Sex, and Integration range from .62 to .75. The lowest correlation for the 17 variables studied was .50 for Barrier. These results were achieved in a cross-validation of the scoring method by applying it to 101 Form A protocols obtained from college students tested by Swartz and Holtzman (1963). Cross-validation on 84

Form B protocols yielded equally high correlations between computer scoring and hand scoring of the same records.

In some situations it is not possible to set aside a minimum of one
hour for administration of the HIT. Some interest has been shown in a
short form containing the first 30 cards in either A or B. Herron (1963)
conducted a study to determine the loss of information resulting from
a 30-item HIT. He discovered that if .70 is accepted as a minimum
value for adequate split-half reliability, the Short Form may be used
successfully for at least the following variables: Rejection, Location,
Form Definiteness, Form Appropriateness, Color, Pathognomic Verbalization, and Human. The same can probably be said for factor
scores, since they are derived from more than one inkblot variable.

Each of the above variations in the standard method still has as a
major goal the production of inkblot protocols and scores which are as
close as possible to the standardized individual method in their
psychological meaning. When one has special purposes in mind, a
number of other variations is possible. Special subsets of inkblots can
be drawn up using published item statistics for the 90 inkblots as a
basis for selection. For example, figure-ground reversals (Space)
occur rather rarely in the standard version of the HIT. But it would be
a simple matter to select a dozen inkblots which have a high degree of
"card pull" for such responses and then ask the subject to give two
responses per card rather than one. The resulting scores on Space as
an inkblot variable would be better distributed and more reliable,
permitting special study of the psychological meaning of figure-
ground reversals. On the basis of experimental studies dealing with
the arousal of affect by color, Hill (1966) has proposed that the ten
most brilliantly colored inkblots in the HIT be considered a special
subset for measuring affective response to color.

In studies in which many repeated measures of inkblot perception are needed, the 90 inkblots can be divided into smaller parallel
subsets containing 10 or 15 blots each. Palmer (1963) and Simkins
(1960) have employed this procedure quite successfully in several
experiments. Two, or even three, responses per card can be required
of each subject if necessary to insure sufficient information for reliable measurement. Still another possibility that has not been sufficiently explored as yet is the development of special-purpose multiple-choice forms for measuring variables of particular interest. A
multiple-choice test would have the advantage of complete objectivity, although such a derivation would probably bear little resemblance to the standard individual method.

CONCLUSION

The rapidly expanding literature of the Holtzman Inkblot Technique shows considerable promise for the method when used appropriately. The availability of a large number of standardized inkblots opens a new field of research in this important area. While it is unlikely that all 22 standardized variables will remain unchanged in the face of new evidence from research, there is much to be said for adhering carefully to the detailed instructions for administration and scoring. Only in this manner can one take full advantage of the established norms and related procedures for interpretation.

Several promising variations in the method of administration and scoring have been developed which appear to adhere fairly closely to the original aims of the technique. It remains to be seen, however, whether group administration and computer scoring alter the qualitative aspects of the HIT to such an extent that its value is diminished in personality assessment. As with any new technique for the assessment of personality, the final verdict of its utility can be reached only after much investigation in a wide variety of situations, both experimental and clinical.

REFERENCES

Barger, P. M., & Sechrest, L. Convergent and discriminant validity of four Holtzman Inkblot Test variables. *J. Psychol. Studies*, 1961, *12*, 227–236.

Barnes, C. Prediction of brain damage using the Holtzman Inkblot Technique and other selected variables. Unpublished doctoral dissertation, University of Iowa, 1963.

Beck, S. J. *Rorschach's Test, Vol. I, Basic Processes* (ed. 2, revised). New York: Grune and Stratton, 1949.

Chasey, W. C., Swartz, J. D., & Chasey, C. G. Effect of motor development on body image scores for institutionalized mentally retarded children. *Am. J. Mental Deficiency*, 1974, *78*, 440–445.

Clark, C. M., Veldman, D. J., & Thorpe, J. S. Convergent and divergent thinking of talented adolescents. *J. Educ. Psychol.*, 1965, *56*, 157–163.

Cleveland, S. E., & Fisher, S. A comparison of psychological characteristics and physiological reactivity in ulcer and rheumatoid arthritis groups. *Psychosom. Med.*, 1960, *22*, 283–289.

Cleveland, S. E., & Morton, R. B. Group behavior and body image: A follow-up study. *Hum. Relations*, 1962, *15*, 77–85.

Cleveland, S. E., & Sikes, M. P. Body image in chronic alcoholics and non-alcoholic psychiatric patients. *J. Proj. Tech. & Pers. Assess.*, 1966, *30*, 265–269.

Codkind, D. Attitudes toward the imaginary: Their relationship to level of personality integration. Unpublished doctoral dissertation, University of Kansas, 1964.

Connors, C. K. Effects of brief psychotherapy, drugs, and type of disturbance on Holtzman Inkblot scores in children. *Proceedings of the 73rd Annual Convention of the American Psychological Association*, Washington, D.C.: APA, 1965, pp. 201–202.

Cook de Leonard, C. Problems in the translation of Spanish (Mexican) protocols into English. *Proceedings of the Ninth Congress of the Interamerican Society of Psychology*. Miami, Fla., 1964, pp. 271–277.

Cook, P. E., Iacino, L. W., Murray, J., & Auerbach, S. M. Holtzman Inkblot anxiety and shading scores related to state and trait anxiety. *J. Pers. Assess.*, 1973, *37*, 337–339.

Cronbach, L. J. Statistical methods applied to Rorschach scores: A review. *Psychol. Bull.*, 1949, *46*, 393–429.

Currie, S. F., Holtzman, W. H., & Swartz, J. D. Early indicators of personality traits viewed retrospectively. *J. School Psychol.*, 1974, *12*, 51–59.

Darby, J. A. Alteration of some body image indexes in schizophrenics. *J. Consult. Clin. Psychol.*, 1970, *35*, 116–121.

Elizur, A. Content analysis of the Rorschach with regard to anxiety and hostility. *Rorschach Res. Exch.*, 1949, *13*, 247–284.

Fehr, L. A. Construct validity of the Holtzman Inkblot anxiety and hostility scores. *J. Pers. Assess.*, 1976, *40*, 483–486.

Fisher, S. *Body Experience in Fantasy and Behavior*. New York: Appleton-Century-Crofts, 1970.

Fisher, S., & Cleveland, S. E. *Body Image and Personality*. Princeton, N.J.: Van Nostrand Co., 1958.

Gamble, K. R. The Holtzman Inkblot Technique: A review. *Psychol. Bull.*, 1972, *77*, 172–194.

Gardner, R. W., & Moriarty, A. Individuality in the Holtzman Inkblot test. In *Personality Development at Preadolescence: Exploration of Structure Formation* (Chapter 7). Seattle, Wash.: University of Washington Press, 1968.

Gorham, D. R. Development of a computer scoring system for inkblot responses. *Proceedings of the Ninth Congress of the Interamerican Society of Psychology*. Miami, Florida, 1964, pp. 258–270.

Gorham, D. R. Validity and reliability studies of a computer-based scoring-system for inkblot responses. *J. Consult. Psychology*, 1967, *31*, 65–70.

Gorham, D. R., Moseley, E. C., & Holtzman, W. H. Norms for the computer scored Holtzman Inkblot Technique. *Perceptual and Motor Skills* Monograph Supplement, 1968, *26*, 1279–1305.

Hartmann, H. A., & Rosenstiel, L. V. (Eds.). *Lehrbuch der Holtzman-Inkblot-Technik (HIT)*. Bern/Stuttgart/Wien: Hans Huber, 1977.

Herron, E. W. Psychometric characteristics of a thirty-item version of the group method of the Holtzman Inkblot Technique. *J. Clin. Psychol.* 1963, 19, 450–453.

Hertz, Marguerite R. The use and misuse of the Rorschach method. I. Variations in Rorschach procedure. *J. Proj. Tech.*, 1959, 23, 33–48.

Hill, E. F. Affect aroused by Color, a function of stimulus strength. *J. Proj. Tech. & Pers. Assess.*, 1966, 30, 23–30.

Hill, E. F. *The Holtzman Inkblot Technique: A Handbook for Clinical Application*. San Francisco: Jossey-Bass, 1972.

Hill, E. F., & Peixotta, H. E. *Workbook for the Holtzman Inkblot Technique*. New York: The Psychological Corporation, 1973.

Holtzman, W. H. New developments in the HIT. In P. McReynolds (Ed.), *Advances in Psychological Assessment*, Vol. 3. San Francisco: Jossey-Bass, 1975.

Holtzman, W. H. Inkblots through the looking glass. In M. H. Siegel & H. P. Ziegler (Eds.), *Psychological Research: The Inside Story* (Chapter 15). New York: Harper and Row, 1976.

Holtzman, W. H., Diaz-Guerrero, R., & Swartz, J. D. *Personality Development in Two Cultures: A Cross-cultural Longitudinal Study of School Children in Mexico and the United States*. Austin: University of Texas Press, 1975.

Holtzman, W. H., Diaz-Guerrero, R., Swartz, J. D., & Lara-Tapia, L. Cross-cultural longitudinal research on child development: Studies of American and Mexican school children. In J. Hill (Ed.), *Minnesota Symposia on Child Psychology*, Vol. II. Minneapolis: University of Minnesota Press, 1968, pp. 125–129.

Holtzman, W. H., Gorham, D. R., & Moran, L. J. A factor-analytic study of schizophrenic thought processes. *J. Abnormal & Social Psych.*, 1964, 69, 355–364.

Holtzman, W. H., Moseley, E. C., Reinehr, R. C., & Abbott, E. Comparison of the group method and the standard individual version of the Holtzman Inkblot Technique. *J. Clin. Psychol.*, 1963, 19, 441–449.

Holtzman, W. H., Santos, J. F., Bouquet, S., & Barth, P. *The Peace Corps in Brazil*. Austin, Tex.: University of Texas, 1966.

Holtzman, W. H., Thorpe, J. S., Swartz, J. D., & Herron, E. W. *Inkblot Perception and Personality*. Austin, Tex.: University of Texas Press, 1961.

Iacino, L. W., & Cook, P. E. Threat of shock, state anxiety, and the HIT. *J. Pers. Assess.*, 1974, 38, 450–458.

Kidd, A. H., & Kidd, R. M. Relation of Holtzman scores to rigidity. *Perceptual and Motor Skills*, 1971, 32, 1003–1010.

Knudsen, A. K., Gorham, D. R., & Moseley, E. D. Universal popular responses to inkblots in five cultures: Denmark, Germany, Hong Kong, Mexico, and United States. *J. Proj. Tech. & Pers. Assess.*, 1966, 30, 135–142.

Lord, Edith. Experimentally induced variations in Rorschach performance. *Psychol. Monogr.*, 1950, *64*, No. 10 (Whole No. 316).

Megargee, E. I. The performance of juvenile delinquents on the Holtzman Inkblot Technique: A normative study. *J. Proj. Tech. & Pers. Assess.*, 1965a. *29*, 504–512.

Megargee, E. I. The relation between Barrier scores and aggressive behavior. *J. Abnormal Psych.*, 1965b, *70*, 307–311.

Megargee, E. I. Uncontrolled and overcontrolled personality types in extreme antisocial aggression. *Psychol. Monogr.*, 1966, *80*, 1–29.

Megargee, E. I., & Cook, P. E. The relation of TAT and inkblot aggressive content scales with each other and with criteria of overt aggressiveness in juvenile delinquents. *J. Proj. Tech. & Pers. Assess.*, 1967, *31*, 48–60.

Megargee, E. I., Lockwood, V., Cato, J. L., & Jones, J. K. The effects of differences in examiner, tone of administration, and sex of subject on scores of the Holtzman Inkblot Technique. *Proceedings of the 74th Annual Convention of the American Psychological Association*, 1966, pp. 235–236.

Megargee, E. I., & Swartz, J. D. Extraversion, neuroticism, and scores on the Holtzman Inkblot Technique. *J. Proj. Tech. & Pers. Assess.*, 1968, *32*, 262–265.

Moseley, E. C. Psychodiagnosis on the basis of the Holtzman Inkblot Technique. *J. Proj. Tech.*, 1963, *27*, 86–91.

Moseley, E. C. Multivariate comparison of seven cultures: Argentina, Colombia (Bogota), Colombia (Cartagena), Mexico, Panama, United States, and Venezuela. *Proceedings of the 10th Congress of the Interamerican Society of Psychology*, Lima, Peru, 1966. In C. F. Hereford & L. Natalicio (Eds.), *Aportaciones de la Psicologia a la Investigacion Transcultural*. Mexico City, Mexico: Trillas, 1967, pp. 291–304.

Moseley, E. C., Duffey, R. F., & Sherman, L. J. An extension of the construct validity of the Holtzman Inkblot Technique. *J. Clin. Psychol.*, 1963, *19*, 186–192.

Moseley, E. C., Gorham, D. R., & Hill, E. Computer scoring of inkblot perceptions. *Percep. Motor Skills*, 1963, *17*, 498.

Mueller, W. J., & Abeles, N. The components of empathy and their relationshp to the projection of human movement responses. *J. Proj. Tech. & Pers. Assess.*, 1964, *28*, 418–428.

Murstein, B. I. The projection of hostility on the Rorschach, and as a result of ego-threat. *J. Proj. Tech.*, 1956, *20*, 418–428.

Otten, M. W., & Van de Castle, R. L. A comparison of set "A" of the Holtzman inkblots with the Rorschach by means of the semantic differential. *J. Proj. Tech. & Pers. Assess.*, 1963, *27*, 453–460.

Palmer, J. O. Alterations in Rorschach's Experience Balance under conditions of food and sleep deprivation: A construct validation study. *J. Proj. Tech. & Pers. Assess.*, 1963, *27*, 208–213.

Phillips, L., Kaden, S., & Waldman, M. Rorschach indices of developmental level. *J. Genet. Psychol.*, 1959, *94*, 267–285.

Rapaport, D., Schafer, R., & Gill, M. *Diagnostic Psychological Testing*, Vol. II. Chicago: Year Book Publishers, 1946.

Rosenstiel, L. V. Increase of hostility responses in the HIT after frustration. *J. Pers. Assess.*, 1973, *37*, 22–24.

Ruebush, B. K. Children's behavior as a function of anxiety and defensiveness. Unpublished doctoral dissertation, Yale University, 1960.

Sells, S. B., Frese, F. J., Jr., & Lancaster, W. H. Research on the psychiatric selection of flying personnel. II. Progress on development of SAM Group Ink-Blot Test. Project No. 21-37-002, No. 2. Randolph Field, Texas: USAF School of Aviation Medicine, 1952.

Simkins, L. Examiner reinforcement and situational variables in a projective testing situation. *J. Consult. Psychol.*, 1960, *24*, 541–547.

Swartz, J. D. Performance of high- and low-anxious children on the Holtzman Inkblot Technique. *Child Devel.*, 1965, *36*, 569–575.

Swartz, J. D., & Holtzman, W. H. Group method of administration of the Holtzman Inkblot Technique. *J. Clin. Psychol.*, 1963, *19*, 433–441.

Swartz, J.D., Witzke, D. M., Holtzman, W. H., & Bishop, C. *Holtzman Inkblot Technique Annotated Bibliography* (ed. 3) Austin, Texas: Hogg Foundation for Mental Health, 1978.

Tamm, M. Resultadoes preliminares de un estudio transcultural y desarrollo de la personalidad de ninos mexicanos y nortearmericanos. In C. F. Hereford & I. Natalicio (Eds.), *Aportaciones de la Psicologia a la Investigacion Transcultural*. Mexico City: F. Trillas, 1967, pp. 159–164.

Thorpe, J. S. & Swartz, J. D. The role of intelligence and social status in rejections on the Holtzman Inkblot Technique. *J. Proj. Tech. & Pers. Assess.*, 1963, *27*, 248–251.

Thorpe, J. S., & Swartz, J. D. Level of perceptual development as reflected in responses to the Holtzman Inkblot Technique. *J. Proj. Tech. & Pers. Assess.*, 1965, *29*, 380–386.

Thorpe, J. S., & Swartz, J. D. Perceptual organization: A developmental analysis by means of the Holtzman Inkblot Technique. *J. Proj. Tech. & Pers. Assess.*, 1966, *30*, 447–451.

Whitaker, L., Jr. The Rorschach and Holtzman as measures of Pathognomic Verbalization. *J. Consult. Psychol.*, 1965, *29*, 181–183.

Zubin, J. Failures of the Rorschach technique. *J. Proj. Tech.*, 1954, *18*, 303–315.

Zubin, J., & Eron, L. *Experimental Abnormal Psychology* (preliminary edition). New York: New York State Psychiatric Institute, 1953.

4

The Thematic
Apperception Test (TAT)

Bertram P. Karon

The Thematic Apperception Test (TAT) was developed by Morgan and Murray (1935) and the workers at the Harvard Psychological Clinic in the 1930s as a method to elicit within a few hours the information that ordinarily might require a protracted psychoanalytic investigation (Murray, 1938; 1943). The earliest validations were to compare the reconstruction from the TAT with that made in a protracted psychoanalytic or psychotherapeutic investigation or with that made from extended clinical investigation of normal subjects by a variety of techniques. Unlike the Rorschach, which began in Hermann Rorschach's observations on the differential responses of psychiatrically classified patients, the TAT was not tightly tied to the Kraepelinian categories. Insofar as psychologists felt that their job was to classify people according to the most recent set of psychiatric nosologies (e.g., DSM-II or -III), the TAT was not felt to be as useful as the Rorschach. Moreover, insofar as the behavioristic ideology predominated in American psychology, the TAT was not felt to be useful. Even though predicting overt behavior is often best undertaken with an understanding of psychodynamics, the investigation of the inner world, including fantasies, wishes, motives, conscious and unconscious, seemed irrelevant to a doctrinaire behaviorist. Recent trends toward so-called cognitive behaviorism reflect a change in that view.

The first manual for the TAT (Tomkins, 1947) made many of the basic issues clear. The Kraepelinian categories were dismissed with the statement that to tie the future of projective tests to their ability to classify patients according to these psychiatric categories would be to

limit the future, because of the inadequacies of the psychiatric classification schemes. That statement is as true of current schemes (e.g.,
DSM-III) as of earlier ones. What must be done is to make statements
from the projective test which are true, and then perhaps to use these
statements to arrive at a better set of categories.

Nonetheless, the TAT is an extraordinary tool, enabling both the
clinician and the researcher to investigate aspects of the human
personality which are not easily investigated in other ways.

THE STIMULI

The TAT consists of 20 pictures with alternatives on some cards for
men and women, and for boys and girls. They are intended to be
varied in content, to include pictures that should give rise to fantasies
concerning most areas of importance in the subject's life, and that are
sufficiently structured for the subjects to find it easy to tell stories
about them, but sufficiently unstructured so that stories told by different subjects will differ widely. The current set is the third published
revision and seems to be suitable for most purposes. Other sets of
pictures for specialized purposes or to remedy some real or fantasied
omission in the original set are available.

The use of alternate stimuli is not, in general, of great importance.
The critical issue is to get the subject to tell stories. If one could say to
a subject, "Tell me 20 different stories," and get compliance, that
would be an adequate protocol. Almost no one could do it, however.
The pictures allow them a place from which to take off. As Tomkins
(1947) has noted, most people do not have anything like 20 stories to
tell, despite the fact that they usually feel as if they could tell an
infinite number of stories.

For research, or for specialized clinical applications, it is
nonetheless permissible, and sometimes even advisable to use different pictures. Thus, anthropologists have used pictures drawn in culturally relevant forms (e.g., Henry, 1947). This may go so far as using
pictographs for cultures where realistic photograph-like art is not
culturally common. The principle is to use what gets the best set of
stories, although cross-cultural comparison is easier if the stimuli are
the same.

Similarly, specialized pictures may be used to elicit fantasies
concerning specific issues of importance to the researcher or clinician. Such stimuli should be structured enough to suggest the area of

interest, but not too structured; otherwise, one reduces the variability of response and hence the discovery of individual variation. Moreover, there are three drawbacks to using special "relevant" stimulus pictures. The first is that pictures which are responded to by most people as irrelevant to the area of investigation yield the most important information when relevant fantasies occur, since those fantasies have to be of importance to the subject. Second, subjects may be alerted by structured stimuli to the area of concern, so that they reveal only conscious fantasies, and may consciously screen out material so as to give one the impression they would like to give. (Of course, this is a general problem, but it is less serious when subjects are not aware at the time of testing which aspects of their dynamics are under investigation.) Third, one must gain experience with the individual variation in stories to these stimuli and cannot readily utilize prior norms nor one's experience with stories told to standard stimuli in evaluating the subjects.

INSTRUCTIONS

When administering the TAT, one should always start by asking for a certain amount of background information if it is not already known, namely, the age, sex, education, occupation, marital status, number, ages, and sex of children, number, age, and sex of siblings, and who lived in the subject's household during childhood. In other words, one needs to know both the family of origin and the current family situation. To understand the stories one will need to know who the probable characters are likely to be.

In the Murray manual, standard instructions occur as follows:

> Form A (suitable for adolescents and for adults of average intelligence and sophistication). "This is a test of imagination, one form of intelligence. I am going to show you some pictures, one at a time; and your task will be to make up as dramatic a story as you can for each. Tell what has led up to the event shown in the picture, describe what is happening at the moment, what the characters are feeling and thinking; and then give the outcome. Speak your thoughts as they come to your mind. Do you understand? Since you have fifty minutes for ten pictures, you can devote about five minutes to each story. Here is the first picture."
>
> Form B (suitable for children, for adults of little education or intelligence, and for psychotics). "This is a storytelling test. I have

> some pictures here that I am going to show you, and for each picture I
> want you to make up a story. Tell what has happened before and what
> is happening now. Say what the people are feeling and thinking and
> how it will come out. You can make up any kind of story you please.
> Do you understand? Well, then, here is the first picture. You have five
> minutes to make up a story. See how well you can do."

The exact words of these instructions may be altered to suit the
age, intelligence, personality, and circumstance of the subject.

However, it is our experience that standardized instructions are
not important except for research purposes on the test itself. What is
important is for the subject to tell you a good story. Our preference is
as follows:

> "I'm going to show you a set of 10 pictures, one at a time. I want
> you to tell me what's going on, what the characters might be feeling
> and thinking, what led up to it, and what the outcome might be. In
> other words tell me a good story."

At the end of the first story,

> "O.K., that was pretty good. Now let's see what you can do with
> this one."

The important issue is to get the subject involved in telling a
story. Unlike other tests, the TAT should not be a stress situation.

The examiner should get interested in a story as a story. He
should applaud the good qualities of the story. This should not be
difficult. Human beings enjoy telling stories and enjoy being told
stories. The more rapport between examiner and subject, the more the
examiner is concerned with the quality of story as story, and the more
the subject and examiner enjoy the stories as story, the better (more
interpretable) the protocol (set of responses) will be.

Alternative instructions exist in various manuals as to having the
subject turn away from the examiner or turn toward the examiner.
The issue, however, ought to be one of keeping the subject as relaxed
and comfortable as possible.

SELECTED SUBSETS OF PICTURES

The more cards one uses the better. The original instructions were to
use 20 cards, 10 in the first administration and 10 in the second
administration, each to be no more than an hour and on separate days.
If for some reason it is necessary to give them continuously, it is a
good idea to take a short break at the end of the tenth card and then

continue. Most clinical psychologists tend to use a selected subset of cards from the TAT, because it is usually only part of the examination. Nonetheless, it is still true that the more cards one gives, the more material one gets, and the easier and more certain are one's inferences. One can, however, make certain recommendations for an optimally abbreviated set of cards. The following are the cards that I recommend in an abbreviated set in the order of the importance of their inclusion. Whatever cards are included in the set should, if possible, be administered in the order of their numbering, since there does seem to be a logic to that order which makes it easier for the subject, and more revealing. Alternate cards with the same number are designated M (Man), F (Woman), B (Boy), G (Girl) to indicate for whom Morgan and Murray consider that card appropriate.

Card 3BM (a figure huddled against a couch).   This is the single most useful card in the TAT and should always be included. It tends to elicit the most pressing present problem of the subject. It works equally well with both men and women. The huddled figure is seen about equally often as being a man or a woman.

Card 3GF (a woman looking unhappy in a doorway).   This card is nearly as useful for women as 3BM, and in testing women I ordinarily use both 3BM and 3GF.

Card 1 (a boy and a violin).   This card is useful for two reasons: (1) it is very easy for most subjects to tell a story about it without being threatened, and hence makes a good beginning; (2) it reveals childhood as it actually was experienced. Even when the parents are not mentioned, it is usually possible to infer what the nature of the relationship of the child to the parent was from the nature of the story.

Cards 6 and 7.   These cards were intended to elicit fantasies about the relationship with the mother and the father. Since any psychodynamic view of human beings considers the nature of those relationships important to understanding the individual, one almost always would like to include these cards. However, the age difference on card 6GF (older man, younger woman) is not large enough to be sure that the associative material is necessarily to a parent figure.

Card 4 and Card 13MF.   These cards relate to heterosexual relations. For most patients information about difficulties in this area is a matter of interest, and hence, these cards would be included.

Card 12M (a hypnotist).   This card is very useful if the subject is either in psychotherapy or about to go into psychotherapy in terms of revealing the nature of the transference relationship and the difficulties which either are being encountered or will be encountered. If the patient's therapist is female and the patient is female, it is useful to administer 12F (older woman, younger adult woman). The elucidation of the transference difficulties may occur then on either card or on some psychological integration of the contents of both.

Card 11 (science fiction card).   This card is usually productive of a remote story. Frequently it is said that this produces deeply repressed material. The material from this card is not usually highly revealing, but it serves to reduce the defensiveness of the subject. In beginning the second series of cards (or any subset of them), it is my practice to say, "Those stories (to the first ten cards, or some subset) were really very good. Now I'm going to show you another set of cards. The first set of stories were pretty realistic. But these pictures are far out, and you can really let yourself go." Showing Card 11 at this point helps set the mood for the subjects to open themselves up to deeper, more speculative fantasies.

Card 14 (silhouette of a boy in a window).   This card was originally designed to get at the inner contemplative life of the individual. However, it is a card that should always be used if suicide is a matter of interest. For a suicidal patient it is obvious that this is someone about to jump out the window. Patients usually are not suspicious or upset about this as long as this is not the first card administered. After all, the psychologist has showed them a picture of a man jumping out the window. What could there be self-revealing about saying so. For the suicidal individual, it is obvious that someone in a window is there to jump.

Card 16 (blank card).   Obviously, this is the most self-revealing. It is sometimes held that you get a cherished fantasy. The card should always be introduced, e.g., "Up to now I have asked you to tell stories. I would like you to make up a picture. It can be a picture you've seen or one that's entirely yours."

After the subject has described the picture, "Now take the picture you've described, and use it like the other ones and tell me a story about it."

Card 10 (two people embracing).   This usually gets associations concerning tenderness. How an individual handles tenderness or affection is often a matter of great importance in understanding that person.

Card 20 (figure under a lamppost).   This usually gets associations concerning loneliness, and this too is an aspect of human existence that frequently is of importance.

For clinical uses, one should approach the matter flexibly, being willing to give any set of cards that might be revealing as the material indicates. For research purposes one may use either the standard set or a subset or a modified set, which will elicit fantasies relevant to whatever is under investigation.

Recording the Stories

In the early days the stories were recorded by a stenographer behind a screen. Since that is outside of most people's technical facilities, the alternatives became recording by hand what the subject said or, for research purposes, having the subject record their own responses. It is possible to administer the TAT to a group and have them record their own responses in writing. They should write in ink and be instructed that they can change anything, but not cross it out, to simply strike it out with a single line and correct it.

However, one generally gets shorter, less elaborated stories when the subjects write their own stories than when the stories require no such effort on their part.

When the examiner records the responses manually, it often seems as if some subjects work out their sadism by telling long, elaborate stories, and enjoying the examiner's effort, but this is a useful sublimation.

Nowadays the simplest procedure is to have the subject talk into a tape recorder. This permits the examiner to concentrate on what the subject is saying, and at eliciting open and full stories. The tape recording may later be transcribed if a written transcript is wished. Most subjects these days are not at all disturbed by a tape recorder. The tape recorder should be in full view and explained before the testing begins.

MORE ON ADMINISTRATION

The subject should be praised for his/her productions. If the story seems incomplete, pressing for more details is not a good idea. In the first story one might remind the individual of the instructions that were ignored, like what the characters' feelings and thoughts might be, or what led up to it, or what the outcome might be. After that, simply accept the story that the subject gives. If one asks detailed questions, one usually can get more information; however, the information is frequently "tacked on," not really part of the spontaneous fantasy of the subject. Moreover, pressing for information generally makes the subject more defensive and resistant. It is a better practice to accept what the subject gives you and use more pictures to get more information.

If one accepts and praises what the subject gives you, typically the subject gets more and more open as the testing continues. It is not infrequent that a subject says, "I didn't intend to tell you about this, but by time the testing was over, I guess I told you all about it."

Such information about not asking questions should not be followed slavishly. If the answer to a specific question, e.g., "Did he actually jump out the window?" would seem to clarify interpretation of the protocol greatly, one, of course, asks the question. But such questioning should be infrequent and as pleasant and unthreatening as possible.

The early manuals emphasize that a story should be about 300 words in length. This makes good sense when you realize that the original subjects were Harvard undergraduates, an intelligent, verbal, highly motivated group of people. For clinical use it will be found that even one sentence per card can be extraordinarily valuable.

MANUALS

Of the books available on the use of the Thematic Apperception Test, the best is still the first, Tomkins (1947). It is the most thorough and is the only one which considers the issue of levels. It is recommended that anyone seriously interested in using the TAT read at least that book. Its limitations seem to be three:

1.   The scoring system is such that one could not score the TAT in a reasonable amount of time. This is illustrative of the general problem of scoring schemes. There is no scoring scheme for the TAT which is both usable and sufficiently inclusive to be clinically relevant. For clinical use one must approach the material in the TAT clinically. The human mind is the only computer which can consider alternative hypotheses in sufficient complexity and diversity to winnow through the information involved in the TAT. If one were to use a scoring system, one would have to use a scoring system at least as complex as the one presented by Tomkins. The recommendation is that one read that scoring system in order to gain a feel for the complexity of the variables that one would want to take into account, but that one ignore any temptation to use the scoring system as given.

It is also recommended that one not use any other scoring system except for research purposes. This issue will be returned to below.

2.   The stimulus material is not described. This is important in that the less determined by the stimulus, the more significant is an element of the story. This lack can be remedied by one's own experience, although descriptions of the stimulus value of the TAT cards have been presented by Stein (1955) and by Rosenzweig and Fleming (1949).

3.   The Tomkins manual highlights Mill's methods for inductive reasoning. This may reflect the early date of publication of the book when psychodynamic psychology, projective tests, and clinical inference needed still to establish their legitimacy. Recognizing that deriving inductive conclusions from psychological data about psychological processes was no different from the general scientific problem of inductive reasoning was part, undoubtedly, of a process of legitimation of the status of psychodynamic psychology. Most current psychologists find Mill's methods and general philosophic arguments uninteresting. The reader is urged, however, to go beyond this framework into the very specific and detailed comments about the TAT.

PRINCIPLES OF INTERPRETATION

There is only one generally valid, most powerful principle of interpretation. It is a procedure which frightens most novices and many experienced psychologists.

One must take the stories one sentence at a time and ask, "Why would a human being say that, out of all the possibilities that exist?" If one allows oneself to think clinically, that is, to use all one knows about human beings, from common sense (general information), from life experience, and from one's psychological training, one will be led to inferences. Obviously, such inferences are nothing more than tentative hypotheses. However, if one repeats this process with each sentence from each story, considering also the possible implications of the relationships of each sentence to the total story, one eventually finds that certain hypotheses keep coming up, become more consistent and detailed, and others are contradicted and disappear. By the time one has worked through the total protocol, one usually can make very strong statements about the subject with considerable certainty.

Such a process of purely clinical inference is frightening for a number of reasons. One is that most psychologists are aware that they may be revealing their own dynamics as well as that of the subject. For another, they are faced with having to go into their understanding of themselves in order to understand another human being. Nonetheless, it can be demonstrated that even novices when required to use their clinical understanding arrive at conclusions with surprising accuracy.

It is always an enlightening experience to ask new graduate students to commit themselves publicly to what they would see in the TAT of a subject whom they do not know, and then to investigate by a protracted series of interviews and experimental conditions what the person is like. The graduate students are usually startled to discover how accurate their reconstructions were.

Obviously, however, the more knowledgeable the interpreter, the better the interpretations. Experienced clinicians will be more accurate, and clinicians who are familiar with whatever criterion or aspects of personality they are attempting to predict will be more accurate. While the TAT may be used with any theoretical position (as can free association, for that matter), a knowledge of psychodynamic psychology is particularly useful. The novice should have read at least Freud (1916/1963), and further psychodynamic understanding is useful, e.g., Freud (1933/1966), Sullivan (1953), Fairbairn (1952) or Guntrip (1969), and Tomkins (1962, 1963).

The reason there is no substitute for a clinical process of inference with the TAT is that the variables of interest in personality theory are literally infinite. There is an infinite number of aspects of the human personality about which we might be interested. Each of the constructs of most personality theories are themselves subdivisible into any number of aspects, which may or may not be of importance or interest. Thus, for example, the concept of aggression may be useful as a unitary variable for some purposes, but in different individuals aggression toward others and toward the self may be handled the same or differently. Aggression toward inferiors or superiors and/or equals; aggression toward strangers and toward friends; verbal aggression, thought aggression, and physical aggression may be handled the same or differently. Conscious and unconscious aggression may be handled differently. Which distinctions are important to make will depend both upon the person one is studying and the purpose for which one is studying that personality.

These considerations immediately reveal why scoring systems are of little or no use. An adequate scoring system is so complex that no one has the time to score the protocol. Tomkins (personal communication) told me that in attempting to derive an adequate scoring system one graduate student spent a year on Card 1 developing 500 scores. At that point the project was abandoned, since life is too short to develop an adequate scoring system for the entire TAT, or to employ it even if one existed. Simple scoring systems (cf. Bellak, 1971) throw away most of the information in the process of scoring, and hence turn out not to be clinically useful.

In doing research, however, where one wishes to investigate only a single specified aspect or a few simply specified aspects of a personality, it is possible to carefully define a scoring system for research purposes. One can develop as high a degree of reliability and accuracy as one cares to take the trouble to develop. One can also use such a scoring system in clinical applications where one is interested in a single predetermined aspect of personality. But a generally useful scoring system is not only nonexistent, in principle it cannot be found.

There are certain additional principles which are useful. First of all, the shorter the story, the more weight should be placed on what the individual says. Thus, very disturbing material in a very brief protocol should be considered much more carefully than when embedded in very long and elaborate stories. Very short stories represent a process of screening, and if this material comes through even after screening, it should be considered very seriously. Bright people who give elaborate stories may give content that is very disturbing without it being a matter of serious concern, simply because it is part of an elaborate developed context of material being openly revealed. In general, not only do brighter and more motivated people give longer stories, but healthy people also tend to give longer stories. Most serious psychopathology tends to interfere with the length of the story. While the TAT was not desgined to classify according to the Kraepelinian categories, Rapaport, Gill, Schafer, and Holt (1968) provide information on what patients of known diagnostic categories do typically yield in their TAT stories.

The stimulus material of the cards is not of primary importance, as mentioned before, even though certain cards tend to arouse fantasies concerning certain issues. It is the story and not the card which is of importance in the TAT. Relevant material may occur on any card. However, the more unusual the content of a story is for a given card, that is, the less it is determined by the stimulus-value of the card, the more weight one should attach to that in drawing inferences, since the content is more obviously derived from the subject. Something which is a usual description of the card should be given little weight in trying to understand the subject's dynamics. This is why cards that are too highly structured turn out not to be highly revealing. The ideal card should be structured enough so that the subject can get started in telling the story, but not so structured as to determine too much of the detail of that story.

The Harvard group (Murray, 1938) developed a language of needs, presses, and themas to summarize the content of the TAT. A need is an internal state, a press is an external force in the environment, and a thema is the interaction of one or more needs with one or more presses and their resolution. While this language is of some use, the TAT may be used with any psychological language or theory that the investigator finds useful.

However, if the psychological language used does not make distinctions which are critical to the phenomena being investigated, the conclusions may be in error. Thus, if one codes as suicidal stories in which people kill themselves, think of killing themselves, or symbolically kill themselves, one will end up with a code that predicts nothing. The level (physical action, verbalization, conscious ideation, unconscious) of the suicidal fantasy is critical.

Similarly, the Rosenzweig Picture Frustration Test (a TAT-like test aimed at aggression) consists of a set of cartoons of someone being frustrated (Rosenzweig, 1978). For each situation, the subject is asked, "What does this person say?" Responses are scored as "Extrapunitive" (aggression toward others), "Intropunitive" (aggression toward the self), or "Impunitive" (not aggressive). The test will be found to be "invalid" because Extrapunitive responses are not high in physically aggressive juvenile delinquents (Lindzey & Goldwyn, 1954). But clinicians familiar with physically abusive juvenile delinquents know that they are not verbally aggressive people. They are typically verbally inchoate. For them physical aggression is the outlet for their hostility and is negatively related to their verbal hostility. Thus the test is valid, but the scoring system is too gross to describe what is going on for these subjects. It assumes that verbal and physical aggression are the same thing.

In general, the question of level must be considered in detail. To this day, Tomkins' (1947) is the only manual which tends to make detailed statements about the matter of level. For any impulse or tendency or wish or fantasy, one must attempt to establish on what psychological level it operates. The general principles are these: behavior is predicted by behavior, verbalizations are predicted by characters who say something, thoughts are predicted by thoughts, and insofar as there is a discrepancy between the level of the stories and the subject's life, the stories will be more overt in their level of expression than in the subject's life.

The first four stories told correlate more with external current behavior than does the whole protocol (Kagan & Lesser, 1961). In general, the later the story in the series, the less it correlates with current overt functioning behavior. It seems as if the early stories get the most dominant tendencies, and later stories get less and less surgent impulses.

Critical in understanding the TAT is the concept of distance. The more the hero of a story is like the subject in age, sex, immediate circumstance, the more likely the things described refer to current surface psychological functioning. The more different the hero is, the deeper the psychological functioning. Distance can be created by sex, by age, but most importantly by circumstance, and by special states (drugs, alcohol, illness), geography, time, unusual conditions, and so forth. While opposite-sexed characters may be used to express distant impulses, they more often represent opposite-sexed individuals in the patient's life.

THE UNCONSCIOUS AND THE TAT

One question of interest is whether unconscious processes are revealed on the TAT. Certainly, processes about which the individual is unable to give a coherent account do occur on the TAT. In some cases it may be that the variable of interest (for example, "Pathogenesis") may not be a construct about which the individual thinks, but if they did, they would probably be unaware of their habitual mode of functioning. More interesting, however, is the question of whether some idea, memory, or impulse of which the individual might be or has been clearly conscious, but which is no longer available in consciousness, is represented in the TAT. The author's clinical experience is that it is. The most dramatic evidence comes from patients who have been given electric shock (ECT) treatment after a suicidal attempt. As a result of the organic interference, the patient may not remember what led up to the suicide and to the electric shock treatments. Nonetheless, when such a patient is administered the TAT, the full story of the precipitating events will generally be found in the TAT protocol. The patient will have no conscious awareness that these stories pertain to their actual life experience.

CONSCIOUS WITHHOLDING

Very closely related to this issue is the issue of how much the patient puts into the TAT and how much the patient consciously withholds. As Tomkins (1949) has pointed out, the evidence is that a subject taking the TAT can withhold from the protocol anything they wish consciously to withhold. In order to do so, they must have a clear, conscious idea about this aspect of themselves and have the wish not to reveal it.

Thus, criminals may or may not include details of their crimes in the TAT. Usually they do not, if they are being examined before standing trial. Usually they do after all sentencing or parole considerations have been settled, or if they do not see the psychologist as having any possible influence on their disposition, or if they see the psychologist as having only a favorable influence on the disposition of their case.

Even more revealing is the question of masturbation. Most Americans have conflicts about masturbation. These conflicts almost never appear on the TAT. The exceptions are two: (1) schizophrenics, and (2) patients who are in intensive psychotherapy or psychoanalysis. The explanation for this is simple. Most Americans have some conflict about masturbation of which they are fully conscious and which they do not feel it is socially appropriate to share with a stranger. Schizophrenics are frequently so devoid of appropriate awareness or of usual social concern that they will share such conflicts with a stranger either because they are unaware of the effect it would have on a stranger, or because of some paradoxical motive, such as to demonstrate their sickness, badness, or sexuality, or even the wish to irritate the other person. The person in intensive therapy or psychoanalysis identifies the testing psychologist as being like their therapist, who may well have taught them that all things should be handled consciously, and that one does share at least in the privacy of psychotherapy those things about which one is anxious, guilty, embarrassed, or concerned. In using the TAT to evaluate the effectiveness of psychotherapy or any other treatment, it is therefore important to ask what differences the experiences of psychotherapy will have in the test-taking set of the patient. Thus, the presence or absence of so-called primary process material cannot be used as a criterion of treatment. For people not in psychotherapy, its presence may represent a breakdown in defenses. For patients in psychotherapy it may represent a mode of functioning which they have learned to use constructively.

SUICIDE

One of the most important and frightening clinical judgments that diagnosticians and therapists are required to make is whether a patient is suicidal, how dangerous the patient is, and under what circumstances the patient will or will not be deadly. While there is no procedure which is absolutely accurate, the TAT provides material which allows for much greater certainty in evaluation than can be attained without this technique. Unlike other procedures, not only does the TAT give some measure of dangerousness, it gives an indication of the circumstances under which the patient may or may not be dangerous, and of the underlying fantasies. It may even reveal suicidal dangers under circumstances which are now remote, but may not be remote at some future time in the patient's life. Consider, for example, the ECT-treated suicidal patient who clearly describes the dynamics of the suicide attempt and its precipitants on the TAT while consciously having no idea what led up to the ECT, who can report only being told that he/she made a suicide attempt and now is unaware of the interpersonal precipitants. Such a patient can be predicted to be a suicidal danger when the organically induced amnesia recedes sufficiently so that the precipitants are once more in awareness, particularly if those precipitating circumstances still exist. Thus, a patient who had attempted suicide when her husband told her he was involved in a long-term relationship with another woman and wanted a divorce had no memory of the circumstances or of her suicide attempt after ECT, but clearly told the whole story on the TAT. It could be predicted that when her memory returned, this woman, who now consciously prided herself on how wonderful her marriage was, would once more be at risk.

In examining a patient for suicide it is my usual procedure to at least include Cards 1, 3, 6, 7, 12M, 14, and 16. After the projective test one should always conduct a direct interview with the subject about the subject of suicide. The fear that one will precipitate a suicide by raising the issue is nonsense. Very often the subject will tell you clearly that they intend to kill themselves, why, and how. Such patients should be taken seriously. The projective examination should be carried out first rather than the interview, because the subject will be very guarded when taking the projective test if the interview is carried out first. Card 14, which should always be included, must not be the first card presented.

The principles of interpretation are very simple. Suicide is predicted by suicide stories. A suicide story is one in which a hero of the same age and sex as the patient under circumstances similar to those of the patient actually kills him/herself. Stories about people who think about suicide or who talk about suicide do not predict suicide. Those stories predict suicidal thoughts or suicidal verbalization, respectively. Stories which are supposedly symbolic of suicide, for example, "There is darkness, then there is light," may or may not be symbolic of suicide. Even if they are symbolic of suicide, they do not predict suicide. Patients who describe suicide symbolically are like patients who describe sex symbolically. Those are not subjects comfortable with sexuality, but rather those who are repressing sexual impulses and expressing them symbolically. Those for whom the sexual impulse is egosyntonic do not express sex symbolically but in stories with overt sexual content. Similarily, symbolic suicide may predict a suicidal impulse, but one which is not egosyntonic.

In addition to whether or not the subject is dangerous at the moment, one also can get an idea of the circumstances under which the subject will or will not be dangerous. This may lead to effective intervention. Three illustrative examples may be useful.

A male reformatory inmate was referred on his third incarceration. He had made suicide attempts his first two times in jail. When given the TAT, two things seemed to appear in the stories. In several stories the heroes were imprisoned and developed psychotic breaks. In other stories individuals who were sick or out of their heads tried to kill themselves. When interviewed directly about suicide, the subject partially confirmed the TAT and said, " I won't do it if I know what I'm doing, but if I get into one of those states again, I don't know what I'll do." It was clear from the TAT that incarceration was likely to precipitate a psychotic break, and from both TAT and interview that, when psychotic, he was likely to kill himself. It was then possible and necessary to try to intervene. Discussing the meaning of incarceration for him and dealing with the rage that was involved in killing himself seemed to be sensible. After three sessions the subject had been sent to "solitary." He had been sent there because he had gone temporarily psychotic and smashed something in the so-called "cottage." The inmate revealed some cuts on his neck which he had inflicted with a piece of a light bulb that he had hidden when searched. He said, "I'm sorry, Doc. Look at what I've done after all your work." It was possible to point out to him, however, that he had stopped himself this time as opposed to being stopped by other people on previous attempts, and the psychotherapeutic work continued. Such a benign outcome would not have been possible if the suicidal impulse and its probability had not been known in advance.

Another reformatory inmate was referred for evaluation immediately after a serious suicide attempt, as soon as he had been patched up by the physician. Despite the immediate serious suicide attempt, the evaluation showed on Card 3BM, Card 14, and the blank card stories about a man and his brother planning and executing a burglary for money. No suicidal stories occurred. It was possible to say with some degree of certainty that whatever suicidal impulses the inmate had were no longer active, since he was concerned with something more important to him. No further suicide attempts were made.

The third example is a private psychotherapy patient who showed no suicidal impulses and prided himself on the "sweet reasonableness" of his marriage. That TAT, however, showed a number of stories involving suicidal impulses. In each case they were precipitated by the loss of a love object. In those cases in which the hero killed himself, the hero was always childless. In those cases where the hero did not kill himself, it was because it was not fair to a child and nobody would care anyway. The subject was asked about whether he thought of killing himself and he said, "No." About a month after entering therapy, his wife informed him that she was leaving him and had stayed with him this long only because she was afraid that he might go crazy or kill himself if she left; now that he was in therapy she was no longer responsible. He then became depressed, decided to kill himself, went up to his child's room, looked in and decided it would not be fair to the child and as he left said to himself, "Anyway, nobody would care." He came in to his psychotherapy session the next day and described the whole sequence of thoughts which had been laid out in his TAT.

Such clinical views are of course validatable by systematic research if carefully done. Vogel (1967/1968) undertook systematic comparison of suicidal and nonsuicidal patients on the TAT and found that suicidal patients did indeed give overt suicidal stories in which the hero actually committed suicide.

HOMICIDE

Perhaps the most frightening evaluation is that of homicidal danger. As in any evaluation, one must first start with a clinical view of what the patient is like who is dangerous and then use the TAT to evaluate the relevant aspects of the personality. In clinical experience, murderers are always individuals who cannot tolerate conscious anger. They either attempt to keep the anger unconscious and, when it spills into awareness, it has immediate access to motility, that is, they act on the anger rather than feeling it without acting. Or in some cases they do not feel the anger consciously at all, but simply act out the murderous impulse.

McKie (1971/1972) used the TAT to investigate this systematically, comparing murderers with other prisoners of similar socioeconomic circumstances. The TAT showed less overt aggression and less feelings of anger than in nonmurderous criminals. What aggression occurred was lethal in its consequences; there were fewer stories told by murderers of one man hitting another with his fist, but if physical aggression occurred, it would be of a kind that would likely be lethal, that is, a man shooting or stabbing someone. Typically, murderous individuals give you a TAT in which no aggression or anger occurs at all, or one in which violence of the sort that they will or have committed is carried out by a hero similar to themselves under similar circumstances.

The use of the TAT in criminal situations is always subject to the previously mentioned principle that the subject can keep out of the TAT anything of which they are consciously aware and which they do not wish to reveal. But, in general, material will be represented in the TAT to the extent that it is important in the functioning of the individual, unless it is fully conscious and the individual wishes to keep it out.

RESISTANCE

One of the most useful possibilities of the TAT is predicting or discovering what it is that is going wrong in psychotherapy. As with so many other questions the answer is, in many cases, revealed simply and clearly. In the answer to Card 12M, (or to cards 12M and 12F if both the therapist and patient are female) the therapist may be described as a hypocrite, as dumb, as a financial exploiter, as a homosexual or heterosexual seducer, or as rejecting, revealing some aspect of the transference resistance which may never have been talked about in therapy, but which the therapist can now bring into the therapeutic process in a constructive fashion. One may discover the belief that either the therapy will kill the patient, or that the end of the therapy will kill the patient or, indeed, whatever conscious and unconscious fantasies are involved around the therapeutic relationship. The important principle, however, is that in addition to looking at one card one should always try to get a general overview of the individual's functioning.

RELIABILITY

The reliability of the TAT is a question that has many answers depending upon what it is one means by reliability. The first meaning is *scorer reliability*: do two people looking at the same protocol come to the same conclusions? The answer to that depends on whether the two people are looking for the same information, since two people looking for different aspects of personality may not find the same information relevant. Similarly, two people working with different psychological theories may find different aspects of the personality to be relevant. Usually, scorer reliability is only an issue in research, and the evidence there is that one can get as much scorer reliability as one cares to get by defining carefully the scoring system. Such scorer reliability has been found in the range of .90 for Pathogenesis, for example. However, it is only for research purposes that one usually has a single delimited concept in mind and therefore would take the trouble to develop a highly reliable scoring system.

It is useful to use specific words in deriving a scoring key, and for each rater to reread the key each day before scoring stories. If scoring a series of stories from more than one group of subjects, the stories should be randomly intermixed and scored blindly, that is, without knowledge of the group to which they belong. Stories which are easily scored should be scored first, and difficult decisions laid aside.

On each successive run-through more difficult decisions are made. This procedure should be repeated until all tests are scored. The decisions will become less and less difficult, and the arbitrary decisions can be made all at once. If a modification of the scoring key is necessary, it can be made at that time.

In devising a scoring key, one generally starts with a clear theoretical concept. On the first run-through, one makes easiest decisions, recording the specific bases. On successive run-throughs, one adds to and clarifies the key as specifically as possible.

The second meaning is *temporal reliability*: do you get the same thing over time? Now, the same thing over time is not a simple concept. Many aspects of personality vary over time either in a meaningful or cyclical way. If one used the TAT to measure hunger, if the measure was at all accurate it would vary over the course of the day. Similarly, if one measured mood, it would fluctuate as the individual's mood fluctuated. A mood measure which did not fluctuate could not possibly be valid. In some areas of human personality, we do not know what the temporal stability of the trait measured is. Temporal stability in general is to be investigated, not assumed. The TAT, by permitting us to measure many aspects of personality which are not readily measurable in other ways, may allow us to investigate the temporal patterning of these characteristics.

In dealing with reliability one must make a distinction between the repetition of the same specific story or the repetition of stories which would lead to similar inferences about the personality. Only the latter is important. Interpreting the stability of the TAT to be a question of the stability of the same specific story leads to relatively trivial results: the TAT is either highly reliable, or not at all reliable depending upon what the subject perceives the instructions to be when taking the TAT a second time. If the subject perceives the task as, "Tell the same stories you told before," then a protocol will in general result with the same specific story. If the subject perceives the task to be an imaginative one in which he/she is not to tell the same stories told before, the same specific stories will not occur. Note that the critical factor is what the subjects believe they are expected to do, not necessarily what they are told. However, the repeat reliability of the TAT when we are considering that as the temporal consistency of the inferences to be drawn can be demonstrated in many instances to be quite solid. Tomkins (1947) reports average temporal consistency using the Murray need, press scoring for 18- to 20-year-old women subjects to be .80 for a two-month interval, .60 for a six-month interval, and .50 for a ten-month interval. He also reports differences in temporal consistency for the TAT with the plasticity of the individual being examined. People who are undergoing personality changes have TATs that change, rigidly consistent individuals yield TATs with similar consistency.

A third meaning of reliability is *internal consistency*: do different items within the same test correlate with each other at a moment in time? But the TAT is not simply a psychometric test and does not conform to a simple psychometric model of parallel items within a test. With the TAT (and similar personality tests), there is the problem that each picture and its associated fantasy may be a very specific situation, whose specifics will determine a true but different pattern. The fact that later items get more and more distant from the surface of behavior suggests again that changes between cards do not represent unreliability necessarily, but different facets of that complex organization we understand as the human personality. Moreover, there is a patterning to the fantasies within the TAT such that if a need is expressed on one card, there is a tendency for it not to be expressed strongly on the next card, and then to be reexpressed on the third card and so forth. Such patterning is meaningful if one thinks of the role of fantasies in human beings as partially satisfying "needs," according to most psychological theories.

The concepts we use in personality theories are complex constructs, to some extent arbitarily defined, chosen for some purpose from the infinite number of possible aspects of personality. The components of such a concept do not necessarily correlate with each other. As in the example of "aggression" described above, what is the variable will depend on whether you wish to study displacement as the psychoanalysts did, in which case it was useful to consider aggression a unitary concept, or whether you wish to predict murder or physical violence, in which case the psychological level of the aggression (unconscious, conscious thought, verbal, physical nonlethal, physical lethal), kind of person directed toward, and conditions of instigation become critical.

In psychometrics, reliability became an issue because there were many instruments, such as intelligence tests, for which there were no good criteria of validity. It can be demonstrated mathematically, if one makes the arbitrary assumption that a test contains an error component uncorrelated with anything, that an increase in reliability will increase the validity for predicting all criteria. If one assumes each item to be a miniature of the test, then internal consistency measures how much is "true" variance and how much is "error" variance. It was possible to make progress in intelligence testing, and in mental tests in general, by increasing the reliability of the tests, and, indeed, validities for many purposes were increased. It is this relationship between reliability and validity which intially gave the concept of reliability, measured by internal consistency, such a useful and central role.

Nonotholess, random orror uncorrelatod with anything and para llel subtests or items are assumptions only approximated in reality with some tests. Without these arbitrary assumptions there is no necessary mathematical relationship between internal consistency and validity (Karon, 1966).

Since, according to psychometric theory, a lack of reliability will make it impossible to predict any criteria, reliability need be a concern only when a test is not valid, that is, when it does not predict a criterion it ought to predict. A lack of reliability cannot, in a blind prediction, account for the ability of a test to predict. It can only account for the failure of a test to predict criteria. A test which is valid therefore must be reliable.

A traditional theorem of classical psychometric theory is that the highest "validity" coefficient serves as an estimate of a lower bound to the square root of the reliability. ("Validity" coefficient as used in this sentence means simply a correlation coefficient between the test and any other independent measure of *any* variable, and *not* the more specific meaning of validity as correlation with the particular specified characteristic that the test is supposed to measure.)

This may be equivalently stated as the reliability must be greater than the square of *any* "validity" coefficient. This procedure for determining a lower bound to reliability is a well-established part of classical mental test theory (Gulliksen, 1950, pp. 23–28).

Therefore, students who work with the TAT or other personality tests may take the highest validity coefficient (the highest correlation of their test score with anything), square it, and report this estimate of a lower bound to the reliability, which indeed it is. That this lower bound to the reliability, so estimated, is frequently higher than the internal consistency directly measured, is simply evidence of the fact that mental test theory, with its assumption of random error uncorrelated with anything, does not apply to their domain. If the theory were not procrustean, such discrepancies would be impossible. Of course, this is not to advocate capitalizing on chance by scanning 100 validity coefficients and choosing the largest. But, in the ordinary course of research, one has one, two, or three validity coefficients, and capitalizing on chance is not a problem.

Preferable, however, is the more straightforward recommendation that the student simply report the validity coefficients and let these coefficients speak for themselves.

VALIDITY

The clinical validity of the TAT needs to be established for each investigator, because the measuring instrument is not the test, but the test plus interpreter. The blind interpretation of the protocol followed by an intensive investigation of the individual is the best way to convince oneself of the utility of this source of clinical material. This was the kind of validation which occurred in the early days and continues to occur. Some examples have been given above.

A more systematic report has been given by Kardiner and Ovesey (1951), who reported that when TATs were independently analyzed, as were the Rorschachs of the same subjects, the results of each of the projective tests separately coincided with the conclusions independently arrived at by a clinical psychoanalyst on the basis of 25 to 100 interviews of each subject.

The general literature on the TAT, like that on most projective tests, shows a wide range of validity. One can with equal ease seek out and find studies in which the TAT does not seem to be valid and studies in which it is found to be highly valid. In general, most of this seemingly contradictory literature can be made to make sense on the basis of one variable: the training and/or experience of the individuals interpreting the TAT. In those studies where the individuals had training and/or experience in using the TAT and are predicting a criterion about which they know something, the TAT turns out to be valid. In those studies where the interpretation is made by people without any training or experience, who are trained by people without training, or who are predicting a criterion about which they know nothing, the TAT turns out not to work very well. Clinical processes require relevant training and/or experience.

A relevant study is that of Karon and O'Grady (1970), in which two graduate students in Clinical Psychology with training in the TAT blindly rated TATs of schizophrenic patients for Emotional Health. They used a psychological scaling technique to quantify their judgments. The ratings were to be made clinically and were to reflect the following: the ability to take care of oneself, ability to work, sexual adjustment, social adjustment, absence of hallucinations and delusions, degree of freedom from anxiety and depression, amount of affect, variety and spontaneity of affect, satisfaction with life and self, achievement of capabilities, and benign versus malignant effect on others. In addition they were to assume that the following also indicated healthy development: length of the protocol, absence of stereotyped responses and more varied material, presence of benign fantasies and helping nurturant parent figures, self-confidence, reality testing, direct representation of problems. Their blind ratings correlated with each other .94 and .81 in two replications. The correlation with ratings of emotional health from the Rorschach was .64 and .80. The correlation with emotional health ratings on the basis of a detailed clinical status interview was .55 and .57. Since these patients were schizophrenic, intellectual tests were used as a measure of the thought disorder. Number of errors on the Drasgow-Feldman Visual-Verbal test, a concept formation test designed to be specifically vulnerable to the schizophrenic disorder, correlated with the TAT ratings −.41 and −.74 in the two replications. Wechsler-Bellevue scores correlated .55 and .65. Porteus maze scores correlated .44 and .45. This pattern of validities is impressive.

Even more impressive was the ability to predict the number of days in the hospital in the six-month period after the TAT was administered. Since none of the testing material was used to determine hospitalization or day of discharge (the testing had been gathered for research purposes), it was impressive that the TAT ratings of emotional health correlated −.63 with days hospitalized in the ensuing six months in the first replication, and −.64 in the second replication.

It should be noted that in this appropriate validity study there are the following critical elements:

1. The raters were allowed to use the TAT as a clinical instrument.

2. The raters had been trained in using the TAT as a clinical instrument.

3. The judges were rating a criterion, Emotional Health, about which they had relevant training and experience.

4. A psychological scaling technique was used to reduce the clinical judgments to appropriate quantitative numbers.

It should not be construed that this is the only appropriate study. It is simply illustrative of the kind of study which will yield positive findings. There are many other studies showing the TAT appropriately used to be a highly valid clinical and research instrument.

THE RESEARCH USE OF THE TAT

It is the feeling of the author that one can appropriately use the TAT as a research instrument only if one is familiar with its clinical use and the kind of reasoning that is involved in its appropriate clinical use. Nonetheless, there are many aspects of the human personality worth studying systematically about which information is not readily obtainable by other techniques, or about which one could obtain information only by an extensive psychotherapeutic investigation. As mentioned above, Kardiner and Ovesey (1951) discovered that the use of either the Rorschach or the TAT would have yielded the same results as their extensive psychoanalytic investigation of their subjects on an individual basis. Obviously, the TAT is much easier and more practical to use than psychoanalysis as a research tool.

It is also possible to examine cultures by taking samples of people within different cultures and noticing how their modal assumptions about the world differ. Anthropologists have in fact carried out such studies, using the TAT to study both groups and individuals within those groups, for example, Henry (1947), Lindzey (1961), Hanks and Phillips (1961).

One can use TAT-like materials even to investigate supposed universal dynamics, if the relevant aspects of the response to the cards is seemingly not determined by the stimulus. Thus, a modified Blacky "castration" card (Blum, 1949), showing a blindfolded dog with a knife about to fall on its tail, was used to investigate alternative universal theories of the source of castration fears in men. The finding for both schizophrenics and normals was that this differs with actual life experience, but the most usual is a fear of both parents, with the fear of the father serving in part as a defense against a deeper more frightening fear of the mother (Karon, 1964; 1970). Of course, this did not examine whether castration fears exist or are important. That would require a stimulus to which castration fantasies would be almost certain if they exist, and yet would not seemingly be required by the stimulus. Unfortunately, the nearest approximation is still free association sessions over a long period of time (psychoanalysis).

In using the TAT for research one needs to define what it is that one wishes to measure. In the Karon and O'Grady study, for example, what was meant by Emotional Health was clearly specified by the investigators and checked with other psychoanalytically oriented professionals familiar with the patient population as to the meaningfulness of such a measure before it was employed.

If one can clearly conceptualize what it is that one wishes to measure, one can in general derive a relevant TAT measure. If one cannot clearly conceptualize what it is one wishes to measure, then one will have no luck in deriving a TAT measure. Thus, a model of good clinical research is provided by Wynne and Singer (1963), who observed the interaction of families of schizophrenics and were able to note a deviant pattern of communication. Once they had observed this pattern of deviant communication in the actual familial interaction, they were also able to define criteria for scoring this communication deviance from the Rorschach and from the TAT.

Both projective tests now differentiated parents of schizophrenics from parents of delinquents or normals (Singer & Wynne, 1965). Wender, Rosenthal, Zahn, and Kety (1971), in a widely cited "definitive" study of genetic factors, contrasted children adopted at an early age whose biological parents were schizophrenic with adopted children whose biological parents were not schizophrenic. All cases of schizophrenia, approximately 10 percent, occurred in the group whose biological parents were schizophrenic. Adoptive parents were interviewed, as well as tested with the Rorschach, TAT, MMPI, and Word Association Test. It was claimed that there was no difference between the two groups of adoptive parents which would account for the difference in the rate of schizophrenia.

However, when the Rorschachs of all the adoptive parents were scored blindly by Singer, she identified with complete accuracy (no false positives or negatives) every adoptive parent whose adopted child became schizophrenic, suggesting non-random factors in adoption, rather than genetics. However, Wender, Rosenthal, and Kety (1976) reported that the TAT did not differentiate the adoptive parents, suggesting that the Rorschach findings were a fluke, or that the TAT was not valid.

But the TATs were not made available to Singer. They were scored by research assistants of Wender and co-workers, who had found nothing on the Rorschach protocols (or anywhere else).

The Singer scale is complicated; serious researchers (Doane, West, Goldstein, Rodnick, & Jones, in press) reported that it required a year's work to develop adequate scoring procedures for their use. In a unique prospective study casting light on the direction of causality, they found that if the parents of maladjusted, but not psychotic, adolescents gave TATs that were scored on the Singer criteria as being like parents of schizophrenics and were intrusively hostile ("Expressed Emotionality"), then every adolescent in their sample was psychotic or borderline five years later; no adolescent was psychotic or borderline five years later if their parents neither showed communication deviance on the TAT nor were intrusively hostile; where the parents were in the destructive direction on one variable and not on the other, there was an intermediate frequency of psychotic or borderline individuals.

Following a different line of reasoning, we considered the unusual pattern of unconscious interaction between parents and children that schizophrenic patients in psychotherapy seemed to describe consistently. The question was whether the retrospective investigation in psychotherapy was yielding reliable results that were meaningful, or whether these findings were an artifact of reconstruction and that these families were not really different from families where the children did not develop subsequent pathology, as some investigators have maintained. But much of the research on familial factors was irrelevant, because it was superficial. The problem was that the specific behavioral interactions that seemed to lead to the pathology were different in different families. Thus, one mother might have burned her son's hand to teach him not to steal. Another mother might have taken her son's paintings to show people how gifted he was while he begged to be allowed to keep them. Still another mother might toilet train her child incredibly early, and so on, but no one of these patterns of destructive parenting would occur uniformly across families. It seemed also that the parents were not consciously malevolent nor destructive people, but were acting out some unconscious problem or defense, for which no one could legitimately blame them.

To deal with this issue systematically, it seemed clear that one had to get at some level of generality, such as motivation, which could be investigated across families, and use a procedure which would tap unconscious processes. The TAT seemed obvious. The concept of Pathogenesis was defined as the degree to which one acts in terms of one's own needs when those needs and the needs of someone who depends on the person conflict. Parents of schizophrenics, it seemed from the case material, tended to act, albeit without awareness, in terms of their own needs, disregarding the needs of their child, more frequently than parents of normals.

A scoring system for Pathogenesis was worked out. Each story is scored P (Pathogenic), B (Benign), or U (Unscorable). The story is scored P if there is an interaction with potentially conflicting needs and the dominant person does not take the dependent person's needs into account. The story is scored B if there is an interaction with potentially conflicting needs and the dominant person takes the dependent person's needs into account. The Pathogenesis score is the ratio: $P/(P + B)$, that is, the percentage of scorable stories in which the dominant individual in the story acted in terms of his/her own needs, ignoring the potentially conflicting needs of a dependent person. The latest version of the scoring key is available from the author on request.

The TATs of parents of schizophrenics and of parents of normal children of the same age and sex were scored blindly. In a series of studies it was discovered that parents of schizophrenics generally average around .75 on the Pathogenesis scale. Parents of normals tend to average around .35. Thus, nobody is perfectly destructive, and nobody is perfectly good, but a lifetime of living with such a parent does leave one vulnerable. Meyer and Karon (1967) differentiated mothers of schizophrenics from mothers of normals. Mitchell (1968) replicated this with larger samples. Mitchell (1974) also differentiated fathers of schizophrenics as well as mothers in another study. Mitchell (1974) also reports that fathers of male delinquents are high in pathogenesis, but the mothers are almost down to normal levels. Nichols (1970/1971) found that degree of Pathogenesis on the TAT of their mothers correlated with severity of thought disorder and length of hospitalization among hospitalized male schizophrenics. Melnick and Hurley (1969) and Evans (1976/1977) found that Pathogenesis scores differentiated child-abusive mothers from normal mothers. Pathogenesis also differentiated good from bad therapists in one study (VandenBos & Karon, 1971).

Thus, two different aspects of personality functioning, the Wynne and Singer communication deviance measure and the Karon Pathogenesis index, both differentiate parents of schizophrenics. In both cases the concepts were derived from clinical observations and theory. The clinical concept was first clearly delineated, and then a technique of scoring for that well-delineated clinical concept was derived. This is the procedure that one would recommend in using the TAT for research.

A well-known example of an alternative procedure is the McClelland (1953) use of the TAT for measuring the Need for Achievement. The need for achievement had been defined in the early Murray studies on the basis of fantasies concerning the wish to achieve. McClelland (1953), using an experimental paradigm, instigated a set to achieve in one group of undergraduates and not with another group. He scored whatever increased as being the Need for Achievement and developed an elaborate scoring key. Research (Ricciuti, 1954; Ricciuti & Sadacca, 1955; Ricciuti & Clark, 1957; Entwistle, 1972) has suggested that simply counting the number of stories in which any achievement imagery occurs, plus the length of the story, will predict most criteria as well as the careful scoring scheme developed by McClelland. In some situations so may appropriately phrased direct questions (Holmes & Tyler, 1968). Nonetheless, this scheme has demonstrated a measure of validity in a number of situations, although there are also negative validity studies.

Most important was the finding from the beginning that this score worked only for men, but not for women. Clearly this must mean that we had only begun to approach the conceptual problem. Today we would never make the mistake of accepting a psychological theory as adequate that worked for only half of the human race.

A further difficulty with this experimental paradigm for determining the scoring is that the complexities of human achievement motivation are such that momentary instigation will not affect those people whose needs for achievement or lack of such needs are so determined that they cannot be turned on or off by momentary stimulation. Such people exist, and we would not expect the experimentally derived scoring system to reflect such dynamics as Jones's (1915) concept of "urethral eroticism," or Fenichel's (1945) "Don Juan of Achievement." But such clinical ideas can be investigated by the TAT nonetheless, as did Murray (1955) in describing an "Icarus" complex, which he delineated in the TAT as well as in case history material.

An illustration of the weakness of correlative ways of arriving at a scoring system is exemplified by further research carried out by some of McClelland's collaborators (Clark & Sensibar, 1955). Their hope was to find an empirical measure of the need for sex using similar procedures. Two groups of male undergraduates were compared. One saw a set of pictures of landscapes, and then were administered the TAT. The other group saw a set of pictures of sexy, nude females and were then administered the TAT. The assumptions were that male undergraduates in general could not see such pictures without becoming sexually aroused, that this would then be reflected in the TATs, and that one would then have an empirically derived score for the Need for Sex, similar to the Need for Achievement.

The finding was just the opposite. Those who had seen the sexy pictures actually had less sexual content in their stories than the male undergraduates who had not seen such pictures. The investigators sensibly enough assumed that these subjects must have been sexually aroused, but that the arousal must have also made them anxious or guilty. Their anxiety or guilt inhibited them from including as much sexual content in their stories as they would ordinarily. To test this out, the experiment of showing the sexy pictures and then giving the TAT was repeated in a different context, namely, at a fraternity beer party where the social setting and the alcohol could be depended upon to inhibit the anxiety or guilt about telling sexy stories. Indeed, the subjects told stories that were full of overt sexual content.

The investigators then realized they had data for examining two theories of symbolism (as used in the psychoanalytic sense) which were put forth by different clinical theorists. The one view is that symbolism is a special or primitive language used in dreams and fantasies in which people say what they need to say. Such a view has been put forth by such diverse theorists as Carl Jung (1920), Erich Fromm (1951), and Calvin Hall (1953a; 1953b). The other view is that symbolism is used to express what is there but cannot be expressed directly, that is, that symbolism has a disguise function. Such a view is put forth by Freud (1900/1950) and even more clearly by Ferenczi (1913/1950). If the first view is correct, the stories that have the most overt sex should also have the most sexual symbolic content, and the stories which have the least overt sex should have the least symbolic sexual content. If, on the other hand, symbols are used to express with disguise, then there should be the most symbolic sexual content in the stories told by the subjects who were sexually aroused, but not telling sexual stories, and there should be least symbolic sexual content in the fraternity beer party subjects who were telling overt sexual stories. The TATs were scored for symbolic sexual content blindly, and the finding was that symbolism is used to express what cannot be expressed openly. The beer party stories had the least symbolic sexual content and the most overt sexual content. The stories told by subjects after seeing the sexy female pictures, but who did not tell overtly sexy stories because of anxiety or guilt, were full of symbolic sexual content. As is so often the case when carefully investigated, psychoanalytic clinical theory was confirmed.

TAT DERIVATIVES (ALTERNATE STANDARDIZED STIMULI)

Perhaps the most important alternate stimuli are Symond's (1949) series of cards intended for adolescents, focusing on a wider variety of situations that are of importance to adolescents. The set seems to be useful, although the standard set seems adequate for most purposes with adolescents.

Bellak (1971) developed the Children's Apperception Test for young children using pictures involving animals. Research (e.g.,

Armstrong, 1954; Light, 1954), however, has indicated that children tell better stories to the standard set. Now there is a version of the Children's Apperception Test having the same animal picture situations, but with human figures. However, we know of no evidence that it is more revealing than using the standard set of TAT pictures.

The Blacky test (Blum, 1949) shows pictures of dogs aimed at specific psychosexual problems from Freudian analytic theory. This is useful for research purposes, but for clinical work it is usually more revealing to use the standard set, in which psychodynamic conflicts may be evaluated within their full interpersonal setting.

Thompson developed a set of TAT cards in which the protagonists are Black. Early research (Cook, 1953; Light, 1955) seemed to indicate, however, that use of the Thompson TAT did not significantly alter the responses of Black subjects, but did make a difference in responses of White subjects. One recent research study (Karon & O'Grady, 1970) showed that clinical inferences drawn from the standard TAT administered to Black psychiatric patients were valid.

Other available standard pictures for storytelling tests include the African (Black) TAT, Family Relations Indicator, Four-Picture Test, Make a Picture Story Test, Michigan Picture Test, Object Relations Technique, Pickford Projective Pictures, Picture Impressions Test, School Apperception Method, Senior Apperception Test, South African (White) Picture Analysis Test, and the Vocational Apperception Test. Descriptions, reviews, and bibliographies of each of these (as well as other personality tests) can be found in Buros (1970; 1975).

MULTIPLE-CHOICE ADAPTATIONS OF THE TAT

In general, most attempts to develop multiple-choice versions of the TAT have turned out to be of little validity. Thus, for example, the Blacky test has both a free-response and a multiple-choice section. The use of the Blacky free response as a TAT has often proved very useful. The use of the multiple choice in general does not yield as much (e.g., Young, 1959). There is, however, one demonstratedly valid multiple-choice technique based on the TAT, the Tomkins-Horn Picture Arrangement Test, a test consisting of 25 sets of three line drawings. The task is to put them in order so they tell the story that makes the best sense and in three sentences tell the story. This test was designed to be scored objectively, and a rationale based on the TAT rationale, plus a conceptualization of the special difficulties involved in multiple-choice adaptations of projective tests, was used to evolve a scoring procedure, which is presented along with validity data and national norms by Tomkins and Miner (1957; 1959). Tomkins' theory was that multiple-choice projective tests fail because most of the responses are stimulus-determined, and hence can be given for many different reasons. By focusing *only* on rare responses (and considering combinations of responses across cards to find unusual responses) one can avoid this pitfall. Results seem to support this view. "Rare" responses are operationally defined as occurring in less than five percent of the normal population of the same age, education, and vocabulary level.

Using the PAT on a small number of subjects to derive conceptually meaningful motivation measures empirically, Miner (1960; 1961a; 1961b) obtained validity coefficients, in larger-sample cross-validation studies, against real job performance of .57 (for sales personnel) and .72 and .61 (for tabulating machine operators). Using a more conservative coefficient, the point bi-serial R, reduces the latter two to .58 and .48, which are still impressive.

An illustrative use of the PAT as a large-scale research instrument was *Black Scars* (Karon, 1975) in which a nation-wide Gallup sample was tested to investigate the effects of suffering discrimination on Black personality, and the effects of participating in a system of discrimination on White personality.

CONCLUSION

The TAT is a sample of human fantasy that allows us to investigate aspects of the personality which are often not easily investigatable otherwise. It is both a valuable clinical tool and an extraordinary tool for research, because it allows us to investigate any personality variable that we can clearly define.

REFERENCES

Armstrong, M. A. S. Children's responses to animal and human figures in Thematic Apperception. *Journal of Consulting Psychology*, 1954, *18*, 67–78.

Bellak, L. *The TAT and CAT in Clinical Use.* New York: Grune & Stratton, 1971.

Blum, G. A. A study of the psychoanalytic theory of psychosexual development. *Genetic Psychology Monographs*, 1949, *39*, 3–99.

Buros, O. K. *Personality Tests and Reviews*. Highland Park, N.J.: Gryphon
Press, 1970.

Buros, O. K. *Personality Tests and Reviews II*. Highland Park, N.J.: Gryphon
Press, 1975.

Clark, R. A., & Sensibar, M. R. The relationship between symbolic and manifest protections of sexuality with some incidental correlates. *Journal of
Abnormal and Social Psychology*, 1955, *50*, 327–334.

Cook, R. A. Identification and ego-defensiveness in Thematic Apperception.
Journal of Projective Techniques, 1953, *17*, 312–319.

Doane, J. A., West, K. L., Goldstein, M. J., Rodnick, E. H., & Jones, J. E. Parental
affective style and communication deviance as predictors of subsequent
schizophrenia spectrum disorders in vulnerable adolescents. Manuscript submitted for publication, 1979. (Available from Dr. Goldstein,
Dept. of Psychology, UCLA.)

Entwistle, D. E. To dispel fantasies about fantasy-based measures of achievement motivation. *Psychological Bulletin*, 1972, *77*, 377–397.

Evans, A. L. Personality characteristics of child-abusing mothers. (Doctoral
dissertation, Michigan State University, 1976). *Dissertation Abstracts
International*, 1977, *37*, 6322b–6323b (University Microfilms No. 77-11,
642).

Fairbairn, W. R. D. *Psychoanalytic Studies of the Personality*. London: Tavis-
tock, 1952.

Fenichel, O. The Don Juan of Achievement. *Psychoanalytic Theory of Neurosis*. New York: Norton, 1945, pp. 502–504.

Ferenczi, S. The ontogenesis of symbols (1913). In *Sex in Psychoanalysis
Selected Papers*, Vol. I. New York: Basic Books, 1950, pp. 276–281.

Freud, S. *The Interpretation of Dreams*. New York: Macmillan, 1900/1950.

Freud, S. *A General Introduction to Psychoanalysis*. New York: Liveright,
1916/1963.

Freud, S. *New Introductory Lectures on Psychoanalysis*. New York: Norton,
1933/1966.

Fromm, E. *The Forgotten Language*. New York: Rinehart, 1951.

Gulliksen, H. O. *Theory of Mental Tests*. New York: Wiley, 1950.

Guntrip, H. *Schizoid Phenomena, Object Relations, and the Self*. New York:
International Universities, 1969.

Hall, C. S. A cognitive theory of dream symbols. *Journal of Genetic Psychology*, 1953a, pp. 169–186.

Hall, C. S. *The Meaning of Dreams*. New York: Harper, 1953b.

Hanks, L. M., & Phillips, H. P. A young Thai from the countryside. In B.
Kaplan (Ed.), *Studying Personality Cross-Culturally*. Evanston, Ill.: Row,
Peterson, 1961, pp. 637–658.

Henry, W. E. The Thematic Apperception Technique in the study of culture personality relations. *Genetic Psychology Monographs*, 1947, *35*, 1–134.

Holmes, D. S., & Tyler, J. D. Direct versus projective measure of achievement motivation. *Journal of Consulting and Clinical Psychology*, 1968, *32*, 712–717.

Jung, C. G. *Collected Papers on Analytical Psychology*. London: Bailliere, Tindall, and Cox, 1920.

Jones, E. Urethralerotik and Ehregeiz (Urethral eroticism and ambition), *Internationale Zeitschrift für Psychoanalyse*, 1915, *3*, 156–157.

Kagan, J., & Lesser, G. S. *Contemporary Issues in Thematic Apperceptive Methods*. Springfield, Ill.: Charles C. Thomas, 1961.

Kardiner, A., & Ovesey, L. *The Mark of Oppression*. New York: Norton, 1951.

Karon, B. P. An experimental study of parental castration phantasies in schizophrenia. British Journal of Psychiatry, 1964, *110*, 67–73.

Karon, B. P. Reliability: Paradigm or paradox, with special reference to personality tests. *Journal for Projective Techniques and Personality Assessment*, 1966, *60*, 223–227.

Karon, B. P. An experimental study of parental castration phantasies. *British Journal of Psychiatry*, 1970, *117*, 69–73.

Karon, B. P. *Black Scars*. New York: Springer, 1975.

Karon. B. P., & O'Grady, P. Quantified judgments of mental health from the Rorschach, TAT, and Clinical Status Interview by means of a scaling technique. *Journal of Consulting and Clinical Psychology*, 1970, *34*, 229–235.

Light, B. H. Comparative study of a series of TAT and CAT cards. *Journal of Clinical Psychology*, 1954, *10*, 179–181.

Light, B. H. A further test of the Thompson TAT rationale. *Journal of Abnormal and Social Psychology*, 1955, *51*, 148–150.

Lindzey, G. *Projective Technique and Cross-Cultural Research*. New York: Appleton-Century-Crofts, 1961.

Lindzey, G., & Goldwyn, R. M. Validity of the Rosenzweig Picture-Frustration study. *Journal of Personality*, 1954, *22*, 519–547.

McClelland, D. C. *The Achievement Motive*. New York: Appleton-Century-Crofts, 1953.

McKie, R. R. A clinical study: Relationships of anger and fear to aggression, in murderers and in non-violent offenders. (Doctoral Dissertation, Michigan State University, 1971). *Dissertation Abstracts International*, 1971/1972, *32*, 7312-B, (University Microfilms No. 72-16, 477).

Melnick, B., & Hurley, J. R. Distinctive personality attributes of child-abusing mothers. *Journal of Consulting and Clinical Psychology*, 1969, *33*, 746–749.

Meyer, R. G., & Karon, B. P. The schizophrenogenic mother concept and the TAT. *Psychiatry*, 1967, *30*, 173–179.

Mill, J. S. *A System of Logic*. London: 1843.

Miner, J. B. The concurrent validity of the PAT in the selection of tabulating machine operators. *Journal of Projective Techniques*, 1960, *24*, 409–418.

Miner, J. B. The validity of the PAT in the selection of tabulating machine operators: an analysis of predictive power. *Journal of Projective Techniques*, 1961a, *25*, 330–333.

Miner, J. B. Personality and ability factors in sales performance. *Journal of Applied Psychology*, 1961b, *25*, 6–13.

Mitchell, K. M. An analysis of the schizophrenogenic mother concept by means of the Thematic Apperception Test. *Journal of Abnormal Psychology*, 1968, *73*, 571–574.

Mitchell, K. M. Relationship between different levels of parental "Pathogenesis" and male children's diagnosis. *Journal of Clinical Psychology*, 1974, *30*, 49–50.

Morgan, C. D., & Murray, H. A. A method for investigating phantasies: The Thematic Apperception Test. *Archives of Neurology and Psychiatry*, 1935, *34*, 289–306.

Murray, H. A. *Explorations in Personality.* New York: Oxford University, 1938.

Murray, H. A. *Thematic Apperception Test Manual.* Cambridge: Harvard University, 1943.

Murray, H. A. American Icarus. In A. Burton & R. E. Harris (Eds.), *Clinical Studies of the Personality.* New York: Harper, 1955, pp. 615–641.

Nichols, N. H. The relationship between degree of maternal pathogenicity, and severity of ego impairment in schizophrenic offspring. (Doctoral dissertation, University of Michigan, 1970). *Dissertation Abstracts International*, 1971, *31*, 5003B, (University Microfilm No. 71-4693).

Rapaport, D., Gill, M. M., Schafer, R., & Holt, R. P. *Diagnostic Psychological Testing.* New York: International Universities, 1968.

Ricciuti, H. N. *The prediction of academic grades with a projective test of achievement motivation: I. Initial validation studies.* Technical Report No. 1, ONR Contract Nonr—694(00). Princeton, N.J.: Educational Testing Service, 1954.

Ricciuti, H. N., & Sadacca, R. *The prediction of academic grades with a projective test of achievement motivation: II. Cross-validation at the high school level.* Technical Report, ONR Contract Nonr—694(00). Princeton, N.J.: Educational Testing Service, 1955.

Ricciuti, H. N., & Clark, R. A. *A comparison of need achievement stories written by experimentally "relaxed" and "achievement-oriented" subjects: Effects obtained with new pictures and revised scoring categories.* Technical Report, ONR Contract Nonr—694(00). Princeton, N.J.: Educational Testing Service, 1957.

Rosenzweig, S. *Aggressive Behavior and the Rosenzweig Picture-Frustration Study.* New York: Praeger, 1978.

Rosenzweig, S., & Fleming, E. E. Apperceptive norms for the Thematic

Apperception Test: II. An empirical investigation. *Journal of Personality*, 1949, *17*, 483–503.

Singer, M., & Wynne, L. Thought disorder and family relations of schizophrenics: IV. Results and Implications. *Archives of General Psychiatry*, 1965, *12*, 201–212.

Stein, M. I. *The Thematic Apperception Test*. Cambridge, Mass.: Addison-Wesley, 1955.

Sullivan, H. S. *The Interpersonal Theory of Psychiatry*. New York: Norton, 1953.

Symonds, P. M. *Adolescent Fantasy*. New York: Columbia University, 1949.

Tomkins, S. S. *The Thematic Apperception Test*. New York: Grune and Stratton, 1947.

Tomkins, S. S. The present status of the Thematic Apperception Test. *American Journal of OrthoPsychiatry*, 1949, *19*, 358–362.

Tomkins, S. S. *Affect, Imagery, Consciousness*, Vols. I & II. New York: Springer, 1962, 1963.

Tomkins, S. S., & Miner, J. B. *The Picture Arrangement Test*. New York: Springer, 1957.

Tomkins, S. S., & Miner, J. B. *PAT Interpretation*. New York: Springer, 1959.

VandenBos, G. R., & Karon, B. P. Pathogenesis: A new therapist personality dimension related to therapeutic effectiveness. *Journal of Personality Assessment*, 1971, *35*, 252–260.

Vogel, R. B. A projective study of dynamic factors in attempted suicide (Doctoral dissertation, Michigan State University, 1967). *Dissertation Abstracts*, 1968, *28*, 4303B. (University Microfilms No. 68-4230).

Wender, P. H., Rosenthal, D., Zahn, T., & Kety, S. The psychiatric adjustments of the adopting parents of schizophrenics. *American Journal of Psychiatry*, 1971, *127*, 1013–1018.

Wender, P. H., Rosenthal, D., & Kety, S. S. Wender et al. reply. *Contemporary Psychology*, 1976, *21*, 74.

Wynne, L., & Singer, M. Thought disorder and family relations of schizophrenics. II. A classification of forms of thinking. *Archives of General Psychiatry*, 1963, *9*, 199–206.

Young, M. F. An investigation of narcissism and correlates of narcissism in schizophrenics, neurotics, and normals. (Doctoral dissertation, Temple University, 1959). *Dissertation Abstracts*, 1959, *20*, 3394. (University Microfilms No. 59-06465).

5

Completion Methods: Word Association, Sentence, and Story Completion

A. I. Rabin and Zoli Zlotogorski

This chapter is devoted to the presentation and discussion of three different, but related, projective methods. The first, the word-association technique has been "hindsightedly" adopted and admitted into the projective compound. As is indicated in the subsequent discussion, the method of word association was used in experimental as well as clinical settings long before the advent of the concept and the term of *projective techniques*. In a sense it may be called the progenitor of these methods. Whereas word association dates back to the 19th century, sentence completion and story completion methods are of a later vintage.

What do these methods have in common? First, they all present verbal stimuli. Word association, however, is generally presented orally, while in the other two methods the stimuli are generally presented in printed form (often supplemented by the examiner's reading). Second, the responses are similar, with the verbal (oral) response expected in the word association and, generally, written ones to the sentence and story completion. Third, in all three instances the stimuli impose certain expectancies as to the content of the response; relevant, related, or associated content is expected. The sentence and story completion methods, however, place additional constraints on the respondent. The structure of the sentence stub or the beginning of the story have certain syntactical and grammatical demand characteristics beyond the content.

Finally, in the case of the completion methods the purpose and intent of the examiner are not as disguised as in the case of the major projective techniques such as the Rorschach and the TAT. In the case of the Rorschach, for example, the respondent is ordinarily unaware of the meaning and interpretation of his responses. Completions of verbally presented stimuli that have a certain "face validity" are such that the respondent is fully aware of their meaning and their message to the examiner. Thus, under these conditions the examinee reveals as much or as little of his "private world" as he consciously wishes or allows himself to do.

WORD ASSOCIATION

The word-association method has been called the oldest of all projective techniques (Peck & McGuire, 1959). Jung carried out a series of investigations using word associations to confirm Freud's theory of repression. The Kent-Rosanoff Free Association Test was published shortly thereafter, and, although Jung's work is cited as a source (Rosanoff, 1927, p. 371), it appears to have been developed relatively independently. The 100 words comprising the Kent-Rosanoff list were developed with a sample of 1000 normal subjects, and a frequency tabulation of responses was reported (Rosanoff, 1927, pp. 546–604).

During the early years of psychoanalysis, word-association techniques flourished. Kraepelin and Bleuler employed word association as an improved tool for psychiatric description and classification. Others, including both Wundt and Galton, experimented with the word-association technique. The increasing popularity of this technique reached its zenith with Rapaport's studies of projective techniques. Rapaport and his associates conducted an intensive study of diagnostic testing and used word associations as one of their techniques (Rapaport, Gill & Schafer, 1946).

In the decades following Rapaport's major study, word-association techniques have been largely supplanted by other methods. Barely 15 years after the Rapaport studies, Sundberg

(1961) ranked the Kent-Rosanoff Free Association Test as twenty-ninth in reported clinical usage. Despite its demonstrated value as a clinical and research instrument, the past decade has witnessed few current contributions to applied and clinical research.

Materials

The materials needed for a word-association test are paper and pencil, a timing device, and an appropriate list of words. One such list is reproduced in Table 5.1. The Rapaport list of 60 nouns contains a number of emotionally loaded words with direct denotative meanings. The earlier Kent-Rosanoff list of 100 words contains nouns, adjectives, verbs and fewer words with double meanings.

Table 5.1. Revised Word List from Rapaport et al.[1]

1. rat	21. suicide	41. cut
2. lamp	22. mountain	42. movies
3. love	23. smoke	43. cockroach
4. book	24. house	44. bite
5. father	25. vagina	45. dog
6. paper	26. tobacco	46. dance
7. breast	27. mouth	47. gun
8. curtains	28. horse	48. water
9. trunk	29. masturbation	49. husband
10. drink	30. wife	50. mud
11. party	31. table	51. woman
12. spring	32. fight	52. fire
13. bowel movement	33. beef	53. suck
14. rug	34. stomach	54. money
15. boy friend	35. farm	55. mother
16. chair	36. man	56. hospital
17. screen	37. taxes	57. girl friend
18. penis	38. nipple	58. taxi
19. radiator	39. doctor	59. intercourse
20 frame	40. dirt	60. hunger

[1] From Rapaport, Gill and Schafer, *Diagnostic Psychological Testing*, Vol. 2 Chicago: Year Book, 1946, p. 84. Reprinted with permission of the publishers.

Administration

In a quiet and comfortable setting the word stimuli are almost always presented orally (Lindzey, 1959), although administration can be visual (Rotter, 1951). Daston (1968) recommends that the word association test be given relatively late in the testing session. He cites two good reasons for delay. First, given the threatening nature of the task, good rapport with the client should be established beforehand. Second, it offers the examiner the opportunity of adding words with idiosyncratic loadings based on the clinical hunches gleaned from the initial contact with client.

Instructions to the client are fairly standard. The examiner reads the words one at a time, slowly and clearly; generally, beginning with a statement such as, "I am going to read you a list of words, one at a time. Please answer with the first word that comes into your mind." He records the word response plus the time that elapses between the stimulus word and the client's response. Naturally, other behaviors, such as fidgeting, explosive speech, flushing, and slurring should be recorded as well. Practice trials to help the client understand what is expected of him or her are usually recommended. These words are not from the list to be used nor is the response or latency time recorded.

Rapaport and co-workers (1946) elaborated on the above administration by adding a reproduction trial. The subject is instructed "to respond with the very same words you did before." Reproductions are recorded only if they deviate from the original reaction words. Appelbaum (1960a; 1960b; 1963) follows the Rapaport procedure with an additional trial, asking the subject to respond with a word that is different from the original response.

Evaluation and Interpretation

The word-association technique is ordinarily used in conjunction with other projective techniques and in that role provides additional data and insights on the client. The proper use of these data is dependent on experience and good clinical judgment. However, there are ways in which the responses may be categorized so as to be helpful in clinical interpretation.

Daston (1968) reviews four of these methods and is recommended reading for the beginning clinician. According to him, Symonds concentrates on qualitative signs and includes: repetition of the stimulus word, misunderstanding of the stimulus word, apparently senseless reaction, preservation, defective reproduction, and long reaction time.

The Kent-Rosanoff system focuses on response content using normative tables based on the responses of 1000 subjects allowing estimates of commonness and acceptability of response. The responses are then classified as "common reactions" or "individual reactions." Individual reactions include such categories as: juvenile reactions, neologisms, repetitions, particles of speech, associations to preceding stimulus or preceding reaction, and word complements.

The Rapaport schema is, like the Kent-Rosanoff, content based. In addition to the first reading, the examiner reads the list a second time, so there is analysis of reproductions. Rapaport's classification of associative responses focuses on formal characteristics of the response. Responses are classified as "close reactions" (e.g., "house"— my house), "distant reactions" (e.g., "book"—turkey), "content disturbances" of S or R, and reproduction disturbances. The system includes 25 types of association disturbances and six reproduction disturbances.

Finally, the Appelbaum addition deserves note. He has used it primarily with brain-damaged populations. His scoring system includes: repetitions, blockings, multi-words, self-reference, perseverating, and repetitions of the stimulus word. This procedure can differentiate among brain-damaged, psychiatric, and normal populations, equated roughly on intellectual, educational, and age factors.[1]

Research and Developments

Word-association techniques have in general declined in usage. There are a number of problems which may limit their research value. One is the problem of response set in general and social disability in particular. Both responses and response latencies seem highly susceptible to these factors. Another problem is the appropriateness of norms, which have lost their reliability as language and usage continues to change over time.

[1]For a more detailed treatment of scoring procedures the reader is well advised to review Daston's (1968) work cited earlier.

A third problem inheres more in the researchers themselves, rather than in the materials. The psychodynamic model which stimulated the growth of the word-association technique is less popular today. As interests have changed so have the research tools employed for assessment.

With the advance of other tools it seems that the "sire" (Daston, 1968) of projective techniques has fallen into relative disuse. Yet the very brevity of the word association is still appealing to the clinician. The fruitful combination of this brevity and the freedom of response is represented in the Sentence Completion Test.

SENTENCE-COMPLETION METHODS

History

Daston (1968) notes two precursors to the present-day sentence-completion technique. The first, the word-association method introduced and furthered by the work of Jung, Kent, Rosanoff, and others, has already been discussed. The second has its origins in the work of Ebbinghaus (1897), Kelley (1917), and Trabue (1916), who used it to measure intellectual variables. In the early study of memory, incomplete sentences were employed as recall measures or recognition measures. The subject was instructed to fill in the blanks from memory (recall) or he was instructed to select from alternative completions (recognition), following learning.

Though there have been a number of studies employing the sentence-completion methods as a research instrument, it has been primarily used as a clinical assessment tool. As early as 1910, Wells (1954) reports its use as a "series of phrase-completions." Most reviewers, however, agree that their first systematic use in the area of personality assessment was in the late 1920s and early 1930s (Payne, 1928; Tendler, 1930). These early investigations found them valuable as indices of response styles and emotional reactions with rather diverse populations (Bell, 1948; Sacks & Levy, 1950; Rotter, 1951; Rhode, 1957; Forer, 1960).

Wide use of the sentence completion method, as well as of most projective techniques, actually began as a result of the demands engendered by the Second World War. Flexibility and economy were two features of the sentence-completion method which greatly enhanced its popularity. Murray and MacKinnon (1946) used a sentence-completion form to evaluate candidates in the classic Office of Strategic Services Studies. The OSS sentence-completion technique covered 12 areas of personality. A response was considered "significant" either by its rarity with regard to normative expectations or by its frequent use with different sentence stubs. These significant responses were then used as a "springboard" for the subsequent interview of candidates.

The use of the sentence-completion technique was not limited to the "cloak and dagger" of the OSS but quickly spread to other branches of the armed services. It was employed to predict the success of flight cadets in the Air Force (Holtzman & Sells, 1954; Guilford, in Rhode, 1957), while the Rotter Incomplete Sentences Blank (ISB—Rotter & Willerman, 1947) was used in convalescent Army Air Force settings. Though stemming from work done in the Army, the ISB and other sentence-completion methods were extended to work with adolescent, college, and adult populations.

In the past three decades, there appeared a spate of sentence-completion devices in addition to those already mentioned. The development of the sentence-completion technique has proved a useful tool for both research and clinical purposes. Rather than confuse the reader by sheer enumeration, we will attempt to refer to as many as are appropriate. The very fact that psychologists continue to employ these devices, and are creating new ones, indicates confidence in the sentence-completion method.

Underlying Assumptions

Commmon to all sentence-completion methods as well as other projective methods is the projective hypothesis (see Chapter 1). The subject is said to reveal general personality styles as well as clues about specific conflicts and problem areas. Rhode states that, "In unconstrained response to sentence beginnings, the subject inadvertently reveals his true self, since there is no way in which he can anticipate the significance of his answers for personality study" (Rhode, 1947, p. 170).

Incomplete sentences are less amorphous than inkblots, yet they allow greater variability of subject response than do such procedures as word associations. Sacks and Levy (1950) cite ten responses they obtained to the stub, "The way my father treated my mother made me feel . . ." Five of the responses were positive in tone, five were negative. Content ranged from ". . . very happy," through ". . . rather indifferent," to ". . . like killing him," and ". . . he was a sucker." Response latencies varied from four to 35 seconds. This is an impressive demonstration of individual differences with personality implications.

In our earlier discussion of word-association techniques we noted the close link to psychoanalytic theory. This is not the case with sentence-completion methods. Dynamic considerations may well enter into the construction of a sentence-completion test, but other areas may be examined as well. The test can be focused on specific criteria, and items with content validity can be developed. Clinically oriented techniques, like the Sacks Sentence Completion Test (SSCT) or the Stein Sentence Completion Test, contain items specific to personality-relevant areas. Others, such as the Stotsky and Weinberg (1956) test and the Miner Sentence Completion Scale (1976), measure worker and managerial attitudes, respectively.

Another assumption is that the subject's responses to the sentence stubs are not consciously shaped by attitudes and beliefs that are devoid of deeper psychic meaning. Goldberg (1965) notes the theoretical controversy underlying this assumption. What level of personality does the sentence completion tap? In other words, if we conceptualize different levels of psychic functioning and organization, then where do the subject's responses to the sentence stubs fit in? Meltzoff (1951) attacked the problem experimentally by manipulating situational factors. He found that response set and social desirability were factors in the obtained results. Siipola (1968) imposed time pressure and found a significant increase in ego-alien content as a result. Jourard (1969) investigated the effect of the experimenter's self-disclosure on subject responses, while Wood (1969) noted the effect of pronoun stems, standard nonpersonal stems, and impersonal stems upon projection.

An interesting investigation was conducted by Stone and Dellis (1960), who gave a series of tests to a group of hospitalized psychiatric patients. The researchers hypothesized an inverse relationship between the depth of personality tapped and the degree of stimulus structure for a given test. The tests employed were the WAIS, the Forer Sentence Completion Test, TAT, Rorschach, and Draw-a-Person, presented here in descending order of relative structure. Stone and Dellis hypothesized that the unstructured tests (Draw-a-Person, Rorschach) would elicit a greater degree of psychopathology. The blind ratings of judges as to the degree of psychopathology agreed precisely with the order predicted by the researchers. These results, though criticized by Murstein (1965) for lack of adequate control, seem to support the position that the sentence-completion technique "elicits materials from a range of levels but with the bulk of it being fairly close to awareness" (Hanfmann & Getzels, 1953, p. 290).

To summarize, it is not necessary to subscribe to the assumptions of any one theory to use sentence-completion tests. The method is valuable in obtaining information. The purpose of the investigator determines his dependency on theory and the materials he employs (cf. Rabin, 1961).

Materials

By now it should be apparent that while there may be one sentence-completion method, there are many sentence-completion tests. Materials depend on the focus of the inquiry. In other words, the sentence stems vary according to the questions of interest and concerns of the researcher or clinician.

Most tests contain between 40 and 100 stubs. The format is fairly consistent across sentence-completion tests. Instructions and demographic information are normally followed by a numbered list of sentence stems. Stubs are printed on the left side of the page with sufficient but limited space for the subject's response. Finally, it should be noted that an adequate supply of writing materials (pencils, erasers, etc.), should be provided.

Administration

The Sentence Completion Test can be administered individually or to groups of varying size. In a quiet, comfortable, and well-lit room the subject writes his or her own sentence completions. Instructions are printed on the sentence completion blank and may be repeated aloud by the examiner.

Sentence completions are usually power rather than speed tests. Although it is valuable to note the time taken, the clinician should be aware that time saving is directly related to response brevity (Cromwell & Lundy, 1954; Goldberg, 1965). The Rotter Incomplete Sentence Blank (Rotter & Rafferty, 1950) instructs the subject to express his "real feelings" while the Rhode (1957) Sentence Completion Method combines the speed criterion with the instruction to write the "first thing that comes to mind," as does the Forer (1960) Structured Sentence Completion Test. Finally, the Miale-Holsopple (Holsopple &

Miale, 1954) Sentence Completion Test instructs the subject to complete each sentence in whatever way he wishes.

As a final point on administration, it is always valuable for the clinician to note any individual or idiosyncratic reactions to a particular sentence stem. Both observable reactions and subject comments often add further data to support clinical hypotheses and inferences.

Evaluation and Interpretation

A number of ways of evaluating responses are reported in the literature. The assessment of noncontent properties of the sentence-completion response is called formal analysis. Benton, Windle, and Erdice (1957) have reported seven such methods including length of completion; use of personal pronouns; times of reaction and completion; verb/adjective ratio; range of words used; grammatical errors; and first word used. Though some early research was conducted using formal analysis, the majority of evaluation and interpretation in clinical settings is carried out via content analysis.

Content analysis of sentence-completion responses are many and varied. Our review will include some which are highly subjective and impressionistic and those that have developed objective scoring procedures.

The impressionist's view is well presented by Holsopple and Miale (1954). Objective scoring, they feel, is premature at our current level of sophistication in personality. At present, a sentence-by-sentence interpretation seems most appropriate for building global descriptions of personality (Holsopple & Miale, 1954). The Miale-Holsopple Sentence Completion Test consists of 73 unstructured sentence stems. A few representative items are:

Children are usually certain that _____.
A large crowd _____.
People shouldn't _____.
A woman's body _____.

The authors suggest the following questions be kept in mind in evaluating the sentence completions:

1. Was the completion positive or negative in tone?
2. Was the subject's role active or passive?
3. Was the completion specific or qualified?

4. Was the response imperative? Declarative?

5. What was the temporal orientation: past, present, or future?

6. Were there differences in the subject's identification from one completion to another?

7. Did responses reflect wholehearted commitment or was there hedging?

8. Were there differences in definiteness or vagueness of responses from one completion to another?

9. Was there wide variation in the amount of verbalization to a sentence stem?

After reading through the entire record to gain a global impression, a second reading should give a feel for sequence, response clusters, and outstanding properties. In the third reading the clinician examines individual sentences which lay the groundwork for setting down hunches and inferences. Employing a combination of insight, empathy, and experience, a personality picture emerges in terms of "basic conflicts, ways of handling conflict, limitations, and defects, as well as positive resources" (Holsopple & Miale, 1954, p. 43). The intuitive approach they espouse epitomizes the art of clinical work and its richness. It also emphasizes the dangers inherent in such subjectivity. Goldberg notes that there is meager empirical support for the impressionistic approach. Further, he observes that "the validity and power of a sentence-completion test analyzed impressionistically can be no greater than the skill of the clinician using the instrument" (Goldberg, 1965, p. 27).

A more rigorous and objective system of scoring content has been presented by Rotter and Rafferty (1950) for the Incomplete Sentence Blank (ISB). The ISB consists of 40 items where the subject is instructed to express his/her "real feelings." A few representative items are:

I like _____.
What annoys me _____.
Marriage _____.
I secretly _____.

Most of the items are short and relatively unstructured, and many use first-person pronouns. Each completion is scored on a 7-point scale (0 to 6) for degree of conflict (C). There are three classes of C responses, three classes of positive (P) responses, and a class of neutral (N) responses. A manual is provided with the ISB which contains a number of examples to help the examiner assign the appropriate rating.

After the responses are rated individually, an overall adjustment score is arrived at by totaling the weighted ratings. Interscorer reliability using the ISB has indeed been impressive, ranging from .89 (Chance, 1958) to .97 (Churchill & Crandall, 1955).

Though Rotter and Rafferty achieved success in developing reliable scoring methods, they do not propose an actual system for qualitative interpretation of the protocols. Once again the authors emphasize that the interpretation depends to a great degree on the preferences and experience of the clinician.

A more ambitious scoring system was developed by Rhode (1947; 1957) in her Sentence Completion Method (SCM). The SCM consists of 65 items plus an open-ended question at the end of the test. The stems chosen represent a broad range of stimuli, some of which are conflictual in nature. A few representative items are:

    The future _____.
    I remember _____.
    My mother _____.
    Most people _____.
    My worst _____.

Responses to each of the sentence stems are then analyzed with respect to the motivational forces of the individual. Murray's (1938) conceptual schema of needs and presses provides the framework for the analysis of the data. Rhode employs 38 categories of needs, inner integrates, inner states, and general traits. The evaluation and assignment of responses eventually results in a final determination of an individual's dynamic functioning. Although she provides many scoring examples in her book, Rhode has purposely not attempted a formal scoring manual.

The final example of a sentence-completion test presented here is less formal than either the SCM or the ISB, while providing a more structured analysis than the Miale-Holsopple Sentence Completion Test. The Forer Sentence Completion Test has no formal scoring system, Forer prefering to describe rather than quantify. Nonetheless, the evaluational schema he provides is detailed enough to make quantification a relatively easy next step. The Forer test contains 100 purposely structured stems, forcing the patient to deal with specific material. A few representative items are:

When he was completely on his own, he _____.
I was most depressed when _____.
While he was speaking to me, I _____.
Most women act as though _____.

Forer groups responses into four categories:

1. Interpersonal attitudes
2. Wishes
3. Causes of one's own feeling or action
4. Reaction to external states

A specifically designed checklist is used to help organize the materials gathered from the test. The structure of the test allows the assignment of specific items to specific attitudes, reactions, and motivational areas. Given this structure any deviation from the formal aspects of completion normally indicates "the presence of highly personalized elements in the associative process" (Forer, 1950, p. 25).

The four sentence-completion tests presented above are but a sampling of a large and growing number of sentence-completion forms. As noted earlier, sentence-completion tests are as varied as the investigators employing them. For the clinician the power of these tests lies in the generation of hypotheses and inferences regarding his identified client. For the researcher a single-variable orientation is more likely to maximize data relevance and facilitate replication. In his review of 50 studies bearing on the validity of the sentence completion method, Goldberg notes that "many tests, scored in many ways, using a variety of criteria, applied to a variety of populations, have yielded a variety of data" (Goldberg, 1965, p. 30).

Recent Clinical Research

Sentence-completion methods are often used as preliminary screening devices and as part of a battery. As part of a battery, the clinician and researcher often wonder what level of personality is tapped by any given projective technique. Murstein and Wolf (1970) tested the levels hypothesis in terms of stimulus structure of different projective techniques. This study was a replication of an earlier investigation by Stone and Dellis (1960) but used a widely varying psychiatric population and normal population. The results supported the hypothesis that less stimulus structure led to increased judgment of pathology for the normal population. In the psychiatric population no significant differences were found in the rating of pathology as the structure of the tests was lessened. Murstein and Wolf explain these findings in terms of differing sensitivities and desires to respond to cue properties between the psychiatric and normal populations. In a sense the patient projects his inner world and conflicts on an array of tests regardless of degree of structure. This response style reflects need to follow internal cues rather than external cues. Normals, on the other hand, are much more apt to respond to external stimuli, projecting less pathology on structured tests and more on ambiguous unstructured tests.

Watson (1978) has observed that these findings have interesting implications for the semistructured sentence-completion methods. These tests offer a middle range where the subject may choose to follow the structure of the stimuli or may choose to project more dynamic issues on the moderately structured stimuli. Coleman (1969) views this as a product of the varying structure of a projective technique and the resulting awareness or unawareness on the part of the subject in regard to his or her own response to test stimuli.

The degree of subject awareness has remained a debatable issue and, thus far, the sentence-completion technique has resisted consensual typological classification. However, the subject's responses to the relative structure and awareness engendered on the test serve as a source of differential diagnosis. The degree of control versus the degree of projection of idiosyncratic issues are valuable pieces of information in the clinician's attempt to understand the subject's personality structure.

Exner (1973) designed the Self Focus Sentence Completion (SFSC) so as to create nomothetic base for comparison of individuals and groups. While recognizing the idiographic source of data, Exner's work provides normative data for 2952 nonpsychiatric subjects and 273 psychiatric patients. The SFSC is a 30-item sentence-completion blank which began as a cross-validational study of egocentric or narcissistic Rorschach responses. Responses to the SFSC are rated as either clearly self-focusing (S), clearly external-world oriented (E), or not fitting into either (0). A fourth category for ambivalent (A) responses was added later so as to include responses containing both E and S statements. Finally two subscores were added, one which represents negative self-focusing responses (Sn) and the other for marked emotional E responses (Ea). Three scoring-reliability studies were conducted using three sets of judges varying in degree of training, and the reliability coefficients reported were impressively high ($S = .94$, $E = .91$, $A = .93$, $N = .89$, $Sn = .86$, $Ea = .81$).

Exner's hypothesis was that in normal individuals a balance should exist between self-focus and external-world focus. Difference scores (d) between the S and E score for each group were calculated and subjected to a Mann-Whitney U test for all groups. All five nonpsychiatric groups ranked lower in mean d scores than did the nine psychiatric groups ($p < .01$ level). In other words, problems of adjustment seem to be related to an excess of concern or involvement with the self at the expense of effective environmental interaction. Alternatively, problems of adjustment were also related to an excess of concern with the individual's environment at the expense of adequate concern with the self. Several validation studies were conducted on the SFSC, the most interesting of which were pre–post intervention design studies. Statistically significant changes in the d scores from pretreatment scores were reported for both an improved adolescent group and a group of psychosomatic clients reporting symptom remission (Exner, 1973).

The importance of the above study is that it provides a normative base against which individual responses or group responses to a sentence-completion technique can be compared. The value of the sentence-completion technique as part of a test battery should now be apparent to the reader. Nystedt, Magnusson, and Aronowitsch (1975) reviewed the contribution of the Sentence Completion Test, the Rorschach, and the TAT using a multitrait multimethod matrix. Although the three tests demonstrated low convergent validity, each test contributed to a thorough understanding of the individual. The value of the sentence completion method is clear, but as Goldberg (1968) concludes in his excellent review "more research is needed."

Methodological Research

The sentence stub dictates, to a considerable degree, the obtained response. Stub length, affective tone, content, and person reference are all important variables. Getzels and his collaborators contend that private attitudes are more easily revealed to third-person stubs (Getzels, 1951; Hanfmann & Getzels, 1953; Getzels & Walsh, 1958). More socially questionable responses were provided to SCT third-person stubs; and the disparity between socially unacceptable responses on a direct questionnaire and third-person stubs was greater for high-prejudiced than for low-prejudiced subjects.

The studies showing a preference for third-person sentence stubs are discrepant with earlier clinical research findings favoring first-person stubs (Sacks, 1949; Morton, 1949; Arnold & Walter, 1957; Cromwell & Lundy, 1954). It may well be that an answer to the discrepancies lies in the population employed. Clinical populations act ostensibly as their own agents, seeking help with their problems. It would therefore make sense for them to reveal themselves on first-person stubs. For those groups who are less self-revealing, their private attitudes must be assessed more indirectly.

Finally, caution has been expressed by Stricker and Dawson (1966), who varied first- and third-person stems on the Rotter ISB. Their subjects were psychiatric patients, who ought to have favored first-person stubs. They found, alas, that neither instructions nor first or third person of the stub had differential effects and concluded that variations along these dimensions may be gratuitous.

Another important concern in constructing a sentence-completion test is the amount of structure found in the stems. Nunnally defined structure as "an agreed-on public meaning for a stimulus" (Nunnally, 1959, p. 339). A highly structured stem would then tend to establish narrow response sets. As we have noted earlier, some researchers prefer a good deal of structure while others prefer the idiographic data provided by a minimally structured stem. Peck and McGuire (1959) reported that stuctured stems result in less ambiguous responses. Rozynko (1959) studied the rated social desirability of sentence-completion responses obtained from 50 psychiatric patients. His findings indicated that the social desirability of the responses was directly related to the social desirability of the sentence stem. These and other studies clearly indicate that the content of a response is directly related to the structure of the stem. The advantage of structure is content control, while the disadvantage is the loss in response significance.

A related issue is the effect of the tone of the sentence stem on the responses of the subject. In an early study of stimulus "pull," Meltzoff (1951) found that positive-pull stimuli resulted in more positive responses. On the other hand, negative-pull or unpleasant stimuli content evoked negative responses and greater levels of judged maladjustment. Stephens (1970) used the ISB on 345 male and 245 female subjects and found stimulus pull factors clearly present only for males. Murstein and associates (1972) studied the effects of positive, negative, and neutral pull on the projected and rated adjustment of the resulting responses. Adjustment ratings were higher for the positively toned stems, but neutral stems elicited more projection. Both the Stephens (1970) and Murstein and associates (1972) studies indicate the need for caution in analyzing sentence completion data, especially in light of the effects of stimulus pull. In view of our earlier discussion of the projective hypothesis, the optimum design for a sentence-completion test then might be a majority of neutral stimuli to allow for a greater degree of projection.

Personality Research

Goldberg (1968) in his review of the status of sentence-completion methods notes that it is used relatively more as a clinical than as a research instrument. Given the flexibility and ease of construction of the instrument, this is something of a puzzle. In recent years there has been evidence of greater interest in sentence-completion methods, especially in the area of personality research. Here, we will review three distinct areas of personality research which employ the versatility of sentence-completion methods.

Rabin (1977) in a 20-year longitudinal study explored the consistency of sentiments from late adolescence to adult maturity. The focal question of his study was how this enduringness compares with the reported data that deal with stability and consistency of broader personality characteristics over time. A 51-item adaptation of the Sacks and Levy Sentence Completion Test was administered to both kibbutz and non-kibbutz subjects both at t_1 (1955) and at t_2 (1975). The subsample on which the data were obtained consists of 18 persons equally divided as to sex. The subjects were 17 to 18 years old during the original testing and in their late 30s upon retest.

The items in the test were grouped into eight different areas (i.e., father, mother, family, past) and the completions were rated with respect to affect involved—positive, negative, or neutral. Data analysis revealed two coefficients of correlation of the eight total areas which were statistically significant. Attitudes toward father changed in a direction opposite to the original ones held during late adolescence, while attitudes toward sex were significantly consistent over the 20-year time span. In addition to this study Rabin (1965) has conducted a series of cross-sectional comparative studies of kibbutz and non-kibbutz children, using sentence-completion techniques as one of his instruments. The SCT proved a useful tool in evaluating differences along personality dimensions between these groups from different environments. In effect the kibbutz studies showed the versatility of the sentence-completion test in both a cross-sectional and longitudinal study.

In a series of studies, Loevinger and her colleagues have used the sentence-completion test to evaluate levels of ego development. This work by Loevinger, Wessler, and Redmore (1970) is based on the assumption that each person has a core level of ego functioning. Loevinger's hierarchy of stages of ego development includes nine basic levels (presocial/symbiotic, impulsive, self-protective, conformist, self-aware, conscientious, individualistic, autonomous, and integrated) spanning the lifetime. The strategy of the Washington University Sentence Completion Test is to determine this core level based on the distribution of ratings of a subject's responses to the 36 sentence stems. The authors provide a detailed scoring manual complete with numerous examples of each level being presented. Interrater reliability for both expert and less experienced raters was studied and found to be quite good. Median interrater correlations for items were .75 and .85 for the core ego level score.

Validity studies (Loevinger & Wessler, 1970) of the scoring system involved structured interviews of adults and of children at different age levels. Ego development ratings were then compared to the levels obtained from the sentence-completion test and found to correlate quite highly. Redmore and Waldman (1975) reported on two studies evaluating the reliability of the test as a function of subject responses. Their findings indicate some susceptibility of the sentence-completion test to systematic error stemming from the subject's motivational set. Despite these difficulties the test and scoring system devised by Loevinger and co-workers (1970) would appear to have considerable potential as a clinical as well as research instrument.

Loevinger has repeatedly suggested that her hierarchy is conceptually distinct from the concept of psychological adjustment. However, she has speculated that, "there may be differences in the kind of pathology or present symptom characteristic for different ego levels" (Loevinger & Wessler, 1970, p. 427). Gold (in press) designed a study to assess the relationship between Loevinger's hierarchy of ego development stages and symptom patterns as measured by the Minnesota Multiphasic Personality Inventory. A total of 250 high school students between the ages of 14 and 15, 125 boys and 125 girls, served as subjects. Gold hypothesized that certain symptom patterns were more prevalent at certain points of the ego development hierarchy than at others. The existence of all but one of these parallels was supported by the data. These results clearly indicate a greater degree of maladjustment among preconformists than at other levels of ego development. Clearly the Washington University Sentence Completion Test may prove to be a useful tool for the study of the developmental ego levels of patients in different diagnostic categories.

The third set of studies using the sentence-completion method has focused on the assessment of safety and esteem motives, as characterized by Maslow (1970). In two naturalistic studies, Aronoff (1967; 1970) using a sentence-completion test distinguished reliably between safety- and esteem-oriented individuals. Aronoff (1970) reported that the motivational level of a group's membership can affect significant aspects of the existing social structure. In a later study, Aronoff and Messe (1971) composed five-man groups homogeneous with respect to either safety or esteem needs on the basis of their responses to the sentence-completion test. Again they found that groups developed types of social structures similar to those found naturalistically. These findings corroborated an earlier investigation relating cognitive complexity and social structure. Here, Tuckman (1964) had formed three-man groups based on their cognitive complexity scores as rated by their responses to a sentence-completion test. The results indicated that the level of cognitive complexity was inversely related to the degree of social structure (hierarchical-egalitarian).

Wilson and Aronoff (1973) carried out a study in order to establish the construct validity of the sentence-completion test for assessing safety and esteem motives. A large number of students were given the test and 36 safety-oriented and 36 esteem-oriented subjects were selected and given the manifest anxiety, dominance, and dependency subscales from the MMPI. The results indicated that safety-oriented subjects were significantly higher on manifest anxiety and dependency and lower on dominance than esteem-oriented subjects. These studies provide evidence in support of the assumption that the Sentence Completion Test (Aronoff, 1967) measures motivational variables and helps to establish the construct validity of scores derived from the SCT.

STORY COMPLETION TECHNIQUES

The third method to be described in this chapter is that of story completion. As is the case with the word-association and sentence-completion techniques, we cannot refer to *the* story-completion technique, but to a group of techniques or "tests" which have the principle of story completion in common. It is only in the last two decades that this method has been included in texts of projective techniques. Examples of such publications are Wursten's work on the "Madeline Thomas and Similar Methods" (1960) and Lansky's more general chapter on "Story Completion Methods" (1968). The former deals primarily with the clinical and research applications of the method with children, while the latter concerns itself with a wider spectrum of age, techniques, and applications. In his pioneering review of projective techniques, however, Bell (1948) combined a discussion of the method in a chapter on storytelling and completion.

A story-completion technique may be defined *as a verbal stimulus consisting of at least one complete sentence which represents the beginning of a story plot to be completed by the examinee.* There are, therefore, three elements in the definition. First, the stimulus is to consist of one or more sentences. Second, this "prose" is to constitute a coherent beginning of a plot. Third, the subject's or client's task is to complete the story as best he or she sees fit. Some methods leave the completion task entirely open; the examinee is free to respond. Many others structure the completion task in different ways, as we shall see presently.

It is well to quote Lansky (1968) with respect to the differential nature of the stimulus and task of examinee in the story completion methods:

> A story beginning or plot is not equivalent to a fraction of a sentence, even when the fraction is "once upon a time. . . ." One obvious difference is that the sentence stub invites completion of that sentence, whereas "What happened next?" after a story beginning asks for a confirmation of the plot, a feeling for consequences, and the like [p. 291].

In the section that follows some examples of incomplete stories used with children and adults will be cited. Subsequently, the rationale, clinical and research applications, and potential will be briefly reviewed.

Incomplete Stories for Children

Two sets of incomplete stories were developed some time ago and have been employed quite frequently, especially in clinical settings. The two methods are the Madeline Thomas Stories and the Duss (Despert) fables. Both were described in some detail elsewhere (Wursten, 1960). However, it would be quite appropriate to illustrate with some material from both techniques.

The following are a few of the 15 stories from the Madeline series.

1. A boy (or girl) goes to school. During recess he (she) does not play with other children; he (she) stays by himself (herself) in a corner. Why?

2. A boy fights with his brother. Mother comes. What is going to happen?

7. It is Sunday. This boy has been taken for a ride with mother and father. Upon their return home, mother is sad. Why?

Here are a few incomplete stories or "fables from the Duss (Despert) series, translated from the French by Wursten (1960):

1. A daddy and mommy bird and their little baby bird are sleeping in a nest on a branch of a tree. All of a sudden a big wind comes along and shakes the tree, and the nest falls to the ground. The three birds wake up brusquely. The daddy flies to a pine tree, the mother to another pine tree—what is the little bird going to do? He already knows how to fly a little bit.

8. A boy (or girl) took a very nice walk in the woods alone with his mother (or her father, for the girl). They had lots of fun together. When he returned home the boy found that his father did not look as he usually did. Why? (Similarly, upon returning the girl finds that the mother does not look the same as usual.)

9. A child comes home from school. Mother says to him (her), "Don't start your homework right away—I have something to tell you." What is the mother going to say to the child?

The purpose of the first Madeline Thomas story, quoted above, is fairly clear. The child is given an opportunity to explain trends of withdrawal from the group—possible fears, shame, or guilt, etc. Story No. 2 of the same series obviously may involve sibling rivalry and possible feelings about differential treatment by mother, and item No. 7 of the same group of stories gives the child the opportunity to interpret the mood of the mother and project some of the concerns in his (her) relationship with her. The major implication here is that some issues may be described and reacted to by the child more readily in the "game" of completing stories than in response to direct questioning by a clinician.

The intent of the "fables" (the second series listed above) is also to provide the opportunity to project dynamically meaningful material. Stories are a bit longer and are less direct. The first story, or fable, is intended "to investigate the child's attachment to one of the parents, or his independence." Oedipal issues or problems are the focus of story No. 8 of the series. Finally, story No. 9 is intended to uncover some of the possible fears and desires of the child.

For the most part these methods with children are employed clinically and qualitatively as an extension (and deepening) of the diagnostic interview. They may help pinpoint some focal problems in the child's world and his or her attempts to cope with them. The stories are, by and large, used idiographically. Although nomothetic and quantitative approaches are possible by focusing on specific classes of response. Very little has been done along these lines so far.

Research Application with Adolescents and Adults

Despite the attempts to introduce standard incomplete stories for clinical use (e.g., Sargeant, 1944; Lansky, 1968) most of the reported findings with this method were obtained with adolescents and adults in research settings. For the most part, incomplete stories were targeted to elicit information on some particular variable or group of variables. In most instances a problematic or conflictual situation is presented and specific questions are asked about resolution. In other instances, the stimulus (incomplete story) attempts to direct the respondent's attention to a specific area of concern to the investigator.

Wallace (1956), for instance, was interested in the assessment of future time perspective. He instructed his subjects (schizophrenics) as follows: "I want to see what kind of a story you can tell. I'll start one for you, and then let you finish it in any way you wish. I'll start it now. . . ." One of the brief stories is presented below.

> "Joe is having a cup of coffee in a restaurant. He's thinking of the time to come when . . ." [p. 241].

This story clearly directs the subject to be future oriented ("time to come"). The measure of "extension" of future time perspective was simply derived from the story by determining the length of time, or duration of action in its completion.

A similar approach to the study of the "learning of moral standard" was employed by Allinsmith (Miller & Swanson, 1960). The incomplete stories used in this instance present situations which describe a moral violation (e.g., theft, disobedience, death wishes) and the examinees are asked to complete the stories. The completions were to give information concerning the severity of guilt and the attendant defensive operations. Here, as in the case of Wallace's study, no specific questions were asked. But the criteria for devising the stories were much more complex. The incomplete stories that were employed had to meet several such criteria. The act described involved a secret violation of a moral teaching and expressed a motive in "a defined situation." Adaptation of this method in research in another cultural setting proved quite fruitful (Rabin & Goldman, 1966).

An even more focused approach to the study of specific variable is found in the monograph "Prediction of Aggression" (Olweus, 1969). In this carefully designed study of Swedish adolescents, Olweus used four incomplete stories "all of which concern the relationship between two characters only. A male adult and a boy roughly of the same age as the subject." Several specific questions are expected to be answered after reading the incomplete stories. In one of the stories Uncle Lars, who promised to take Peter sailing in his new boat, decides to sail without him because Peter clumsily knocked down a bucket of dirty water in the boat. Respondents were asked to react to the following questions:

How did Peter feel then?
What did Peter think?
What did Peter do?
What happened then? (continuation of story)

Detailed discussion of the statistical findings and theoretical implications of this study would take us far afield. Suffice it to state that the method was very useful in focusing upon the relationship between fantasy and aggressive behavior—an important issue in the psychology of personality.

In a cross-national project children's approach to the resolution of social conflict was studied by means of six story completions by the Andersons (1954). One sample story is paraphrased as follows:

> Mother sent Michael to the butcher. He got two fine sausages. On the way home he puts the wrapped sausages on the edge of the sidewalk and plays with his friends for a while. A shepherd dog darts out quickly, grabs a sausage out of the package and disappears. Michael wraps up the remaining sausage and goes home. What does Michael say to his mother? How does mother behave? How does Michael feel about it? Think about these questions, and *finish* the story quickly.

Here, again, the response of the examinee is directed toward specific issues, involving the perception and resolution of social conflict. A *post hoc* content analysis of the completions yielded numerous scoring categories in order to determine quantitatively the dominant patterns of resolution in the presented conflict situation.

Finally, an early experiment by Sargeant (1944) comes close to the examples enumerated above. Under the disguised title of a "Test of Insight into Human Motives," Sargeant presented 15 "armatures" to her subjects. The armatures are "bare framework" . . . "without elaboration or qualification" in which persons in a variety of conflict situations are described and the subjects are asked to describe actions and feelings, and the reasons for them. Here is an example of one of these "armatures":

> A girl who is working or studying away from home gets a letter from her mother, after her father's death, asking her to move back home.
> a. What did she do and why?
> b. How did she feel? [p. 32]

Several discrete response categories were developed—"normal" feeling, cognitive expression, indicators (elaboration, qualification, etc.), and conflict solutions. High scoring reliability (judges) is reported as is other detailed statistical information and comparative data on a normal and a hospitalized sample. The method enjoyed a brief period of use as a clinical test, but has not been employed much in recent years.

SUMMARY

Story completions have been used fairly extensively in a number of research projects in which the content of the stimulus can be designed to meet the specific needs of the problem(s) under investigation. In addition to the custom-designing for specific research purposes, incomplete stories of a standard nature have also been used clinically, especially with children.

REFERENCES

Anderson, H. H., & Anderson, C. L. Children's perception of social conflict situations: a study of adolescent children in Germany. *American Journal of Orthopsychiatry*, 1954, *23*, 246–257.

Appelbaum, S. A. Automatic and selective processes in the word associations of brain-damaged and normal subjects. *Journal of Personality*, 1960a, *28*, 64–72.

Appelbaum, S. A. The word association test expanded. *Bulletin of the Menninger Clinic*, 1960b, *24*, 258–264.

Appelbaum, S. A. The expanded word association test as a measure of psychological deficit associated with brain-damage. *Journal of Clinical Psychology*, 1963, *19*, 78–84.

Arnold, F. C., & Walter, V. A. The relationship between a self- and other reference sentence completion test. *Journal of Counseling Psychology*, 1957, *4*, 65–70.

Aronoff, J. *Psychological needs and culture systems*. Princeton, N.J.: D. VanOstrand, 1967.

Aronoff, J. Psychological needs as a determinant in the formation of economic structures. *Human Relations*, 1970, *23*, 123–138.

Aronoff, J., & Messe, L. A. Motivational determinants of small group structure. *Journal of Personality and Social Psychology*, 1971, *17*, 319–324.

Bell, J. E. *Projective techniques*. New York: Longmans, Creen, 1948.

Benton, A. L., Windle, C. D., & Erdice, E. A review of sentence completion techniques. Project NR 151–175. Washington, D.C.: Office of Naval Research, 1957.

Chance, J. E. Adjustment and prediction of others' behavior. *Journal of Consulting Psychology*, 1958, *22*, 191–194.

Churchill, R., & Crandall, Y. The reliability and validity of the Rotter incomplete sentence test. *Journal of Consulting Psychology*, 1955, *19*, 345–350.

Coleman, J. C. The levels hypothesis: A re-examination and reorientation. *Journal of Projective Techniques and Personality Assessment*, 1969, *33*, 118–122.

Cromwell, R. L., & Lundy, R. M. Productivity of clinical hypotheses on a sentence completion test. *Journal of Consulting Psychology*, 1954, *18*, 421–424.

Daston, P. G. Word associations and sentence completion techniques. In A. I. Rabin, (Ed.), *Projective techniques in personality assessment*. New York: Springer, 1968, 264–289.

Ebbinghaus, H. Uber eine neue Methode in Prufung Geistiger Fahigkeiten und ihre Anwendung bei Schulkindern. *Zeitschrift fur Psychologie und Physiologie des Sinnsorganen*, 1897, *13*, 401–457.

Exner, J. E. The self focus sentence completion: A study of egocentricity. *Journal of Personality Assessment*, 1973, *37*, 437–455.

Forer, B. R. A structured sentence completion test. *Journal of Projective Techniques*, 1950, *14*, 15–30.

Forer, B. R. Word association and sentence completion methods. In A. I. Rabin & M. R. Haworth (Eds.), *Projective techniques with children*. New York: Grune and Stratton, 1960.

Getzels, J. W. The assessment of personality and prejudice by the method of paired direct and projective questionnaires. Unpublished doctoral dissertation. Harvard University, 1951.

Getzels, J. W., & Walsh, J. J. The method of paired direct and projective questionnaires in the study of attitude structure and socialization. *Psychological Monographs*, 1958, *72*, 1, (Whole No. 454).

Gold, S. N. Relations between level of ego development and adjustment patterns in adolescents. *Journal of Personality Assessment* (in press).

Goldberg, P. A. A review of sentence completion methods in personality assessment. *Journal of Projective Techniques and Personality Assessment*, 1965, *29*, 12–45.

Goldberg, P. A. The current status of sentence completion methods. *Journal of Projective Techniques and Personality Assessment*, 1968, *32*, 215–221.

Hanfmann, E., & Getzels, J. W. Studies of the sentence completion test. *Journal of Projective Techniques*, 1953, *17*, 280–294.

Holsopple, J. Q., & Miale, F. *Sentence completion*. Springfield, Ill.: Charles C. Thomas, 1954.

Holtzman, W. H., & Sells, S. B. Prediction of flying success by clinical analysis of test protocols. *Journal of Abnormal and Social Psychology*, 1954, *49*, 185–190.

Jourard, S. M. The effects of experimenter's self-disclosure on subject's behavior. In C. D. Spielberger (Ed.), *Current topics in clinical and community psychology*, Vol. 1. New York: Academic Press, 1969, pp. 109–150.

Kelley, T. J. Individual testing with completion test exercises. *Teacher's College Records*, 1917, *18*, 371–382.

Lansky, L. M. Story completion methods. In A. I. Rabin (Ed.), *Projective techniques in personality assessment*. New York: Springer, 1968.

Lindzey, G. On the classification of projective techniques. *Psychology Bulletin*, 1959, *56*, 158–168.

Loevinger, J., & Wessler, R. *Measuring ego development. 1. Construction and use of a sentence completion test*. San Francisco: Jossey-Bass, 1970.

Loevinger, J., Wessler, R., & Redmore, C. *Measuring ego development 2. Scoring manual for women and girls*. San Francisco: Jossey-Bass, 1970.

Maslow, A. H. *Motivation and personality*. New York: Harper & Row, 1970.

Meltzoff, J. The effect of mental set and item structure upon response to a projective test. *Journal of Abnormal and Social Psychology*, 1951, *46*, 177–189.

Miller, D., & Swanson, G. E. (Eds.). *Inner conflict and defense*. New York: Holt, 1960.

Miner, J. B. Relationships among measures of managerial personality traits. *Journal of Personality Assessment*, 1976, *40*, 383–397.

Morton, R. A controlled experiment in psychotherapy based on Rotter's Social Learning Theory of Personality. Doctoral dissertation, Ohio State University, Columbus, Ohio, 1949.

Murray, H. A., & MacKinnon, D. W. Assessment of OSS personnel. *Journal of Consulting Psychology*, 1946, *10*, 76–80.

Murstein, B. I. (Ed.). *Handbook of projective techniques*. New York: Basic Books, 1965.

Murstein, B. I., Colon, R. M., Destrexhe-deLeval, N. & Vanhoof-VanParys, M. Influence of stimulus properties of the sentence-completion-method on projection and adjustment. *Journal of Personality Assessment*, 1972, *36*, 241–247.

Murstein, B. I., & Wolf, S. R. Empirical test of the "levels" hypothesis with five projective techniques. *Journal of Abnormal Psychology*, 1970, *75*, 38–44.

Nunnally, J. C. *Tests and measurements*. New York: McGraw-Hill, 1959.

Nystedt, L., Magnusson, D., & Aronowitsch, E. Generalization of ratings based on projective tests. *Scandinavian Journal of Psychology*, 1975, *16*, 72–78.

Olweus, D. *Prediction of aggression*. Stockholm: Scandinavian Test Corporation, 1969.

Payne, A. F. *Sentence Completion*. New York: New York Guidance Clinics, 1928.

Peck, R. F., & McGuire, C. Measuring changes in mental health with the sentence completion technique. *Psychological Reports*, 1959, *5*, 151–160.

Rabin, A. I. Custom-built projective methods: a symposium. *Journal of Projective Techniques*, 1961, *25*, (1), 6–10.

Rabin, A. I. *Growing Up in the Kibbutz*. New York: Springer, 1965.

Rabin, A. I. Enduring sentiments: the continuity of personality over time. *Journal of Personality Assessment*, 1977, 41(6), 564–572.

Rabin, A. I., & Goldman, H. The relationship of severity of guilt to intensity of identification in kibbutz and non-kibbutz children. *Journal of Social Psychology*, 1966, 69, 159–163.

Rapaport, D., Gill, M., & Schafer, R. *Diagnostic psychological testing*, Vol. 2. Chicago: Year Book, 1946.

Redmore, C., & Waldman, K. Reliability of a sentence completion measure of ego development. *Journal of Personality Assessment*, 1975, 39, 236–243.

Rhode, A. R. *Sentence completions test manual*. Beverly Hills, Calif.: Western Psychological Services, 1947.

Rhode, A. R. *The Sentence completion method: its diagnostic and clinical application to mental disorders*. New York: Ronald Press, 1957.

Rosanoff, A. J. *Manual of Psychiatry* (Rev. Ed.). New York: Wiley, 1927.

Rotter, J. B. Word association and sentence completion methods. In H. H. Anderson & Gladys L. Anderson (Eds.), *An introduction to projective techniques*. New York: Prentice-Hall, 1951, pp. 279–311.

Rotter, J. B., & Rafferty, J. E. *Manual: The Rotter Incomplete Sentences Blank*. New York: Psychological Corporation, 1950.

Rotter, J. B., Rafferty, J. E., & Schachtiz, E. Validation of the Rotter Incomplete Sentences Blank for college screening. *Journal of Consulting Psychology*, 1949, 13, 348–366.

Rotter, J. B., & Willerman, B. The incomplete sentences test. *Journal of Consulting Psychology*, 1947, 11, 43–48.

Rozynko, V. V. Social desirability in the sentence completion test. *Journal of Consulting Psychology*, 1959, 23, 280.

Sacks, J. M. The relative effect upon projective responses of stimuli referring to the subject and of stimuli referring to other persons. *Journal of Consulting Psychology*, 1949, 13, 12–20.

Sacks, J. M., & Levy, S. The sentence completion test. In L. E. Abt & L. Bellak (Eds.), *Projective psychology*. New York: Knopf, 1950.

Sargeant, H. An experimental application of projective principles to a paper and pencil personality test. *Psychological Monographs*, 1944, 57, (Whole No. 265), 1–57.

Siipola, E. M. Incongruence of sentence completions under time pressure and freedom. *Journal of Projective Techniques and Personality Assessment*, 1968, 32, 562–571.

Stephens, M. W. Stimulus pull as a determinant of individual difference in sentence completion responses. *Journal of Projective Techniques and Personality Assessment*, 1970, 34, 332–339.

Stone, H. K., & Dellis, N. P. An exploratory investigation into the levels hypothesis. *Journal of Projective Techniques*, 1960, 24, 333–340.

Stotsky, B. A., & Weinberg, H. The prediction of the psychiatric patient's work adjustment. *Journal of Counseling Psychology*, 1956, 3, 3–7.

Stricker, G., & Dawson, D. D. The effects of first person and third person instruction and stems on sentence completion responses. *Journal of Projective Techniques and Personality Assessment*, 1966, *30*, 169–171.

Sundberg, N. D. The practice of psychological testing in clinical services in the United States. *American Psychologist*, 1961, *16*, 79–83.

Tendler, A. D. A preliminary report on a test for emotional insight. *Journal of Applied Psychology*, 1930, *14*, 123–126.

Trabue, M. R. *Completion test language scales*. New York: Columbia University Press, 1916.

Tuckman, B. W. Personality structure, group composition and group functioning. *Sociometry*, 1964, *27*, 469–487.

Wallace, M. Future time perspective in schizophrenia. *Journal of Abnormal and Social Psychology*, 1956, *52*, 240–245.

Watson, R. I. The sentence completion method. In B. Wolman (Ed.), *Clinical diagnosis of mental disorders*. New York: Plenum Press, 1978.

Wells, F. L. Foreword. In J. Q. Holsopple & Florence R. Miale, *Sentence Completion*. Springfield, Ill.: Charles C. Thomas, 1954.

Wilson, J. P., & Aronoff, J. A. sentence completion test assessing safety and esteem motives. *Journal of Personality Assessment*, 1973, *37* (4), 351–354.

Wood, F. A. An investigation of methods of presenting incomplete sentences stimuli. *Journal of Abnormal Psychology*, 1969, *74*, 71–74.

Wursten, H. Story completions: Madeline Thomas and similar methods. In A. I. Rabin & M. R. Haworth (Eds.), *Projective techniques with children*. New York: Grune and Stratton, 1960.

6

Projective Drawings

Emanuel F. Hammer

Anthropologists have demonstrated how a past world may be imaginatively reconstructed from one of its products, even if it be only a fragment of a tool, a pot, or some drawings left on walls. Similarly, an individual's inner world may be understood through a sensitive reading of a series of his projective drawings—free renditions of a house, a tree, a person, a family, an animal, his favorite doodles, and so on.

Since their birth almost two decades ago, projective drawings as a clinical tool have moved relatively rapidly into a secure niche in the projective battery. By virtue of their time economy, ease of administration, and rich clinical yield, projective drawings appear to be the most frequent supplement, along with the TAT, to the Rorschach in the clinician's work-a-day projective armamentarium. In addition to Buck's House–Tree–Person and Machover's Figure Drawing techniques, various clinicians employ one or more of the following: the Draw-A-Person-in-the-Rain modification of Abrams, which attempts to elicit clues to the self-concept under conditions symbolizing environmental stress, Schwartz's Draw-an-Animal approach (useful for disclosing the biological side of the biosocial coin), the Draw-a-Family procedure, Harrower's Unpleasant Concept Test, Kinget's Drawing Completion Test, and free doodles.

In projective drawings, the subject's psychomotor activities are caught on paper. The line employed may be firm or timid, uncertain, hesitant, or bold, or it may consist of a savage digging at the paper. In

151

addition, as we shall later see, the subject's conscious and unconscious perception of himself and significant people in his environment determine the content of his drawing. In such expression, the unconscious levels of the subject tend to utilize symbols—symbols whose meanings can be unraveled through study and understanding of dreams, myths, folklore, psychotic productions, and so on. The illustrations that follow will support and elaborate the thesis that drawing productions are employed by a subject as one of the many forms of symbolic speech.

THE CLINICAL BEGINNINGS

Florence Goodenough, having devised an intelligence scale based mainly on the number of details put into the drawing of a man, became aware, along with other clinicians, that her test was tapping personality factors in addition to intellectual capabilities of her child subjects. The present writer, for example, in using the Goodenough "Draw-a-Man Test" also became aware of the fact that emotional factors, more so than intellectual ones, were constantly pressing into view. In checking a drawing for credit for the inclusion of a hand, it soon became apparent that whereas the same quantitative IQ credit was given for a balled-up, clenched fist, or a delicate and open hand in a feminine gesture patting the cheek, produced by a male subject in his drawing of a male, more important qualitative clues to the functioning of the total personality were being ignored. The subject was granted identical quantitative credit whether he drew his person with the arms crossed defiantly over the chest, hanging flexibly at the sides, or placed timidly behind the back, but the fact that these several arm positions had vastly different qualitative implications was not taken into account, and much valuable diagnostic, and even prognostic, material was overlooked. Similarly, the large range of facial expressions, size, placement on the page, and so on, seemed to offer more information about nonintellectual components than about the intellectual capabilities.

Many clinicians have had similar experience with drawings, experience expressed in the rule so often quoted: "Children draw what they know, not what they see."

Both the House–Tree–Person Drawing device (H-T-P) and the Figure-Drawing procedure, as personality tools, were an outcropping of intelligence scales. Machover's (1949) Figure-Drawing technique grew from her experience with the Goodenough tool for appraising children's intelligence. Similarly, Buck's (1948) H-T-P procedure grew out of an intelligence scale upon which he was working at the time Wechsler came out with his Intelligence Scale. Buck, having had the same experience observing the flooding of the drawings with nonintellectual personality factors, salvaged the H-T-P drawing test from his other intellect-tapping subtests and developed it into the productive projective technique it has, by now, become.

MATERIALS AND ADMINISTRATION

A No. 2 pencil and a sheet of paper are handed the subject. His or her drawing of a house is requested with the longer axis of the sheet placed horizontally before the subject. His drawings of a tree and person, in turn, are then obtained on separate sheets of paper with the longer axis placed vertically. The subject is asked to draw as well as he can, but he is not told what kind of house, tree, and person to draw. If the subject protests that he is not an artist, he is assured that the H-T-P is not a test of artistic ability at all but that we are interested, rather, in how he does things. Any questions he asks are reflected back to him in such a way as to indicate that there is no right or wrong method of proceeding but that he may do the drawing in any manner he wishes.

After he or she draws the person, the subject is then handed another sheet of paper and this time asked to draw a person of the sex opposite to that of the first person drawn. The pencil and the pencil drawings are then taken away, crayons (a 15-cent box of eight Crayola crayons obtained at any five-and-ten-cent store) are substituted, and a chromatic set of drawings of house, tree, and person of each sex obtained. The subject is allowed to use the crayons in any way he wishes, as few or as many as he chooses, to shade in or draw only the outline as he elects to, and all questions are handled nondirectly. In addition, in pencil again, the subject may be asked to draw the most unpleasant thing he can think of, to draw a person in the rain, or to complete or make a drawing from certain lines which serve as stimuli (The Drawing Completion Test). With children, we may occasionally also ask for a drawing of a family and/or a drawing of an animal (Hammer, 1958).

UNDERLYING HYPOTHESES

Projective drawings tap the stream of personality needs as they flood the area of graphic creativity. Certain concessions must, however, be made to psychology's demand for standardization: hence, the same concepts (house, tree, person, animal) are asked for from the subject, on the same size paper with standard material.

Armed with the knowledge that man's deeper needs (1) color creative efforts and (2) show an affinity for "speaking" in pictorial images, the clinician and/or experimenter has at his or her disposal a rapidly and easily administered technique for eliciting submerged levels of human feelings. Basically, the subject's relative emphasis on different elements within the drawings, in addition to global drawing performance, tells us a good deal of what matters to him or her, what it does to him or her, and what he or she does about it.

In the field of projective drawing, interpretation empirically rests upon the following foundation stone: (1) the use of common psychoanalytic and folklore meanings of symbols, derived from study of dreams, myth, art, fantasy, and other such activities steeped in unconscious determination; (2) clinical experience with the mechanisms of displacement and substitution as well as a wide range of pathological phenomena, especially the conversion symptoms, obsessions, compulsions, and phobias—all of which become understandable only within the framework of the concept of symbolism; (3) unraveling of the symbolization employed in drawings by inviting the patient's associations; (4) empirical evidence with previous patients' drawings; (5) following the lead provided by the flooding of symbolization onto the drawing page, from the unconscious of psychotics, the possibility of detecting more subtle murmurings in the same tongue of symbolism in the drawings of nonpsychotics; (6) the correlation between projective drawings made at intervals during the course of therapy and the clinical picture at the times the drawings were produced; (7) internal consistency between one drawing and another, between the drawings and the other techniques in the projective battery, between drawings and dreams, between drawings and the behavioral picture, and between drawings and the case history; (8) and lastly, but most importantly, experimental studies.

The field of projective drawing interpretation also rests upon several theoretical postulates: (1) There is a tendency in man to view the world in an anthropomorphic manner, that is, in his own image.

(2) The core of the anthropomorphic view of the environment is the mechanism of projection. (3) Distortions enter into the process of projection to the extent to which the projection has a defensive function; that is, the projection is in the service of ascribing to the outer world that which the subject denies in himself.

Distortions in the mechanisms of projection are very much like the situation of a man who, according to the analogy of Gondor (1954), "has only a limited number of slides for a projection machine, and, no matter what the situation or the type of screen, can project only his available pictures" (p. 11).

The emotionally disturbed person's perception of the world is not always accurate. It may give him distorted views—and one's characteristic distortions of the world are sampled by projective drawings.

HOW IT WORKS: SOME ILLUSTRATIONS

While it is beyond the space allotted to this chapter to attempt to illustrate in any meaningful way the array of various projective drawings commonly used, perhaps the operant flavoring and "feel" of one aspect of it can be conveyed by focusing on the drawing of a person. But even the use of just the drawing of a person as a projective technique can be presented, within the space limitations, only in a most introductory way. For deeper treatment of the Draw-a-Person and for an extension of the presentation to include the other related drawings, the reader is referred to *The Clinical Application of Projective Drawings* (Hammer, 1958).

One woman, a 25-year-old school teacher, had entered therapy because she had a problem relating to men and a block against getting married. She sensed that her moderate obesity might be a defense against males. After approximately a year-and-a-half of treatment, she was able to reduce, had begun going out, and had established a "going steady" relationship with one young man. One day, she came to the therapy session, proudly showed an engagement ring, and announced jubilantly that she was to be married.

Feeling that she had accomplished her goals in therapy, but also having some marginal doubts, she asked if she might retake the H-T-P to compare it with the one she had initially taken upon entering treatment: to thus assess what the test revealed and to see if it matched her subjective feeling of how far she had come and where she now was. The drawing of a female she now produced (Figure 6.1) was better integrated, prettier, more feminine, and certainly no longer the representation of the obese woman it had been. The figure, like the earlier one, still stood on phallic feet, however, and the hands now were drawn into a position of "pelvic defense." Both hands, in spite of the ring now conspicuous on the third finger of one of them, were drawn to a position of guarding the genital area. Whereas noteworthy gains in self-image were apparent, the projective drawing cried out with the problem of fear of intercourse and some underlying masculine identification still unresolved.

In support of the implications of the fear of sexuality which the impending marriage was now crystallizing, there were two parataxic slips made by the patient during that session. When I had asked her when she was getting married, she answered, "I'm getting engaged in June" instead of "married" then, thus revealing her inner desire to put the marriage further off. Relating the slip to the drawing, it was not difficult to help her to sense that her treatment was not yet complete.

Figure 6.1.   Drawing by a 25-year-old school teacher after becoming engaged, suggesting sexual panic at impending marriage

As the session ended and we walked to the door, I happened to have asked her how much Christmas vacation, which she was then on, she had. She replied, "My vacation ends June 3rd, I mean January 3rd!" Our eyes smiled, she then burst into laughter, and in the sessions which followed, we settled down to the work remaining to be done.

The reader might find it instructive to be able to view drawings, side by side, made by individuals suffering from the same symptom. In this manner, common denominators may become apparent. Figures 6.2 and 6.3 were both offered by male alcoholics, one in his early 40s and one in his late 40s. Both had a long history of drinking finally producing the chronic alcoholic pattern, which now assumed the center of their existence. In their perception of women, we note strikingly threatening, repellent aspects which may have contributed—among the other motives—to their initial need to retreat into the all-male atmosphere of bars, and there to dilute their fear of females and to quiet the inner voice of doubt regarding their masculinity.

The awareness of these two men's perception of women as over-

Figures 6.2 and 6.3.   **Drawings by two male alcoholics reflecting their view of women**

whelmingly hostile, powerful, scary, and even ghoulish suggests that their turning to drink may be in the service, among the other needs, of achieving a pleasant plateau from which to survey the world of men and women with some equanimity, to handle their harsh perceptions so that the edges are blurred and threatening figures made softer. Emboldening themselves with whiskey, their problems may diffuse, and the world of females which they cannot handle (both men are married) fades, leaving them in a solitary haze.

Figure 6.4 was drawn by an overt homosexual and labeled by him a man. In spite of the man's hat, the rest of the figure conveys an impression of a female in slacks, with feminine hip curve, a hint of a breast delineation, lipsticked mouth, delicate nose, and emphasized eyebrows. His feminine identification—of being a woman merely dressed in male clothing—is compellingly conveyed in the projective drawing.

Figure 6.5, in contrast, was drawn by an overtly heterosexual, even Don Juan, individual who was rather frantically pursuing one affair after another. Following one such affair in which, to his amazement, he suddenly found himself impotent, he then exhibited his penis on a subway on his way home—an offense for which he was referred for psychological examination. Among other things, we particularly note the high heel he gives the shoe, the shading around the buttocks area indicating anxiety, and the hint of a phallic protrusion showing at the genital area. The fear of attack from the rear, conveyed by the excessive and inappropriate shading at the buttocks, is supported by the heavy collar pulled up around the back of his neck, as if to protect a vulnerable rear, up and down.

The demonstrative efforts at masculinity which unwittingly escape him as he draws the front of the trousers (as they did in his recent offense) thus suggest that compensatory efforts at proving himself more of a male than he inwardly feels serve as a defensive maneuver to handle and subdue his covert homosexual panic.

Profiting from the understanding of the communication of the previous drawing, we can now more readily decipher the next one (Figure 6.6). This was drawn by a 17-year old adolescent boy who, on the surface, was a wincingly self-conscious young man. Shy and retiring, his was a cautious and hampered adaptation as he related to peers at school and at home. Yet on paper he draws a large male crowding the edges of the page, one with over-expanded shoulders, the suggestion of a mustache, and simultaneously carrying not one, but two, symbols of athletic prowess, a tennis racket in one hand and a baseball bat in the other—this in spite of their incongruity for simultaneous use. What is perhaps even more noteworthy, against this backdrop, is that the baseball bat appears to emanate directly from the fly of the trousers, and then at the other end has a hint of a urethral-like indentation or opening. The entire rendition could not be more phallic if such an attempt had been deliberately and consciously made. His loud protesting on paper that "I am indeed a man!" and the directly phallic direction these efforts took were later confirmed. This youngster, having entered therapy for problems of incapacitating shyness, within several weeks confided to the writer that he also wished help for his exhibitionistic behavior, for a tendency he had to wait for young girls to pass outside his window, for him then to drop his pants and knock on the window to attract their attention.

To illustrate the way projective drawings may mirror affective states, note Figure 6.7, drawn by a narcotic addict suffering a depressive reaction. The subject is a 21-year-old male, a withdrawn individual feeling unhappily alone, isolated from others, and panicky and fearful in his efforts to escape from human advances of even a gentle and friendly kind. His whole life pattern demonstrated a weakly adaptive style of interpersonal relationships. The withdrawn quality reflected in the almost back view, the regressive aspects connoted by the figure all but curled up, the abject feelings of despondency, despair, and hopelessness are conveyed in every line. The figure drawing suggests a crushed self-esteem and the agonized state of a self beaten down. (The drawing was supported by his TAT performance where futility ran through all the stories to embrace one protagonist after another in failure.)

The figure drawing thus reflects his need, behind his use of narcotics, to withdraw into a silent, cushioned solitude. The absence of clothing mirrors his tendency to remove himself from the conventions of the jarring social world he experiences around him.

The next illustration was offered by a 28-year-old female, a concert pianist who had begun to develop a feeling of awkwardness and lack of flexibility in her hands which was currently interfering, disasterously, with her performances. Numerous neurological examinations had all yielded consistently negative findings, and hence she was referred for a psychological examination.

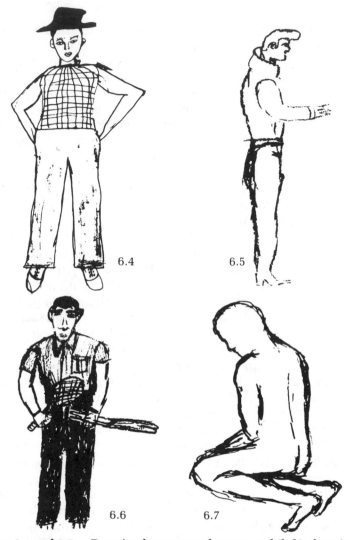

6.4

6.5

6.6

6.7

Figures 6.4 and 6.5. Drawing by an overt homosexual (left); drawing by a latent homosexual male using Don Juanism as a defense (right)

Figure 6.6 Drawing by an adolescent boy with conspicuous compensatory defenses and also symptoms of exhibitionism. On the original drawing, the figure crowded the margins and the shoes extended beyond the lower edge of the page.

Figure 6.7. Drawing by a narcotics addict with depressive reaction

On the Rorschach, the writer found her as he described in the following excerpts:

> Intense feelings of anger, struggle and competition define her inner psychological state. The perception of people on the Rorschach as "resisting each other, working against each other, rather than together," the perception of animals as "angry, struggling, fighting," and the projection, "two people pulling against each other" all combine to convey the flavoring of her inner competitive struggle and hostility. Her major defense at this time is to attempt to employ repression to manage and contain these unacceptable feelings underground. The "blood" and "fire" images in her Rorschach further imply that intense, primitive affects are associated with major tensions. She responds to one of the chromatic cards (Card IX) by offering the following: "Fire . . . two witches . . . smoke . . . conflict . . . eruption . . . volcano . . . hatred . . . and hell . . . and here is the Greek God of Wrath." The sequence from fire to hell and the God of Wrath illustrate the strong sense of guilt which caps off the feeling of aggression symbolized by the initial association of fire. The "conflict" in the middle of this stream of associations, which then goes on to "eruption" and "volcano," further emphasizes the strong struggle she is attempting in order to keep her anger from breaking forward into overt behavior. The inference of aggression pressing forward becomes considerably less speculative when she adds "hatred" to the more symbolic "eruption" which preceded it.

In keeping with the above, her projective drawing provides a rather important clue to the block and inhibition in performing as a pianist from which she is suffering. The patient draws someone (Figure 6.8), essentially well-rendered and effectively presented except for one glaring exception. The hands are drawn in such a way that they don't like human hands at all, but much more like an animal's paws—with the claws extended. She had commented, while drawing, "I just couldn't draw the hands." The subject then describes the drawn person as "She wants to move, but doesn't know how."

The freezing of her movement—out of the pervading fear that angry, savage, animalistic, hostile impulses may be released in these movements—the drawing suggests, may be what interferes with the smooth and fluid execution of hand motions so necessary to her as a pianist. It is in the area of angry feelings, hence, that the therapeutic focus will be most rewarding, in the interests of helping her to face, and then resolve, her secret rage behind her block as a pianist. We may

Figure 6.8.   Drawing by a concert pianist suffering a performance block

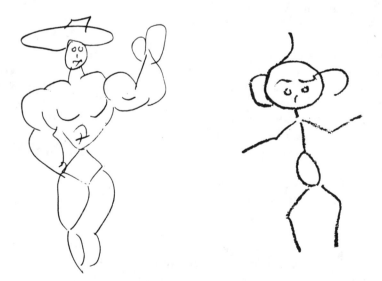

Figures 6.9 and 6.10.   Drawings by an 18-year-old male showing surface and subsurface personality levels

also note the flowing skirt presented as if thrown into motion by stirred up, churning feelings beneath it, which may suggest the impulses of sexuality as an attendant problem.

The nuanced language of drawing projection is particularly suited for stating the complexities and human contradictions as they balance and interrelate within a single personality. At such times, the apparent contradictions can be seen to possess an inner harmony, as in the musical statement and counterstatement of a fugue. Figure 6.9, drawn by an 18-year-old male caught stealing a TV set, constitutes such a pictorial statement. Beneath the obvious attempts at an impressive figure of masculine prowess, there are more subtle trends of the opposite: of inadequacy and inconsequentiality. The muscles of the drawn figure have been inflated, beyond the hard and sinewy, into a puffy softness as if it is a figure made of balloons; the legs taper down to insubstantiality and, finally, absent feet, and an incongruous hat is placed on the boxer making comical his lifting of one gloved hand in victory.

The same dichotomy can be seen in his projections onto Rorschach Card V: "looks like a wasp." The popular response to this card is a bat or a butterfly. The subject, instead, projects an index of felt smallness, while at the same time attempting to make up for this by aggressiveness. Thus he is saying, in effect, "I may be small, but I'll show you I can be something to be reckoned with."

His passive-aggressive strategy becomes all the more dramatically apparent in the comparison of his pencil- and later crayon-drawn persons.

On the one hand, emblematic of his defenses, his drawn achromatic person is the "20-year-old" boxer with muscles flexed and a weight-lifter's build. Beneath this inflated image, however, on the crayon drawing of a person (which, due to the impact of color, tends to tap the relatively deeper levels of personality) (Hammer, 1958) he offers now only a "six-year-old boy" who then looks even more like an infant than a child: with one curlicue hair sticking up and the suggestion of diapers on (Figure 6.10, shown here in black-and-white). The ears are rather ludicrous in their standing away from his head and, all in all, the total projection in this drawing is that of an infantile, laughable entity, rather than the impressive he-man he overstated on the achromatic version of a person. Beneath his attempts to demonstrate rugged masculinity (which may have culminated into the offense with which he was charged), the patient experiences himself as actually a little child, dependent and needing care, protection, and affection.

Projective drawings may, we see from this and the next drawing, sometimes provide a highly personal statement. I don't believe I have ever seen a Rorschach response which can match a drawing such as Figure 6.11, for communicativeness of intimate expression. This is because a subject, while drawing, can, in a relative sense, exclude the examiner—can immerse himself more deeply and become more absorbed in the unfolding graphic projection than he ever can in directly relating to the examiner and telling him what he sees in one response after another on Rorschach stimuli.

Intertwined in this drawing of a person are masochistic, homosexual, and exhibitionistic needs, in that order of dominance. The exhibiting of the buttock area combines the last two mentioned trends. The manacling of the hands and the tying of the feet apparently expressed and, in cyclic fashion, further produced so much masochistic involvement and excitement, that in an orgiastic-like

Figure 6.11.   Drawing in which masochism, homosexuality, and exhibitionism are evident

mood he wanted more. He then provided this for himself in the blown-up addition of the large foot to the side of the drawing proper, with (one is tempted to say) loving-care emphasis upon the enslaving chains and encasing metal bands.

For contrast, Figure 6.12 presents the sadistic side of the sadoma-sochistic coin. The subject offering this drawing had been Head Disciplinarian of a boys' reformatory for some years until he was suspended for uncontrollably striking the youngsters. He described himself as having, boot-strap-fashion, mastered his early difficulties as a youth. As to his description of his drawn person, he said it "looked like a Prussian or a Nazi General." (Consistent with this identification, his TAT themes were smeared with gore and strident with sadism.)

To illustrate, at this point, the range along the continuum—from schizoid to schizophrenic conditions—on which the clinical psychologist is most often asked to make his diagnostic contribution, Figures 6.13 through 6.19 are presented.

Figures 6.13 and 6.14 represent the drawing of a male and female by a schizoid patient. The drawn male (Figure 6.13) is more manne-quin-like than human and actually suggests a store dummy. Figure

Figure 6.12.   Drawing by an authoritarian and sadistic male

6.14 was described as, "She looks like a paper doll." His projections thus are not of flesh and blood beings, but of derealized humans who cannot engage in emotional give and take. Within the patient, the sap of affect has grown thin. He feels himself to be a somewhat synthetic being, rather than a full or living person. This is an individual who does not appear to be buoyed by any connection he feels with the human environment. He appears to have lost the sensations of spontaneity, play, warmth, autonomy, or even of emotional authenticity. The "bloodless" man and woman drawn suggest the feelings of alienation within the subject. A sense of isolation, of distance, aloneness, and separateness from the human environment appears central to his portrait of himself. He lives beside life more than in it.

Consistent with his drawings, on the TAT he demonstrated a failure to include much about the relationship between the people shown in the stimuli. On the Rorschach, the number of his movement responses was diminished, and when they were given, the forms were static. The humans or animals did not act, but were only about to act or were acted upon. Color was also absent, vitality low, and zest for living muted. Emphasis was almost exclusively on Form as a determinant, again implying minimal feelings of emotional life within.

Figures 6.13 and 6.14.   Drawings by a schizoid individual

The implications for therapy are that his sterility and restriction of personality as well as his markedly schizoid structure will limit and define his behavior in the therapeutic situation. A long period of treatment would be necessary to achieve a gradual melting through the wall of his detachment by human warmth and interest; and it would have to be extended with care to avoid stimulating further protective withdrawal.

To move further along the continuum, we may next observe Figure 6.15.

The patient who drew this person is a well-built, immaculately dressed, 37-year-old Negro man. He had served in the Navy and received an honorable discharge, having attained the rank of an officer. He then attended college and received his B.A. After this, he was an assistant preacher in a Southern church for several years, and then came to the North. He was referred for examination because he was convicted on three counts of assault, involving two men and a woman. The police officer had found a straight razor, a packing knife, and a pen knife on the defendant's person. The complainants had never seen the defendant before. The men and woman were standing near a candy booth when the defendant pushed his way between them, knocking the woman off balance and causing her to fall. One man—according to his story—shouted, "Are you crazy or something?" which enraged the defendant who then struck the man on the side of the head and the woman about the mouth. At that point, the second man appeared, came to their assistance, and the defendant pummeled him with his fists.

The defendant's version was that the man who had exclaimed, "Are you crazy or something?" had added, "you black nut!" Thus the referring probation officer raised some question concerning a racial issue having inflamed the defendant's reaction. The diagnostic query which accompanied the referral for an examination was, "Is this man emotionally sick, is there any presence of significant pathology, and is he capable of peculiar reactivity?"

On the Rorschach, the patient emerged as a borderline schizophrenic individual. Primary thinking processes seeped through to color his perception of the world in raw, primitive terms. His drawings of people were both of nudes, his drawn female a massive, threatening figure, whereas his drawn male (Figure 6.15) stands timidly with hands behind his back, eyes suspiciously and paranoidally alerted, and chin exaggerated in a demonstration of compensatory needs to prove himself assertive. What is more important, however, is the reality-testing impairment. He describes his drawn male as "standing there and talking . . . talking to a neighbor or someone he sees passing on the street." Here, the strikingly inappropriate description of a nude male standing and talking to a neighbor or passer-by on the street conveys the impaired reality testing and dissociative capacities of the subject. The Form Minus responses, which accumulate on his Rorschach (responses where the percepts do not fit the outline of the blot), further convey the level of diminished reality-testing on which this man operates.

Past the borderline range and well into the schizophrenic domain, Figure 6.16 stands as a reflection of frank pathology. The geometric rendition of hands, feet, and ears suggest an arbitrary perceptual tendency (to overabstract and possibly also to rely upon magical signs). The robot-like head and neck add to the autistic quality, while the absence of a mouth and the pupil-less eyes reflect the communication difficulties schizophrenics so agonizingly experi-

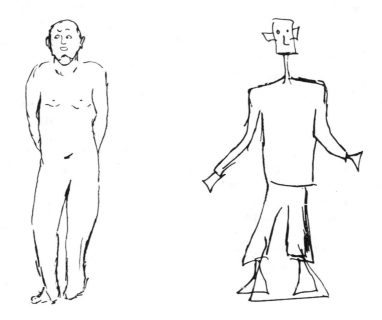

Figures 6.15 and 6.16.   Drawing by a man suffering from a borderline schizophrenic condition (left); drawing by a schizophrenic patient (right)

ence. The line for the ground suddenly comes up in a rather peculiar way as if to add some stability to his footing, no matter how artificially.

This is an individual who, at the most, has a pseudo-integration of personality, with the frail links barely keeping him together. His illness appears to serve, at best, as a mere expedient for survival amid the contradictions within him. The patient appears to have constructed an unreal world into which he is retiring from sanity.

Figure 6.17 carried the reflection of the depersonalization process still further. This patient's identification is with a fluid and formless being; a truly tragic conception of personal identity. Ego boundaries fade and the figure melts away. Haunted by a picture of himself as a creature whose outlines blur, he has eventually given in, and by now, a back ward patient of a mental hospital, has lost sight of who and what—and if—he is.

A search through the hospital folder revealed a Draw-a-Person projection done, upon admission, many years earlier. His person was standing rigidly at attention, body and head very stiff, legs pressed closely together, arms straight and held to the body.   The kinesthetic emphasis was on the rigid posture and on the tension with which the posture was held, keeping the self closed off against the world around. The overall impression was of a person frozen into a posture, unable to move over the threshold of action.

Figure 6.17.   Drawing by a highly depersonalized schizophrenic individual

Still further along the continuum to massive deterioration, Figure 6.18 reflects an individual with body image totally gone, with peripheral lines no longer present around the face, and a body wall through which the intestines have spilled.

Figure 6.19 stands as an extreme example of one particular type of schizophrenic reaction, the paranoid subtype. The savage mouth expresses the rage-filled projections loose within him. The emphasized eyes and ears with the eyes almost emanating magical rays reflect the visual and auditory hallucinations the patient actually experiences. The snake in the stomach points up his delusion of a reptile within, eating away and generating venom and evil.

At times, issues of life-and-death import themselves may be picked up by the projective drawings. Figure 6.20 was drawn by a man suffering from an involutional depression. He draw the large figure first; then when he saw that he could not complete the entire figure on the page, he drew the smaller figure. He momentarily paused, looked at both figures, said that the larger figure lacked a collar, picked up the pencil he had laid down, and drew the "collar" by slashing the pencil across the throat of the drawn male. It was almost as if, the writer got the eerie feeling, the patient were committing suicide on paper. Along with this, the patient offered a story to TAT Card 1 which consisted of the boy picking up and smashing the violin. We recall Bellak's theory of the violin's representing the body image and here find consistency with the suicidal impulses acted out on the drawing page. The witnessing of this man slashing his drawn throat on paper was too vivid a demonstration to take lightly. Conferring with his psychiatrist resulted in the patient being institutionalized. Some time later the patient actually made a suicidal attempt, but fortunately, owing to the protective surroundings of the institution, this was detected, and the bathrobe belt with which he attempted to hang himself was cut down in time.

Generally, regarding acting-out, we may state that *the stronger, the more frank, the more direct (and hence unsublimated) the expression of impulses which break through in the projective drawings, the more the defensive and adaptive operations of the ego may be presumed to be insufficient in their assimilative function, and the more the likelihood of acting-out.*

A word of caution: although the previous examples were presented as graphic illustrations of projection in drawing, they were meant to be exercises only. In actual clinical practice, the dangers of basing interpretive deductions on isolated bits of data are obvious. In

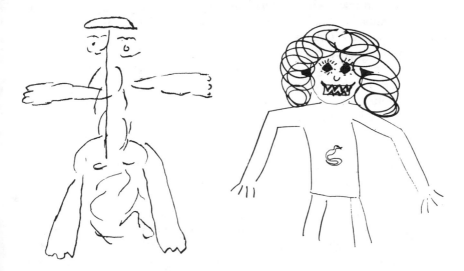

Figures 6.18 and 6.19. Drawing by an extremely deteriorated back ward patient (left); drawing by an acutely paranoid, psychotic man (right)

Figure 6.20. Drawing prophesizing a suicide attempt

practice, confirmation of interpretive speculation on the basis of one drawing must be checked against not only the other drawings, but the entire projective battery, the case history, the clinical impression gleaned during the interview with the subject, and all other available information. If, for example, a subject for his Most Unpleasant Concept draws someone having run over someone else in an automobile, for his house drawing sketches a picture of a cathedral, and for his animal drawing offers a lamb, the sequence suggests a common denominator that one might *speculatively* read as follows: I attempt to conquer the anger and hostility within me by denial and reaction-formation (that is, I say that the most unpleasant thing for me would be to aggressively harm someone else), by restricting myself to what is pure, innocent, good and holy (the drawing of a cathedral), and gentle (the choice of a lamb for an animal drawing) in interpersonal exchange. Rage will not erupt (the most unpleasant thing I can think of, as reflected in the Most Unpleasant Concept Test) if I cling to a saintly ideal (the cathedral drawing and to a lesser degree, the lamb drawing) to see me through crises which may, at times, arise.

This tentative formulation must then be checked against the Rorschach and the clinical impression. On the behavioral level, the subject may assume a self-effacing, Pollyanna role in which he attempts to present himself as being good, sweet, and noble. The projective drawing induction may be offered further support by the Rorschach content of aggressive hostility. Thus, if the drawings fit in, persuasively, with the overt behavior and the Rorschach content to make a continuous pattern of the reaction-formation variable within the subject's personality, we may, with greater confidence, accept their implications.

Interpretations should ordinarily represent the convergence of several sources of data. This *principle of convergence* is essentially no different from that which guides dream analysis, psychoanalytically oriented therapy, Rorschach interpretation, and thema analysis of Thematic Apperception Test data. In fact, it is a basic principle of all scientific methodology.

RESEARCH: STUDIES AND CHALLENGES

The research studies in the field of projective drawings are, by and large, so contradictory that the writer finds himself taking a deep breath as he settles down to try to make sense of the mosaic. On the one hand, a number of studies have failed to demonstrate that psychologists are able to make accurate diagnoses on the basis of figure drawings (Sherman, 1958a, 1958b; Sipprelle & Swensen, 1956; Swensen, 1957; Whitmyre, 1953). Some of Machover's (1949) interpretive hypotheses, when put to the experimental test, have emerged lacking in validity (Blum, 1954; Fisher & Fisher, 1950; Grams & Rinder, 1958; Hammer, 1954; Reznikoff & Nicholas, 1958; Ribler, 1957).

On the borderline, yielding both negative and positive results, Hammer and Piotrowski (1953) found (1) a relatively high degree of both reliability in the judgments of the degree of aggression and its validity as manifested in a subject's free-hand drawings of a House–Tree–Person; (2) in spite of this high degree of reliability and validity, on a secondary level the clinicians' interpretations appear to have been also influenced by their own projections and areas of sensitivity. Perhaps the second finding raises the question of the possibility of a personal psychotherapeutic experience for the clinician serving as diagnostician, as it has long since been advocated by many for the clinician serving as therapist.

On the positive side, numerous studies have demonstrated clear-cut differences between "normal" (or random selections of people) and various pathological groups (Anastasi & Foley, 1941; Berrien, 1935; Eigenbode, 1951; Goldworth, 1950; Gunzberg, 1954; Holzberg & Wexler, 1950; Hozier, 1959; Plaut & Grannell, 1955; Reznikoff & Tomblen, 1956; Schmidl-Waehner, 1942; Singer, 1950; Springer, 1941; Wexler & Holzberg, 1952). Substantiating correlations have been found between ratings of personality traits based on figure drawings and ratings based on case histories, other tests, and interviews (Katz, 1951; Mott, 1936; Richy & Spotts, 1959; Singer, 1957; Spoerl, 1940; Tolor & Tolor, 1955; Witkin, Lewis, Hertzman, Machover, Meissner, & Wapner, 1954). Steinmann (1952) devised a scoring system which was found by Graham (1955) to correlate quite highly (r = .70) with degree of pathology in psychosis. Hiler and Nesvig (1965), using adolescent subjects, showed that normals and psychiatric patients could be differentiated on the basis of their drawings. The valid criteria of pathology which were substantiated were drawings revealing the following characteristics: "bizarre," "distorted," "incomplete," and "transparent." The most valid of the four criteria was "bizarreness," under which heading were subsumed: "schizy," "grotesque," "inhuman," "sinister," "sick," "ghoulish," "wierd" and "gnome-like." In the cross-validation sample, 46 percent of the patients and only 2 percent of the controls produced a drawing which was by independent judgment described as "bizarre."

Goldworth (1950) found 32 percent of his sample of schizophrenics and 58 percent of his sample of people with organic brain damage drew heads which were characterized by the judges as "bizarre" or "grotesque." In contrast, none of his sample of 50 normals and only four of his group of 50 neurotics drew heads so characterized.

Waehner's (1946) results support small size and insufficient pressure as typifying anxious, constricted children. Alschuler and Hattwick (1947) demonstrate that small figures are associated with withdrawn or emotionally dependent behavior; light strokes with low energy level, inhibitions, and depression; and heavy strokes with more self-assertive tendencies. Lack of restraint revealing itself in an overexpanding drawing size was correlated with aggressiveness and a tendency toward release of it into the environment (Zimmerman & Garfinkle, 1942).

Albee and Hamlin (1950), having devised a scale for the ratings of drawings which correlated .62 with the patient's case history, applied this scale to three groups: normals (a group of dental patients), anxiety cases in treatment, and schizophrenics in treatment. It was found that the scale did not differentiate beween the two subtypes of patient groups, the schizophrenics and the anxiety cases, but that it did reliably differentiate between the normals and each of the groups of patients.

Whereas this study by Albee and Hamlin did not find differences between anxiety neurotics and schizophrenics, Griffith and Peyman (1965) did find support for the hypothesis that eye and ear emphasis in the drawing of a person is associated with ideas of reference. This study is noteworthy in drawing to our attention the superiority of actual overt behavior to official psychiatric classification in attempts to validate projective techniques. The authors point out that Swensen's judgment (1957) that figure drawings are of use in clinical work only "as a rough screening device" was based on studies with certain defects of design. Most of the studies Swensen reviewed used psychiatric diagnoses as the criteria. The reliability of psychiatric diagnoses, however, has been more and more questioned of late. Had psychiatric diagnosis been the criterion in the Griffith and Peyman study, nonsignificant, rather than significant, results would have been the yield.

Also avoiding psychiatric diagnosis as the criterion, Schmidt and McGowan (1959) demonstrated the relationship between drawn persons and the traits of the subject offering the drawing: figure drawings by physically disabled persons could be distinguished by judges from figure drawings by physically normal persons.

Perhaps the most jolting marshalling of negative results was provided by Swensen in his *Empirical Evaluations of Human Figure Drawings* (1957) alluded to above. How then are we to explain the striking inconsistencies and contradictions in the research findings on projective drawings? The fallacy of employing psychiatric diagnoses as the criteria has already been mentioned as one explanation among several.

In a study of the psychologists themselves, Schmidt and McGowan (1959) found that the clinician-judges they employed to evaluate the drawings tended to fall into two categories: (1) those whose orientation might be considered "affective," who employed an impressionistic or "feeling" approach to the drawings, and (2) a "cognitive" group who displayed a tendency to evaluate the drawings more in terms of specific signs. The first group, the one using a more artistic, intuitive approach, they found could diagnostically sort the drawings into the correct group successfully. The more "scientific" and "intellectualized" group of judges could not. Those who relied on their feelings apparently could receive the subtle kinesthetic communication embedded in the figure drawing; those who attempted to merely use their heads were, we might deduce, on a different wavelength. It may be, then, that the contradictory findings in the field of figure drawings are as much dependent upon what type of judge is used in the study as they are upon errors in criteria employed, research design, or matching of samples from one experiment to the next.

My own experience, derived from teaching the Annual Summer Workshop in Projective Drawings, is that in the hands of some students projective drawings are an exquisitely sensitive tool, and in the hands of others, those employing a wooden, stilted approach, they are like disconnected phones. It may be because of this that, in spite of the contradictory research findings, clinicians who can use drawings with some artistry—those whose everyday clinical experience demonstrates the frequently remarkable and compelling congruence between the dynamics of patients and their figure drawings—continue to use them in the projective battery. In fact, at one time (Sundberg, 1961) projective drawings had risen to become the second most frequently used projective tool, preceded only by the Rorschach. The remarkable staying power of the projective drawing tool attests to the unshakable conviction of clinicians that this technique has within it the capacity to provide them with useful information about clients.

To return to Swensen's (1957) review: Several fallacies are expressed which invite correction before other research workers fall into the use of the same misconceptions. In the face of so comprehensive and integrated a review of the literature, criticism of Swensen's article is perhaps superderogatory, but because his paper has become so pivotal a survey in the field, several points of clarification must be made.

Swensen reports that Holzberg and Wexler (1950) found no significant difference between normals and schizophrenics in drawing naked feet with the toes delineated, in drawing feet with the toenails indicated, or in a tendency to begin a drawing on one part of the page and then start some place else on the page, turning the page over, or showing other signs of disorganized sequence. Also, no significant differences were found between normals and schizophrenics in the frequency of drawing internal organs which showed through a transparent body wall. Swensen interprets these findings as contradicting Machover's hypotheses concerning these signs' suggestion of schizophrenic processes in the subject.

The occurrence of naked feet with toenails delineated, the occurrence of disorganized and bizarre sequence in the order of the various parts of the human figure drawn, and the representation of internal organs almost invariably, in my experience, are associated with schizophrenia. In view of this experience, I cannot help suspecting that the responsibility for the lack of statistical support for these clinical findings lies with the experimental approach rather than with the hypotheses: All of these three "schizophrenic signs" are relatively infrequent in projective drawings of the human figure, but where they do occur, they occur in the drawings of schizophrenics. Thus, to test these hypotheses adequately, only instances where the sign occurs should be included. For example, to wait to accumulate 20 such drawings and then determine the incidence of schizophrenia in the subjects who submitted these drawings would be the only way to assess fairly the validity of the sign. If one had to wait until 200 drawings were accumulated in order to obtain 20 in which these signs occurred, and then one found that in 18 of the 20 the subject was actually schizophrenic, this would then constitute an investigation of the meaning of such a sign. However, to investigate a relatively infrequent occurrence by comparing 50 "normals" with 50 schizophrenics and deducing from the respective instance of zero and two frequencies of such signs that there is "no statistically significant difference" between the two groups does violence to the actual clinical use of such signs and to the statistically sophisticated investigation of their meaning.

The next point of clarification concerns those studies investigating hypotheses which are formulated on a not-too-careful reading of Machover's contribution. Swensen states that Machover reports that the drawing of knee joints suggests a faulty and uncertain sense of body integrity and occurs chiefly in schizoid and schizophrenic individuals. Swensen then interprets Holzberg and Wexler's (1950) finding, that normal women show the knee joint significantly more often than hebephrenic schizophrenic women, as a direct contradiction of Machover's hypothesis.

Actually, a reading of the section of Machover's book in which the meaning of "joints" is discussed (and it is only one paragraph) will find the following sentences: "The schizoid, the frankly schizophrenic individual, and the body narcissist in decline, will lean on joint *emphasis* [my italics] in order to stave off feelings of body disorganization," and "Most drawings that involve joint *emphasis* [my italics]. . . ." Thus, the flavor of the hypothesis concerns overemphasis on detailing of joints in the drawings. The mere *inclusion* of the knee joints in the drawings, without overemphasis, is consistent with the better reality contact and assessment of the normal women as compared with the hebephrenic schizophrenic women and is not research data opposing the hypothesis as clinically employed.

Elsewhere Swensen points out that "erasures are considered an expression of anxiety" but that Goldworth (1950) found that, in general, normals employed more erasures than other groups. Swensen concludes that, "These results appear to contradict Machover."

This type of research reasoning embodies a popular fallacy in which groups of subjects are compared with other groups of subjects, and extremes in each group tend to cancel each other out, thus yielding a more benign mean for the group. But clinicians find that neurotic and psychotic groups tend to deviate from the norm in either direction. Thus, sick individuals will draw a figure much too large (at the grandiose end of the continuum) or much too small (reflecting direct feelings of inferiority and inadequacy); they will either draw with too light a line (reflecting anxiety, hesitancy, and uncertainty) or too heavy a line (reflecting aggression and inner tension); similarly they will erase too much or not erase at all. As with all areas of behavior, it is the deviation in either direction from the mean which is clinically noteworthy. Group comparisons, then, on any variable, tend to obscure the extreme emphasis, in both directions, of that group and to cancel out the noteworthy occurrences.

In regard to the specific hypothesis about erasures, some erasure, with subsequent improvement, is a sign of adaptiveness and flexibility. Overemphasis upon erasure, particularly in the absence of subsequent improvement in the drawing, is the correlate of excessive self-doubt, self-disapproval, and conflicts which result from perfectionistic demands upon oneself. A total absence of erasures, on the other hand, many denote a lack of adaptive flexibility.

In cases such as this, a comparison of means has no valid meaning. The only research design that is applicable would involve employing a three-point (or five-point) rating scale: (1) overemphasis, (2) "normal" emphasis, and (3) underemphasis and absence. Then the comparison between groups which is appropriate would be in regard to percentages falling in the extreme categories, not with the obscured picture of the means.

Cronbach, in his American Psychological Association Presidential Address, took researchers to task for treating individual differences as a merely bothersome variation—to be reduced by adequate controls or treated as mere error variance. Such assumptions cannot help but lead to an oversimplified set of results, because the simplification is built into the experiment before it gets off the ground. Schafer (1954) has expressed a similar criticism:

> Recognizing and specifying complexity [in a projective record] is objectionable only to those clinicians who cling to mechanical "sign" interpretation and to those score-oriented researchers who naively expect that dumping all patients described as "paranoid" [or "anxious," "schizophrenic," "well adjusted," etc.] into one group will consistently yield highly instructive means, variances, or correlations, and whose conception of test theory and research stops right there.

In a charming and lively paper, Dunnette (1966) refers to some of the sterile exercises which sometimes pass as research as "methodologically our favorite *pets*." Naming the game "Tennis Anyone?" he defines it as:

the compulsion to forget the problem—in essence, to forget what we are really doing—because of the fun we may be enjoying with our apparatus, our computers, our models or the simple act of testing statistical hypotheses. Often, in our zest for this particular game, we forget not only the problem, but we may even literally forget to look at the data!

As David Campbell (Dunnette, 1966) has remarked, "We seem to believe that *truth* will be discovered somehow through using more and more esoteric techniques of data manipulation rather than by looking for it in the real world."

It is my own feeling that projective drawings, resting on repeated clinical verification, will survive to eventually stimulate more knowledgeable experimental approaches and the devising of less crude nets through which the elusive complexities of clinical data will slip less easily.

The fact that present correlations are low between ratings of traits reflected in drawings, on the one hand, and personality characteristics of the subject, on the other, should not be surprising. A drawing of a man and a drawing of a woman are, after all, a pretty small sample of an individual's expressiveness. The use of a *battery* of drawings therefore is suggested for research approaches, as it is used clinically by those who employ the H-T-P, rather than only the Draw-a-Person. In fact, the drawing of a house, tree, and person of each sex, and then four crayon drawings, a house, tree, male and female person, provide eight drawings, which when rounded out with the Draw-a-Family procedure, the Draw-an-Animal, the drawing of the Most Unpleasant Concept a subject can think of, and the other miscellaneous drawings would *only then* actually provide a pool of data sufficient to more validly "test" projective drawings. Otherwise, it is much like testing the validity of a Rorschach examination by employing only the first two cards.

To take the implication in the other direction, the shaky results of research studies based merely on the Draw-a-Person test suggest that clinicians, in their everyday work, should employ a wider projective drawing net than just the two drawings of the human figure. Caligor (1952) found that paranoid trends could be detected in only 25 percent of a group of paranoid schizophrenics when only one drawing was used but could be detected in 85 percent of the cases when a series of eight drawings was employed.

In terms of experimental design, what we need currently are more multivariate statistical methods which incorporate the uniqueness of the pattern of the individual's behavior, as it is the pattern rather than individual elements which are really what emerge in projective technique assessment. It is the harmony or lack of harmony between various elements which form the essence of personality, not the individual traits per se. Swensen (1957) himself points out that studies which attempt to evaluate the significance of patterns of signs on the Draw-a-Person test appear to be more promising than attempts to evaluate the significance of individual signs. This, of course, has also been maintained by Buck (1948) and by Machover (1949).

The last point that requires clarification in Swensen's review concerns the very basic premise of projective drawings as a reflection of the self. Swensen reports Berman and Laffal's (1953) comparison of figure drawings with the body type of the subjects offering the drawings. A Pearson r of .35, significant at the .05 level of confidence, was yielded on the basis of Sheldon's body types. In inspecting Berman and Laffal's data, Swensen points out that "only" 18 of their 39 subjects drew figures that were judged to be of the same body types as the subject's body type, and concludes that for some subjects, the figure drawn represents the subject's own body, but for the majority of subjects, the figure drawn represents something else. Swensen deduces, "Since in clinical work the reliable diagnosis of the clinical case is of paramount importance, this lack of consistent evidence supporting Machover . . . suggests that the DAP is of doubtful value in clinical work."

Here Swensen is entangled in a relatively unsophisticated notion of the concept of the self. Some subjects tend to project themselves as they experience themselves to be, while other subjects tend to project themselves as they wish to be. The idealized version of the self is an integral component of the self-concept and is necessary in describing personality. In actual clinical context, most drawings are neither one nor the other, but represent a fusion of both the realistic perceptions of oneself and the ego ideal. In addition, the picture is further complicated by the fact that the perceptions of oneself as one fears one might be also color the total picture. Since the self actually includes what we are, what we wish to be, and what we fear we might sink to, we must expect all three to appear in projective drawings and not regard any deviation from perfect correlation on any one of these variables between the drawing and the subject as a contradiction of the basic hypothesis.

The trouble with Swensen's interpretation of the results of Berman and Laffal's study is that he too narrowly defines the self as both experienced by the subject and as projected in his drawing. As the present writer points out elsewhere (1958), an additional facet that must be reckoned with in the understanding, and investigation, of projective drawings involves a perception of significant figures in one's early developmental years. Thus, the projective drawing interpreter and/or research worker must grapple with the problem of disentangling the influences of four different projections on the drawing page: What one *feels* oneself to be, *fears* oneself to be, *wishes* to be, and perceives *others* to be.

For example, a subject who suffers from "castration anxiety" will reveal the *fear of what he may become* in his drawing. A subject who feels himself to be obese may draw a fat person *(what he feels himself to be);* another subject who suffers from obesity but who has not yet lost the capacity to year for, and strive for, an ideal figure, will draw a very shapely person *(what he wishes to be).* A child who experiences his father as threatening may, as one subject recently did, draw a male with teeth bared, a dagger in one hand, and scissors in the other, with a generally menacing facial tone and violent look in the eyes *(his perception of others).*

In the face of a complex world, the research worker is obliged to recognize the complexity of the variables he attempts to come to grips with in his investigations and steer vigorously away from the dangers of atomistic studies, naively conceived and dogmatically interpreted.

REFERENCES

Albee, G. W., & Hamlin, R. M. Judgment of adjustment from drawings: The applicability of rating scale methods. *J. Clin. Psychol.*, 1950, 6, 363–365.

Alschuler, A., & Hattwick, W. *Painting and Personality.* Chicago: University of Chicago Press, 1947.

Anastasi, Anne, & Foley, J. P., Jr. A survey of literature on artistic behavior in the abnormal: Experimental investigations. *J. Gen. Psychol.*, 1941, 23, 187–237.

Berman, S., & Laffal, J. Body type and figure drawing. *J. Clin. Psychol.*, 1953, 9, 368–370.

Berrien, F. K. A. A study of the drawings of abnormal children. *J. Educ. Psychol.*, 1935, *26*, 143–150.

Blum, R. H. The validity of the Machover DAP technique. *J. Clin. Psychol.*, 1954, *10*, 120–125.

Buck, J. N. The H-T-P technique, a qualitative and quantitative scoring method. *J. Clin. Psychol. Monogr.*, 1948, No. 5, 1–20.

Caligor, L. The detection of paranoid trends by the 8 Card Redrawing Test (8 CRT). *J. Clin. Psychol.*, 1952, *8*, 397–401.

Dunnette, M. Fads, fashions, and folderol. *Am. Psychol.*, 1966, *21*, 343–352.

Eigenbode, C. R. Effectiveness of the Machover signs and others in differentiating between a normal group and a schizophrenic group by use of the projective drawing test. Unpublished master's thesis, George Washington University, 1951.

Fisher, S., & Fisher, Rhoda. Test of certain assumptions regarding figure drawing analysis. *J. Abn. Soc. Psychol.*, 1950, *45*, 727–732.

Goldworth, S. A. A comparative study of the drawings of a man and a woman done by normal, neurotic, schizophrenic, and brain damaged individuals. Doctoral dissertation, University of Pittsburgh, 1950.

Gondor, E. *Art and Play Therapy.* New York: Doubleday, 1954.

Graham, S. Relation between histamine tolerance, visual autokinesis, Rorschach human movement, and figure drawing. *J.Clin. Psychol.*,1955,*11*, 370–373.

Grams, A., & Rinder, L. Signs of homosexuality in human figure drawings. *J. Consult. Psychol.*, 1958, *22*, 394.

Griffith, A., & Peyman, D. Eye-ear emphasis in the DAP Test as indicating ideas of reference. In Murstein, *Handbook of Projective Techniques,* New York: Basic Books, 1965.

Gunzburg, H. C. Scope and limitations of the Goodenough drawing test method in clinical work with mental defectives. *J. Clin. Psychol.*, 1954, *10*, 8–15.

Hammer, E. Relationship between diagnosis of psychosexual pathology and the sex of the first drawn person. *J. Clin. Psychol.*, 1954, *10*, 168–170.

Hammer, E. F. (Ed.). *The Clinical Application of Projective Drawings.* Springfield, Ill.: Charles C. Thomas, 1958.

Hammer, E., & Piotrowski, Z. Hostility as a factor in the clinician's personality as it affects his interpretation of projective drawings. *J. Proj. Tech.*, 1953, *17*, 210–216.

Hiler, E., & Nesvig, D. Evaluation of criteria used by clinicians to infer pathology from figure drawings. *J. Consult. Psychol.*, 1965, *29*, 520–529.

Holzberg, J. D., & Wexler, M. The validity of human form drawings as a measure of personality deviation. *J. Proj. Tech.*, 1950, *14*, 343–361.

Hozier, Ann. On the breakdown of the sense of reality: A study of spatial perception in schizophrenia. *J. Consult. Psychol.*, 1959, *23*, 185–194.

Katz, J. The projection of assaultive aggression in the human figure drawings of adult male Negro offenders. Unpublished doctoral dissertation, New York University, 1951.

Machover, Karen. *Personality Projection in the Drawing of the Human Figure.* Springfield, Ill.: Charles C. Thomas, 1949.

Mott, S. M. The development of concepts: A study of children's drawings. *J. Genet. Psychol.*, 1936, *48*, 199–214.

Plaut, Erika, & Crannell, C. W. The ability of clinical psychologists to discriminate between drawings by deteriorated schizophrenics and drawings by normal subjects. *Psychol. Rep.*, 1955, *1*, 153–158.

Reznikoff, M., & Nicholas, A. An evaluation of human figure drawing indicators of paranoid pathology. *J. Consult. Psychol.*, 1958, *22*, 395–397.

Reznikoff, M., & Tomblen, D. The use of human figure drawings in the diagnosis of organic pathology. *J. Consult. Psychol.*, 1956. *20*, 467–470.

Ribler, R. I. Diagnostic prediction from emphasis on the eye and the ear in human figure drawings. *J. Consult. Psychol.*, 1957, *21*, 223–225.

Richey, M. H., & Spotts, J. V. The relationship of popularity to performance on the Goodenough Draw-a-Man test. *J. Consult. Psychol.*, 1959, *23*, 147–150.

Schafer, R. *Psychoanalytic Interpretation in Rorschach Testing.* New York: Grune and Stratton, 1954.

Schmidl-Waehner, B. Formal criteria for the analysis of children's drawings. *Am. J. Orthopsychiat.*, 1942, *17*, 95–104.

Schmidt, L. D., & McGowan, J. F. The differentiation of human figure drawings. *J. Consult. Psychol.*, 1959, *23*, 129–133.

Sherman, L. J. Sexual differentiation or artistic ability? *J. Clin. Psychol.*, 1958a, *14*, 170–171.

Sherman, L. J. The influence of artistic quality on judgments of patient and non-patient status from human figure drawings. *J. Proj. Tech.*, 1958b, *22*, 338–340.

Singer, R. H. A study of drawings produced by a group of college students and a group of hospitalized schizophrenics. Master's thesis, Pennsylvania State University, 1950.

Singer, R. H. Various aspects of human figure drawings as a personality measure with hospitalized psychiatric patients. Unpublished doctoral dissertation, Pennsylvania State University, 1957.

Sipprelle, C. N., & Swensen, C. H. Relationships of sexual adjustment to certain sexual characteristics of human figure drawings. *J. Consult. Psychol.*, 1956, *20*, 197–198.

Spoerl, D. T. Personality drawing in retarded children. *Character Pers.*, 1940, 8, 227–239.

Springer, N. N. A study of the drawinags of maladjusted and adjusted children. *J. Genet. Psychol.*, 1941, 58, 131–138.

Steinmann, K. The validity of projective technique in the determination of relative intensity in psychosis. Unpublished doctoral dissertation, School of Education, New York University, 1952.

Sundberg, N. I. The practice of psychological testing in clinical services in the United States. *Am. Psychol.*, 1961, 16, 79–83.

Swensen, C. H. Empirical evaluations of human figure drawings. *Psychol. Bull.*, 1957, 54, 431–466.

Tolor, A., & Tolor, B. Judgments of children's popularity from their human figure drawings. *J. Proj. Tech.*, 1955, 19, 170–176.

Waehner, T. S. Interpretatation of spontaneous drawings and paintings. *Genet. Psychol. Monogr.*, 1946, 33, 3–70.

Wexler, M., & Holzberg, J. D. A further study of the validity of human form drawings in personality evaluation. *J. Proj. Tech.*, 1952, 16, 249–251.

Whitmyre, J. W. The significance of artistic excellence in the judgment of adjustment inferred from human figure drawings. *J. Consult. Psychol.*, 1953, 17, 421–424.

Witkin, H. A., Lewis, H. B., Hertzman, M., Machover, K., Meissner, P. B., & Wapner, S. *Personality Through Perception*. New York: Harper, 1954.

Zimmerman, J., & Garfinkle, L. Preliminary study of the art productions of the adult psychotic. *Psychiat. Quart.*, 1942, 16, 313–318.

ADDITIONAL RECENT PUBLICATIONS
ON PROJECTIVE DRAWINGS

Apfeldorf, M., Walter, C., Kaiman, B., Smith, W., & Arnett, W. A method for the evaluation of affective associations to figure drawings. *J. Pers. Assess.*, 1974, 38, 441–449.

Cauthen, N., Sandman, C., Kilpatrick, D., & Deabler, H. D-A-P correlates of Sc scores on the MMPI. *J. Proj. Tech.*, 1969, 33, 262–264.

Coopersmith, S., Sokol, D., Beardslee, B., & Coopersmith, A. Figure drawing as an expression of self-esteem. *J. Pers. Assess.*, 1976, 40, 368, 374.

Davis, C., & Hoopes, J. Comparison of H-T-P drawings of young deaf and hearing children. *J. Pers. Assess.*, 1975, 39, 23–33.

Golstein, H., & Faterson, H. Shading as an index of anxiety of figure drawings. *J. Proj. Tech. and Pers. Assess.*, 1969, 33, 454–465.

Irgens-Jensen, O. *Problem drinking and personality: A study based on the Draw-a-Person Test.* Oslo: Universitetsforlaget, 1971.

Klopfer, W. "Will the real Rorschach please stand up?" *Contemp. Psychol.*, 1972, *17*, 25–26.

Lord, M. Activity and affect in early memories of adolescent boys. *J. Pers. Assess.*, 1971, *35*, 418–456.

Ludwig, D. Self-perception and the Draw-a-Person Test. *J. Proj. Tech.*, 1969, *33*, 257–261.

7

The Intelligence Test in Personality Assessment

Sidney J. Blatt and Joel Allison

The conceptualization and application of the intelligence test has gradually but persistently evolved and expanded in scope. This has been reflected in part in a shift away from a limited preoccupation with the global IQ score to a broader focus on the diverse tasks of an intelligence test as an assessment of ego functions. Increased interest has also been shown in the principles and patterns in which these various ego functions are organized and integrated into various types or modes of adaptation. Thus, while the purpose of early intelligence testing was to evaluate an individual's general intellectual capacity by comparing it to appropriate norms and standardization groups, more recent conceptualization and utilization of intelligence tests have increasingly questioned the arbitrary separation of intelligence, as a functional concept, and personality. To some extent the interrelationship of intelligence and personality was recognized at the outset, but in the somewhat static concept that personality factors could influence and interfere with test efficiency. For example, it was noted relatively early that many patients showed a decline or deterioration

This chapter was written with the support of the Cooperative Research Program of the Office of Education, United States Department of Health, Education and Welfare, Project No. 1931, "Non-Intellectual Factors in Cognitive Efficiency." We are indebted to Roy Schafer, Cynthia Wild, and Alan Feirstein for their comments on drafts of this chapter.

187

as well as marked variability in their intellectual functioning, and interest was focused on the relationship between the range of the scores and various psychopathological conditions. This conceptualization of the relationship of psychopathology to gross scatter of test scores was then refined to include the hypothesis that the variability (or scatter) reflected selective impairments that were specific to various psychopathological states. The development of the Wechsler-Bellevue in the mid-1940s with its subtests, each of which was administered to all subjects, was an important stimulus to this revised, more refined concept of test scatter because the Wechsler scales permitted more specific and consistent comparisons (Rabin, 1965). It was also with the development of the Wechsler scales that some of the guideposts were established for clarifying the inseparability of intelligence and total personality functioning. The addition of a theoretical analysis of the various psychological functions assessed by the different subtests (Rapaport, Gill, & Schafer, 1945; Wechsler, 1944) supplied an interpretive rationale for viewing the interrelationship of the various psychological functions reflected in subtest scores with personality organization. In large measure, this new approach reflected the systematic application to intelligence tests of the hypothesis that each act of the individual bears the imprint of his unique personality organization (the projective hypothesis). This more dynamic conception of intelligence as an integral aspect of personality organization has been reemphasized, expanded, and extended in more recent years (Fromm, Erika, 1960; Fromm & Hartman, 1955; Fromm et al., 1954; 1957; Mayman, Schafer, & Rapaport, 1951; Waite, 1961).

This chapter will also deal with the integral relatedness of intelligence and personality, primarily as seen on the Wechsler scales. First, the role of the intelligence test in personality assessment and how the projective hypothesis applies to intelligence testing will be considered. Then an analysis of the psychological functions assessed by the individual Wechsler subtests and how scores, and the patterns of scores, can be interpreted, will be presented. This will be followed by a detailed discussion of the WAIS of one individual to demonstrate how various sources of test data—the scores on the subtests, attitudes toward one's responses and being tested, and the content of the responses and of asides and gestures during testing—interweave to give insight into the complexities of unified psychological functioning. Last, there will be a review of recent research on the relevance of the WAIS to personality.

THE WAIS AND PERSONALITY ASSESSMENT

There are essentially three ways in which the projective hypothesis can be applied to intelligence tests.

1.   The *content of responses* can contain personalized concerns and idiosyncratic preoccupations.

2.   The *style of responses* and the quality and nature of the clinical transaction represent aspects of personality organization.

3.   The *structure or organization of psychological functions* as indicated in the patterning of diverse abilities, both between and within subtests, is an integral aspect of personality organization.

1.   The *content* of specific test responses including asides and comments can reflect important areas of concern and preoccupation. Unlike the Rorschach and the TAT, the intelligence test assesses adaptive potential in situations that involve relatively habituated, routine functions and past achievements. A number of tasks are presented with the demand and expectation that responses be organized and realistic, and that they remain relatively free of personal issues and of primitive wishes and fantasies. In contrast to the Rorschach and TAT, which permit less logical thought organization and encourage the embellishment and enrichment of responses by fantasies, the intelligence test requires functioning which is logical, organized, and relatively attuned to reality.

In general, personalized concerns tend to interfere with efficient functioning on the intelligence test and their presence invariably serves as a harbinger of their prominence as situations become less restrictive and less structured and require the individual to organize his responses according to his inner world. Thus, minor content variations on the WAIS often appear in major proportions on the TAT and Rorschach. The intelligence test, therefore, is not a test of central importance if one is primarily interested in learning about various content concerns of an individual. Content in the intelligence test is more relevant to assessing the degree to which such concerns enter into and interfere with cognitive efficiency in relatively routine, impersonal situations. Psychological functions such as perception, memory, and visual-motor organization play important roles in adaptation (Hartmann, 1958) and for these processes to be effective they must remain relatively free and undisturbed by the various pressing concerns of the individual (Rapaport, 1958). When these cognitive functions are infused by drives and personalized preoc-cupations and organized by less logical principles (as in psychosis), efficiency is sharply curtailed. It is primarily in the severely neurotic and particularly in psychotic conditions that psychological function-ing in the routine and relatively neutral situation of the intelligence test is undermined by personal preoccupations or autistic elabora-tions. For example, a girl with intense depressive concerns received only partial credit on the sixth Picture Arrangement of the WAIS (the flirt sequence) by arranging her cards in the order of JNAET. She explained her sequence by stating that the King has gotten out of his car because of his interest in the "hat" rather than in the girl, thereby revealing her feelings that any interest on the part of men does not reflect recognition of her essential worth. This same patient in relat-ing a fly and a tree on Similarities revealed another aspect of her depression—her oral neediness—by seeing the similarity in the fact that "both require food to live." A more severe intrusion of a personal nature occurred in the WAIS of a chronic schizophrenic young man beset by feelings of unreality. When asked why we should keep away from bad company, he responded, "because from Confucius on down it is bad to associate with people more confused than yourself." Not only do the concerns expressed about confusion suggest the possibil-ity of impaired reality testing, but the clang association and the symbolic and nonrelevant thinking in the blending of "confusion" and "Confucius" indicates that thinking can be alogical and governed by rather primitive principles.[1]

Though effective functioning on the WAIS generally requires a minimal intrusion of irrelevant material into responses, this does not mean that a well-intact WAIS protocol should contain only perfect "textbook" responses. Such records can be banal, trite, and unin-teresting and reflect a highly conventional individual who may find difficulty in expressing personal feelings, interests, and needs. Highly

---

[1]Although the relationship between "Confucius" and "confusing" might well appear in humor, this response was not presented as humor but rather as a serious attempt to cope with demands of the question. The attitude and mood tone which accompany a response are an important aspect of the response process. A somewhat alogical answer could be offered as a humorous alternative or it can represent more pathological thinking when it has a forced quality or where the individual is unable to establish distance and juxtapose the humor with a more appropriate response.

Attitudes taken toward responses can aid in the differentiation of momentary playful and controlled regression from less voluntary and more persistent regressed modes of functioning (Holt & Havel, 1960; Kris, 1952; Schafer, 1958; Wild, 1965).

organized skills and psychological functions should have a degree of autonomy from drives but it is equally important that a degree of autonomy be maintained from the environment as well (Rapaport, 1951, 1958). Though the degree of autonomy from the environment can be assessed most readily in an individual's capacity to give imaginative and creative responses to the Rorschach and TAT, the degree of autonomy from environmental demands can also be considered to some extent on the WAIS. The structure of the WAIS tends to limit the range of cognitive strategies that can be employed, but the subtests differ in the limitations and restrictions they place in defining an acceptable response. Subtests such as Information require circumscribed, precise responses while subtests like Comprehension and Vocabulary require more verbalization and have a wider latitude of acceptable responses. The content of responses on these subtests may reflect unique aspects of personality without necessarily indicating a disruption of functioning or pathology.[2] For example, in defining travesty, both "a mocking imitation" and "burlesque" receive full credit, but it is of some interest when "burlesque" (a less usual response) is offered by a young man whose father is an accomplished actor whom he feels able to imitate only weakly but angrily in the caricatured style of an old, decrepit vaudevillian. Another example: in response to the question, "What is the Vatican?" subjects often allude only to its being the home of the Pope. It is less common to have included in the response—still accurate, however—the fact that the Vatican is an enclosed city, as in the following response: "The Vatican is a city enclosed . . . which is within the confines of Rome and in which the Papacy of the Catholic Church has its seat." In this instance the reference to enclosure raises specific questions as to the relevance for this subject of issues of protection and a felt need to maintain an internally imposed barrier against certain aspects of experience.

Generally, however, the WAIS tells us more about autonomy

---

[2]Assessing the individual's relative position in reference to conventional environmental demands is important in at least one other respect. The reality presented by the WAIS involves procedures and ways of perceiving and organizing experiences which are crucial for success in the "usual" tasks of our culture. Some members of our society live essentially in subcultures which are somewhat removed from the mainstream of middle-class experience and from conventionally learned approaches to cognitive tasks. The WAIS (and most intelligence tests) presents a more novel situation to such people than it does to people schooled in the types of procedures and tasks presented by the tests. It is important to remember that though the WAIS is generally considered to be more structured than most other psychological procedures, it can also be experienced in very different ways depending upon earlier educational experiences.

from drives than from the environment since it places such a high premium on habituated, logical thinking. Successful, efficient WAIS functioning occurs within a structured and organized context, and we must look to the results of a battery of tests which include a diversity of types of thinking, some of which permit relatively little variation in cognitive approach and discourage any embellishment of responses by drives, and others which permit and even encourage more variation in style of approach and enrichment by drives. In this way we can observe a broader spectrum of a subject's adaptive efforts and note the degree to which he is equally at home with thinking which is based on more primitive principles of organization and contains drive content (primary process thinking) as he is with a more rigorous, logical, and drive-free approach (secondary process thought).

2.   The subject's style of responding to the WAIS items is also relevant for personality assessment. Are the verbalizations, for example, pedantic, overdetailed, and marked by incessant qualification (obsessive style); or hesitant, blocked, and interspersed with self-depreciatory remarks (depressive style); querulous, distrustful, and legalistic (paranoid style); or expansive, outpouring, and excited (hypomanic style)? More subtle aspects of stylistic differences are also apparent in consistent approaches to the solution of a problem, e.g., when a subject routinely relies on trial and error behavior to solve certain Performance subtests, or shows a tendency to be inflexible in trying new alternatives when an initial effort at solution is found to be incorrect.

There is often no clear distinction between style of responding and the content of a subject's responses and comments. Content features interact with functioning and often reflect not only the concerns of a subject but also the specific and habitual modes or styles of response to internal and environmental stimulation. Relevant in this regard are statements to the tester which can reveal a variety of interpersonal styles. Schafer (1954) has discussed at length the varied styles of interpersonal relatedness which can occur in the Rorschach testing situation—styles which he has classified as involving projection, isolation, intellectualization, compulsive perfectionism, repression, denial, reaction formation against hostility or dependent needs, passive demandingness, counterphobic defenses, or masochistic, ingratiating, or rebellious attitudes.

It is revealing to assess such stylistic variations in the WAIS situation as well. A subject confronted with the Picture Completion item (a woman looking in the mirror) states, ". . . the front leg on the left hand side is too short. Also, though the woman is powdering her nose you can't see the reflection of her hand or the powder puff in the mirror. Nor can you see her right arm, which should be visible in the perspective as it is." (What was intended to be missing?) "The reflection in the mirror. As I look at the leg now its just a crude drawing." By shifting the locus of his difficulty from his own indecisiveness to the deficiency of the drawing, this subject is, through his emphasis on orderliness, implicitly blaming the tester for confronting him with a crude, i.e., primitive and possibly messy stimulus. We can hypothesize further that it may be the "too short" leg and its suggestion of body deficit and castration which is disturbing to the subject. Instead of acknowledging to himself his upset in this regard or his indecisiveness when faced with this stimulus, he devalues the external stimulus and the tester. With this subject we would be alert to other indications of a similar style of response, namely becoming indecisive and meticulous and blaming others when faced with his own felt shortcomings or deficiencies.

3. *The organization of specific cognitive functions*, as measured by the subtests, is another source of data for understanding personality organization. The patterns of diverse abilities (intersubtest scatter) and the patterning of success and failure within a single subtest reflect the organization of a number of ego functions which are important aspects of the capacity for adaptation. Recent research on cognitive styles and cognitive control principles has indicated that the organization of these ego functions reflects consistent modes of adaptation which include general cognitive abilities as well as the styles of mediating, filtering, and controlling drive and impulse expression in a wide variety of situations (Gardner, et al., 1959; 1960; Kroeber, 1963; Witkin, et al., 1962). Cognitive variables like those involved in the WAIS (e.g., anticipation, planning, attention, and concentration) are believed to represent the basic functions which are integrated into the broad principles of organization that appear early in development and are involved in psychological defenses as well as the processes which cope realistically with external reality.

It is important to stress that the various aspects of psychological functioning do not exist in isolation; rather, one is always observing and assessing the balance among affects, drives, defenses, and cognitive controls.

If the pattern of scores on the WAIS subtests reflects general modes of adaptation, then there should be close concordance between the principles which account for the organization of these various psychological functions and other aspects of the WAIS protocol, such as the content of the responses and the style of the clinical transaction. Such consistency has been found between style of response, content of personal concerns and their psychosexual emphasis, symptom formation, psychological defenses, and cognitive abilities. These consistencies have been called character styles (e.g., Fenichel, 1945; Reich, 1949; Shapiro, 1965) and they are based in part on diagnostic concepts, but in an expanded sense. The concept of character is an attempt to differentiate general modes of adaptation on the basis of the styles of thinking, perceiving, and experiencing rather than solely on the basis of manifest behavior, such as symptom formation. For example, a paranoid style will reflect a style of response that is cautious, rigid, and legalistic; the content of concerns will tend to focus on insulation and protection, and comments to the tester will often involve suspiciousness regarding the verbatim recording, feelings of being tricked, and efforts to externalize and project blame for difficulty onto the tester and/or the test; the content of concerns, moreover, is likely to revolve around power (who is in control). As for the specific cognitive abilities, scores related to functions involving hyperalertness to details (Picture Completion and/or Picture Arrangement) and a heightened emphasis on bringing together and relating disparate things (Similarities) are usually intact and somewhat elevated compared to other functions in a paranoid character structure although not necessarily in a paranoid psychosis. The unique contribution of the WAIS in this evaluation, however, is the understanding of the organization of the psychological functions assessed by the various subtests.

By using the WAIS to study organization of cognitive processes and the relative balance of primary and secondary process thinking, intellectual processes are considered to be a more integral part of personality. A great deal of understanding about the organization of ego functions can be achieved through an analysis of the patterns of subtest scores. Inasmuch as the scaled scores reflect an individual's standing on a number of specific abilities and psychological functions, variations between and within the different functions do occur as a result of the individual's uniqueness, whether the variations in adaptive capacity are because of strengths or because of weaknesses due to pathological impairment of certain processes. Each of these sources can contribute to variations in the subtest scatter and in each case they reflect the organization of psychological functions we call personality. The weighted subtest score, however, becomes meaningful only in the context of the total score pattern, for it is in the variation among scores that the particular organization of psychological processes is expressed and not in the absolute level of the scores.

Thus, two people may have identical scores on a subtest, but for one it may be his highest subtest score, and for the other it may be his lowest subtest score. In interpreting a WAIS profile, then, a baseline must be established from which the variation in subtest scores can be viewed. This baseline assesses the general intellectual level of the individual and variations in subtest scores are considered in relation to it.

There are several baseline measures. The one most widely used is the Vocabulary subtest, since it is usually the single best estimate of intelligence and is relatively impervious to the effect of functional and organic conditions and to the overall decline in functioning which accompanies age. The subtests may be viewed as having positive or negative deviation from the Vocabulary score.

In order to fully utilize the concept of scatter, one must understand the particular psychological processes tapped by each of the subtests. In the section to follow, the psychological functions assessed by the subtests will be discussed. These interpretive rationales have been greatly influenced by the theoretical ego psychological formulations of David Rapaport and his colleagues (1945, 1951)" [Allison, Blatt, & Zimet, 1967].

It should be stressed that these interpretive rationales represent assumptions derived from extensive clinical experience. As yet, many of these assumptions have not been adequately evaluated in research. Research on these hypotheses will be more fully discussed in a later section of this chapter.

INTERPRETATIVE RATIONALE FOR WAIS SUBTESTS[3]

Verbal Subtests

Vocabulary.   As indicated previously, this scale correlates most highly with the Total IQ. This is so primarily because it represents the breadth of concepts, ideas, and experience gained during one's lifetime. The acquisition of these concepts and their availability to memory is contingent both on innate ability and on an enriched early life experience. Although emotional conflicts as well as characterological features may affect the acquisition of an adequate vocabulary, it is, in general, still the single best estimate of intellectual capacity, being

[3]From "The Scatter of Subtest Scores." Copyright © 1967 by Joel Allison, Sidney J. Blatt, and Carl N. Zimet. From *The Interpretation of Psychological Tests.* Reprinted by permission of (the authors and) Harper & Row, Publishers.

stable over time and relatively resistent to neurological deficit and psychological disturbance. Because of its relative invulnerability, reliability, and predictive capacity, the Vocabulary subtest offers an excellent baseline to which other tests can be compared.[4] It is in relation to the Vocabulary score that one may consider positive or negative scatter, the elevation and heightened investment in certain ego functions, or the disruption of ego functions due either to temporary inefficiencies or to more marked and permanent organic or psychogenic problems.

Information.   This subtest is seen as measuring the wealth of available information which, like Vocabulary, is acquired largely as a result of native ability and early cultural experiences, but which, unlike Vocabulary, is more alterable by defensive processes or by schooling or persistent efforts at academic achievement. Self-made men, for example, often show a level of Information that exceeds their Vocabulary scores. Rapaport and co-workers (1945) indicated that the effort to acquire a general fund of information is frequently an indicator of "intellectual ambitiousness." Inasmuch as repression is geared toward blocking out memories from awareness, the acquisition of general knowledge is especially hindered by repression when it is a primary mode of defense (Rapaport, et al., 1945). Repression may interfere with the fund of information either in the initial learning process in which the material is acquired or in later attempts to recall the material. This concept of memory further implies that experiences are delivered into consciousness when a situation again appeals to the same needs, strivings, interests, or affects with which the experience is linked in the subject's frame of reference. Repressive people, with their marked degree of memory blockage, therefore, are likely to show disruptions, inefficiency, and variability on a task like Information which concerns long-range memory, relates to active intellectual strivings, and deals with piecemeal, sharply defined bits of experience. The obsessive compulsive, on the other hand, with his characteristic pedantic emphasis on detail and his intellectual strivings, will tend to obtain a relatively high score.

Comprehension.   This subtest presents a subject with a series of

---

[4]An exception to this general rule occurs when early life experiences have been intellectually impoverished in some way, where intellectual stimulation has been minimal, as in many economically and socially deprived families, and where very early school experience has been irregular and disrupted. With such people one must look to scores other than Vocabulary such as the mean of all the subtests, to establish a baseline for comparison.

more or less conventional social situations and asks about appropriate behavior and its rationale. Comprehension, therefore, measures a subject's grasp of social conventionality and social judgment (Rapaport, et al., 1945). This subtest is frequently a very sensitive indicator of maladaptation; low scores may represent a need to defy or ignore social conventionality, or they may indicate an impairment of judgment or a diminished interest in social interaction, as in schizophrenic conditions. Frequently the Comprehension subtest, because it deals with social situations and judgments appropriate to these situations, may yield material related to issues of morality and superego organization. Antisocial trends are frequently expressed in the content of the subtest via such comments as "check to see whether there's any money in it," in response to the envelop item. There are some psychopaths, however, who tend to score very high on this subtest; they are the more glib and socially facile individuals. However, high Comprehension may also represent a push toward hyperconventionality or conformity and reflect the naiveté, conventional thinking, and moral strivings of individuals with hysterical features. High Comprehension, especially coupled with lower Information, therefore, is characteristic for hysterics. The reverse pattern, high Information and lower Comprehension, is generally seen in the obsessive-compulsive, largely because of the obsessive's uncertainty and excessive qualification but excellent fund of information. It is important to note that three items on the WAIS Comprehension subtest require the interpretation of proverbs. These items assess primarily the capacity for abstract thought rather than social judgment. In drawing inferences from this subtest one must consider the extent to which the score is affected by these three items.

Similarities.   This subtest is essentially a measure of verbal concept formation (Rapaport, et al., 1945; Wechsler, 1958). Conceptual abstraction can be carried out on one of three general levels of cognitive development. The concrete similarity between two objects, a specific common feature of the objects (e.g., a table and a chair both have legs or a dog and a lion both have fur) represents the lowest level of cognitive development. This type of concept formation, which is correct in a limited sense, acknowledges a most direct and obvious feature of the objects without attempting to reach for broader and more abstract generalizations. The thinking is unusually specific, direct, and limited in focus and generally constitutes a rather poorly articulated concept which at best receives only a partial score. A second type of concept formation is the functional definition which defines a utilitarian purpose as the basis for the conceptual category (e.g., piano and violin, play them both). Though this type of abstraction of concept formation is more sophisticated than a concrete conceptualization, it still falls short of a high-level abstraction. In terms of personality functioning, the extensive use of functional categories may indicate an inability on the part of the ideational processes to serve as a buffer against impulsive action. Rather than ideation serving as a form of delay and planning, a general move toward activity and acting out may be indicated. The third type of concept formation is the abstract level, which captures the essential common characteristic of the objects. This is the highest level of thought and stands in marked contrast to the prior two forms of more concrete thought processes (Rapaport, et al., 1945). From the general level of abstraction on the Similarities subtest, and also from its relationship to the Vocabulary baseline, and the qualitative features of the derived concepts, valuable clues can be derived concerning the level, flexibility, and appropriateness of conceptual thinking and the role of abstract ideational processes in the subject's total psychological organization.[5] When Similarities fall exceptionally low within the scatter, one may suspect central nervous system impairment. In acute schizophrenic states, impaired thought processes would not be limited to Similarities, but, as will be discussed shortly, would also affect such other scales as Comprehension (judgment) and possibly Arithmetic (concentration). Similarities, because of its demand for abstraction, tends to be elevated in character styles such as the obsessive and the paranoid where there is an emphasis on abstract and symbolic modes of thought.

Digit Span.   In presenting a subject with increasing lengths of rote material for immediate memory and recall, this subtest generally taps passive reception of stimuli and the automatic effortless process called attention (Rapaport, et al., 1945). Attention functions best when it is not disrupted by preoccupations, anxiety, or the intrusion of drive derivatives. A Digit Span score which is markedly below the Vocabulary level tends to indicate the presence of anxiety, whereas a Digit Span score which is high in relation to Vocabulary indicates blandness of affect and is frequently found in detached, schizoid people. In schizoid records the blandness usually represents a lack of conscious anxiety, chronicity, and an acceptance of pathology. High Digit Span, which indicates a lack of anxiety, may also be seen in psychopathic protocols and in hysterics characterized by "la belle

---

[5]Concrete and functional responses may also be a function of impoverished educational experiences rather than a reflection of psychopathology or intellectual limitations.

indifference." Conversely, a low Digit Span may suggest a more positive prognosis, since it reflects an acute state of subjective distress in which the disorder has not become ego-syntonic or the person comfortable with it and unmotivated to change. A one- to three-point difference may be expected in favor of digits forward over digits backward. If this pattern is reversed, one should also be alerted to blandness or negativism.

In other contexts, low Digit Span may have yet another meaning. One of the primary features of central nervous system damage is a severe distractability which accompanies diminished cortical control. The capacity to attend is adversely affected by distractability, and, therefore, an impoverished Digit Span with added indications of concrete concept formation and unusual motor impairments frequently is seen in brain-damaged patients.

Arithmetic.   Complex arithmetical reasoning requires extensive concentration and attention (Rapaport, et al., 1945). Concentration is foremost in this task, since the subject has to actively focus his attention in order to acquire the information within the problem and to manipulate meaningfully its complex dimensions. The subject must attend to the specific numbers of the problem and maintain an overview so that various elements are seen in their relative positions in the problem matrix, and the interrelationship between the various elements must be manipulated in order to arrive at a solution. The tasks on the Arithmetic subtest require the subject to utilize skills that have been attained comparatively early in development and during the educational process. In this sense the subject has to turn back to prior skills and apply them to a particular task. The test also introduces time pressures for the first time, and the subject is forced to apply himself actively to the problem while reducing distracting elements from within the problem or from the total environment. Arithmetic is like Vocabulary and Information in that it depends upon memory and prior learning, but it differs markedly in the fact that it requires concentration and active application of select skills to cope with a new and unique situation.

By comparing functioning on the Digit Span and Arithmetic subtest, the relative balance between attention and concentration can be ascertained. Attention is the relatively passive and automatic reception of stimuli without effortful attempts to organize the material or to establish mnemonic devices. It is usually a one-step assimilation of a stimulus field which can be disrupted by internal preoccupations. Concentration is a more active, effortful process, and though it depends on attention to some degree, it goes beyond it in organizing and manipulating a complex series of events. The relative balance and interweaving of these two psychological functions have important implications for understanding psychological organization (Rapaport, et al., 1945). Efforts to compensate for disruptions in attention, for example, often involve extensive efforts at concentration to bolster processes which should occur in a relatively automatic way. Lapses in attention usually occur as a function of anxiety, whereas difficulties in concentration indicate more serious thought disorder. This interpretation of possible thought disorder, however, may be made only when Arithmetic and Digit Span are widely disparate. A low score solely on Arithmetic relative to Vocabulary, for example, is typically found in hysterical and narcissistic individuals who avoid active, effortful ideation and the elaboration of internal experience. The diagnostic implication of an Arithmetic score lower than Digit Span becomes all the more critical when Digit Span is higher than Vocabulary, for then it indicates a lack of anxiety and a blandness when there are difficulties in concentration (Rapaport, et al., 1945). Should both Arithmetic and Digit Span be low, as frequently occurs in anxious, unreflective hysterics (or in brain damage), impairments both in active concentration and attention are present. The differential relationship between Arithmetic and Digit Span and their relationship to the Vocabulary baseline, therefore, are most important diagnostic considerations.

Performance Subtests

Picture Arrangement.   In arranging a series of sketches into a sequence which creates a meaningful story, the subject is required to understand the inner relationships of a series of events and to grasp the essential message of social interaction. The skill necessary for seeing the inner connections between sequences of enduring, continuing, and causally related events, is really a capacity to recognize what effects one event has on the next. Meaningful continuity in everyday experiences is largely dependent on the capacity to anticipate, judge, and understand the possible antecedents and consequences of any event. Poor performance on this subtest frequently reflects an impaired capacity to anticipate events and their consequences and to plan effective courses of action (Rapaport, et al., 1945). On the other hand, subjects with cautious, guarded, hyper-alert paranoid features are frequently extremely sensitive to social events and consequent behavior and are highly involved in an attempt to anticipate the future. Their psychological orientation may be reflected in an elevation of the Picture Arrangement subtest score.

The Picture Arrangement subtest also reflects, as does the Comprehension subtest, the response to stimuli that are concerned with social interactions. These two subtests allow comparison of well-learned social conventionalities (Comprehension) with the capacity to anticipate and plan in a social context (Picture Arrangement). A profile containing high Picture Arrangement but low Comprehension scores may be seen in a character disorder where there is sensitivity to interpersonal nuances, but a disregard for social conventionality. The glib psychopath with a social facade may receive high scores on both the Comprehension and Picture Arrangement subtests. It should also be noted that Picture Arrangement is the only subtest that contains an element of humor. Frequently the inability to see the humorous aspects of life interferes with an optimum capacity to function on this subtest.

Picture Completion.   This subtest requires visual organization and the capacity to attend to and observe the inconsistencies and incongruities within a picture. One must focus attention on the details of the picture and actively examine and check the drawing, either in terms of its symmetry or in terms of an internalized image of the object. In this sense the major function seems to be, again, concentration, but in contradistinction to Arithmetic, the concentration is directed toward an externalized form and there is only minimal demand for the more internalized processes required in the Arithmetic subtest (Rapaport, et al., 1945). As in Arithmetic, the time limit is of considerable importance in placing additional demands upon the subject. The instructions of this subtest ask the subject to appraise critically and look for defects within the stimuli. Occasionally this subtest may be affected by a subject's reluctance to criticize, to assert himself, to attack actively or find fault with an aspect of his environment. The Picture Completion score will be high and frequently have positive Vocabulary scatter in paranoid subjects for whom hyper-alertness and hyper-vigilance is a prime mode of functioning. Obsessive compulsives may also have inflated scores because of their pedantic, meticulous examination of every aspect of the picture. Since the objects or people are shown in an incomplete state, a low score may reflect concerns over bodily intactness with a possible emphasis on castration concerns; a low score may also be seen as a function of passivity. Specific conflictual issues may be reflected in long delays, failures on relatively easy items, or failures involving particular content. This latter type of failure often takes the form of an emphasis on "supports" missing, e.g., someone holding a pitcher, or the flag, or else in an emphasis on people missing, e.g., no one in the rowboat. Depending on the context, missing supports may reflect feelings of helplessness and passivity and missing people may reflect feelings of estrangement from people and a need for contact.

Object Assembly.   In dealing with jigsaw puzzles, subjects are required to grasp a whole pattern by anticipating the inner relationship of the individual sections. On some items and for some subjects, anticipation of the final pattern is immediate and the task is one of simple visual-motor coordination (Wechsler, 1958). On more difficult items within the subtest, some subjects may not have immediate insight into the final pattern, in which case the subject frequently resorts to trial-and-error behavior. Bringing subparts together often furthers the progressive emergence of the total pattern, and in this press toward solution one can observe the subject's capacities for trying new leads, for shifting set, and for functioning on minimal cues. Equally important is observing the smoothness, accuracy, and rapidity of a subject's visual-motor coordination, which may express habituated and stereotyped motor actions. Also, in presenting an object which has been broken apart, we implicitly confront the subject with something dismembered. Performance on this test, therefore, is adversely and particularly affected by intense concerns over bodily integration and intactness and/or inadequate defenses against these concerns. It should be noted that on occasion blocking occurs on specific items which may also be related to conflictual issues (e.g., on the hand in subjects with concerns over aggression or masturbation).

Block Design.   In this test of visual-motor organization (Wechsler, 1958), the subject is presented with a pattern which he is asked to reconstruct out of blocks that are identical to each other in size and design. Block Design differs markedly from Object Assembly: in Object Assembly the end product must be anticipated from the part objects; in Block Design the final pattern is presented and must be broken down and then reconstructed in block size units (Rapaport, et al., 1945; Wechsler, 1958). The differentiation of a part of a design and the specification of its interrelationships with other parts is essentially a concept formation task involving both analysis and synthesis. The visual organization demanded to differentiate partially a total design and the motor action needed to integrate the blocks is frequently interfered with by central nervous system damage. Since anxiety interferes with attention to small details, performance is facilitated by the blandness and lack of anxiety frequently seen in schizoid personalities. It is important to note the procedure which the subject uses to duplicate the pattern, that is, whether it is orderly and follows along the outline of the blocks or is haphazard and goes from one section of the design to the other in a random pursuit to find the "magical" clue.

Digit Symbol. In comparison to the other performance tests, Digit Symbol is generally a measure of the capacity for imitative behavior (Rapaport, et al., 1945). It requires relatively little learning, concept formation, anticipation, planning, or analytic-synthetic functioning; rather, it involves the simple utilization of energy for a smooth and unhesitating duplication of simple patterns (Wechsler, 1958). In the past the Digit Symbol subtest was thought to be a measure of learning ability. Recent research, however, has indicated that a minimal degree of learning takes place during this task and also that few subjects rely on memory; therefore, we see the test primarily as a measure of the capacity to utilize energy in a simple task. Inasmuch as the subject is required to muster up energy and to apply it, this task reflects the amount of energy output a subject can generally bring to his work and his activities. Thus, a low Digit Symbol, markedly below Vocabulary, is frequently a sign of a depressive lack of energy output, whereas Digit Symbol above Vocabulary may be evidence of an overcompliant striving and a desire for achievement going beyond one's intellectual capacities. It is also noteworthy that this is the first subtest in which subjects are asked to write, to use a pencil. Particularly for school-age subjects this test may arouse feelings about classroom demands. Digit Symbol, when it is elevated above other Performance tests, indicates that reduced functioning in the other Performance tests may not be due to a lack of speed and low energy output, but rather to specific problems related to the unique functions tapped by these other subtests.

The relationship of Digit Symbol to Digit Span is often of particular diagnostic import. We have observed a frequent pattern in which Digit Span is relatively low and suggests considerable anxiety and Digit Symbol is relatively high and reflects a marked energy output. In these cases, the individual seems to be controlling strong and pressing anxiety by excessive activity. This activity may represent an attempt to conform and win approval and acceptance. Such passivity, conformity, and even ingratiation could be in the service of reducing the level of anxiety by minimizing the possibility of attack and criticism.

When we find the reverse pattern, a high Digit Span and a low Digit Symbol, we are usually confronted with an essentially depressed person who is attempting to ward off recognition of depressive affect perhaps in a hypomanic way, usually via denial, but not necessarily through activity and acting-out behavior.

Digit Symbol, also, like Digit Span and Block Design, deals with essentially neutral, content-less material, and it may be for this reason that some people, for example, schizophrenics, at times do especially well on these subtests despite the fact that these patients clinically may show highly anxious behavior and despite the finding that performance on these subtests is particularly vulnerable to the effects of anxiety. With such schizophrenics it is their basic blandness, their isolation from, and lack of relatedness to, their seemingly intense affects and also their heightened powers of attention and passive receptivity in contrast to their impaired concentration that is revealed through their high scores on these subtests.

Differences in Verbal and Performance IQ

In addition to evaluating the specific subtests, inferences can be obtained from the comparison of the Verbal and Performance IQs. In the Bright Normal and Superior ranges, the Verbal IQ usually tends to be a little higher than the Performance IQ, and the difference increases as the Full Scale IQ rises because marked abilities and accomplishments in one area lead to a relative de-emphasis on the development of other functions. Thus, for the highly ideational person, efficiency in motor activities will often lag behind verbal efficiency. An eight- to ten-point difference between Verbal and Performance IQs where there is, for instance, a Total IQ of 135 (e.g., Verbal IQ, 138, Performance IQ, 127, Full Scale IQ, 135) is of limited diagnostic significance and indicates only a highly verbal subject with possible obsessive-compulsive tendencies. When the Verbal IQ begins to show a marked imbalance over the Performance IQ (by greater than 15 points), more serious pathological trends may be considered. A markedly obsessive concentration on words and thoughts or an extreme variability in functioning such as might result from a psychotic condition may be apparent. Usually, however, and depending on the subtests scores, two additional possible inferences are suggested by a marked elevation of the Verbal over the Performance IQ: depression and/or central nervous system pathology. Depression often involves psychomotor retardation, and tasks with time limits and those subtests which require active manipulation tend to reflect this retardation. On the Performance scale, Digit Symbol in particular but also Object Assembly and Block Design are generally lowered. The Performance IQ is also lowered in brain-damaged patients, but rather than solely affecting subtests on which speed is an issue, brain damage involving visual-motor deficits is reflected on those Performance subtests which require planning, organization, concept formation, concentration, and attention. Block Design in particular is a difficult task for these patients, and the score on this test is usually lower than any of the other Performance subtests. Several Verbal subtests, Vocabulary and Information, are often unaffected in brain-damaged patients, since much of the material is explicitly contingent upon prior experience and has been overlearned. Thus, while there may be some decrements in the Verbal IQ of organic patients because of low scores on Digit Span, Arithmetic, and Similarities, the Verbal IQ is maintainted at a level closer to the premorbid intellectual level than is the Performance IQ.

In the lower intelligence ranges, the Performance IQ tends to be a little higher than its Verbal counterpart, largely because the emphasis on motor functioning tends to be associated with a reduced investment in ideational modes. But a Performance IQ greater than a Verbal IQ in individuals of at least average intelligence is atypical. Three major diagnostic trends, all of which have acting-out as a primary feature, are suggested by such a pattern: hysteric, narcissistic, and psychopathic character disorders. In the hysteric, the repression of impulses and impulse derivatives usually results in restriction of intellectual and cultural interests and pursuits. Functioning on the Verbal scales of the WAIS is often strikingly influenced by repression, naiveté, and inability to remember, and although hysterical women from rich cultural backgrounds may acquire a superficial cultural and intellectual veneer that can lead to an elevated Verbal IQ, this "modern" hysterical pattern still maintains much of the subtest scatter seen in the more classic hysterical states (especially the Comprehension above Information). Performance IQ is also often higher in narcissistic character disorders and in individuals with psychopathic trends (Wechsler, 1958), since these are generally "action-oriented" people who are unable to establish the delay necessary for dealing with questions requiring thought and concentration and internal elaboration. They are much more comfortable with tasks which require external manipulation and action, and thus function better on the Performance subtests. The comparison of the Verbal IQ and Performance IQ and the examination of the pattern of the subtests of the WAIS is an important step in the diagnostic process. It allows the clinician to describe the individual's unique organization of psychological functions and from this to infer the defenses, the nature and quality of the drives and impulses, the degree and type of pathology, as well as his assets and capacities for adaptation and coping.

Intra-subtest Scatter

Since each subtest of the WAIS presents items of increasing difficulty, there should be a tapering off of efficiency and accuracy. However, some test records, particularly of patients, show a certain degree of variability of passes and failures within some subtests. Occasionally this takes the form of missing easy items initially but at other times the pattern is more one of intermittent fluctuation. In general, marked intra-subtest variability indicates a considerable degree of psychological disruption due to temporary inefficiencies or to a permanent loss of capacities, such as in organic brain damage. On occasion, variability also can occur in a person with consistently disturbed school experiences where information and ways of coping with the various tasks of an intelligence test will have been acquired in a sporadic and uneven way. In hysterical patients it is usual to find variability primarily on the Information subtest since in these patients repression often serves as a general defensive orientation and serves to block out access to information even distantly associated with particular areas of conflict. Variability and disruption on Blocks and Similarities likely reflects an organically based problem as does recurrent variability throughout the tests. Epileptics, for instance, have a typical pattern of alternation of passes and fails with a waxing and waning quality usually regardless of the subtest or of the specific content of the items. An important rule of thumb in assessing the degree to which organicity is suggested by intra-subtest variability is whether the test disruptions seem unrelated to specific preoccupations of the individual. Disruptions which are unrelated to specific concerns but are more associated with general cognitive functioning occur in organically based interference with ego functioning. In schizophrenia the fluctuation is likely to be due more to areas of preoccupation, although in more chronic longstanding patients, ego efficiency may be affected in a more global way and result in poorer efficiency with some easier items. In such instances other test data may be crucial for ruling out organic brain damage.

CASE PRESENTATION

In order to illustrate the contribution of the WAIS to diagnostic assessment, sections of a WAIS protocol will be presented and discussed in terms of an analysis of the organization expressed in the subtest scores and in the content and style of the responses.[6] The patient is a 33-year-old housewife, with a history of a possible psychotic episode 13 years previously. She is described as having gradually diminished her activity outside the house in the year preceding her current hospitalization, having increased feelings of inadequacy and crying spells, showing aggression toward her husband and two children, and eating compulsively.

Her WAIS scaled scores follow:

Comprehension	16	Picture Arrangement	9
Information	14	Picture Completion	9
Digit Span	15	Block Design	9
Arithmetic	9	Object Assembly	7
Similarities	13	Digit Symbol	9
Vocabulary	15		

Verbal IQ: 121; Performance IQ: 91; Total IQ: 109

Among the outstanding aspects of these scores is the striking variability: the large discrepancy between Verbal and Performance IQs and the wide range of subtest scores (from 7 to 16). Considering her Vocabulary and other high Verbal subtest scores as a baseline, her intellectual potential would be estimated to be in the high Superior range (estimated Verbal IQ of 129). Since she obtains an overall IQ of only 109, and such low Performance subtest scores, there is obviously a marked degree of inefficiency in this woman's psychological functioning which is of at least severe neurotic degree.

A more detailed consideration of the test variability suggests specific hypotheses regarding the nature of the disturbed functioning. The discrepancy that exists between her Verbal and Performance IQs reflects a marked impairment of visual organization and visual-motor efficiency that is unlikely to occur outside of an organic condition or one of depressive retardation. Some of the test scores, however, tend to contradict the hypothesis of an organic condition: her verbal abstract thinking on Similarities and her attention span on Digit Span,

---

[6] Brief summaries of Wechsler protocols for a variety of psychological disorders are available in Allison, Blatt, and Zimet, 1967; Mayman, Schafer, and Rapaport, 1951; Schafer, 1948; Wechsler, 1958.

as well as an independent assessment of her memory efficiency do not suggest organicity. If such a Verbal-Performance discrepancy were due to organicity then it would be likely that there would be disruption of abstract thinking and attention. Inasmuch as her abstract reasoning and attention are not impaired and by qualitative observation her motor execution is not inefficient in the sense of being tremulous or uneven, the only remaining organic possibility is some visual impairment. This possibility could be evaluated further as we proceed through the WAIS and with other tests.

Because of the extent of the deficit on Performance tests there is also a strong possibility of marked depressive features. The scatter suggests, however, that the picture is not simply one of depressive energy depletion and psychomotor retardation. For the high Digit Span with its suggestion of blandness and lack of anxiety contrasts with the Performance subtests scores and indicates thereby that the depressive features may be masked and superficially defended against, probably be denial. Unlike a person who is consciously beset by anxious and depressive thoughts and feelings (as would be apparent when Digit Symbol—a test of energy output—and/or other Performance subtests are low, as well as Digit Span), this person's scatter suggests efforts to defend against pressing dysphoric concerns.

A further hypothesis which can be derived from the scatter involves the discrepancy between a high Comprehension score and the low Picture Arrangement score. This suggests an adequate adherence to conventional social judgment (high Comprehension) but an inability to act on this judgment through planning, anticipation, and organization of experience. One would hypothesize that her ability to control her experience and to set future goals is limited in comparison with her verbal judgment and that her verbal social capacities may obscure to some extent her deficiency in this regard. One would wonder therefore about an underlying psychotic process which may not be readily apparent because of her heightened awareness of appropriate versus inappropriate behavior as indicated in the high Comprehension score. The low score on Arithmetic is also conspicuous and reflects an interference with concentration which could also suggest either a psychotic process or a more narcissistic or hysterical avoidance of active, effortful ideation.

The relationship between her Comprehension and Information scores (Comprehension > Information) is consistent with the hypothesis of hysterical trends in that conventional, moral, and social knowledge takes precedence over factual information (which is more dependent on memory functioning and more subject to repression [forgetting]). Because her Information score is relatively high and is at her Vocabulary level, we would argue that this function is not disrupted and therefore the imbalance of several points in favor of Comprehension over Information suggests only minor hysterical trends.

To recapitulate: it is possible that some of the lowered Performance scores could be due to an organic visual disturbance but the primary issue is probably a depressive picture with noteworthy efforts to defend against dysphoric feelings and thoughts. A disturbance of concentration and planning ability and a marked variability of psychological functioning raises the possibility of a psychotic condition accompanied by a considerable preservation of verbal reality adherence and social conventionality. Hysterical trends are also suggested. Clearly, intellecual efficiency is interfered with markedly.

At this point we will turn to the individual subtests with these hypotheses in mind in an attempt to glean further material from the more qualitative features of the test responses and from the scatter within each subtest. Because of space limitations, the entire record will not be presented but only those responses with interpretive import will be discussed.

Information.   She misses 18, 20, 22, 23, 26, 29, reflecting a fair amount of variability which could be due to the effect of repression on overall memory efficiency. Asked the height of the average American woman, she responds correctly, "about 5'5" to 5'6"," then adds, "she's getting taller all the time, that's for sure." This response with its specific emphasis on the process of continuous growth suggests a cognitive conception that things (and one's experience) exist in a marked state of flux and transition; it also suggests in its content the conception that women—starting from a possibly smaller and inferior position—are rapidly increasing their stature. This latter conception may be an attempt to contain and ward off depression. It is stressed further by the expression "that's for sure," introducing an attempt to establish a sense of certainty into a situation of rapid changes. These hypotheses will be checked and elaborated as we proceed.

Also noteworthy in the patient's responses to the Information items is a degree of childlike, infantile expressiveness. Her responses are accompanied by mouth noises and coupled with egocentric comments ("geography is my downfall"), and expressions like "pish posh." Usually she does not recklessly guess when she is unsure of an answer; neither is she notably critical of herself or self-disparaging when she is incorrect.

Comprehension.   On the item "Why should people pay taxes?"

her response is, "In order to maintain what we have and improve what we have, and in order to pay for all the things within the bounds of the country we supposedly need." Though this response is scored 1, it is of interest because of its emphasis on maintenance and on the setting of a clear, somewhat constricted boundary to which taxes apply. This response contrasts with her response to the Information item about women's height in which the body boundary seemed rather fluid and changeable. Here the attempt rather is to set clear and even narrow limits. These two responses which are both at least partially correct are nevertheless suggestive of a certain degree of tension between two opposing modes of experience, expansive alteration versus narrow containment. Her reference to things "we supposedly need" also suggests that she is in conflict about, and is attempting to distance herself from, the intensity of her needs. Some effort at containment, in this case of impulsive action, is also apparent in her response to the "movies" item. "What I would do, I would quietly go to the manager and tell him to do something fast." Although this response receives full credit, the special emphasis on control indicated by the word "quietly," contrasts with the final appearance of the urgent action.

Her response to child labor is also of interest. "Many of us, many people might put children to work when mentally and physically they're not ready for it and could be doing far better things in their formative years." Her subtle shift from the more personal "us" to "people" more generally bespeaks of an attempt to whitewash herself belatedly of some felt injustices toward children. This may directly reflect some self-criticism in regard to the treatment of her children. It demonstrates what we hypothesized from the scatter, namely that there will be efforts to defend against pressing depressive concerns.

Another response on which she receives full credit but which contains personalized content is on the "Forest" question. "Well, if the sun sets in the west and I know I could be helped in the west, I would go, I would use the sun as a guide. I hope it is a sunny day. Or, a river can be used, follow it." Her opening remark of "Well, if the sun sets in the west . . .", suggests some uncertainty regarding the trust-worthiness and regularity of her experience. At her level of intellec-tual capacity there can be little doubt that she knows where the sun rises and sets and that the inavailability of this information reflects her feeling in a "lost" situation of being unsure about where the rising and setting of the sun occurs. She adds that she would go to the west if she knew help could be forthcoming there, which suggests her need-fulness, dependency, and confusion when faced with interpersonal isolation. This emphasis on going in the direction of the setting sun also carries the suggestion of a focus on the experiences of setting, getting low, and depressive mood. Later in the response she hopes "it is a sunny day," thereby repeating the hypothesized relationship between a depressive orientation and her efforts at defense by trying to see things as sunny and optimistic.

Her final response of note on Comprehension is to the "swallow" item. "I've never heard it before. It doesn't mean anything to me (what might it mean?). It might mean a person swimming during summer might swallow a gulp of water but he has yet to anticipate more swallows because he has lots more swimming." On the preceding question she also was initially unsure of its meaning, guessed, and closely approximated the answer. Here, however, she personalizes her answer entirely. She construes the swallow as an oral intake and the orality is essentially of a disturbing nature. Thus, despite the fact that the context is a potentially pleasant summer scene a noteworthy dysphoric oral theme intrudes. Once again, as suggested in the scatter, we see a coupling of a depressive theme with an attempt to defend against it by denial (emphasizing the positive, pleasant, hopeful, abundant). Implicitly there is a suggestion of death (suicide?) by drowning. Her defensive efforts at denial are unsuccessful in that she is unable to sustain a pleasant image without letting the depressive theme intrude. The peculiar and somewhat illogical quality of her answer suggests the possibility of psychotic thinking which she is attempting to contain, as suggested by her initial attempts to avoid responding.

Arithmetic. She misses the 10th, 12th, 13th, and 14th questions. She gets 10 when asked to check her response and gets 13 overtime. During the harder questions she immediately and consistently protests her inability to figure out the problems stating that she gives up; but with outside pressure she relents and attempts to solve the problems. Her failures on this subtest thus seem compounded by avoidance of effortful application and hastiness.

Similarities. Several responses are of special interest. To the question, how are air and water alike, she replies, "Free, no that's not the way. Nature's elements. (What did you mean by free?) There are boundless quantities of air and water, salt water anyway . . . yeah, fresh water too." This response recalls earlier concerns with expansive, limitless activity (the growing women, the continuous swimmer). Here the expansive quality is especially prominent; the "boundless quantities" smack of unlimited supplies and are consistent with the defense by denial this patient is employing against her depressive ideas and feelings seen previously, especially in the Swallow item of Comprehension. The effort to present experience as pleasurable, full, and satisfying was noted previously, It is a constellation typically found in a hypomanic patient; that is, an emphasis, usually driven, on those qualities of experience directly in opposition to depression: fullness versus emptiness, energy versus apathy, feeding versus needing to be fed, happy versus sad, innocent versus guilty.

The next response of interest is an incorrect answer and is to poem and statue. "I guess durability, no . . . a beautiful poem and a beautiful statue, enduring; a tribute to, it might be." It is noteworthy that she introduces the concept of durability, of lasting and not wearing out. It reflects a personalized depressive preoccupation with fantasies of death and with what is fleeting or lasting, transient or permanent both regarding her experience of outer reality and her inner resources. On the "taxes" item in Comprehension it will be recalled that she emphasized maintenance and improvement of "what we have," which suggested a similar concern. Consider that there has been an equivalent highlighting of the theme of freedom, boundlessness, and flux which seems an aspect of her hypomanic strivings. The instability of her defenses is again indicated in this case in the expressed depressive fear of wearing out (possibly as regards her age, energy, and attractiveness). Again it is of note that her depressive concerns are juxtaposed with the beauty and attractiveness of the poem and statue and that the sequence of defensive efforts is to deny the initial depressive statement by the emphasis on beauty.

Also noteworthy is her response to fly and tree. "They're nature's, nature's that's all. (What do you mean?) They're something man isn't responsible for, something nature created, not man created." Her intent is to say they are not created by man but her statement about man's responsibility introduces a theme of moral responsibility. In an earlier response she seemed to show concern with injustice toward children. This is an additional reflection of guilty concerns which are verbalized, then modified and backed away from. Her defense, therefore, is shaky in that these concerns are not totally blocked out and instead they break through and only secondarily are defended against.

Picture Completion.   Her failures consist of two responses which she correctly got overtime, several on which she sees supports missing (e.g., no hand holding the pitcher), and some on which she does not see anything missing. Her functioning therefore is made up of ideational retardation, avoidance, and a thematic trend emphasizing need for support. Thus, there is again some suggestion of a breakthrough of depressive feelings.

Block Design.   Her asides are of interest here. Early in this subtest she states, "Oh, this would be great for the kids." A little later she appears very excited and very childlike, and finally after the last design, the third in a series of failures because of a too bold approach (using full color blocks to make stripes instead of red-white ones), she ends by stating "I'm exhausted, truly . . ." Her aside about the meaning of this subtest for children suggests that she may use the maternal posture as part of the denial of needfulness and depression. Her comment about energy depletion is in contrast to her excited, energetic behavior during much of the test and it reveals the driven quality of her energy output and the underlying depression. It is of further interest that she is able to do all ten Block Designs correctly but the last three were completed after she had considerably exceeded the time limits.

Picture Arrangement.   She has some mild difficulty on the 5th item and feels she "must be awfully thick." This aside is another bit of evidence suggesting self-depreciation and depression. Later on the 7th item her interpretation about the story of the king fishing includes the notion that "someone was stocking the pond." The help to the king is seen by her therefore as indirect.

Her interpretation of the last story—her order is incorrect but close—is that the man brings the bust close to him because of a "sense of propriety" rather than a desire to protect the bust. The emphasis therefore as previously in the WAIS, is holding on to what one has and of concern with proper behavior.

As for the rest of the test, her behavior remains consistently excited, jovial, yet complaining and externalizing blame for difficulties. Expressions like "pish posh," "crazy, man, crazy," and "come on fellows, this is silly," are characteristic. Her externalization of blame is an alternate to clearly stated self-blame in other instances and to the concerns with guilt (injustices and responsibility). We would add to her defensive maneuvers the use of projection; but as with most of her current defenses it is unstable and does not ward off a sense of inner disturbance.

Vocabulary.   At one point in this subtest she asks, "Where's Webster?" and when defining "tangible," she demonstrates with her hands and adds, "What would I do without hands?" The need of support and a concern with loss suggested in Picture Completion is reiterated and the explicit theme of body damage (castration) is added, which in retrospect is supported by the fact that Object Assembly was her lowest subtest.

An additional feature of her test performance involves the question of whether a visual disturbance affects her functioning on Performance subtests. There is little in the qualitative features of the tests to indicate a particular visual disturbance. Instead there is often a slowing down of her visual-motor efficiency, which is consistent with the depressive orientation. Fluctuations of mood are probable in the clinical picture because of the unstable appearance of both defense against depression and the occasional emergence of dysphoric ideation. Hypomanic trends appear to be prominent but mild projective trends are also noted. The marked disruption of functioning along with disturbances in concentration (Arithmetic) and anticipation and planning (Picture Arrangement), and the peculiar verbalization to the Swallow item of Comprehension suggests that the patient is probably functioning at best at a borderline psychotic level but this would have to be clarified by material from other sources.

This case illustrates how a systematic analysis of the cognitive processes assessed in the relatively neutral and well-structured context of the WAIS can make a significant contribution to the process of clinical assessment. Rather than being concerned with whether the profile of scores was most similar to the pattern of one diagnostic group or another, an attempt was made to understand the relative efficiency of a number of psychological functions and how these were integrated into unified and organized modes of functioning. The organization of the various psychological functions could have been highly congruent with a standard diagnostic category or it could have involved several types or levels of organization indicating either a complex interaction of Several levels of defense and impulse or that the patient is in the process of transition to a higher or lower level of functioning.[7] The full contribution of the WAIS to clinical assessment, however, depends on careful observation of the processes through which the individual copes with the various tasks and upon a careful analysis of the content and organization of the individual's verbatim responses.[8]

[7]The differentiation of whether a patient is in the process of reintegration or is in danger of potential regression is a complex clinical problem which requires utilizing data from the entire battery of psychological tests.
[8]Extended recording forms and memorization of the instructions for the entire test can enable the clinician to be more available in the clinical transaction.

REVIEW OF RECENT RESEARCH

The preceding analysis of the WAIS protocol also highlights some of the difficulties encountered in attempting to test the process of clinical inference. Though independent clinical material, including additional test data, supports many of the inferences and formulations made from the WAIS, there still remains the critical question of the validity of the conclusions drawn. Disagreement between judges (lack of reliability) can be a function of differences in level of training or orientation. If nosological categories are used as the validating criteria in a research design, should this patient be considered severely neurotic, psychotic, or borderline with both neurotic and psychotic features? Should she be considered a hypomanic patient, and if so, is it clearly understood and accounted for in the research design that this also implies strong underlying depressive features? The suggestion in the material of subtle hysterical and projective trends adds yet another complication in classifying this patient and in defining adequate control groups.

Various tests in the clinical battery evaluate, at least in part, different levels of functioning, and a lack of agreement could represent variations in functioning at different levels of organization as well as suggesting inconsistencies. In the latter case, the question remains: Which segment of the clinical data (interviews or which of the various tests) does one use as the validating criterion?

Rather than attempting to test the final diagnostic formulations of the total clinical protocol, research can be directed at testing individual assumptions made about the various segments of the protocol. This testing of individual assumptions can be made either in a clinical or in an experimental setting. For example, one of the bits of evidence for the formulation of hypomania in the preceding case was the marked imbalance between Digit Span and Digit Symbol. Clinically this has been observed in other cases where denial was a predominant defense mechanism, and denial is theoretically expected to be a major defense in hypomania. The hypothesis about the relationship of the Digit Span to Digit Symbol and about denial as a defense mechanism can be evaluated independently by selecting Ss with this Digit Span–Digit Symbol pattern from the general population or from clinical files. Major difficulties, however, will be the selection and definition of an acceptable independent criterion measure of denial and of adequate control groups.

Despite these and other methodological problems, a great deal of research has been conducted on the role of the intelligence test in clinical settings.[9] Research has included comparisons of the extent of scatter in various pathological groups, attempts to identify specific responses or patterns characteristic of types of psychopathology, and attempts to test underlying assumptions of the various subtests in a variety of ways, including the use of experimentally induced affect states such as anxiety or depression. Generally the research on the subtest scatter has offered little support for the assumption that the simple range or extent of scores is a consistent aid in differential diagnosis. Attempts have also been made to study the concept of differential scatter as presented by Wechsler (1944) and elaborated extensively by Rapaport, Gill, and Schafer (1945), but the results have been mostly contradictory and inconclusive.

As pointed out by Rabin (1965), one of the major stumbling blocks in attempting to evaluate the hypotheses about selective impairment and scatter may be the persistent use of nosological or diagnostic categories as validating criteria. Many problems exist in the use of nosological concepts in clinical research. Studies often use these classifications as if there is a universal agreement about the conceptual definition of the categories. Rarely do investigators indicate their criteria; schizophrenia, for example, is rarely defined or differentiated from other psychotic states. The frequent wide variation in the definition of diagnostic categories is highlighted by the fact that there can be sharp disagreement about definitions and criteria within a single clinical facility.

Even if there were essential agreement about the conceptual basis, these criteria are frequently applied with varying degrees of precision. It is unusual for a research paper to specify the degree of reliability between judges or even simply to indicate how the diagnostic classifications were established. One rarely has a basis for knowing whether a diagnostic classification was established as an admitting diagnosis by a first-year trainee or resident after a brief 20 minute interview or whether it was the considered and joint opinion of a diagnostic council after weeks of intensive study of the patient. With such poorly defined criteria, frequently applied in imprecise ways,

[9]Reviews of the research literature on the Wechsler scales are available in many sources (e.g., Anastasi, 1961; Cronbach, 1960; Guertin, Rabin, Frank, & Ladd, 1962; Littell, 1960; Rabin, 1965). Therefore this review will present primarily recent studies (since 1960) not covered in earlier reviews. There is also extensive literature on the Wechsler scales and central nervous system damage (e.g., Reitan, Heilbrun), but this will not be included in the present paper.

there is little surprise that the research with diagnostic categories has lead to ambiguous findings. The number of studies attempting to compare organics, schizophrenics, character disorders, neurotics, hospital attendants or nurses, and college students are by now legion. These studies continue despite the fact that there is increasing disillusionment with current diagnostic categories which are, at best, a gross classification system. Usually in clinical work, diagnostic assessment involves a dynamic formulation which includes several levels of psychological organization which transcend any single category. Rather than searching for specific patterns for diagnostic categories, a more productive line of research may be to test systematically the assumptions about the processes assessed by individual subtests and how they are organized into consistent modes of functioning. Specification of the individual processes assessed by the subtests and their interrelationships and organization may in turn lead to more meaningful and precise conceptualizations of psychopathology. This approach does not have to be limited to test scores—it can also include qualitative aspects, such as the style of verbalization, content of responses, the tone of the clinical transaction, and the individual's attitudes toward his performance.

There is a trend in recent research to move away from a comparison of diagnostic groups and instead to study the processes assessed by each of the subtests and their relationships to more general psychological organizations. Typical of this trend is the research on measures of anxiety on the Wechsler scales. Much research has been devoted to examining the hypothesis that Digit Span, as a measure of attention, is disrupted by anxiety. One group of studies includes research on patients with varying diagnoses such as anxiety neurosis, anxiety state, or anxiety reaction (e.g., Gilhooly, 1950; Lewinski, 1945; Rashkis & Welch, 1946; Warner, 1950), and these studies have offered little support for the hypothesis that Digit Span is impaired by anxiety. Another group of studies attempted to evaluate this hypothesis by correlating Digit Span performance with traditional anxiety scales, and the results have been contradictory. Many studies have found no consistent relationship between the Taylor Scale and Wechsler scores (e.g., Dana, 1957; Goodstein & Farber, 1957; Matarazzo, 1955) while others report positive findings (e.g., Siegman, 1956; Jurjevich, 1963). A recent and interesting approach has been the attempt to evaluate the hypothesis that Digit Span measures attention as defined as the "effortless, passive, unhampered contact with outside reality . . . a free receptivity" (Rapaport, et al., 1945). Guertin (1959) and Craddick and Grossman (1962) studied the effects of distraction upon Digit Span and neither auditory nor visual distraction seems to affect significantly Digit Span performance. But as pointed out by Allen (1962), both these studies used "external distractors" which may not be the same as internal distraction and anxiety. Maupin and Hunter (1966) attempted, in several ways, to test the hypothesis that Digit Span measures attention, including studying the relationship of Digit Span to subliminal receptivity. Their findings, however, have not supported the hypothesis that Digit Span is related to attention. These studies (Craddick & Grossman, 1962; Guertin, 1959; Maupin & Hunter, 1966) represent an attempt to approach the problem more systematically, first by investigating the assumption that Digit Span assesses attention and if this is supported, then proceeding to investigate the relationship between attention and anxiety.

Another group of studies represents the attempt to induce anxiety experimentally and to study its effects on performance. Though the studies in this approach also present discrepant findings, a number of studies offer some support for the hypothesis that Digit Span is disrupted by anxiety (e.g., Capretta & Berkun, 1962; Griffiths, 1958; Moldowsky & Moldowsky, 1952; Walker & Spence, 1964; Wright 1954). A recent experiment (Sherman & Blatt, 1966) studied Digit Span, Digit Symbol, and Vocabulary performance after experiences of success or failure were induced by presenting anagrams at two levels of difficulty and by intially misinforming Ss as to peer group norms. Consistent with the findings of a pilot study, Digit Span was comparatively elevated after the experience with difficult anagrams. Vocabulary seemed to be relatively unaffected by the experimental manipulation, but Digit Symbol, like Digit Span, was elevated after the failure experience. The result with Digit Symbol, a measure of speed and energy output, could indicate that the experience of the failure increased Ss' involvement in the experiment; that is, both Digit Span and Digit Symbol were elevated because of increased effort and investment in performance. A failure manipulation may cause varying degrees of distress and/or anxiety. Depending upon the meaning of failure for the individual, it may either disrupt or facilitate performance. In this regard, the study by Walker and Spence (1964) found reduction in Digit Span only in those Ss, who reported being distressed by the experimental manipulation. (They were told that they had been selected because of questionable academic performance.) In subsequent research on Digit Span and experimentally induced anxiety, it seems important to assess the predisposition for becoming anxious, to differentiate which Ss are made anxious by the procedures, and to differentiate Ss who may be able to manage anxiety and improve their performance from Ss who may be disrupted by the experience.

Within the Digit Span subtest, Ss usually remember one or two more digits foward than they remember digits backward. A secondary hypothesis about Digit Span is that digits-backward equal to, or greater than, digits-forward, reflects negativism. In a recent study (Fox & Blatt, 1965) three groups of Ss were selected from clinical files: (1) a group which had digits-forward one or two greater than digits-backward; (2) a group in which digits-forward were equal to digits-backward; and (3) a group in which digits-forward were two less than digits-backward. Ss were also selected so that the three groups were matched on age, sex, and Total IQ, and they included in- and outpatients ranging in diagnosis from neurotic to psychotic but did not include any Ss in whom there were questions of organicity or mental retardation. A significant relationship was found between the extent to which digits-backward exceeded digits-forward and two Rorschach expressions of negativism: the number of white space responses (S) and the number of responses with rare detail (Dr). This significant relationship between independent and assumed expressions of negativism on the Wechsler and Rorschach lends support to the hypothesis that digits-backward superior to digits-forward is a possible indication of negativism; this aspect of Digit Span needs more study.

There have been two lines of research which support the hypothesis that Digit Symbol primarily assesses psychomotor speed. Several studies report that Digit Symbol production is unrelated to the extent to which the symbols are learned (Burik, 1950; Luchins & Luchins, 1953). Recently, Murstein and Leipold (1961) found that Digit Symbol performance did not correlate with group tests of intelligence and achievement but did correlate significantly with tests of motor ability. A second line of investigation with Digit Symbol has been based on the assumption that psychomotor speed reflects Ss' willingness to exert energy on a simple imitative task and that, as such it can reflect a degree of motivation for achievement. Several studies report an elevation of Digit Symbol subsequent to failure experience (Gallahar, 1964; Sherman & Blatt, 1966). Wachtel and Blatt (1965) found significantly greater Digit Symbol production in Ss who were in the upper third of their college class, but equal in overall intelligence (as measure by WAIS Vocabulary and by College Boards) to Ss in the lower third of the class. In contrast to the positive relationship of Digit Symbol to achievement motivation, several studies (Matarazzo & Phillips, 1955; Goodstein & Farber, 1957; Wachtel & Blatt, 1965) report no relationship between Digit Symbol and anxiety. Sarason and Minard (1962) also found no relationship between Test Anxiety and Digit Symbol production. They did find, however, that "achievement orienting instructions" (threat of failure) elevated Digit Symbol production in Test Anxious women but lowered it in Test Anxious men. This is consistent with the other studies (Gallahar, 1964; Sherman & Blatt, 1966) which also found an elevation in Digit Symbol after failure instructions.

In addition to the few studies which suggest that Digit Symbol assesses energy output and a motivation for achievement, several studies have been conducted on some qualitative aspects of Digit Symbol performance. Levine, Glass, and Meltzoff (1957) found that the number of "N" reversals on the Digit Symbol was significantly related to intelligence and to the capacity to delay a response. This is consistent with the findings of Wolfson and Weltman (1963), who found that short-term planners (students who applied very late for admission to nursing school) made more errors on Digit Symbol than students who applied early for admission. The study by Wachtel and Blatt (1965), which found a positive relationship between academic performance and Digit Symbol performance, also attempted to examine whether differences between high- and low-achieving Ss was a function of differences in psychomotor speed on Digit Symbol or whether there were also differences in the deployment of energy. Manifold carbon papers, placed under the Digit Symbol form, made it possible to measure the pressure which a subject exerted while writing the symbols. Low-achieving Ss not only completed fewer symbols but they also pressed harder. Thus, the difference in the Digit Symbol was not only a function of speed but also seemed to be a difference in the capacity to direct energy into adaptive endeavors and to restrict relatively undefined and poorly directed efforts (Wachtel & Blatt, 1965).

The Picture Completion subtest requires concentration on a stimulus with careful noting of subtle details and a willingness to comment on inconsistencies and defects in the picture. A factor analysis of the WAIS Picture Completion items (Saunders, 1960) reports three major factors in Picture Completion performance: a maintenance of contact, a maintenance of perspective, and the effect of uncertainty. Saunders concludes that these three factors support the distinction made by Rapaport and colleagues (1945) that failures can result from "increased distance from the picture," "a loss of distance," and where uncertainty causes seeking of information rather than concentration on the item. There has also been a study of the types of errors made on Picture Completion items (Wolfson & Weltman, 1960) which found that patients, particularly psychotic patients, made more unique errors. Wiener (1957) found a positive relationship between a distrustful attitide and the response of "nothing missing" to the Picture Completion items. The total scores for Picture Completion and Vocabulary, however, were not significantly lower for the distrustful group. The fact that distrustful Ss did no worse on Picture Completion is consistent with Rapaport's formulation (1945) that distrustful or suspicious Ss may function effectively on Picture Completion because of their tendency to be hyper-alert to subtle cues and details.

Both Wechsler (1944) and Rapaport and co-workers (1945) agree that the Object Assembly test is essentially a test of visual motor organization. Rapaport and co-workers (1945) reports that Object Assembly can be impaired by depression and/or anxiety. Studies have examined the relationship of Object Assembly to anxiety (Griffiths, 1958; Hafner, Pollie, & Wapner, 1960; Matarazzo, 1955) or to brain damage (Balthazar, 1963; Fisher, 1958; Penfield & Milner, 1958) and the findings are inconsistent. A more recent study (Blatt, Allison, & Baker, 1965), however, indicates that Object Assembly can be disrupted by intense body concerns. Object Assembly scores were significantly lower in children with intense body concerns than in a control group, and there were no significant differences between these two groups on any other WISC subtest. In addition, a group of adult patients with Object Assembly as the highest or second highest subtest were compared with a group comparable in age, sex, and Total IQ, but whose Object Assembly was the lowest or second lowest Wechsler subtest. The group with low Object Assembly had a significantly greater percentage of Rorschach responses indicating intense body concerns (e.g., anatomical, blood, sex, x-ray responses). These findings suggest that Object Assembly may be affected by anxiety which is centered around the particular issue of body intactness. Considering that the objects presented in the Wechsler Object Assembly are primarily dismembered parts involving a specific content, that is, whole bodies and parts of bodies, it seems likely that the items stimulate preconscious thought about body concerns. In subsequent research it would be of interest to examine whether the relationship between Object Assembly and body concerns is a function of the content of the items or whether the relationship exists with dismembered objects of a more neutral content.

The major contribution in the study of the relationship of Block Design to personality has been the work of Witkin and his colleagues on field independence. Witkin (1965) has found the Block Design, with its demand for analytic thinking, to be highly correlated with measures of field independence. The wide range of variables related to field independence are consistent with clinical assumptions that Block Design assesses the capacity for abstract thought. Field independence has been found to relate to a preference for the ideational and conceptual rather than for the sensory, to a tendency to use isolation as a defense as compared to repression and denial, and for a tendency to be less influenced by and less aware of people (Witkin, 1965). Thus, an elevation in Block Design, as compared to other Performance subtests, might be expected in over-ideational individuals and clinically in patients with obsessive and/or paranoid features. Conversely, hysterical features (e.g., use of repression and denial, a heightened social conventionality, memory inefficiencies) would be one alternative suggested by a relatively low Block Design. Sarason and Minard (1962) report a significant negative relationship between Test Anxiety and Block Design scores.

The Picture Arrangement subtest is considered by Wechsler (1944) and Rapaport and colleagues (1945) to assess social judgment, and Rapaport and colleagues thought that it also requires the capacity for anticipation and planning. Several tests of the hypothesis that Picture Arrangement requires a capacity for anticipation and planning have been conducted with findings which consistently support this assumption. In one study (Dickstein & Blatt, 1966) Picture Arrangement was used to investigate the relationship between the degree of conscious concern and preoccupation with death and temporal experience. It was assumed that when death is not a predominant concern, an individual will perceive himself as a participant in life and his temporal experience will extend further into the future. College males, equal in overall intelligence (Vocabulary) but in the upper or lower quartile on a questionnaire about degree of conscious concern about death, were compared on the WAIS Picture Arrangement and on a story-completion technique. Low death-concern subjects had significantly higher Picture Arrangement scores, and their story completions had greater future time perspective than did the high death-concern group. An alternative explanation for the significant relationship between death-concern and lower Picture Arrangement could be that a depressive psychomotor retardation in the high death-concern Ss caused them to lose time bonus points on the Picture Arrangement. This was not the case, however, for low death-concern Ss gained only a total of 11 time bonus points as compared to 10 time bonus points gained by the high death-concern group and no points were lost in either group for exceeding time limits. The lower Picture Arrangement scores of high death-concern Ss, therefore, seems to be a function of a restriction in their capacity for anticipation and planning.

In a second study (Dickstein & Blatt, 1967), a significant and positive relationship was found between Picture Arrangement performance and future time perspective in stories told to TAT cards and to the stems of a story-completion technique. A third study (Blatt & Quinlan, 1967) studied punctual and procrastinating students, selected on the basis of when in the semester they met course requirements. The two groups of students did not differ on measures of general intelligence (Vocabulary and College Board Scores), college grades, and the number of extracurricular activities. The procrastinating students, however, were significantly different on a number of temporal parameters. They had lower Picture Arrangement scores and less future time perspective in stories told to story stems, and they reported greater concern and preoccupation with death than did the punctual group. The significant differences between punctual and procrastinating subjects as well as the findings in the prior two studies support the hypothesis that the Picture Arrangement, at least in part, assesses the degree to which the capacity for anticipation and planning is impeded.

Another aspect of the Picture Arrangement is the fact that the items all deal with social interactions. The performance on this subtest therefore can reflect the degree of involvement in and appreciation for issues in social situations. A study by Schill (1966) offers some support for this assumption. High and low introverts were selected on the basis of the MMPI Social Isolation scale and Ss who were considered social introverts had significantly lower Picture Arrangement scores.

Differences between Verbal and Performance IQ have been examined in a number of studies of individuals with a history of antisocial behavior. Though earlier studies (e.g., Fields, 1960; Foster, 1959) failed to confirm the significant elevation of Performance IQ reported by Diller (1955) and by Wiens, Matarazzo, and Gavor (1959), later studies (e.g., Corotto, 1961; Craddick, 1961; Fisher, 1961; Frost & Frost, 1962; Kaiser, 1964; Manne, Kandel, & Rosenthal, 1962) have all found significant elevation of Performance IQ over the Verbal IQ in antisocial disorders. These later studies, which found Performance IQ greater than Verbal IQ in acting-out individuals, were conducted primarily with adolescents while the earlier studies which did not support the hypothesis (e.g., Fields, 1960), were conducted with adults. The findings that Performance IQ is greater than Verbal IQ in acting-out seem to be very consistent in adolescents, while with adults the findings are more equivocal (Kingsley, 1960). Some of the inconsistency in the findings with adults may be a function of the attempt to differentiate psychopaths from nonpsychopaths (e.g.,

Clark & Moore, 1950; Craddick, 1961; Gurvitz, 1950). In these studies, psychopathic prisoners did not differ significantly from nonpsychopathic prisoners in the extent to which Performance IQ exceeded Verbal IQ. But in most of these studies, the prisoners as a total group had a Performance IQ which was significantly higher than their Verbal IQ. It may be more appropriate to consider Performance IQ greater than the Verbal IQ as indicating a tendency toward acting-out and antisocial behavior which can occur in several types of patients, not just in psychopaths.

A Verbal IQ significantly greater than Performance IQ, on the other hand, has been reported in Yeshiva University students (Levinson, 1959) who, as a group, were considered to be somewhat over-ideational with little tendency for impulsive action.

Though there has been considerable research on the Performance subtests, relatively little research has been conducted on the Verbal Scales other than Digit Span. Several recent studies (e.g., Kaspar, 1958; Ginnett & Moran, 1964) offer further support for the relative stability of the Vocabulary subtest as compared to the other Wechsler scales. Though Vocabulary may decline somewhat with test anxiety (Sarason & Minard, 1962) and in severe organic and functional disturbances (e.g., Blatt, 1959; Rabin, King, & Ehrmann, 1955), possibly in part because of the demand for precise verbalization, Vocabulary remains relatively stable as compared with other WAIS subtests. As such, it offers, in most cases, a reasonable estimate of general intelligence which can serve as a baseline when considering the relative efficiency of the other subtests.

An item analysis of the Information subtest (Norman & Wilensky, 1961) found that schizophrenics, as compared to a large sample of normals, had significantly greater difficulty on eight Information items which seemed to require reasoning rather than pure recall. This suggests support for the assumption (Rapaport, et al., 1945) that schizophrenics have relatively greater difficulty with complex cognitive tasks which require concentration and reasoning.

There has been little research, however, which has investigated the assumption that the Information scale reflects intellectual strivings and ambition. This hypothesis could be studied systematically if the Information subtest were compared in subjects equal to one another in Total IQ (and other control variables) but who varied on independent measures of their emphasis on intellectual achievement and academic strivings.

Two recent studies offer some support for the assumption that the

Comprehension subtest assesses social competence and responsibility. Kippner (1964) reported a significant positive correlation between Comprehension and the Vineland Social Age. The sample in this study was limited and this relationship should be examined further in other samples and with other criteria of social competence. Another study (Hunt, Quay, & Walker, 1966) reported a significant negative correlation between judgments, by clinicians, of an individual's antisocial tendencies and their performance on the Comprehension subtest.

Janet Spence (1963) studied patterns of response to the WAIS Similarities. Brain-damaged patients made fewer conceptual responses, while schizophrenics were more likely to try to respond or to deny that the items were similar than to admit that they did not know. Contradictory findings in one respect, however, have been reported by Watson (1965), who found that schizophrenics, compared to organics, tended not to attempt to respond when uncertain.

Arithmetic seems to have been relatively neglected in terms of recent research, despite Rapaport's (1945) observation that the capacity for concentration demanded by this test can be disrupted by thought disorder. In clinical practice and research with the Arithmetic subtest, it is useful to distinguish between types of errors which occur. Errors can be simple careless computational mistakes (such as multiplying rather than dividing) or the errors can reflect more extensive confusion and an inability to maintain an adequate focus while transforming and manipulating numbers during the various operations of the problem. These two errors can frequently be identified by asking the individual how he arrived at his answer. A factor analysis of the Information and Arithmetic subtests (Saunders, 1960) offers support for differentiating these two groups of errors in the Arithmetic subtest. Saunders found two major factors: a "numerical information" factor and a factor of "numerical operations." It is the latter factor which Saunders interprets as possibly assessing "ideational discipline" or "concentration."

In conclusion, the recent research on the WAIS has shifted away from an interest in signs and patterns associated with particular diagnostic groups to an investigation of the psychological processes assessed by the subtests. Though a few studies using nosological categories as a research criterion have offered interesting and consistent findings, there has been a move toward considering the Wechsler scales in a broader context and toward using more reliable and more precisely defined criteria.

Much of the recent research has evolved from the conceptualization that the WAIS assesses a variety of ego functions, all of which play important roles in adaptation. This ego psychological model has not only contributed to a redefinition and a redirection in research, but as discussed earlier in this chapter, it has made an extensive contribution to clinical practice as well. Rather than viewing psychopathology in terms of discrete and mutually exclusive categories, psychologists can consider individuals according to the variations in the level of efficiency of a number of ego functions. This assessment of ego functions on the WAIS must be integrated with assessment on other procedures which study these and other functions under different conditions and varying degrees of external structure. By assessing the efficiency of ego functions in a variety of conditions, the relative efficiency of each function can be specified—that is, the conditions under which particular ego functions are likely to have a predominant role in adaptation and how and when inefficiencies of specific ego functions might be most manifest. Thus, the organization of psychological processes is conceptualized in a hierarchical fashion with a primary level of organization having secondary features which may be expressed and utilized in different contexts and under different conditions. This type of evaluation and psychological assessment is no longer based primarily upon manifest behavior such as symptom formation, but stems from a consideration of dynamic issues and of the structural organization of psychological functions of the individual. The organization of psychological functions may be congruent with classic diagnostic categories such as obsessive-compulsive neurosis or hysteria, but it is more likely to be a blend of several levels of organization which transcend any specific diagnostic category.

The enumeration of the relative efficiency of the various ego functions from the scatter of subtest scores may seem to be done in a somewhat mechanical fashion, but this is only a preliminary step in clinical assessment. In order to specify how the ego functions are organized into consistent modes of adaptation, the analysis of the variations in ego functions must be integrated with an understanding of the concerns and preoccupations expressed in the content of the responses and in the quality and nature of the clinical transaction. It is the specification of the principles which organize these various facets of the consistent modes of adaptation which requires extensive clinical experience.

Though there is extensive theory and clinical experience with the WAIS, there is a marked discontinuity between the level of clinical experience and theory with the WAIS and much of the research.

Earlier research has generally offered little support for the clinical application of the WAIS and for the basic assumptions about the relationships between cognitive processes and personality. More recent research has been somewhat more encouraging, but there are still many basic assumptions that are made in clinical practice which need systematic investigation. There are also many important clinical observations with the WAIS which should contribute to the further clarification of the integral role that cognitive processes have in personality organization. Research with the WAIS should not only contribute to a refinement of clinical practice but it should also add understanding and knowledge about cognitive processes and how the various ego functions such as memory, perception, concept formation, visual-motor organization, anticipation, and planning are integrated into a variety of modes of adaptation, some limiting and distorting and others allowing for growth and for creative and constructive expression.

REFERENCES

Allen, R. M. The real question in Digit Span performance. *Psychol. Rep.*, 1962, 11, 218.

Allison, J., Blatt, S. J., & Zimet, C. N. *The Interpretation of Psychological Tests.* New York: Harper and Row, 1967.

Anastasi, Anne. *Psychological Testing*, 2nd ed. New York: Macmillan, 1961.

Balthazar, E. E. Cerebral unilateralization in chronic epileptic cases: The Wechsler Object Assembly subtest. *J. Clin. Psychol.*, 1963, 19, 169–171.

Blatt, S. J. Recall and recognition vocabulary: implications for intellectual deterioration. *AMA Arch. Gen. Psychiat.*, 1959, 1, 473–476.

Blatt, S. J., Allison, J., & Baker, B. L. The Wechsler Object Assembly subtest and bodily concerns. *J. Consult. Psychol.*, 1965, 29, 223–230.

Blatt, S. J., & Quinlan, P. Punctual and procrastinating students: a study of temporal parameters. *J. Consult. Psychol.*, 1967, 31, 169–174.

Burik, T. E. Relative roles of the learning and motor factors in the Digit Symbol subtest. *J. Psychol.*, 1950, 30, 33–42.

Capretta, P. J. & Berkun, M. M. Validity and reliability of certain measures of psychological stress. *Psychol. Rep.*, 1962, 10, 875–878.

Clark, J. H., & Moore, J. H. The relationship of Wechsler-Bellevue patterns of psychiatric diagnosis of Army and Air Force prisoners. *J. Consult. Psychol.*, 1950, 14, 493–495.

Corotto, L. V. The relation of performance to verbal IQ in acting out juveniles. *J. Psychol. Stud.*, 1961, 21, 162–164.

Craddick, R. A. Wechsler-Bellevue IQ scores of psychopathic and non-psychopathic prisoners. *J. Psychol. Stud.*, 1961, 12, 167–172.

Craddick, R. A., & Grossman, K. Effects of visual distraction upon the WAIS Digit Span. *Psychol. Rep.*, 1962, *10*, 642.

Cronbach, L. J. *Essentials of Psychological Testing*, 2nd ed. New York: Harper, 1960.

Dana, R. H. Manifest anxiety, intelligence and psychopathology. *J. Consult. Psychol.*, 1957, *21*, 38–40.

Dickstein, L. S., & Blatt, S. J. Death concern, futurity, and anticipation. *J. Consult. Psychol.*, 1966, *30*, 11–17.

Dickstein, L. S., & Blatt, S. J. The WAIS Picture Arrangement subtest as a measure of anticipation. *J. Proj. Tech. Pers. Assess.*, 1967, *31*, 32–38.

Diller, Judith C. A comparison of the test performances of male and female juvenile delinquents. *J. Genet. Psychol.*, 1955, *86*, 217–236.

Fenichel, O. *The Psychoanalytic Theory of Neurosis*. New York: Norton 1945.

Fields, J. G. The Performance-Verbal IQ discrepance in a group of sociopaths. *J. Clin. Psychol.*, 1960, *16*, 321–322.

Fisher, G. C. Selective and differentially accelerated intellectual dysfunction in specific brain damage. *J. Clin. Psychol.*, 1958, *14*, 395–398.

Fisher, G. M. Discrepancy in Verbal and Performance IQ in adolescent sociopaths. *J. Clin. Psychol.*, 1961, *17*, 60.

Foster, A. L. A note concerning the intelligence of delinquents. *J. Clin. Psychol.*, 1959, *15*, 78–79.

Fox, Elizabeth, & Blatt, S. J. WAIS Digits backwards and forwards and Rorschach white space responses. Unpublished manuscript, 1965.

Fromm, Erika. Projective aspects of intelligence testing. In A. I. Rabin & Mary R. Haworth (Eds.). *Projective Techniques with Children*. New York: Grune and Stratton, 1960.

Fromm, Erika, & Hartman, Lenore D. *Intelligence: A Dynamic Approach*. Garden City, N.Y.: Doubleday, 1955.

Fromm, Erika, Hartman, Lenore D. & Marschak, Marian. A contribution to a dynamic theory of intelligence testing of children. *J. Clin. Experim. Psychopath.*, 1954 *15*, 73–95.

Fromm, Erika, Hartman, Lenore D., & Marschak, Marian. Children's intelligence tests as a measure of dynamic personality functioning. *Am. J. Orthopsychiat.*, 1957, *27*, 134–144.

Frost, B. P., & Frost, R. The pattern of WISC scores in a group of juvenile sociopaths. *J. Clin. Psychol.*, 1962, *18*, 354–355.

Gallahar, P. Effects of increased verbal scale difficulty and failure on WAIS digit symbol performance. *Dissert. Abstr.*, 1964, *24*, 179.

Gardner, R., Holzman, P. S., Klein, G. S., Linton, Harriet B., & Spence, D. P. Cognitive control: a study of individual consistencies. *Psychol. Iss.*, 1959, *1*, no. 4.

Gardner, R., Jackson, D. N., & Messick, S. J. Personality organization in cognitive controls and intellectual abilities. *Psychol. Iss.*, 1960, *2*, no. 4.

Gilhooly, F. M. Wechsler-Bellevue reliability and the validity of certain diagnostic signs of the neuroses. *J. Consult. Psychol.*, 1950, *14*, 82–87.

Ginnett, L. E., & Moran, L. J. Stability of vocabulary performance by schizophrenics. *J. Consult. Psychol.*, 1964, *28*, 178–179.

Goodstein, L. D., & Farber, I. E. On the relation between A-scale scores and Digit Symbol performance. *J. Consult. Psychol.*, 1957, *21*, 152–154.

Griffiths, J. S. The effects of experimentally induced anxiety on certain subtests of the Wechsler-Bellevue. *Dissert. Abstr.*, 1958, *18*, 655–656.

Guertin, W. H. Auditory interference with Digit Span performance. *J. Clin. Psychol.*, 1959, *15*, 349.

Guertin, W. H., Rabin, A. I., Frank, G., & Ladd, C. Research with the Wechsler Intelligence scales for Adults. *Psychol. Bull.*, 1962, *59*, 1–25.

Gurvitz, M. S. The Wechsler-Bellevue Test and the diagnosis of psychopathic personality. *J. Clin. Psychol.*, 1950, *6*, 397–401.

Hafner, A. J., Pollie, D. M., & Wapner, I. The relationship between the CMAS and WISC functioning. *J. Clin. Psychol.*, 1960, *16*, 322–323.

Hartmann, H. *Ego Psychology and the Problem of Adaptation.* New York: International Universities Press, 1958.

Holt, R. R., & Havel, J. A method for assessing primary and secondary process in the Rorschach. In M. Rickers-Ovsiankina (Ed.). *Rorschach Psychology*. New York: Wiley, 1960, pp. 263–319.

Hunt, W., Quay, H., & Walker, R. The validity of clinical judgment of asocial tendencies. *J. Clin. Psychol.*, 1966, *22*, 116–118.

Jurjevich, R. M. Inter-relationship of anxiety indices on Wechsler intelligence scales and MMPI scales. *J. Gen. Psychol.*, 1963, *69*, 135–142.

Kaiser, M. The WISC as an instrument for diagnosing sociopathy. *Dissert. Abstr.*, 1964, *25*, 2612.

Kasper, S. Progressive matrices (1938) and emotional disturbance. *J. Consult. Psychol.*, 1958, *22*, 24.

Kingsley, L. Wechsler-Bellevue patterns of psychopaths. *J. Consult. Psychol.*, 1960, *24*, 373.

Kippner, S. WISC Comprehension and Picture Arrangement subtests as measures of social competence. *J. Clin. Psychol.*, 1964, *20*, 366–367.

Kris, E. *Psychoanalytic Explorations in Art.* New York: International Universities Press, 1952.

Kroeber, T. C. The coping functions of the ego mechanisms. In R. W. White (Ed.). *The Study of Lives.* New York: Atherton Press, 1963.

Levine, M., Glass, H., & Meltzoff, I. The inhibition process, Rorschach human movement responses, and intelligence. *J. Consult. Psychol.*, 1957, *21*, 41–45.

Levinson, B. M. Traditional Jewish cultural values and performance on the Wechsler tests. *J. Educ. Psychol.*, 1959, *50*, 177–181.

Lewinski, R. J. The psychometric pattern: I. Anxiety and neurosis. *J. Clin. Psychol.*, 1945, *1*, 214–221.

Littell, W. M. The Wechsler Intelligence Scale for Children: Review of a decade of research. *Psychol. Bull.*, 1960, *57*, 132–156.

Luchins, A., & Luchins, E. Effect of varying administration of the Digit Symbol subtest of the Wechsler-Bellevue Intelligence Scale. *J. Gen. Psychol.*, 1953, *43*, 125–142.

Manne, S. H., Kandel, A., & Rosenthal, D. Difference between Performance IQ and Verbal IQ in a severely psychopathic population. *J. Clin. Psychol.*, 1962, *18*, 73–77.

Matarazzo, Ruth D. The relationship of manifest anxiety to Wechsler-Bellevue subtest performance. *J. Consult. Psychol.*, 1955, *19*, 218.

Matarazzo, J. D., & Phillips, Jeanne I. Digit Symbol performance as a function of increasing levels of anxiety. *J. Consult. Psychol.*, 1955, *19*, 131–134.

Maupin, E., & Hunter, Diane. Digit span as a measure of attention: attempted validation studies. *Psychol. Rep.*, 1966, *18*, 457–458.

Mayman, M., Schafer, R., & Rapaport, D. Interpretation of the Wechsler-Bellevue Intelligence Scale and personality appraisal. In H. H. Anderson & G. L. Anderson (Eds.). *An Introduction to Projective Techniques.* New York: Prentice-Hall, 1951.

Moldowsky, S., & Moldowsky, Patricia C. Digit Span as an anxiety indicator. *J. Consult. Psychol.*, 1952, *16*, 115–118.

Murstein, B. I., & Leipold, W. D. The role of learning and motor abilities in the Wechsler-Bellevue Digit Symbol subtest. *Educ. Psychol. Meas.*, 1961, *21*, 103–112.

Norman, R. P., & Wilensky, H. Item difficulty of the WAIS Information subtest for a chronic schizophrenic sample. *J. Clin. Psychol.*, 1961, *17*, 56–57.

Penfield, W., & Milner, Brenda. Memory deficit produced by bilateral lesions in the hippocampal zone. *AMA Arch. Neur. Psychiat.*, 1958, *79*, 475–497.

Rabin, A. I. Diagnostic use of intelligence tests. In Wolman, B. B. (Ed.). *Handbook of Clinical Psychology.* New York: McGraw-Hill, 1965.

Rabin, A. I., King, G. F., & Ehrmann, J. C. Vocabulary performance of short-term and long-term schizophrenics. *J. Abn. Soc. Psychol.*, 1955, *50*, 255–258.

Rapaport, D. The autonomy of the ego. *Bull. Menninger Clin.*, 1951, *15*, 113–124.

Rapaport, D. The theory of ego autonomy: a generalization. *Bull. Menninger Clin.*, 1958, *22*, 13–35.

Rapaport, D., Gill, M., & Schafer, R. *Diagnostic Psychological Testing*, Vol. I. Chicago: Yearbook Publishers, 1945.

Rashkis, H. A., & Welch, G. S. Detection of anxiety by use of the Wechsler scale. *J. Clin. Psychol.*, 1946, *3*, 354–357.

Reich, W. *Character Analyses.* New York: Noonday Press, 1949.

Sarason, I. G., & Minard, J. Test anxiety, experimental instructions, and the Wechsler Arithmetic, Information, and Similarities. *J. Educ. Psychol.*, 1962, *6*, 299–302.

Saunders, D. A. A factor analysis of the Picture Completion items on the WAIS. *J. Clin. Psychol.*, 1960, *16*, 146–149.

Saunders, D. A. A factor analysis of the Information and Arithmetic items of the WAIS. *Psychol. Rep.*, 1960, *6*, 367–383.

Schafer, R. *The Clinical Application of Psychological Tests.* New York: International Universities Press, 1948.

Schafer, R. Psychoanalytic Interpretation in Rorschach Testing: Theory and Application. New York: Grune and Stratton, 1954.

Schafer, R. Regression in the service of the ego: Relevance of a psychoanalytic concept for personality assessment. In Gardner Lindzey (Ed.). Assessment of Human Motives. New York: Rinehart, 1958.

Schill, T. The effects of MMPI social introversion on WAIS Picture Arrangement performance. J. Clin. Psychol., 1966, 22, 72–74.

Shapiro, D. Neurotic Styles. New York: Basic Books, 1965.

Sherman, A. R., & Blatt, S. J. The effects of success vs. failure experiences on Digit Span, Digit Symbol and Vocabulary performance. Unpublished manuscript, 1966.

Siegman, A. W. The effort of manifest anxiety on a concept formation task, a nondirected learning task and timed and untimed intelligence tests. J. Consult. Psychol., 1956, 20, 176–178.

Spence, Janet T. Patterns of performance on WAIS Similarities in schizophrenia, brain damage and normal Ss. Psychol. Rep., 1963, 13, 431–436.

Wachtel, P. L., & Blatt, S. J. Energy deployment and achievement. J. Consult. Psychol., 1965, 29, 302–308.

Waite, R. R. The intelligence test as a psychodiagnostic instrument. J. Proj. Tech., 1961, 25, 90–102.

Walker, R. E., & Spence, Janet T. Relationship between Digit Span and anxiety. J. Consult. Psychol., 1964, 28, 220–223.

Warner, S. J. The Wechsler-Bellevue psychometric pattern in anxiety neurosis. J. Consult. Psychol., 1950, 14, 297–304.

Watson, C. G. WAIS error types in schizophrenics and organics. Psychol. Rep., 1965, 16, 523–530.

Wechsler, D. The Measurement of Adult Intelligence. Baltimore: Williams & Wilkins, 1944.

Wechsler, D. The Measurement and Appraisal of Adult Intelligence, 4th ed. Baltimore: Williams & Wilkins, 1958.

Wiener, G. The effect of distrust on some aspects of intelligence test behavior. J. Consult. Psychol., 1957, 21, 127–130.

Wiens, A. N., Matarazzo, J. D., & Gavor, K. D. Performance and Verbal IQ in a group of sociopaths. J. Clin. Psychol., 1959, 15, 191–193.

Wild, Cynthia. Creativity and adaptive regression. J. Pers. Soc. Psychol., 1965, 2, 161–168.

Witkin, H. A. Psychological differentiation and forms of pathology. J. Abn. Psychol., 1965, 70, 317–336.

Witkin, H. A., Dyk, R. B., Faterson, H. F., Goodenough, D. R., & Karp, S. A. Psychological Differentiation: Studies of Development. New York: Wiley, 1962.

Wolfson, W., & Weltman, R. E. Implications of specific WAIS Picture Completion errors. J. Clin. Psychol., 1960, 16, 9–11.

Wolfson, W., & Weltman, R. E. Visual-motor proficiency of long and short term planners. Percept. Mot. Skills, 1963, 17, 908.

Wright, M. W. A study of anxiety in a general hospital setting. Canad. J. Psychol., 1954, 8, 195–203.

8

Integration of
Projective Techniques
in the Clinical Case Study

Walter G. Klopfer

THE PURPOSE OF THE CLINICAL CASE STUDY

It is regrettable that as clinical psychologists, so many of us acquire consummate skill in detecting the fine points of interpretation of psychological tests, reading between every line in an interview, and splitting every diagnostic hair without any clear guidelines as to what to do with this information and what the purpose of the evaluation should really be. As scientist-clinicians, we have a nagging curiosity which generates an interest in doing the case study for its own sake, because we hope that it will help us to gain a broader and deeper understanding of any given personality and build up our appercep-tive reservoir. However, in looking at the matter more practically, we see that there are really three parties involved in the clinical case study whose needs must be considered and somewhat met if the whole project is to be worthwhile. These are the examiner, the pa-tient, and the reader of the clinical case study. Each one of these has a stake in the enterprise, although each may perceive his or her in-terests in a somewhat different manner. In addition to rational goals, the examiner, for instance, may want to use the clinical case study as a way of communicating a certain impression to the reader: he might like the reader to consider him erudite, sophisticated, agreeable, gregarious, or intellectually stimulating. It may be that the clinical case study will serve as a political instrument, designed to sell a particular point of view to anyone who may come across it. It is possible that interprofessional or intraprofessional relationships which are currently tense will be influenced indirectly through a description of certain kinds of causality and the prediction of certain outcomes on the basis of the case study.

The reader of the report, too, may have his understanding of the matter obscured by irrelevant considerations. For him the examiner and/or the techniques employed may be on trial; the theory implicit in the report may be either consonant with the reader's point of view or it may not; he may want to use the study as a way of confirming his own views and defending them to some higher authority.

Often lost in the shuffle is the third party, the patient. Both the reader and the examiner may get so interested in their own intellectual byplay and their power struggle that the real question of contributing something tangible and significant to the patient's welfare may be partially lost. The patient has extremely ambivalent feeling about whether he wants to be understood or not. On the one hand, it would seem that the more that is known about him by the professional people involved in his case, the more efficiently they will be able to bring about some happy resolution of his problems. On the other hand, the patient is far from sure that these people will be able to make the kind of use of the information that will enable them to help him constructively in ways in which he is willing to be helped. There is an unresolved question of whether they can be trusted. Perhaps he is enamored of his defenses and loathe to discard them in favor of some unknown, frightening vulnerability. This applies particularly to that part of the case study which is based upon projective techniques. By their very nature, projective methods elicit material that the individual might not be willing to reveal about himself if he had more complete conscious control over what he was communicating; therefore, we are deliberately attempting to get under his guard, reach inside of his character armor, and tease out aspects of his personality. Sometimes we may be pitting ourselves against his conscious will. In order to justify this procedure, we must be very sure that our purpose is genuinely constructive and that the information given will be truly used for the patient's benefit. This implies consideration of the impact of the report upon the primary and the secondary readers. Just as there is little reason to cast pearls before swine, there is no point in presenting information concerning a patient's unconscious life to people who are uninterested or unsympathetic to this view of personality; neither should we supply such information to those who would use it to make unjustified administrative decisions or who would subject the patient to confrontations that might shame or humiliate him.

A clinical study should be a document designed to enable the examiner to use his skill to integrate the results of projective and other methods of personality assessment and to communicate them in a way which is correct not only scientifically, but tactically and politically as well. This requires the use of proper language, the censoring of some material, and the enhancing of those points which are most pertinent to the administrative or clinical problems under consideration. The clinical case study should be made available only to those persons who can make proper use of it in the light of the above considerations. If some part of this material or all of it is to be presented to the patient, this consideration should certainly influence the format of the report. Since it is not customary to give patients written copies of their own case study, however, this point will not ordinarily be an issue.

The next question that might be raised is that of the purpose of the case study in terms of the explicit content, irrespective of what is involved from the viewpoints of the various interested parties. It would seem that there are three different purposes:

1.   The understanding of the patient. This is, of course, the most common purpose of the psychological report and the one that most readily comes to mind. The understanding must originate from the examiner, who is thus enabled to communicate something about the person which is meaningful. Obviously if this understanding is to be transmitted to the readers of the clinical case study, there must be a common frame of reference, which must manifest itself not only in such obvious tools as words and technical terms, but also in the basic assumptions made, the theory assumed, and the connecting links alluded to.

One might make the further assumption that the ultimate purpose of the clinical case study is to give the understanding of the patient back to him or her. The understanding that is gained from interviews and objective personality inventories is often already available to the patient, since he ordinarily has conscious control of the material he provides by the use of these techniques. Thus the conscious material already present in the patient which is transmitted to the examiner and subsequently back to the patient will come as no great surprise. The reader will gain little more information from these sources than is already apparent to the patient. In contrast, the understanding of the patient which comes from the examiner's use of projective methods is often not consciously evident to the patient but could be useful if it could be communicated back to him in more rational (consciously acceptable) form during the course of feedback or subsequent psychotherapy. This presumes that making the patient aware of those motives of which he is unaware will give him more rational choices to make and enhance his mastery of reality. Thus, the potential therapist can gain information of direct use.

2.   The next important purpose of the report is the prediction of future behavior. As the art and science of clinical psychology continue to develop, more and more agencies, institutions, industrial firms, and individuals are looking to the clinical psychologist for concrete help in making decisions. For example, Matarazzo and colleagues (1964) report the use of projective and other techniques of personality assessment as a way of predicting high or low risk of a psychiatric sort for applications for a metropolitan police force. Obviously this is a very important prediction. Other clinical psychologists are taking chances every day predicting that somebody will or will not be able to function outside of a hospital, be a prospect for surgery, be a good candidate for parole, commit suicide, make good managerial material, be a good candidate for graduate work in clinical psychology, etc. Previous research with psychology reports (Ullmann, Berkman, & Hammister, 1958) has indicated that the value of the clinical case study for prediction is limited by the ambiguity and universality of many of the statements made, implying a lack of courage on the part of examiners in using their data to make forthright predictions. The predictive value of the clinical case study has also been limited by the reluctance of many examiners to give feedback to the patient himself. This reluctance has not been displayed in the field of vocational counseling, wherein test scores regarding interests, aptitudes, achievements, and personality traits are regularly supplied to the counselee as a way of helping him or her to set more realistic goals and to be aware of some of the forces within that are likely to sabotage or enhance his or her efforts. Presumably, the examiner who uses projective tests and who thus possesses a greater range of information that he or she can help the patient with can share at least some of it with the party most involved. It seems that sometimes clinical psychologists have a tendency to take over inappropriate medical customs which dictate that a cloak of mystery surround the findings of the (witchdoctor) examiner. Much of the information contained in the clinical case study could be of great value to the patient, not necessarily in profoundly changing his personality or immediately producing a shift in his behavior, but at least showing

him a map so that he can find his way to his own motives if he wishes and thus make decisions somewhat more clear-sightedly than otherwise.

3.   The third purpose of the clinical case study is to serve as a record of the patient's psychological state at a given time. The problem of baseline is an annoying one in clinical research, to say nothing of its being an insurmountable problem in many tasks of clinical evaluation. For example, how can a psychologist accurately answer the question of whether someone has been brain damaged by an accident if there are no baseline data with which to compare the tests given to him or her following the accident? How can the psychologist judge that a given individual has undergone a change in the direction of abnormality or greater pathology, for the purpose of testifying at a trial, for example, when he can say nothing about the patient in his premorbid state? Many diagnostic concepts involve the assumption of "change" and yet our measures are usually crosssectional. One of the regrettable customs within the mental health professions is that information is frequently not shared and that each examiner feels that only he, because of his allegedly superior diagnostic skill, has any understanding of the patient. Thus, he does not take the trouble to study data painstakingly acquired by other professionals and the patient is not as well understood in terms of the sequence of events that have taken place in his or her life. Crude baselines such as number of jobs, previous marriages, or years of school may be as misleading as they may be helpful. Just as a physician should have a record of previous medical examinations and the dentist ought to familiarize himself with a patient's dental history, so should the psychologist consider the patient's history in constructing a clinical case study that can serve as a valuable record of the person's psychological state at a given time and place, and under a given set of circumstances.

THE EXTENT OF THE CLINICAL CASE STUDY

One of the basic fallacies in clinical evaluation and clinical research is that there is such a thing as a "basic" or "true" personality. Frequently, one can see the spectacle of a clinician comparing the results of various tests from various modalities together with the patient's life history and the results of interviews, trying to decide which of these is "correct." It is almost as though he were saying, "Will the real personality of patient X please stand up!" This is a shallow and dangerous game to play. In contrast, the present author would like to make the assumption that behavior is always basically consistent and that every piece of behavior that we collect during the process of acquiring data for the clinical case study must be integrated into a conceptual framework concerning the patient if we are to come up with anything resembling the truth. The only way that the three blind men can tell what the elephant looks like is to compare notes and see whether they can arrive at a superordinate hypothesis concerning the nature of the beast. Within this chapter, an attempt will be made to specify levels of personality by using the multilevel framework first presented by Leary in his book *The Interpersonal Diagnosis of Personality* (1957). One slight modification will be made in Leary's system based upon research which has been carried out since that time. The levels to be alluded to are the following:

Level I

Leary called this the level of "public communication." It is operationally defined as the level at which an individual is perceived by significant others using ranking techniques. Other ways of measuring it include having persons well known to the patient fill out adjective check lists on him, describe him, be interviewed about him, or be observed in interaction with him and then questioned. This may seem to be a strange level to discuss in a chapter focusing upon the use of projective techniques in a clinical case study; however, some of the research reviewed in this book indicates quite clearly that projective methods may sometimes lead to correct prediction of Level I behavior. Conscious self-report on the part of the patient is, of course, distorted by social-desirability factors, but since the interpretation of projective tests is done by others, the relationship between projective tests predictions and predictions based upon direct Level I measures is often higher than might be expected. An example of this is given in the study by McGreevey (1962). "Sometimes Level I descriptions differ among reference groups as described in the discussion of assessing adolescents by the present author" (Klopfer, 1979).

Level Ia

This is the level of public image perceived by the patient herself. This is a level not mentioned by Leary; it has been discovered by research carried on by the present author. Previously it has been assumed that the best estimate that a given patient could make of her public image was her perception of herself. Thus, when she describes her own traits as being radically different from those described by significant others, it was assumed that she was lacking in social awareness and consequently likely to elicit inappropriate and confusing feedback from other people. However, it was felt that perhaps an individual might make a better prediction of her public image if asked to do so directly. In a study by Warren & Klopfer (1965) it was discovered that small groups of subjects who knew each other well were able to predict their own Level I image quite correctly when asked specifically to do so and that this prediction of Level I (herein called Level Ia) was not significantly different from their true Level I, whereas their conscious self-concept (Level II) was significantly different from Level I.

Level II

This is the level of conscious self-concept, the level, of course, at which people perceive themselves. It is operationally defined as their performance on the Interpersonal Adjective Checklist. It can also be measured by objective personality inventories, by direct interviews, and as will be demonstrated below, by certain so-called projective techniques such as the Sentence Completion Test. This level has to serve as a reference point within which one can study the degree of distance from awareness of those thoughts and feelings revealed under projective conditions. Since the controversy concerning the level of awareness of the material elicited by projective techniques rages to this day (witness, for example, Murstein's contention that the TAT measures nothing but what can be elicited in an interview [1963]), it is well to be able to specify this level for the purpose of making a comparison between it and others more public or private.

Level III

The level of "private symbolization" is operationally defined by Leary as the level measured by projective tests. This is a rather broad concept, but he narrows it down somewhat. For example, in the case of the TAT he distinguishes the TAT "hero" and the TAT "other" levels. The assumption here is that even though both of these are slightly distant from awareness, the feelings and thoughts attributed to the "other" figures in the TAT are somewhat more distant from the conscious feelings of the patient than those feelings attributed to the central or "hero" figure. This is somewhat akin to Tomkins' (1947) "distanciation theory" first enunciated in his book some years ago. Within fantasy there may be further distinction between that which is manifest and that which is inferred (latent). Holt (1978) believes that TAT stories are more conscious and less "projective" than fantasy. This concurs with Leary's designation of Level III as preconscious.

The contention which will be elaborated upon in the present chapter is that the clinical case study can be considered complete, can be of value in terms of the objectives enunciated above, only if some attempt is made to measure each of the above levels and to integrate the total picture into something coherent, with clearly defined predictive qualities. In order to illustrate the importance of the multilevel schema, the following illustration is given:

First, take a single personality trait—aggression. Let us further crudely dichotomize aggression by calling the overt presence or manifestation of aggression plus (+), and the absence of overt or manifest aggression minus (−). This violates the actual measuring technique, since we think of a continuum, but this kind of dichotomy will serve for present purposes. Let us further assume that we have only three levels that we want to measure, namely Level I, the trait as viewed by significant others; Level II, the trait as viewed by the individual himself; and Level III, the trait as judged from projective tests. This then leads to eight different combinations. In each case, the first symbol will be that measured by Level I, the second measured by Level II, and the third measured by Level III. These eight combinations will be briefly discussed in terms of the interpretation that would be assigned to each in connection with this one trait.

A: + + +.   This is a patient who demonstrates overt aggression as viewed by other people, as admitted to by himself, and as revealed by projective tests. We may assume that he is an unusually aggressive person, that this aggression is not alien to him, that he may perhaps even possess more of it than is overtly expressed, and that there is no particularly severe conflict about its expression. He may make others uncomfortable.

B: + + −.   In this instance the aggression is perceived by others as well as the individual himself but is not manifest by judgments based on projective tests. Here we may assume that since aggression is not present at the fantasy level that either the individual expresses all the aggression he needs to and gets it out of his system, or else that he may perhaps be demonstrating more aggression than is needed by him in terms of his own value system. It may be that he is part of a subculture in which the presence of aggression is socially sanctioned and even strongly desired, and that therefore he has trained himself to behave and think of himself in this manner.

C: + − +.   This is an individual whose aggression is manifest at the behavioral or public level as well as at the fantasy level, but he himself does not admit it. This is the fairly typical picture of a neurotic individual who has been trained to consider aggression as an evil act, so that taking it into awareness would arouse guilt. However, the fact that he still possesses it and that it influences his behavior is quite evident to others behaviorally and projectively even though it may be obscure to the individual himself.

D: + − −.   In this case the aggression is behaviorly manifest although denied by the individual and absent in fantasy. This may mean that the individual, in terms of pecking order, is the most aggressive person in a generally passive group. It may mean that he is in a situation where he has learned to behave in a pseudo-aggressive manner to conform to the "rules," either explicit or tacit. Perhaps he is a member of the Marines or some other group in which this kind of behavior is absolutely essential. However, he does not find it necessary to deceive himself and his projective tests also reveal the lack of genuine motivation for his behavior.

E: − + +.   This is an individual who does not show behavioral aggression that other people can see, but he deems himself aggressive and also has shown aggression at the fantasy level. Here we may be dealing with an instance of consciously controlled aggression in which the individual realizes that the unrestrained expression of aggression may alienate and antagonize other people, and has chosen to inhibit or control these tendencies. However, they continue to seethe within him and he is very much aware of them, not finding it necessary to delude himself.

F: − + −.   This is a case of an individual who shows very limited fantasy aggression but still deems himself aggressive. This may be because he is in a situation where being aggressive is socially sanctioned and desired, and so, in wanting to be an accepted member of the group, he has managed to convince himself that he is aggressive; however, his basic lack of aggression as demonstrated by fantasy is transmitted into behavior, and he is no more able to delude other people than he is to delude the judge of the projective material.

G: − − +.   This is a fairly standard picture of the neurotically repressed individual who is unable to express aggression or to even permit it full access to awareness, but who turbulently bubbles with it underneath the surface as revealed by the material in the projective tests. The aggression may rise close to the surface but is systematically excluded from self-concept.

H: − − −   Here we have an individual who shows no man-ifest aggression behaviorly, consciously, or projectively. One may well ask what happened to his aggression. Fortunately, Leary has another level to account for this kind of behavior, which he calls Level IV. It is alluded to here only parenthetically because no operational definition of it has been provided. Level IV is the level of the "unex-pressed unaware" which is described as material which is systemati-cally excluded at all other levels. Whether the patient with a picture like this is really lacking in aggression or whether the aggression is so intensely ego-alien that it has to be excluded even from projective material is, of course, hard to say.

From the above illustrations it can be seen that projective mate-rial is most meaningful when looked at within the context of the other sources of information. When projective material is used alone, and when the question of whether we are predicting overt behavior, conscious self-concept, or merely fantasy is left unanswered, the reader may legitimately feel that we are confounding him with our ambiguity. Of what earthly use is it to talk about "latent homosexual-ity" or "masturbatory anxiety" or "confusion about sexual role" when it is completely unclear whether we are talking about one or the other of these different levels? Take for example the matter of "latent homosexuality." Are we talking about a person who is extremely effeminate and makes readily discernible passes at other men and whose latency consists only in the fact that he does not actually engage in anal coitus? Or are we talking about someone who has never engaged in homosexual contacts but who is very much preoccupied with fantasies and ideas and wishes concerning homosexuality which cause him excruciating anxiety? Or are we talking about some-one who merely gets confused about the sex of the figures in the Rorschach and TAT, and who has never had a conscious thought or feeling concerning homosexuality in his life? It may be that some clinical psychologists feel that this is a trivial question and that latent homosexuality is latent homosexuality, no matter at what level you find it. However, with this point of view the present author would take violent exception. Much of the difficulty that clinical psycholo-gists have gotten themselves into with communities and governmen-tal agencies is due to this very kind of slovenliness in making predic-tions. I surely would not want to be evaluated for an important government job or denied access to classified information solely because of someone's interpretation of my projective material. Not enough is known at this point concerning the predictive efficiency of symbolic material to make such use of projective data warranted. However, if the fantasy material is integrated with the objective and behavioral material, we may then be able to come up with an interpretation and prediction which has considerably more justification and reliability.

This argument also applies to the question of whether we should use "blind" interpretations of projective material as part of the case study. I think this would be a legitimate procedure for training purposes, for research purposes, or perhaps for the purpose of playing some kind of power game. However, if our purpose involves recommendations concerning the fate of human beings and of groups of human beings, it would seem that a less risky approach would be indicated. As illustrated by the above examples, a given piece of projective behavior may be interpreted differentially, depending on the context within which it is found in comparison to other levels. If we consider that in the above illustrations only one trait is employed, and even that trait is crudely dichotomized, the number of combinations and permutations that are possible when we compare projective with other materials becomes extremely large.

Thus, it seems that the scope of the clinical case study should be fairly broad, although not necessarily long. The personality assessor should take it as his or her task to say something concerning the individual's interpersonal behavior and his or her perception thereof (Levels I and Ia), his or her conscious view of himself or herself and how similar or different it is from the above (Level II), and his or her fantasies (Level III). Every single aspect of his personality can be discussed at all three levels. His relationship with each one of the significant people in his life can be described in a multilevel fashion. For example, it would be possible to say that he behaves timidly toward his wife, considers himself on good terms with her, but has fantasies in which he behaves quite aggressively toward her. Thus, we are comparing the same relationship at three different levels. Similarly, we can talk about his attitude toward his work. It may be that he behaves as though he did not care whether he did well in college, that he says he wants to do well in college, and his fantasies reveal his basic alienation from intellectual pursuits. Any given point of interpretation made in the clinical case study and, specifically, any contribution made to the clinical study by projective material can be presented in a sophisticated and integrated manner as illustrated above. Thus, it is bound to be of much greater value than the usual naive presentation of projective data as either fantasy or reality, with the reader left to choose and to integrate it with other data as best he or she can.

WHAT LEVEL DO PROJECTIVE TECHNIQUES MEASURE?

Leary (1957) makes the bland assumption that projective techniques measure a single level which he referred to as Level III, or the level of "private symbolization"; however, it is the judgment of the present writer that this assumption will not bear close scrutiny and that, in fact, projective techniques are extremely complex in terms of the levels that they measure and the kinds of predictions that can be made from their data. In order to illustrate the complexity involved, two projective tests will be discussed in detail and some allusion will be made to others.

The Rorschach

The Rorschach consists of two kinds of stimulus elements which lead to different sorts of predictions. First, there are those stimulus elements that can be verified by common consent. These include color, shading, and form. Unless the subject perceiving the blots is color-blind, he will know that some blots are black and white, others contain red, and still others contain many different colors. Consequently, whatever the significance of color reactions may be, the prediction made from such reactions will be in terms of an individual's reaction to commonly experienced aspects of the external environment. Thus, the hypotheses regarding color made in the Rorschach literature are all at Level I—in other words, predictions of publicly observable behavior. This is a reasonable hypothesis, and if color reactions cannot lead to experimentally verifiable Level I hypotheses, the experimenter is justified in considering this as evidence questioning the validity of that aspect of the Rorschach test.

The matter is somewhat different in regard to shading. Although shading nuances are a commonly perceived aspect of the Rorschach stimulus situation, the stimulus involved is sufficiently subtle so that not all subjects perceive them. It may be that some people looking at the blots are not sufficiently perceptive, sensitive, or keen-sighted; hence, they will not be aware of this particular stimulus property of the blot and not respond accordingly. As a result, the clinician tends to be less explicit in talking about what responses to shading stimuli mean. Even though they sound at first blush like Level I hypotheses (the individual is "sensitive" or "sensuous" or "aware of the nuances of the environment"), yet there is a careful avoidance of translating such interpretations into directly observable behavior. There are other kinds of shading reactions (k, K, FK), placed on the left side of the psychogram (Klopfer, et al., 1954), to which no behavioral significance whatever is attached—for example, FK. Here the common interpretation in terms of an "introspective inclination on the part of the perceiving subject" certainly is not something that can be clearly translated into behavior or for which Level I criteria can be explicitly formulated. The same thing is true of the KF response commonly alluded to as "free floating undifferentiated anxiety." This term is rather vague and is not operationalized. No one has claimed that factor analytic studies failing to find a relationship between this kind of determinant and something like the Taylor Manifest Anxiety Scale (TMAS) necessarily invalidate either measure. This is because this is not a measure of manifest anxiety, so it is therefore not at all clear what it is a measure of. Thus, we are forced to conclude that shading is quite unclear in terms of its level of significance and this is probably one of the reasons why its interpretation in Rorschach research has always been somewhat obscure.

The measure of perceptual accuracy (or form level) on the other hand, has been a solid basis for making behavioral predictions. For example, the work of McReynolds (1951) indicates that form accuracy can distinguish between people with greater and lesser reality ties. When a subject says that the side large Ds on card VIII look like animals or that the whole of card V looks like a bat or a butterfly, we consider him as having dealt with his world in a realistic manner. It is essentially a question of whether someone calls a table a table or a chair a chair, according to our common agreement on how we label such objects. If an individual were to refer to a table as a chair, or a chair as a table, we would, by means of our democratic system of consensual validation, rule him psychotic and send him to the state hospital (especially if he hit us with the chair). However, he might have memorized the name "table" for the object usually designated in this manner, and the term "chair" for the object usually designated as such without really believing it privately. This is why it is particularly useful to show him a Rorschach inkblot to which he has had no previously conditioned verbal response. If he looks at the side details on card VIII and calls them "fish," or if he looks at the whole of card V and labels it a "frog," we know that he does not perceive objects, or label them, in a way which is common and that he is likely therefore to get himself into difficulty in our society and end up making other people sufficiently uncomfortable that they will feel that intervention is warranted. We may therefore conclude that form accuracy is an extremely significant aspect of Rorschach interpretation and one from which clear-cut Level I predictions are made. Very few clinical psychologists would make a diagnosis of psychosis on the basis of deviant content alone, unless there were some tangible evidence of the subject's inability to perceive the way others in his society commonly do.

An entirely different frame of reference is involved in connection with movement responses. None of the inkblots typically has been known to move; they do not kiss, they do not kick, they do not have sexual intercourse, nor do they fly about the room; and yet all of these actions are commonly attributed to them by perceiving subjects. When these attributes are imputed to the cards we do not regard this as pathological; rather, we talk about the individual using his inner resources in a way that creatively modifies his perception of the environment. Thus, it would appear that movement responses are clearly Level III responses since they are measures only of the inner world of the subject, and at best can be labeled fantasy; we might validate the interpretive significance of movement responses by correlating them with TAT material (if the latter is indeed a Level III measure), or with manifest dream content. However, even here the evidence is contradictory. For example, a recent study by Bendick and Klopfer (1964) indicates that both sensory deprivation and motor inhibition, when imposed upon subjects, tend to artificially increase the number of movement responses given to standard Rorschach cards under standard methods of administration. This seems to imply that the external environment does influence the projection of movement onto the blots, thus casting some doubt on the interpretation of movement responses as a reaction to internal stimuli alone. In the past it has been common for theorists to poke fun at the idea of Rorschach movement being related to general movement of a motoric sort. A typical caricature of a paradigm that might be thought up is that a pedometer is to be attached to a subject during the day, and that the amount of walking around he does might be correlated to the amount of movement response he produces on the Rorschach. This kind of design was thought up to ridicule the idea that movement might have a literal kind of significance rather than an attributive significance due to the reaction of the individual to an external stimulus on the basis of his inner creative life. However, after obtaining results such as those of Bendick and Klopfer (1964), this design might not appear quite as ludicrous. It appears that as more and more research with the Rorschach test progresses, the number of areas that are strictly Level III diminish.

Certainly the whole area of "manner of approach" is one which has always been presented in a Level I manner. The hypotheses regarding whole and details that have been presented in standard textbooks such as those of Klopfer, Ainsworth, Klopfer, and Holt (1954), and Beck (1945), are all couched pretty much in Level I terms. When the clinician says that the subject is likely (with an over-emphasis on whole responses) to "look upon the situation as a whole" or "deal with life problems in their entirety" or "attack problem-solving in a global, undifferentiated manner," these certainly sound like statements that can be translated into directly observable Level I behavior. Similar statements have been made concerning usual and unusual details and white space (S) responses. In the old days of Rorschach theorizing, when a great deal of attention was paid to Jung's introversion-extratension dichotomy, all sorts of hedging went on in connection with such interpretations. For example, it was assumed that a preponderance of figure–ground reversal in an intro-versive context would have a meaning different from a similar pre-ponderance in an extratensive context. The oppositionalism was assumed in the former case to be directed "against the self." Whatever was meant by that seems to have been dropped from the current literature, and most recent works emphasize figure–ground reversal as having direct behavioral significance and being an analogue to other kinds of figure–ground reversal or oppositional ways of perceiv-ing the world.

When it comes to the area of conventionality or originality, the interpretations are likely to be fairly directly analogous to observable behavior. We refer to people looking at the world the way others do, or having an unusual approach to situations, and we talk about their thought content either as being like that of the average person in their culture or as being very much unlike it; thus, it would appear that we are not dealing with any mysterious Level III area here, but rather a fairly concrete Level I or II area. The area of content analysis, on the other hand, is one in which there may be some legitimate doubt. Certainly, it is in the area of symbolization that the interpretations made would seem rather obscure from the viewpoint of either con-scious self-concept or public image. The kind of statements that one often finds in reports that are based upon the analysis of content are such as these: "The individual has difficulty with his basic sex identification," "there are indications of latent homosexuality," "there seems to be a basic fear of castration on the part of the perceiving subject," or again, "there is a good deal of bodily preoccupation on the part of the subject." The key word in many of these interpretations seems to be *basic*. The word *basic* is kind of a weasel word in personality evaluation. It is referred to here as such because it clouds the issue of the level at which we are doing assessment and making predictions. If we say "basic" and somebody says that they cannot see this behavior taking place publicly, then we have a way out and say that of course we did not mean that. If we use this same word "basic" and the subject subsequently denies having this feeling or experience in an interview situation, then we say that we did not mean that either. So by a process of elimination it would appear that what we mean is that this is a Level III phenomenon of which the individual may not be consciously aware. This gets us into our usual bind—we use psychoanalytic kinds of concepts where we can neither really prove nor disprove our allegations. However, even the area of content analysis has become somewhat less mysterious lately. The research in the area of the prediction of aggression on the basis of content analysis carried on by such authors as Elizur (1949), Finney (1955), and Murstein (1956) indicates that frequently aggressive content is the best-single predictor of aggressive behavior. This is another shattering blow to those who assumed there was no obvious, tangible connection between projective data and actual behavior. It also tends to cast some doubt on the assumption made over many years that we could predict behavior from the Rorschach only on the basis of such consensually validatable aspects of the blot environment as color, form accuracy, and manner of approach. It appears that the veil of mystery is about to be lifted from the area of content and that here, too, we have a reasonably direct bridge between projective data, public behavior, and possibly conscious thought content.

What shall we then conclude about the Rorschach? The Rorschach seems to be a very multilevel kind of instrument. Probably the one level we allude to the least in Rorschach interpretation is Level II, and this is probably why the Rorschach is a particularly useful instrument. There are many aspects of behavior that an individual hesitates to reveal about himself. As we have said, traditionally, a projective test is a test which reveals data which the individual either will not or cannot bear to reveal about himself. Probably most of the confusion arises because of socially desirable traits that the individual has in less abundance than he would like to, or socially undesirable traits that he possesses but that he wishes that he did not. The amazing part of the foregoing analysis is that so much of Rorschach data is transmitted in Level I form. This, however, is not particularly surprising in view of some of the results of research. Take for instance the study by McGreevey (1962). Even though McGreevey's study did not deal with the Rorschach but with other projective tests, it nevertheless has some bearing on the present argument. McGreevey had groups of subjects who were ranked by their peers on four personality traits, two desirable and two undesirable. They also ranked themselves on these same traits. Discrepancies were found in the expected directon; that is, they overevaluated themselves on desirable traits and underevaluated themselves on undesirable traits. Judgments based upon projective tests in this study indicated that even in the case of high-discrepancy groups (large Level I–II discrepancy), the judges using the projective data were able to predict the ranking of the individual on the trait by the peer group (Level I) with greatar accuracy than the individual himself was able to (Level II). We have always known that people, because of their own ego defenses, were unable to predict public image aspects of behavior of which they were ashamed or which for some reason or another have been excluded from awareness. The news is that projective tests enable us to cut through this ego-defensiveness and to make predictions close to the level of public image. Thus, the bridge between projective tests and the kind of administrative predictions that we are often asked to make may be at least halfway built.

The Sentence Completion Test

Another so-called projective test which nicely illustrates some of these points is the Sentence Completion Test (SCT). The SCT has been variously assumed to measure each one of the levels described above. Sometimes it is assumed that the completed sentences reflect behaviors which are publicly observable and which would then be consistently rated by significant others. Sometimes the SCT is assumed to measure the level of conscious perception, in which case the examiner uses it as a structured interview, assuming that all of the statements, including both the stem and the ending, are consciously acceptable and ego-syntonic and would have been elicited by direct questioning as well. Sometimes the SCT is treated as a Level III instrument. Under the latter conditions, it would be assumed that measures tapping other levels of behavior should not be correlated with it and that it measures only unacceptable, nonobservable aspects of personality functioning. In clinical practice the test is often used without any direct references to level of behavior, making it possible to rationalize any given inference at whatever level it happens to fit the best. Therefore, if the individual is described in a certain way by significant others but does not necessarily admit having those traits, the SCT can be assumed to be a Level I test. If the individual admits the trait in himself, the SCT is a Level II test, and if neither of the above situations exists, then the test may still be considered a valuable projective tool. This kind of fuzziness in demarcating the level of behavior predicted by the SCT can only lead to a lack of precision in the clinical use of the test. In a review of projective tests in the *Annual Review of Psychology* (Klopfer & Taulbee, 1976), the authors refer to "the Sentence Completion Test, once considered a projective test now widely regarded as a structured interview."

One of the most puzzling studies ever published in terms of the Levels hypothesis is the one by Stone and Dellis (1960), which used as subjects a group of "pseudo-neurotic schizophrenics." Apparently, the operational definition of such a person is one who looks more confused on the Rorschach than he does behaviorally, although the authors claim to have had independent criteria for making this diagnosis. The authors hypothesize a sort of movement toward greater depth (unconsciousness) from the Wechsler-Bellevue to the SCT to the TAT to the Rorschach, and all the way down to the Draw-a-Person Test. There were 20 persons in this group, and each test was judged on a 100-point scale of health–sickness. The reliability of the judgments was .72 on the SCT. The results indicated that on the basis of these ratings, the Wechsler and SCT were indistinguishable, as were the SCT and TAT. The Rorschach and the DAP test were in a class by themselves in that they were indistinguishable from one another but cut off sharply from the rest. It is difficult to know what to make of these results. There are those who would argue that this indicates that the Rorschach and DAP test were the most sensitive in that they picked up the "true" pathology of these individuals, which had been missed by the rest. But this begs the whole question as to what we are using tests for and what we are really trying to predict. Do we really want to have people condemned to existence in a state hospital because they are having difficulty maintaining our version of reality in tests like the DAP and the Rorschach? This raises the question of why people generally end up in state hospitals in the first place. It is the contention of the present writer that hospitalization most frequently occurs not because of distorted thinking processes but because of disturbed behavior, which makes the individual objectionable to other people and produces a desire on the part of society to cast him or her out. If we assume that the Case History, the Wechsler, and the SCT are more directly related to observable behavior than the Rorschach and the DAP tests, then it would seem that the more direct instruments are more relevant in determining clinically whether someone is in need of hospitalization or not. Thus, it may be that we are hoisting a patient by the petard of our own double-binding way of instructing him on tests.

How many readers of this book have sometimes experienced guilt because of the dishonest instructions they give on tests like the Rorschach? We say to a patient that we are going to show him ten cards with inkblots on them and that what he sees on these blots is an entirely individual matter. We tell him there are no right and wrong answers and that different people see different things. This is all very well, except that it does not happen to be the truth. The fact of the matter is that there *are* right and wrong answers and that an individual who takes us literally and gives his imagination full play and says whatever he would like to and whatever occurs to him spontaneously is likely to end up as one of the subjects in a study such as the one by Stone and Dellis. It is even possible that some psychologists or psychiatrists will make up a diagnosis like "pseudo-neurotic schizophrenia" to account for the fact that the patient has really given a psychotic-appearing Rorschach but does not look that way on other tests or on the basis of his observable behavior. So the present writer is inclined to form quite different conclusions from those of Stone and Dellis. Not necessarily assuming that some tests are more accurate than others (more "real"), he is likely to assume that the SCT, the Wechsler-Bellevue, and the TAT predict judged behavior better than the Rorschach and the DAP.

THE COMMUNICATION OF FINDINGS FROM PROJECTIVE TECHNIQUES AS PART OF THE CLINICAL REPORT

One of the most crucial problems in integrating projective techniques into the clinical case study is communicating hypotheses culled from projective tests in a report which is also based on other sources of information. These other sources may be interviews with the patient himself and significant others, as well as the interpretation of data based on objective personality inventories, intelligence tests, and direct observations. This question will be broken down in several subsections and some suggestions will be made in each category.

How to Avoid Vagueness and Universality

A classic study by Forer (1949) indicates that universality presents a great temptation to the clinical investigator. In his study Forer presented what was described as a projective test to a class of students and subsequently presented them with "reports" ostensibly based on this material. In actuality, the interpretations were identical, each subject receiving the same one. They were asked to specify the degree to which the interpretations were accurate in each one of their cases and how much confidence they had in them. These "psychological reports" were received with great enthusiasm by the class and they were amazed at the specific accuracy of the allegations made concerning their personalities. This study bears a startling and frightening resemblance to many studies actually dealing with the validation of projective tests. The statements made in Forer's standard report were, of course, of a very universal nature. They got by, just as statements of astrologers, crystal-ball gazers, and the makers of Chinese fortune cookies get by. They also got by in the same way that the statements of many clinical psychologists, psychiatrists, psychiatric social workers, vocational counselors, and other legitimate practitioners get by. Regrettably, much of our behavior in communicating psychological findings consists of a kind of weasel-wording and psychological razzle-dazzle which precludes the dissemination of any specific information. Just recently the present author began working as a consultant to a school system in his hometown. After sending his first reports to the teacher in charge of the guidance program, she wrote back saying that she was certainly glad to get some reports that said something about the children instead of the usual standard stereotypes that she has come to know and ignore. It is probably true of most of the people that we test: that they have intelligence beyond that which they are currently employing, that they have difficulty in their relationships with their fellow men and women, that they have some tendency to be immature and do not clearly identify themselves with their appropriate sex role, and that they are sometimes partially immobilized by tension and emotional distress. Surely these interpretations are correct in most instances, and they are undoubtedly appropriate to most of the readers of this book; however, their very universality makes them of very dubious value in a psychological report. Excessive generality as well as universality tends to make communication infinitely less valuable. The classic study is the one by Ullmann, Berkman, and Hammister (1958) in which psychological reports are used in an effort to predict adjustment in an adult nursing home. The findings were most humiliating to the unknown and unspecified authors of these psychological reports. Number of years of hospitalization was found to be a better predictor of adjustment in an adult nursing home than judgments based upon the entire psychological report. Psychologists have frequently been criticized for the universality and ambiguity of their statements, as for instance in the study by Garfield, Heine, and Levanthal (1954).

One of the reasons that psychologists have often felt forced to be universal and ambiguous is because they have not taken into account the possibility of breaking down their data into levels, as has been promulgated in this chapter. It is our contention that a breaking down of projective data into levels will fortify the clinician with courage and enable him to make specific statements for which he is willing to focus his report in some specific manner, either in terms of a diagnostic classification, an administrative decision, or whatever focus is desired by those requesting the report.

How Best to Join the Findings of Projective Tests and Other Methods

The contention in this chapter has been that many of our psychological tests have properties which enable the clinician to make predictions on one or another level, and that sometimes a given test has within it characteristics that lead to predictions at various levels. However, the most refined and sophisticated kind of personality analysis comes from the integration of projective techniques with other methods of personality assessment. The procedure for organizing psychological reports described by the present author (Klopfer, 1960) enables the clinician to make maximal use of all of these data. It has always seemed to the present author that not only can an individual make legitimate inferences from a single modality which he may not want to make on the basis of the overall evidence as it accumulates, but, more important, he may often be able to make superordinate hypotheses on the basis of various types of data which cannot legitimately follow from any single source of information. Thus, a patient with organic brain damage may have a Bender more distorted than his Rorschach, whereas a schizophrenic may have a Rorschach more distorted than his Bender. A schizophrenic who is primarily paranoid may show a much higher level of efficiency in an intelligence test than he does in a test like the Rorschach. A person who shows one kind of test-taking aptitude as revealed by the validity scales on the MMPI may have his projective instruments interpreted quite differently from a person who shows another kind of test-taking aptitude. A protocol from the MMPI characterized by gross pathology and a plethora of symptoms may be interpreted quite differently in the light of a basically solid Rorschach from a protocol in which the reaction to inkblots is as haphazard and peculiar as the reaction to true and false items. Also, the patient's work history, the reactions to him on the part of significant others, and the observations made of him directly by nurses, social workers, and other professional people may have quite a different meaning in the light of one kind of projective performance as opposed to another. Thus, for example, spontaneous, extroverted behavior may be interpreted as genuine interest and liking for people on the one hand, whereas on the other hand it may be regarded as a frantic attempt to maintain some thin hold on reality, with the alternative being a complete schizophrenic withdrawal.

It seems a great mistake to use projective data and other data as equivalent to one another and to be interested only in similarities rather than disparities. Most people will tend to demonstrate interlevel disparity no matter how well-adjusted they are. People who are emotionally disturbed are almost bound to show some differences between their behavior at one level and another. Therefore, the differences between results of projective tests and other sources of information are likely to be one of the crucial sources of information upon which a clinical study can be based. Any psychologist who ignores this point and obscures the differences by focusing upon similarities will soon tire of the use of projective techniques, since it is obvious that they are not as useful in securing Level II data and sometimes Level I data as other techniques are. The best way to find out what a patient thinks is to ask him. The best way to find out what he does is to observe him. To get the latter kind of information indirectly and tortuously, by showing him inkblots and having him make up stories, is certainly doing it the hard way; only if the projective information will lead to a more refined and sophisticated interpretation of that which is directly observed, and only if the directly observed behavior is used to refine and produce a more sophisticated interpretation of the projective data, is it worthwhile to engage in both types of clinical detective work. If the latter course of action is followed, the result is likely to be an extremely sensitive, penetrating, and insightful analysis of the patient's personality which will be of value to all persons concerned with the case. If, in turn, the clinician manages to communicate his findings in some reasonable way which can be generally understood and appreciated by other workers, he will have rendered a great service to all concerned—more specifically, to the patient, who will be understood beyond the usual superficial way in which people regard and judge one another.

The Desirability of Avoiding Statements Which Imply a Level Other than the One Upon Which the Inference Is Based

One of the greatest sources of error in communicating projective findings as part of a clinical case study is statements that set up a false criterion. Let us say, for example, that the individual shows passivity, tenderness, and a generally "feminine" orientation on the basis of his style and content in the Rorschach test. Let us say further that his performance on the TAT implies that he tends to be dependent on others, emphasizing affiliation, softness, and giving in, rather than virility, independence, and possessiveness. Let us assume further that his overt behavior as judged by the examiner during the progress of the evaluation is more like that of a woman, culturally speaking, than like that of a man. It seems justified to many examiners under these conditions to say in the psychological report that this patient has "strong homosexual tendencies." However, the statement "strong homosexual tendencies" may well be interpreted at a level not intended by the examiner and not justified by the data. It is quite possible for all of the above factors to have been correctly and reliably observed and yet for the patient to not have any demonstrable homosexual tendencies. For example, he may never have been erotically stimulated by members of the same sex, may never have had fantasies about sexual activities involving members of the same sex, and there may be no reason to assume that he has been a problem to other men by being seductive in his relationship to them. Yet all of the latter possibilities would be implied by the statement "strong homosexual tendencies." How much better it would be for the psychological report under the above conditions to speak of the individual's softness, tenderness, and passivity directly rather than extrapolating in a manner which can so easily be misinterpreted and misunderstood!

This raises the whole question of whether there is any particular value in shorthand symbolization based upon some particular theory. It is always tempting to the psychological evaluator to conceptualize at a high level of abstraction. For example, he may have a patient who cuts off inconsequential parts of the blot on the Rorschach test, draws a person on the DAP with his hand in his pocket, tells stories on the TAT in which the hero is unable to provide an adequate solution to the dilemma posed, and reacts with panic and fear to failure to answer questions on the WAIS. The examiner may then try to integrate all of this material in the phrase "castration anxiety." Seemingly, this would be very desirable in that it promotes the discourse to a very high level of inference from which, presumably, the primary and secondary readers of the report could draw all sorts of appropriate conclusions in a wide variety of areas. Unfortunately, this is not as self-evident as it would appear at first blush. The phrase "castration anxiety" may lead to any one of the following kinds of predictions:

(1) The individual feels powerless in situations that are intellectually beyond him and reacts by being critical and picayune; (2) the individual is afraid of other people and tends to behave in a placating and subservient manner, constantly abasing himself before they have a chance to injure him; (3) the individual masturbates excessively and is concerned about this because he feels it will injure him either mentally or physically; or (4) he suffers from the psychotic delusion that some person or persons, either known or unknown, are going to take a knife and cut off his genitalia.

It would make it much easier for the reader of the clinical case study if the person preparing the report would specify which of these possibilities he had in mind rather than leaving it to the imagination of the reader to determine the choice. By going directly from the test data to the prediction, and by making the prediction at a specific and verifiable level of interpersonal functioning, much of the above confusion could be obviated. Thus, the subject who cuts off pieces of the Rorschach blots could be described directly as being critical and behaving in a way which wastes time and does not further the purpose, out of fear of being caught short. The person not resolving problems on the TAT could be described as not being able to plan ahead to the solution of dilemmas in which he can conceive himself to be; the person reacting to failure with panic on the WAIS could be described as having a great deal of difficulty maintaining his sense of self-esteem under conditions of apparent failure; and the person with his hands in his pockets could be described by the DAP in some manner congruent with the theory of the examiner. Unfortunately, the present writer has no hypothesis to offer in the latter instance in view of the lack of evidence that this kind of phenomenon is related to any other kind of behavior.

Using projective statements to imply a behavioral condition which can be directly checked is the most common error made in clinical case studies involving confusion among levels. However, it is by no means the only error that is made. As implied earlier in this chapter, it may be possible to make behavioral predictions from projective data which the examiner would be reluctant to make because of his feeling that projective tests can never measure anything except fantasy. For example, the evidence concerning the relationship between aggressive Rorschach content and aggressive behavior would certainly lead the examiner of the patient with aggressive content on the Rorschach to appropriately make the prediction that this patient is likely to behave in an aggressive manner. Thus, if he were to restrict himself in the report to merely pointing out that this patient has aggressive fantasies, he would be depriving the reader of some important predictive information which might possibly be of administrative and clinical value. Similarly, there may be Level II information which can be derived from projective tests, or so-called projective tests, which the reader would benefit from if he were made aware of it. For example, the SCT obviously could give information about a patient's conscious feelings and ideas, especially when a form using first person stems has been employed. Yet the report will often obscure the significance of these data by referring to it as fantasy data or projective data exclusively. Also, the individual may make personal references during the Rorschach test or the TAT which make it quite clear that he is referring to conscious experiences, feelings, and thought which would be important Level II data, and yet are not described as such in the report. There are times when it would be much more accurate and helpful to say "the patient feels that," or "the patient claims that," rather than to say "projective material reveals that," or "the patient's fantasies imply that."

Thus, the communication of findings from projective tests should always deal with the appropriate levels, and a statement should not hint at or imply a level other than the one that is justified by the evidence. This will greatly enhance the possibility of using data derived from projective techniques in an appropriate manner and integrating it properly with data derived from other sources.

The Importance of Clarity of Style and Language in Statements Derived from Projective Techniques

Interpretations of material based upon projective tests can often be recognized in the clinical case study by the peculiar shift in style of language which seems to occur. The style of the report up until a certain point may have been precise, factual, and clear. The reader has probably been told that the individual has a particular level of intelligence, that his behavior during the examination was thus and so, that his relationships with significant others in his life have been of a particular sort, and that he displays the following symptoms. Now we come to the part of the report based upon projective tests. All of a sudden we are in a kind of never-never land in which we hear about "basic regressive goal mechanisms" or "unresolved Oedipal problems which interfere with current heterosexual relationships" or "obsessive fantasies which have a defeatist flavor." Also, instead of hearing about the subject's or patient's relationship with real people, we are now bombarded by information concerning his attitudes and feelings toward "father figures" and "mother figures." Even though the conservatism of the interpreter in referring to these as "figures" rather than actual parents is commendable, the whole style of the report shifts from talking about an individual to talking about mechanisms and symbols which have no clear-cut connection with what has preceded this section.

Particularly difficult is the kind of esoteric language which sometimes creeps into the report when it deals with material derived from projective techniques. Take for example the use of pithy symbols like letters. We may talk about K—now which are we talking about? Are we talking about MMPI K? Are we talking about Szondi K? Are we talking about Rorschach K, or what? Obviously this is a kind of private language which requires more elaboration than it is worth in a clinical case study. Part of the difficulty arises from a basically incompetent examiner who uses projective techniques in a cookbook manner without really understanding their relationship to personality or to behavior. Thus, he may take statements directly from a standard textbook dealing with interpretations of the psychogram, the various percentages and ratios, the card-by-card analysis and put them together in an undigestible hodgepodge. Many such questions of organization and language have been discussed in the book on report writing (Klopfer, 1960). The recommendation the present author would make in this instance is that the statements derived from projective techniques should become indistinguishable from other parts of the report in terms of style and language. That is to say, they should be integrated and become part of a description of personality based upon all the material derived by the clinical psychologist.

By using the multilevel framework, information obtained from observation, objective tests, intelligence tests, and projective tests can all become part of a single description of personality and behavior which is organized along more rational lines than that of sources of

information. I would say that anyone incapable of translating projective material into everyday language has an indadequate understanding of it and of its relationship to personality.

WHY CLINICAL CASE STUDIES ARE NOT COMPLETE WITHOUT PROJECTIVE TESTS

The concluding section of this chapter will deal with the whole
question of whether projective instruments should be included in a
comprehensive case study. The present author feels that no case study
is complete without projective tests, for the following reasons:

1.   It would be very unsafe, unwise, and incorrect to assume that
a patient either can or wants to present all aspects of his or her
personality fully to the examiner at the time he presents himself or
herself for personality evaluation. One possible reason for this is that
he may have been precipitated into the examination through circumstances which make him feel ashamed and defensive. He may
have been referred by a law-enforcement agency, by a dissatisfied
marital partner, or by a disgruntled parent. He may distrust the examiner or the examining situation and want to hold back his full
confidence until he feels more assured that the matters he reveals will
be adequately received and properly and constructively used for his
benefit. Even if he consciously feels totally cooperative and trusting,
there may still be matters which he is unable to communicate because
he himself is unaware of them. Thus, the present writer would argue
that ego-defensiveness precludes the presentation of complete information through interviews or questionnaires. The projective situation is uniquely suited to getting beneath the patient's character armor
and discovering where his vital organs are. This is not to say that this
information cannot be gotten in other ways; however, getting it
through premature direct confrontation with the patient may pose
dangers to the patient's mental health which can be reduced through
the use of projective tests. The projective tests enable one to get inside
and out again quickly before the patient is aware of the fact that he is
being so searchingly investigated.
    The relationship between the examiner and the person being
examined is likely to be one which will not outlast the examination
itself. Sometimes the psychologist doing the evaluation acts as a
consultant and reports the result to someone else, such as an agency
or a potential therapist. Sometimes the evaluation might be part of a

teaching procedure and the feedback will go to trainees rather than to the patient himself. It seems rather irresponsible to expect the patient to become very trusting and involved with the examiner under conditions like this since something will be begun and there will be no opportunity to continue. This makes the evaluation of hidden personality traits through indirect means such as projective techniques a much more attractive proposition than the exposure of the patient prior to his readiness to assimilate the information.

2.   One of the reasons given for the possible exclusion of projective techniques from the clinical case study is that the observations of others will suffice, assuming that these others are sufficiently skilled and professionally competent, and that not enough is added to the total clinical case study by the use of projective instruments to deserve the added expense and trouble. This places a good deal of responsibility upon the judgment of clinicians, which does not seem to be warranted by the evidence concerning the reliability of clinical judgments. All too often, research projects which hinge upon the reliability of clinical judgments end up in chaos. A good example is the study by Filmer-Bennett and Klopfer (1962), which was an attempt to place the SCT and the TAT in a hierarchical continuum in terms of the Levels frame of reference. The study included 20 college students who were asked to rank themselves on four continua which had been pretested in such a way as to assure relative normality of distribution of the self-ratings once they were made. A group of judges, who were considered experts in the two tests mentioned above, were used to provide criterion measures. The hypothesis was that the self-ratings would be predicted with greater accuracy on the basis of the SCT than on the basis of the TAT, the rationale being that the SCT would have greater face validity for use as a comparison with self-ratings than the TAT. However, the study demonstrated that neither the TAT judges nor the SCT judges were able to approximate the self-ratings and, furthermore, that they disagreed with one another. It seems that clinicians have great difficulty in making straightforward judgments such as predicting self-ratings. Reports from the judges indicated that they were unable, for example, to predict whether somebody would deem himself or herself as being overtly aggressive or not. Even when the projective evidence seemed to indicate that the individual was not possessed of aggression, the clinician would say to himself, "I wonder why this patient is assiduously avoiding the expression of aggression. Probably he is seething with aggression which is threatening him to the extent that he is unable to face the possible onslaught of such an ominous and over-

whelming amount of aggression. This is the reason he is deceiving himself, but not me. I will not be fooled and I will rank him high in aggression." The trouble with this reasoning, of course, is that the judge is not sticking to the level of interpersonal functioning at which he has been asked to make predictions. Now there may be some clinicians who can make straightforward predictions at a level which has been specified by the experimenter, but they have not been clearly identified thus far.

Another problem that arises when one relies upon the observation of the patient by others is that no matter how skilled an observer may be, his judgment is likely to be clouded by subjective influences due to his own psychological blind spots and by dyadic interactional influences. To substantiate this point, one need only refer to some of the work of Masling (1959), who demonstrated to the chagrin of a good many people that patients could influence the judgment of examiners in any one of a variety of ways. For example, he demonstrated that such a seemingly objective matter as a WAIS score could be influenced by a female subject's seductive or nasty attitude toward a male examiner. If even this kind of ostensibly objective datum can be influenced by dyadic interactional influences, it would seem very likely that straight observation or the clinical interview could be similarly influenced. The above is not, of course, an argument solely for the inclusion of projective tests, but for the use of multiple measurements from a variety of modalities. Certainly it would appear that projective tests, even though they are capable of being influenced by transient and situational factors, are harder for the patient to manipulate by means of a set than some other kinds of situations in which he might be observed. Surely we have enough questions about the adequacy and completeness of our methods of personality assessment generally to discourage us from discarding a tool with potential value as great as that of a projective test.

3.   One of the most frequently given reasons for not including projective tests in a clinical case study is that they are not standardized instruments and consequently they are more subject to examiner misinterpretation than others. This criticism is justified if the projective instrument is used in a nonstandard manner. Unfortunately, those clinicians likely to be most critical of projective tests are the ones most likely to use them in a haphazard, inappropriate, and slovenly manner. For example, they will give some of the Rorschach cards and not others, or they will use only the free-association part of the procedure and not conduct a proper inquiry. They will give the entire test, but merely subject it to a kind of sign approach for specific

purposes such as the detection of schizophrenia, which hardly exploits the potentialities of the instrument. Similarly, the TAT may be used to get information about the patient's attitudes toward significant others without taking into account the stylistic possibilities of the performance and the possibility of forming superordinate hypotheses from comparing TAT material with interview material and the observations made of the patient directly. The worse offenders are those who use some kind of esoteric system of scoring and classification culled from various sources, and then claim that there are no standards available. Certainly there are no norms available for a system which is original with the particular clinician. However, a test like the Rorschach has definitely been standardized according to certain major systems like those of Beck and Klopfer. Also, there are developmental norms available to compare the performance of children at various ages with their peers. It is only when the projective test is used in a standardized manner that its scientific as well as artistic contribution to the clinical case study is fully exploited.

REFERENCES

Beck, S. J. Rorschach's Test, Vol. II. New York: Grune and Stratton, 1945.

Bendick, M., & Klopfer, W. G. The effects of sensory deprivation and motor inhibition on Rorschach movement responses. Journal of Projective Techniques and Personality Assessment, 1964, 28, 261–264.

Elizur, A. Content analysis of the Rorschach with regard to anxiety and hospitality. Rorschach Research Exchange, 1949, 13, 247–284.

Filmer-Bennett, G., & Klopfer, W. G. Levels of awareness in projective tests. Journal of Projective Techniques, 1962, 26, 34–35.

Finney, B. C. Rorschach test correlates of assaultive behavior. Journal of Projective Techniques, 1955, 19, 6–17.

Forer, B. The fallacy of personal validation; a classroom demonstration of gullibility. Journal of Abnormal Social Psychology, 1949, 44, 118–123.

Garfield, S. L., Heine, R. W., & Leventhal, M. An evaluation of psychological reports in a clinical setting. Journal of Consulting Psychology, 1954, 18, 281–286.

Holt, R. R. Methods in Clinical Psychology, Vol. I: Projective Assessment. New York: Plenum Press, 1978.

Klopfer, B., Ainsworth, M. D., Klopfer, W. G., & Holt, R. R. Developments in the Rorschach Technique, Vol. I. New York: World Book, 1954.

Klopfer, W. G. The Psychological Report: Use and Communication of Psychological Findings. New York: Grune and Stratton, 1960.

Klopfer, W. G. Assessing adolescents at all relevant levels. Academic Psychological Bulletin, 1979, 1, 113–117.

Klopfer, W. G., and Taulbee, E. S. "Projective Tests." In *Annual Review of Psychology*, 1976, *27*, 543–569.

Leary, T. F. *The Interpersonal Diagnosis of Personality*. New York: Ronald, 1957.

McGreevey, J. C. Interlevel disparity and predictive efficiency. *Journal of Projective Techniques*, 1962, *26*, 80–87.

McReynolds, P. Perception of Rorschach concepts as related to personality deviations. *Journal of Abnormal Social Psychology*, 1951, *46*, 131–141.

Masling, J. The effects of warm and cold interaction on the administration and scoring of an intelligence test. *Journal of Consulting Psychology*, 1959, *23*, 336–341.

Matarazzo, J. D., Allen, B., Saslow, G., & Wiens, A. N. Characteristics of successful policemen and firemen applicants. *Journal of Applied Psychology*, 1964, *48*, 123–133.

Murstein, B. I. The projection of hostility on the Rorschach and as a result of ego threat. *Journal of Projective Techniques*, 1956, *20*, 418–428.

Murstein, B. I. *Theory and Research in Projective Techniques: Emphasizing the TAT*. New York: Wiley, 1963.

Stone, H. K., & Dellis, N. P. An exploratory investigation into the levels hypothesis. *Journal of Projective Techniques*, 1960, *24*, 333–340.

Tomkins, S. *Thematic Apperception Test*. New York: Grune and Stratton, 1947.

Ullmann, L. P., Berkman, V. C., & Hammister, R. C. Psychological reports related to behavior and benefit of placement in home care. *Journal of Clinical Psychology*, 1958, 14, 254–259.

Warren, S., & Klopfer, W. G. *Prediction of Public Image by Means of Self-Report*. Unpublished study, 1965.

9

Why and When to Test: The Social Context of Psychological Testing

David Levine

The major contention of this chapter is that errors in the interpretation of psychological test results occur frequently because the psychologist has not concerned himself sufficiently with the general purpose of the psychological evaluation—because he has underestimated the importance of a clear comprehension of the referral question in its broadest possible context. Although I shall be able to present some clinical and theoretical material to support this idea, I am not familiar with any controlled research which is relevant to it.

It is well known, however, that most requests for psychological testing are not presented to psychologists in terms of a question to be answered or a decision to be made. Too many referrals come from anxious psychiatric residents who are not sure how to manage a patient, from school administrators who feel they need test evidence to support a decision they have already made, from teachers who want test data to convince a recalcitrant parent of the seriousness of a child's problem, from parole board members who want to make use of "every available resource" before committing themselves to a final decision, from social workers "because we have always done it this way"—all these referrals illustrate the kinds of non-test considerations which tend to confuse the referral context and to put the psychologist in an ambiguous position.

In this chapter I plan to analyze and to clarify some of the more typical situations in which psychological testing has been employed.

If the major contention is correct, such a clarification will lead to fewer errors in psychological test interpretation, to more meaningful psychological test reports, and ultimately to more effective social use of psychological test results. I shall present an analysis of five institutional settings within which psychological tests are used: the psychiatric setting; the general medical setting; the legal setting; the educational setting; and the setting of the psychological clinic. A clear understanding of these social contexts will not obviate the need for continued care in the selection of appropriate tests, in the administration and scoring of these tests, and in the interpretation of these test results in accord with the most recent information about the tests and about personality theory in general, but it should avoid some unnecessary confusion and—especially among younger psychologists— it may help direct energies toward important considerations, rather than toward irrelevant issues.

THE PROBLEM

Recently—especially during the past few years—attacks on psychological tests have increased in frequency and scope. Moreover, these attacks come not only from extremist groups or crusading journalists (Gross, 1962; Hoffman, 1962); they have come also from well-meaning, thoughtful people in positions of high social responsibility.

On Friday, June 4, 1965, during the hearings of a House Special Subcommittee on Invasion of Privacy of the Committee on Government Operations, Representative Benjamin S. Rosenthal said: "... I am so impressed [by the evidence I have heard today that] I am prepared to offer a bill on Monday to prohibit the giving of psychological tests by any Federal agency, under any circumstances, at any place, and to make it a Federal crime for any Federal official to do it." (Testimony before House Special Subcommittee on Invasion of Privacy of the Committee on Government Operations, 1965, p. 982.)

This point of view was shared by other senators and congressmen during the two weeks of hearings conducted in June of 1965 on the question: Do psychological tests constitute an invasion of privacy?

On April 5, 1966, Representative Rosenthal introduced a bill in Congress (HR 14288) "to prohibit, except in certain circumstances, the expenditure of funds by any department for the acquisition or use of personality inventory tests . . ."

On February 26, 1964, an Illinois Fair Employment Practices Commission hearing examiner issued a "decision and order directing

Motorola to cease the use of Test 10 (a low level test of intellectual ability) because it did not reflect and equate inequalities and environmental factors among the disadvantaged and culturally deprived group" (Motorola's Employment Test Procedure, 1964). Motorola claimed that the applicant scored below the cutoff point on a screening test which all their applicants must take. The Negro applicant did not argue this point, but he claimed that the test was so constructed as to be unfair to Negroes.

At about the same time, in response to the criticism that group intelligence tests were unfair to Negroes and Puerto Ricans, the Board of Education of the City of New York outlawed the use of group tests of intelligence in its public school system. In a small town in Texas, the same end was achieved by burning psychological tests. Although these are attacks on intelligence tests, projective tests are also open to the criticism that the responses are interpreted in terms of white middle-class norms (Auld, 1952). Thus, although some people may have accepted the social contribution of psychological testing, many are becoming concerned about the possible harm which psychological testing can do as a result of invasion of privacy and because of the possibility of discrimination.

Testing procedures are also criticized on theoretical grounds. As the result of a careful analysis of measurement and decision making, Churchman (1961) concludes:

> In this sense, of measurement taken as a decision-making activity designed to accomplish an objective, we have as yet no theory of measurement. We do not know why we do what we do. We do not even know why we measure at all. It is costly to obtain measurements. Is the effort worth the cost? [p.102]

There is also a problem, however, of an excessive reliance on psychological tests. Although psychological tests are under attack by lay people, an increasing number of social workers, psychiatrists, physicians, judges, educators, and businessmen seem to be placing more faith in psychological testing than many psychologists feel is justified, or using psychological testing for a host of inappropriate reasons, rather than for information about a patient or client. This problem will be discussed in greater detail when we analyze the five institutional contexts.

Attacks on psychological testing come not only from outside psychology; they come from psychologists as well. Meehl (1960), during the course of the clinical-actuarial controversy, wrote:

My advice to fledgling clinical psychologists is to construct their self concept mainly around "I am a researcher" or "I am a psychotherapist," because one whose self concept is mainly "I am a (test oriented) psychodiagnostician" may have to maintain his professional security over the next few years by not reading the research literature, a maneuver which has apparently proved quite successful already for some clinicians. Personally, I find the cultural lag between what the published research shows and what clinicians persist in claiming to do with their favorite devices even more disheartening than the adverse evidence itself [p. 26].

Although Meehl (1965) has pointed out that "commentators have tended to polarize and oversimplify my . . . views," his writings have left many young psychologists and graduate students much bewildered. They were taught in graduate school to give tests; they are hired to give tests; they spend much time testing; they try to arrive at meaningful conclusions about their patients or clients; and their reports are considered seriously as part of the decision-making process. Yet Meehl's data and arguments that personality tests are invalid seem extremely persuasive (Meehl, 1954; 1960).

It is interesting to observe the kinds of reactions which psychologists adopt in response to this conflict and to the threat to their professional self-esteem.

Holzberg (1961) in an analysis of "defensive reactions to research role conflicts" among young psychologists describes several kinds of adjustments which are analogous to what is experienced by psychologists confronted with this threat to their psychodiagnostic self-esteem. Holzberg describes the defenses of withdrawal, projection, denial, identification, and intellectualization.

The psychologist who *withdraws* decides to abandon the function of psychological testing completely, declaring that society will benefit more by the therapy and research that will be done. The psychologist who falls back on "clinical intuition" to the extent that he feels he has a special talent and does not need to concern himself with research being done in assessment, generally combines *identification with a psychologist* whom he tries to emulate and *projection*—"no other tests or psychologists can do the job as well as we can."

The *intellectualizer* takes full responsibility for very few psychological referrals, but is always available to consult on someone else's case. He can shift ground very easily depending on the particular situation in which he finds himself.

The reactions to this conflict by psychologists are not difficult to understand; the implications for the larger social good are, however, difficult to determine. Would society be better off if psychological testing were abandoned? This question will be raised again in terms of the specific social institutions we will explore.

Thus many psychologists, through ignorance, apathy, insecurity, or rigidity, approach their patient or client with little concern for the purpose of the evaluation. The following incident illustrates how futile a psychological examination can be when the psychologist is oblivious of the purpose of his task.

During a consulting visit to a hospital, I agreed to observe a psychology student administer a WAIS. Since the student was ready to begin, I went into his office, followed almost immediately by the supervising psychologist and the patient. The supervising psychologist introduced the patient and the student and then left. The following is a description (as nearly as I can recall it) of what took place:

T (trainee) : Name?
P (patient): Joseph Burns.
T: Birthdate?
P: August 6, 1923.
T: Age?
P: Forty three.
T: Married?
P: No, single.
T: Nationality?
P: American.
T: Occupation?
P: Truck driver.
T: Education?
P: One year of high school.
T: What does rubber come from?
P: Trees.
T: Name four men who've been president of the United States since 1900.
P: Truman, Kennedy, Eisenhower, Johnson.
T: Who was Longfellow?

. . . and so on through the entire WAIS.

This exchange took place in a formal atmosphere, the trainee asking the questions in a precise, businesslike manner and the patient giving his responses laconically. As I recall, the patient was not especially tense at the start of the testing; he was cooperative and his affect was flat. The trainee went through the 11 WAIS subtests in order, generally reading the instructions, and as the examination progressed, the patient became increasingly terse in his responses. He didn't talk at all during the performance tests, started smoking in an agitated manner, and, by the time he was doing the Block Design Test, was obviously making no serious attempt to solve the more difficult items. After the last item on the Object Assembly was completed, the trainee said, "Thank you, we're finished," and the patient got up and walked out without a word.

The trainee had received instructions at the university concerning "establishing rapport" and "understanding the referral." He had been told by his supervisor at the hospital that he would be assigned a patient to test and that he was to give a WAIS because it was the only test he had learned, but he had not been told why this patient was to be tested—nor did he ask. He had previously been told by the supervising psychologist that he should interview patients he would test. The student was highly recommended by his undergraduate instructors and is expected to do well in graduate school. He will learn. He had apparently not yet learned, however, that psychological testing is an interaction between human beings.

It should be clear that on the basis of his hour and a half with the patient, this student is in no position to make much of a contribution. It is my contention that he doesn't even know how intelligent the patient is, let alone know how to begin to formulate a "working image" (Sundberg & Tyler, 1962) of him. Furthermore, I suspect the patient distrusts him and that the trainee would have a very difficult time gaining the patient's confidence in the future. This kind of situation occurs more often than we would like to admit. The bulk of this chapter is devoted to an attempt to analyze how this kind of situation has come about and what can be done to change it. The analysis of the five social contexts will be simplified if we first review some recent developments in "decision theory."

DECISION THEORY AS A THEORY OF MEASUREMENT

What has been called "classical measurement theory" considers the psychological test as a measuring instrument, analogous to a ruler or a thermometer, with test theory "directed primarily toward the study of accuracy of measurement on a continuous scale" (Cronbach & Gleser, 1965). This kind of measurement theory necessarily centers on the classical problems of reliability and validity—with the ultimate criterion of a good test being its use as an accurate predictor. The philo-

sophical position in which this approach is rooted is logical positivism and operationism and the accomplishments of this school of
measurement have been great.

Within the past decade, however, there has been an important
new development in test theory. Cronbach and Gleser (1965) describe
this new approach:

> The value of a test depends on many qualities in addition to its
> [predictive] accuracy. Especially to be considered are the relevance of
> the measurement to the particular decision being made, and the loss
> resulting from an erroneous decision. Recommendations regarding
> the design, selection and interpretation of a test must take into
> account the characteristics of the decisions for which the test will be
> used, since the test that is maximally effective for one decision will
> not necessarily be most effective elsewhere.
>
> An appropriate test theory can evolve from a general and sys-
> tematic examination of the decision problems for which tests are used
> and of the demands these problems placed upon the test [pp. 1–2].

The present chapter may be considered a part of such an examination.

Cronbach and Gleser's point of view is shared by many psychologists (e.g., Sundberg & Tyler, 1962; Levy, 1963). Although no attempt
will be made to review in detail the history or mathematics of decision theory, some landmarks should be mentioned.

The modern history of decision theory begins with the publication of von Neumann and Morgenstern's *Theory of Games and Economic Behavior* in 1944. A game is conceived of as "any situation in
which money (or some valuable equivalent) may be gained as the
result of a proper choice of strategy" (Edwards, 1954, p. 406). Edwards
summarizes von Neumann and Morgenstern's contribution as follows:

> It is of course impossible to condense a tremendous and difficult
> book into one page. The major points to be emphasized are these: the
> theory of games is not a model of how people actually play games
> (some game theorists will disagree with this), nor is it likely to be of
> any practical use in telling you how to play a complicated game; the
> crux of the theory of games is the principle of choosing the strategy
> which minimizes the maximum expected financial loss; and the
> theory defines a solution of a game as a set of imputations (a set of
> payments made as a result of a game, one to each player) which
> satisfies the principle for all players [p. 408].

Although the theory of games seems to have no immediate relevance to our problem, Wald's extension of game theory to the problem of decision making has. Decision making is defined as deciding

> . . . on the basis of observations which cost something to make, between policies, each of which has a possible gain or loss. In some cases, all of these gains and losses and the cost of observing can be exactly calculated, as in industrial quality control. In other cases, as in theoretical research, it is necessary to make some assumption about the cost of being wrong and the gain of being right [Edwards, 1954, p. 409].

The emphasis in decision theory has been on attempts to specify utilities or payoff functions which will enable the decision maker to make the decision which minimizes loss, maximizes gain, or minimizes regret, where "regret is defined as the difference between the maximum which can be gained under any strategy given a certain state of the world and the amount gained under the strategy adopted" (Edwards, 1954, p. 409).

In 1957, the first edition of Cronbach and Gleser's *Psychological Tests and Personnel Decisions* appeared, presenting an analysis of decision theory and psychological testing. The revised edition, which appeared in 1965, includes a chapter which covers the intervening years. We are now beginning to see a way in which decision theory may be of some value to decisions based on psychological tests. The "observations which cost something to make" may be viewed as the psychological tests while the "policies each of which has a possible gain or loss" are the alternatives open to the decision maker.

To facilitate the later discussion, let us briefly define some terms which have been developed in decision theory and redefine some other concepts in terms of decision theory.

Tests.   Any "information-gathering procedures including interviews, biographical inquiries, and physical measurement" (Cronbach & Gleser, 1965, p. 7).

Institutional vs. individual decision.   An institutional decision is one in which one person (or group of persons) makes many comparable decisions. An individual decision "is one in which the choice confronting the decision maker will rarely or never recur" (Cronbach & Gleser, 1965, p. 7). Institutional decisions are made in regard to many people and the decision maker will make decisions which will—in the long run—be best for the institution, be it a large corporation, mental hospital, penal complex, or large community.

In an individual decision, the best choice "depends on the individual's value system and varies from one individual to another" (Cronbach & Gleser, 1965, p. 8).

Values.   Since decisions are good or bad depending on the outcome of the decision, much of decision theory has been concerned with the study of outcomes or, as they are called in decision theory, *payoffs* or *utilities.* For almost all kinds of payoffs, however, the nature of the payoff functions is difficult to specify and the study of values becomes—for the first time in measurement theory—a crucial problem. It may be that the greatest contribution of decision theory will be that it forces the decision maker to be explicit about his value system.

Girshick (1954) writes:

> ... decision theory demands a great deal of the decision maker. It demands that he be in a position to evaluate numerically for every possible state of nature in the situation under consideration the consequences of any of the actions he might take. ... The inability of the decision maker to formulate clearly the loss function is, in fact, a stumbling block in determining what a rational mode of behavior is for him. ... It is impossible to tell a person what is an optimal way for him to behave if he is unable to formulate clearly what he is after. ... [p. 463].

To paraphrase Girshick: Decision theory is a gadfly for the psychodiagnostician. It says to him: You cannot be of any service to the person making the referral unless you can specify what decision he is facing, what alternatives are available to him, what the utility or value of these alternatives is, and finally, what relevance test data and observations have in terms of specifying outcomes for each of the alternatives once they are adopted.

The problem of values is especially difficult because the values of one decision maker may differ from the values of another decision maker. As Bross (1953) writes:

> I have already noted that the various rules for action reflect various attitudes that might be taken toward the real world—optimism, pessimism, and the like. So presumably we should select the rule which comes closest to expressing the outlook of the customer, the person who has come for advice on decision. While this procedure is plausible, it is not very practical. The statistician would have to find some device for measuring the customer's general outlook on life. Things are complicated enough with predicting systems and value systems without having to take this further step—although it may come about someday [p. 110].

Maximization.   The strategy of maximizing the average gain (or minimizing the average loss) over many similar decisions, according to Cronbach and Gleser (1965, pp. 8–9), is not generally relevant for individual decisions. Ward Edwards (1963; 1966) disagrees, emphasizing that our opinions about (our probabilities for) various possible events may be relatively clear or relatively vague but are never utterly clear or utterly vague and that individual decisions should be made on the same basis as institutional decisions.

Sequential strategy.   Classical test theory generally assumed that a final decision was made on all individuals at one time on the basis of a single test battery. Sequential strategy involves several stages of information-gathering at each of which some decisions are reached, but other decisions put off.

Bandwidth.   This term—taken from information theory—refers to the scope of information which the test is designed to obtain. Achievement tests have narrow bandwidth; projective tests are wide-band procedures. Generally, greater bandwidth is achieved by sacrificing accuracy of measurement.

Incremental validity.   The extent to which a test improves decisions over the strategy which would have been employed without the test should be contrasted with comparing the test-based strategy with a random strategy.

Bounded vs. unbounded problems.   The distinction between bounded and unbounded problems is described by Levy (1963):

> The bounded problem is one involving a discrete prediction or decision, usually circumscribed in time and most often concerned with the classification or disposition of a case, whereas the unbounded case involves problems of case management such as in psychotherapy, where the therapist requires of psychodiagnosis a formulation that will serve as a continuing guide in his moment-to-moment and day-to-day decision making. While in the bounded case we know in advance the conditions under which the psychodiagnostic product will be used, in the unbounded case such information is generally lacking or of the most diffuse sort. Considering the distinctive characteristics of each, the formal approach to psychodiagnosis, of which the actuarial method of prediction is one example, is found most appropriate and efficient when dealing with bounded problems, while the interpretive approach offers distinct advantages in the case of unbounded problems [p. 194].

Conclusion vs. decisions.   Tukey (1960) has formulated a distinction between decisions and conclusions. Decisions involve acting "for the present as if" the outcomes of different alternatives are known because a decision between alternatives is necessary at the time. The decision maker weighs

> . . . both the *evidence* concerning the relative merits of A and B and also the *probable consequences in the present situation* of various actions (actions, not decisions!). Finally, we have decided that the particular course of action which would be appropriate if A were truly greater than B is the most reasonable one to adopt in the specific situation that faces us.
>
> A conclusion is a statement which is to be accepted as applicable to the conditions of an experiment or observation unless and until unusually strong evidence to the contrary arises. . . . These characteristics are very different from those of a decision-theorist's decision [pp. 2–4].

Decision to do nothing.   The decision to do nothing has received little attention in decision theory, but Tukey quotes Barnard as saying:

> The fine art of executive decision consists in not deciding questions that are now not pertinent, in not deciding prematurely, in not making decisions that cannot be made effective, and in not making decisions that others should make [p. 5].

The decision to do nothing occupies a special place in decision theory.

The model of testing which I have adopted, then, is based on a decision theory which requires that (1) a decision must be made; (2) psychological tests can be expected to contribute information which will enable the decision maker to maximize his strategy; and (3) the decision maker will actually alter his strategy to coincide with this new information.[1]

It should be noted that some psychologists hold that testing not be limited in this way. Sundberg and Tyler (1962) cite "twin functional goals of clinical assessment as the process used for decision making and for developing a working image or model of the person-situation." They write:

---

[1] It has been suggested that, since the criterion problem remains, decision theory does not represent a conceptual advance over classical measurement theory. Even if this turns out to be the case, our analysis of the social context of psychological testing has been facilitated by conceiving of it in terms of decision theory.

The making of decisions is not all there is to clinical assessment. . . . To some degree the clinician always builds up a *picture* of the person with whom he is dealing. . . . This function of assessment is what we have called the development of a working image or model. By the working image or model we mean the *clinician's set of hypotheses about the person and the situations in which he presently or potentially operates.* . . . The working image is the best approximation a clinician can achieve of a representation of the other human being [pp. 84–85].

Levy's concept of "unbounded psychodiagnostic problems" seems to be dealing with the same kind of approach and to fall logically outside a formal decision theory model as presented here. His "interpretive approach"—which he says is appropriate for unbounded problems—" . . . is found to culminate in a set of assertions (not decisions) based upon the clinician's experience, observations, theories, and beliefs. . . . "

The logic and mathematics of decision theory are intriguing in their own right and the implications are likely to be of value to psychology in a way that far transcends test theory. Good starting points for the reader who is interested in exploring this material further are Cronbach and Gleser (1965), Bross (1953), or Churchman (1961).

THE PSYCHIATRIC SETTING

"We regard the human brain as the *chef d'oeuvre*, or masterpiece of creation. . . . Insanity is but a disease of this organ, and when so regarded, it will often be prevented, and generally cured, by the early adoption of proper methods of treatment" (*American Journal of Insanity*, 1844, back cover).

This point of view—the manifesto of the officers of the New York State Lunatic Asylum—was probably shared by the majority of physicians who met in 1844 to establish the American Association of Mental Hospital Superintendents—later the American Psychiatric Association. However, the cure of syphilis (and subsequent decline of paresis), the advent of psychoanalysis, the introduction of the tranquilizers, and recent developments in psychology, sociology, and anthropology have led most psychiatrists to adopt a much broader perspective to their work. The establishment within the past few years of community mental health centers illustrates this broadening of perspective in psychiatry from the study of the brain to the study of the individual in transaction with family, society, and culture.

These multiple developments make it difficult to speak of a single psychiatric setting and, for purposes of our discussion, we will speak of the psychologist in relation to the psychiatrist as ward administrator; the psychiatrist as psychotherapist; and the psychiatrist as physician.

Psychiatrist as Ward Administrator

The psychiatrist as hospital administrator or ward administrator is a clear example of a decision maker. He is responsible for the health and well-being of his patients; he has the authority to administer a wide variety of medical procedures; he has the authority to say whether a patient will be free or locked up. Shall I discharge the patient? Shall he be transferred to an open ward? Is he a suicide risk? And so on. As with most people in positions of authority, the hospital administrator will utilize help to assist in making these decisions. Why then is the psychologist in the mental hospital so often the one most frustrated in his role as psychodiagnostician?

There seem to be several reasons. First, these decisions are difficult ones in the sense that the base rates are not well established. We don't know how many patients who attempt suicide will eventually be successful. We don't know how many patients who have threatened to kill somebody will actually commit murder. But we do know that these are rare occurrences and the prediction of rare occurrences is an extremely difficult task.

Second, when evaluated in terms of classical measurement theory, our projective tests have often been found wanting. Psychologists have been taught in graduate schools that the goal of measurement is prediction, but find that in practice the procedures they employ are not accurate predictors.

Third, many psychiatrists ignore at times the results of psychological examinations without discontinuing the practice of asking that these examinations be made.

Why do hospital administrators continue to hire psychologists as psychodiagnosticians? Most often the psychologist is seen as filling a technician's role—much like an x-ray technician or laboratory technician. The possible seeds for the growth of tension and dissatisfaction for the Ph.D. psychologist in this kind of situation are obvious.

From the point of view of the physician, biochemical analyses are done by laboratory technicians, not by Ph.D.'s in biochemistry. Why then should he not expect that psycological tests be done by psychological technicians with the integration of all findings being left up to the physician? He has learned what a 10,000 white blood cell count means, why can't he learn what an M:C ratio of 1:4 means? Why does the psychologist insist on long-winded descriptions when all he wants is a diagnosis?

But is that really all he wants? As Szasz (1963) has pointed out, the psychiatrist as ward administrator has altered his major professional responsibility from treatment to custody and his major decisions involve, not diagnosis and treatment, but questions of the freedom of the patient and the safety of society. To the extent that psychiatric diagnosis is helpful in making these social decisions, diagnosis is an important step. But classical psychiatric nosology has been found to be irrelevant to these decisions. Whether or not a patient is schizophrenic is not helpful in deciding whether he is dangerous to himself or others.

If the decision is made to keep the patient in the institution, a host of subsequent decision must faced: To what kind of ward shall he be assigned? To what kind of activities? Which of the available "therapies" is likely to be of benefit to him?

The psychologist working in a mental hospital who receives a referral for "psychologicals" with no further information may respond in accordance with his own needs, the defensive reactions I described earlier in this chapter—withdrawal, rationalization, projection, etc. Or he can attempt to determine what the relevant and important decisions are which will have to be made with respect to the patient and then try to obtain information relevant to these decisions. The first step in finding answers is to determine the appropriate questions.

But, to the extent that the psychologist is unwilling to accept the fact that the psychiatrist as hospital administrator has been charged by society with the legal responsibility for decisions about patients—to that extent the psychologist will be unable to use psychological testing procedures to help the psychiatrist. In a decision-making model of testing, the importance of knowing the decision maker's values has been clearly demonstrated.

Psychiatrist as Psychotherapist

Much difficulty develops when the psychiatrist confuses his own roles. When a psychiatrist attempts to function as both therapist and caretaker or when he shifts haphazardly from one role to another, the nature of his relationship with the patient—and with the psychologist—is likely to become ambiguous at best and tense and distorted at worst. Many psychological referrals are outcomes of difficult situations which psychiatrists have gotten into because of their attempt to play several conflicting roles in relation to their patients.

However, let us try to explore the situation in which a psychotherapist refers a patient for testing at some point during psychotherapy. A referral *before* psychotherapy asks the question, "Is this patient suitable for psychotherapy?" and has been one of the traditional functions of psychological assessment. This kind of referral is clear-cut and, to the extent that the psychologist is willing to accept it, generally presents few problems.

A referral made during the course of psychotherapy is generally more complex because it frequently reflects anxiety on the part of the therapist, whose expectations about what the patient should be doing are not being fulfilled. Frequently, if the psychologist is to make an honest evaluation of the situation, he must communicate to the psychotherapist that the therapist's expectations are unreasonable, rather than that the patient is not being a "good patient." This "diagnostic triad" is the kind of situation which Towbin (1960) has analyzed so lucidly.

Psychiatrist as Physician

Special problems ensue from the basically different frames of reference which psychiatrists and psychologists bring to understanding the patient. Although there is clearly much overlap between the two frames of reference, most psychiatrists view their patient's problems in terms of a disease model while most psychologists see the patient's problems as arising from his difficulties in living with people and in society. The psychologist—as tester—needs to be able to communicate with the psychiatrist. If the psychiatrist asks the question, "Is this patient schizophrenic?" of a psychologist who feels that the concept "schizophrenia" is vague, confused, oversimplified, and stupid, the psychologist will have difficulty answering the question. The question "Is the patient schizophrenic?" may, however, be one of several different questions. The psychiatrist may be saying:

"This new patient must be classified because of legal statutes and hospital regulations. I know as well as you do that 'schizophrenia' is a philosophically embarrassing concept, but we have a job to do, so let's do it."

Or, "This patient can only give vague explanations for coming to the hospital. I suspect he has a lot of very peculiar ideas which he is not talking about and I'm worried that he might behave in a way to hurt himself or someone else on the basis of these peculiar ideas. On the basis of a psychological evaluation, what is your opinion of the nature and quality of his thinking processes?"

Or, "I know the scientific research on this is very poor, but I have to decide whether to give this patient tranquilizing medication, electric convulsive therapy, or psychotherapy and it is my best opinion that patients diagnosed schizophrenic, rather than neurotic or brain damaged, can be treated most efficiently (in decision theory terms, the payoff is best) by tranquilizers. What is your opnion about the best classification of this patient?"

A psychologist who views his role in psychological assessment as a "technician" rather than as a "consultant" (Towbin, 1960) will not be able to distinguish among these three possibilities. The psychologist qua psychologist, i.e., a person trained and experienced in the scientific study of behavior, will make a serious attempt to understand the psychiatrist's frame of reference and is likely to formulate his contribution in terms of the psychiatrist's constructs— not because he feels they are most heuristic, but because he realizes that the job at hand requires the maximum communication. He may have to translate the psychiatrist's concepts into terms which he feels are scientifically meaningful and then retranslate them so as to communicate his findings to the psychiatrist; this may be difficult— certainly more difficult than finding a recipe for a cake which doesn't exist.

GENERAL MEDICAL SETTING

This discussion of theoretical models and formal language is important for the effective functioning of the psychologist as psychodiagnostician in a general medical setting. The medical psychologist not only needs to learn a complex and extensive medical vocabulary, but he needs also to appreciate that a medical decision is different from a scientific decision (or conclusion); the loss function of not rejecting a null hypothesis because of insufficient data is different from the loss function of not performing an operation because of insufficient data. Furthermore, the loss function of not performing one kind of operation is likely to be different from the loss function connected with not performing another kind of operation, or with not performing an operation when the patient is showing one set of symptoms as compared with not performing the operation when the patient is showing a different set of symptoms. Rarely in medicine are these loss functions specifically stated. How then are medical decisions arrived at?

I am familiar with no systematic study of this question. But it is well known that physicians are trained to make these decisions, to use all possible resources to aid in making these decisions, but to assume final responsibility for them. The fact that the physician is the person who is licensed under the Medical Practices Act and who therefore has the legal responsibility for these decisions is a social factor that the psychologist must be prepared to accept if he is to function as efficiently and constructively in the medical setting as in the psychiatric setting. The responsibility and authority for the decision rests with the physician, not with the psychologist. When we are reminded, however, of the estimate that two-thirds of the patients a physician sees in his regular medical practice have a significant emotional component in their illness, the potential contribution of a clinical psychodiagnostician to medical decision making is obvious. Good medical practice is based on an awareness of the psychosomatic factors, the unity of mind and body.

The kind of referral from a physician that is likely to present most difficulties for the psychologist is the one which asks him to "evaluate the emotional factors" in a patient who complains of low back pain, or stomach distress, or headaches but for whose symptoms the medical examination has failed to reveal any organic etiology. The physician is faced with the problem of recommending some kind of treatment, but in the absence of positive signs of mental disorder is hesitant to recommend psychotherapy. If the psychologist could find a psychological disorder, the medical decision would be simplified. Can a psychologist ever fail to find some sign of emotional upset? Especially in someone who is physically ill? On the other hand, can psychological tests rule out organic factors? It appears as if—in this kind of referral situation at least—the professional roles are reversed. Instead of having the psychologist diagnose and the physician do the treatment, it would seem more logical for the physician to diagnose, i.e., rule out organic factors, and for the psychologist to treat those patients for whom no organic etiology can be established.

A common referral in the medical context which makes more sense is the one which asks the psychologist to evaluate the possibility of neurological involvement. Here the psychologist is able to supplement the information obtained in the neurological examination. Whereas the neurological examination focuses primarily on the peripheral nervous system, the psychological examination is concerned with determining whether the higher mental processes are intact. However, even this referral is relevant primarily when the physician has a decision to make. If the presence or absence of neurological involvement would not alter the treatment program, there seems little point in the referral. At times, however, signs of deterioration of the higher mental processes may point toward the need for more refined and risky evaluative procedures, such as a ventriculogram or explorative surgery. Here psychological tests may be seen as one stage in sequential decision making, a common kind of decision making in medical practice.

Increasingly, psychologists have become involved in psychological testing prior to surgery. Here the surgeon is interested in evaluating the risk of a stress reaction consequent to the operation. Although the research in this area is at a preliminary stage (Janis, 1958), this kind of question appears to be a logically appropriate one for a clinical psychologist.

A final illustration of the kind of referral which psychologists receive from physicians is the one from the pediatrician, whose contacts with a family have led him to suspect the beginnings of a serious psychological disorder, and who wants to have this hypothesis explored. This kind of referral stems from the widely accepted emphasis on preventive medicine. In this case, it is often helpful—if not essential—to evaluate the difficulty which the pediatrician may face in confronting the parents with the psychologist's findings and with their resistance to the psychologist's recommendations. Thus, it is not of much help merely to confirm or disconfirm the pediatrician's hypotheses; rather it is necessary to go beyond confirmation and assist in planning for the next step in intervention. Often this next step is the one which requires the greater clinical judgment and psychological wisdom.

THE LEGAL CONTEXT

Of the two disciplines—law and psychology—law has the grander tradition and the more awesome stature. Yet, within the past ten years, psychologists have entered legal chambers with increasing frequency and, even if at times psychologists have appeared inept or stupid, the courts in general afford psychologists much respect.

Law is a system of regulating man's relations in society and it "aims at the just resolution of human conflict" (Cowan, 1963). As such, the study and practice of law by attorneys and jurists encompasses a wide range of human knowledge, not only in the scientific sense, but also in the broader humanistic tradition. Modern legal philosophers are much concerned, for example, with the results of historical studies, sociological research, philosophy, and cultural anthropology (Northrop, 1959).

The law evolves as society evolves. Hence the law is generally cognizant of the contributions to knowledge which are made by other disciplines. But law is also conservative and changes in legal procedure will be slow. We may expect, therefore, that the psychologist's contribution to the legal process will be marked with difficulties and will be characterized by ups and downs.

Probably the most striking advance in the stature of psychologists in the court came in connection with the Jenkins case (Hock & Darley, 1962) during which the "acceptibility of testimony by properly qualified psychologists in cases involving the determination and meaning of mental disease or defect as productive of criminal acts" was sustained by a 7–2 vote of the United States Court of Appeals for the District of Columbia (p. 626).

A low point—the lowest with which I am familiar—took place in the District Court of the District of Columbia during which

> . . . the witness [a psychologist] testified that a psychologist could diagnose illness by the pictures a subject selected as those he liked or disliked [the Szondi test]. At this point the judge threw the cards down. At a Bench conference the defense attorney asked: "May the record reflect that after the last question the Court slammed the cards down?"
>
> Court: "The record may reflect it but the record may show I am throwing it all out. That will take care of that session" [Jeffery, 1964, p. 843].

The role of the judge in a jury trial and in legal decision making in general is a controversial one in legal philosophy and jurisprudence (Wasserstrom, 1961). What is not controversial, however, is that legal decisions, whether they are made by judge, jury, or attorney, are not made in the same way that scientific decisions or medical decisions are made and the psychologist who expects the court or the jury to make use of his contribution to the decision-making process will need to be familiar with the legal system and to have a clear understanding of the specific contribution he is being called upon to make.

Cowan (1963) has presented a most careful analysis of decision making in the legal context and writes:

> The scientist *generalizes*; the lawyer *individuates*. It would take a lifetime to substantiate this bald assertion, but since none of us has a lifetime to give to it, I shall confine myself to a summary statement: *Litigation aims to individuate, and the judicial process is most at home when it disposes of a unique conflict situation uniquely.* . . . I believe that the law will warp and twist the facts, sometimes in an apparently shameless manner, if necessary, to obtain what it thinks of as the *just* result. . . . True equality in law might almost be said to consist in the maxim: *no two cases are ever really alike* [pp. 1065–66].

If no two cases are ever alike what we need is a theory of individual decisions, not institutional decision. Cowan's conclusions are relatively pessimistic in this regard:

> . . . there is nothing in present technology or theory, or even in the minds of the investigators of decision making, that suggests that the *individual decision* will ever become the object of scientific investigation. I should like to be able to report that some scientific interest in this matter does exist. But if it does I have not come upon it. . . . Among the "homely truths" to be borne in mind are the following:
> 1. No general theory of social action exists that has received widespread acceptance even among social scientists. . . .
> 2. No general theory of human motivation in the individual exists . . . [p. 1072].

It may be that Cowan is unfamiliar with the psychological and social-psychological literature or that his standards for a "general theory" are more stringent than the standards of most psychologists. Theories of individual motivation do exist; scientific validation of these theories may not reach the standards Cowan has set up. Nevertheless, the psychologist who is aware of these theories and who is aware, at the same time, of the nature of the evidence which is available to support aspects of these theories is in a position to serve society by furnishing an expert opinion to the courts.

What is expert testimony?

> To warrant the use of expert testimony, then, two elements are required. First, the subject of the inference must be so distinctively related to some science, profession, business or occupation as to be beyond the ken of the average layman, and second, the witness must have such skill, knowledge or experience in that field or calling as to make it appear that his opinion or inference will probably aid the trier

in his search for truth. The knowledge may in some fields by derived from reading alone, in some from practice alone, or as is more commonly the case from both" [McCormick, Evidence (1954)].

The trial judge should make a finding in respect to the individual qualifications of each challenged expert. Qualifications to express an opinion on a given topic are to be decided by the judge alone. The weight to be given any expert opinion admitted in evidence by the judge is exclusively for the jury [United States Court of Appeals. No. 16306, cited by Hoch and Darley, 1962, pp. 648–650].

Many psychologists express the opinion that the psychologist will make his contribution most efficiently if he is used as a "friend of the court." He can thus avoid being involved in legal tangles or appearing foolish when a colleague employed by the "other side" presents an opposing opinion.

Much as the psychologist may prefer to be called into a case as a "friend of court," our system of jurisprudence is based on the advocacy principle—that truth and justice are most likely to emerge when opposing attorneys engage in a legal contest.

In terms of criminal law, the psychologist may be called in at almost any stage of the proceedings: During the investigatory stage by the police (though rarely); by the prosecuting attorney to assist in determining what crime has been committed (e.g., manslaughter or first degree murder); by the defense attorney (often as a last resort); by the judge to contribute to the presentation of evidence; by the judge after the trial to assist in determining the sentence; by the penal officer to plan for the criminal's prison term; by the parole board to assist in their decision; or by the parole officer to assist in rehabilitation planning.

Frequently the psychologist is called into a case by a defense attorney who is trying to establish an innocent verdict by reason of insanity. The many discussions of the M'Naughten rule, irresistable impulse, and the Durham decision are controversies with which legal psychologists must be familiar (Leifer, 1964). Whether or not a psychologist is willing to give an opinion about these issues in any particular case is up to his individual conscience. But he must be prepared to be cross-examined: that is the nature of our legal system. As Harry S. Truman said, "If you can't stand the heat, get out of the kitchen." But if a psychologist believes that our legal system is of value, he will probably feel that there is a legitimate place in it for his expert opinion.

THE EDUCATIONAL CONTEXT

The role of education—especially public education—in our society has been expanding, not only since Sputnik, but for hundreds of years. President Johnson's Great Society, with programs such as the Job Corps, Project Head Start, and the Elementary and Secondary Education Act of 1965, gave an added impetus to this development. In a social institution which is changing rapidly, the role of psychological testing can be expected to be changing as well.

The nature of psychological testing in schools is much less uniform than it is in hospitals, but many of the issues are the same. There is the need for the psychologist to be able to understand the educator's decision problems and the language in which he formulates his alternatives. When a teacher refers a child to find out if he has a "learning block," he is probably trying to get more information so that he can decide whether this child should be retained in grade, transferred to a slower educational program, or advanced in grade but recommended for psychotherapy. The school psychologist needs to know what alternatives are available to the educator and what non-test considerations may be involved in the decision-making process.

The recent policy statement made by the senior staff specialist of Project Head Start describing the psychologist's function in the program deemphasizes the role of psychologist as tester and places much more emphasis on the psychologist's functioning as a consultant to the teacher (Spickler, 1966).

It is unfortunate that so many educators have adopted a medical model of human behavior without fully comprehending the implications of such a model. By so doing, they have made the assumption that "early identification" (which is seen as analogous to early medical diagnosis) is always a desirable goal—that early identification of problem children will lead to the early institution of treatment procedures and that early treatment will lead to early "cure." But there are dangers associated with labelling a potential "problem" too early. The Society for the Psychological Study of Social Issues (SPSSI) Council statement issued in connection with the use of the Glueck Prediction tables for the early identification of potential juvenile delinquents points out that

> . . . unless the utmost caution and care are taken, children who are "identified" and labelled as probable future delinquents are likely to be treated and isolated as "bad" children by teachers and others who are now subjected to the virtually hysterical climate of opinion

concerning juvenile delinquency. Such treatment is likely to increase
the child's sense of social alienation and thereby, increase the probability of his becoming delinquent or of developing other forms of
psychological maladjustment [SPSSI Newsletter, 1960].

This is an example of the self-fulfilling prophecy which makes it
difficult to assess scientifically the validity of psychological test procedures. The SPSSI statement also pointed out that the predictive
claims associated with the Glueck tables were based primarily on
extreme base rates.

The analogy of "early identification" of behavior problems with
the "early diagnosis" of medical illness is, moreover, what
Oppenheimer (1956) calls a "disanalogy." Except for some cases of
mental retardation and organic brain damage (and probably fewer of
these than we believe), the problem of diagnosing educational problems is not analogous to medical diagnosis. Among other differences,
a medical problem involves a single individual while an educational
problem generally involves a family constellation. Further, an educational problem can be understood only in terms of a complex of
variables within the individual, while a medical diagnosis may hinge
on a single factor. Oppenheimer has pointed out that when a model
has more disanalogous elements than analogous elements, a new
theoretical model is generally found. A theory is available to educators, i.e., that educational problems are part of a more global failure of
the child to create a socially effective life-style because of disturbed
interpersonal relations in the family. This model is not as simple and
straightforward as a disease model, but it does seem generally more
consistent with observations.

The adoption of this model, however, would introduce some
difficulty for the psychological tester in the school system: no longer
would it be desirable simply to test the "slow learner" and make a
diagnosis. It would now be necessary to evaluate the total family
picture for a clear understanding of the factors involved in the learning problem. Whether or not the family was willing to cooperate in
such an enterprise would become an important consideration.

An especially difficult situation exists when a disruptive family
is combined with an emotionally disturbed teacher. Towbin's diagnostic triad of psychiatrist, patient, and psychologist presents problems for the psychologist, but the configuration of people involved in
most school referrals is much more complex and involves many more
possible sources of tension and misunderstanding. Besides the child,
his parents, and the teacher, also involved may be the principal, a

guidance counselor, and, in a small community, members of the school board. Each of these people represents a possible source of conflict and every combination of forces may need to be understood. In addition, the hierarchical and authoritarian structure of most school systems makes the nature of these tensions especially difficult to uncover and—if uncovered—to deal with.

A related problem for the school psychologist which does not exist to any great extent as yet in the medical or legal setting is the question of group testing. The question then becomes "When and why to give group tests." If it is good to identify disturbed youngsters as early as possible, why not "institute a large-scale group testing program and really handle the problem."

The evidence presently available does not support the notion that early identification leads to more effective treatment (Levitt, 1957; 1963). Most theories of psychotherapy, especially recent ones developed in the framework of community mental health programs, stress the importance of timing in therapeutic intervention. Although the timing of intervention needs to be studied further, the idea that therapeutic effectiveness is based to a considerable extent on motivation for change and that motivation for change exists at times of crisis is gaining wide acceptance.

One implication of this discussion is clear: the question for the psychologist is not simply "How disturbed is this youngster?" or even "What is the nature of his disturbance?" The additional question "Is there sufficient motivation in this family at this time so that therapeutic intervention should be recommended?" must be considered. As Cole and Magnussen (1966) have suggested, evaluation must be geared to action.

THE PSYCHOLOGICAL CLINIC

In the medical, legal, and educational institutions, the psychologist functions as a consultant to the decision maker; in the psychological clinic, the psychologist is himself often the decision maker. Although he must operate under legal restraints, it is primarily his value system which will effect the decisions. What are the implications of this for the question of "why and when to test?" What kinds of decisions does the psychologist in a psychological clinic make? What kinds of questions is he asked? What kinds of clients does he see?

First, there is the sizable group of "self-referrals," people who are uncomfortable or dissatisfied and who have heard about psychotherapy. They come to the clinic hoping to be relieved of their misery. In most of these situations, psychological testing is irrelevant; it is necessary to agree on a workable psychotherapeutic relationship and to start the treatment process. Generally the client is in some kind of a crisis and is well-motivated so that the time is propitious for starting psychotherapy.

There will be some self-referrals, however, which the psychologist feels—for one reason or another—are not suitable cases for a psychological clinic: either the medical factors are too prominent; there are legal implications which must be clarified first; or the nature of the client's psychological disturbance is such that institutionalization may be necessary during the course of the treatment. In these cases, the psychologist may feel the need for more information before making a decision about psychotherapy. Psychological testing is an appropriate way to get this information. It is important that the client realize that the tests are being given to help the psychologist decide how to proceed. The tests are not being given to help the patient directly.

A second category of psychological clinic cases are children brought to the clinic by parents, because either the youngster is not doing well in school, has gotten into trouble with the police, or is in some way not living up to parental expectations. These cases require special precautions before testing is begun. As indicated in the discussion of the educational setting, this kind of referral needs to be understood in the broadest terms. What other agencies has the family worked with? What relationship exists between the school and the family? The court and the family? More often than not, the specific incident which finally led the parents to seek professional help is only one event in a long pattern of social disturbance. If the psychologist were to take a parent's request at face value, he might test the child, give a diagnostic interpretation to the parents, and make a recommendation. This procedure would be the one followed in a narrowly conceived medical model, although now even physicians and psychiatrists realize that a narrow disease model is inappropriate for problems of this kind. What is needed is a global evaluation of the family dynamics: the family's relation to the community and the relations of members of the family to one another.

To illustrate this kind of situation: I received a call from a woman who asked if the Psychological Clinic gave aptitude tests; she said she wanted to have her 16-year-old son receive aptitude tests because he couldn't make up his mind about what kind of work he wanted to do. I replied that we did give aptitude tests if we felt that they would help answer a relevant question, but that I would first want to discuss with her in more detail what aptitude testing might be expected to accomplish. An appointment was set up with her for the following week.

At the interview I learned that her son did not attend the regular public school, but was in a private home for boys in a nearby town; apparently he had been having trouble in school and with the police. Her lawyer and the juvenile judge had reached an agreement that he be sent to this Boys' Home. Why couldn't he profitably remain at home with his family and receive professional help? She then told me that she had three younger children and was working full-time because she was in the process of getting a divorce from her husband, who was in the state hospital where he had been for about a year. During the preceding year the boy had been in individual therapy at the local Child Guidance Clinic; she had attended several group therapy sessions for parents, but had stopped going because she didn't feel she could benefit from group therapy.

I decided that vocational aptitude testing was irrelevant to the problems which this mother was presenting and discussed with her the possibility of trying to get a better understanding of the total family situation. She agreed to such a plan and a case conference was arranged. Attending this conference were the therapist from the Child Guidance Clinic, the probation officer from the Juvenile Court, the social worker from the Boys' Home, the guidance counselor from the public schools, the mother's attorney, the State Hospital psychiatrist working with the boy's father, and a representative of the Psychological Clinic. At the conference it became clear that there were important decisions to be made: Should the father be released from the State Hospital? Should he be allowed to visit his son at the Boys' Home? What kind of educational program was appropriate for the boy? Should he be allowed home visits? Should the mother be encouraged to resume psychotherapy?

Psychological evaluations of the boy, the mother, and the father were carried out and were part of the information available for discussion at a follow-up conference—at which tentative decisions were reached—but the final decisions generally rested with agencies other than the Psychological Clinic. Does this procedure make more sense than giving the youngest aptitude tests and handing out some test scores? I think so, but I'm not sure how one would proceed to study this issue scientifically.

In a psychological clinic, a psychologist will also receive referrals from other decision makers, especially when these decision makers do not employ their psychologists. It is sometimes possible in the clinic to consider the problem in a broader perspective than when one is closely involved with an agency. We received a referral from the local Sanity Board—a Board consisting of a psychiatrist, lawyer, and Clerk of the District Court—which has the legal responsibility for committing patients to the state mental hospital. The Board wanted us to test a man whose wife had filed a sanity complaint against him; they questioned his sanity but found the decision a difficult one to make. Although the results of psychological testing revealed no clear evidence of psychosis, they were difficult to interpret with much confidence until we decided to ask the wife to come in for an evaluation. As a result of this evaluation the entire situation became clearer. Although not overtly psychotic, on projective test performance the wife was revealed to be a profoundly disturbed woman who had very meager psychological resources. In this case, by the way, a follow-up is available. The couple were seen jointly in psychotherapy, but after about six or seven sessions, the wife started complaining that the therapy sessions were too upsetting; soon after, she stopped coming. The husband continued for about ten more sessions, which he seemed to use in a moderately productive way.

IMPLICATIONS

We have sampled the kinds of institutional settings in which psychologists work in an attempt to understand under what conditions psychological testing will improve decision making. Although I might have discussed other settings, such as industry, university counseling centers, welfare departments, prisons, and so on, I have decided to stay close to my own experience. This excursion has led me to arrive at several judgments about the process of psychological evaluation—judgments which I think can be generalized to other work settings and to other social institutions.

First, a decision-making model for psychological testing is a heuristic one. It will often assist the psychologist in dealing with the individual case in a more constructive way than would otherwise be possible. It will help him focus on the essential aspects of the problem and avoid digressions and irrelevancies.

Second, the complex context of most psychological testing requires careful analysis to determine the essential referral question and the nature of the available alternatives. It is an essential—perhaps crucial—part of the psychologist's job to understand this complex situation. It is unrealistic to expect that the decision maker will always be able to formulate the referral question in a clear and concise manner. In fact, psychologists are called upon generally only in the most difficult or complex cases. If a patient is obviously psychotic, no referral may be made. If, however, there are serious doubts about the patient, the psychologist is expected to contribute to the decision-making process. The person who views his role simply as a tester will be unable to make this analysis. But a psychologist, a person trained in the study of behavior and skilled in the understanding of interpersonal factors in a complex social setting, will be equipped to analyze the total referral context.

Third, the clinical psychodiagnostician must consider himself responsible for learning the theories and the language of the institutional setting in which he works. He must be more than a psychologist; he must also be knowledgeable about the realistic alternatives available to the decision maker. Emphasis should be given to the great responsibility which the clinical psychologist assumes when he undertakes to provide "service" of any kind, even to the extent of admitting that his efforts provided no answers to the question. This responsibility is primary to the referred patient, child, or whoever it is, not to his favorite tests, his professional status, or the field of clinical psychology.

Fourth, new measurement techniques emphasizing interpersonal interactions rather than individual dynamics need to be developed. At the University of Nebraska Psychological Clinic we have found the Family Relations Test (Elias, 1949) and the family diagnostic interview (Tyler, et al., 1962) useful, but these kinds of techniques are at too early a stage of development.

Fifth, the training of clinical psychologists should continue to be broad in scope, consistent with the Boulder scientist-professional model, and we should resist suggestions that we train psychodiagnosticians at a technicians' level. Although it is possible to teach a person to administer tests, to score them accurately, and to "interpret" them according to some cookbook principles, this use of psychological tests is not flexible enough to assist in individual decisions nor sophisticated enough to develop tests which will be useful in institutional decisions. Further, this kind of tester is insufficiently knowledgeable about general and social psychological theory and principles to comprehend the subtleties of complex referrals and to formulate meaningful alternatives.

Sixth, much of the research on test validity is not immediately relevant to the practical use of psychological tests. The question of the value of tests becomes not "Does the test correlate with a criterion?" or

"Does the test accord with a nomological net?" but rather "Does the use of the test improve the success of the decision-making process?" by making it either more efficient, less costly, more accurate, more rational, or more relevant. The clinical-actuarial controversy becomes academic since most of the research in that area is irrelevant in decision making. For example, Lindzey's (1965) demonstration that clinical psychologists can identify homosexuals from the TAT has no decision-making relevance. Furthermore, all the demonstrations that psychological tests do not agree with psychiatric diagnoses fall into the "so what?" category.

Seventh, values held strongly by the psychologist may conflict with the values of the decision maker, e.g., sterilization procedures for the mentally retarded, capital punishment for first degree murder. If this conflict is irreconcilable, the psychologist may have to admit that he cannot function effectively as a psychological consultant in this context. More serious difficulties may ensue if the psychologist is unaware of this conflict in values or insists on arguing that the decision maker change his values. In the latter case he is not functioning as a psychological consultant even though he may be accomplishing a more important social purpose.

Finally, the problems we face in connection with the use of psychological tests will not all be solved by the suggestions made in this chapter. Rather, we face new and perhaps more difficult problems. Attempts to understand the values of the decision maker will present enormous theoretical and practical problems; decision makers generally do not like to be studied. We will probably have difficulty developing psychological tests which measure complex social-psychological variables. Research on the question of whether testing improves the payoff function is difficult because of the impact which the psychological report has on the attitudes of people working with the patient, i.e., the self-fulfilling prophecy. I am personally more excited about these challenges than I was about the clinical-statistical controversy or the argument about construct validity.

REFERENCES

American Journal of Insanity. 1844, back cover.
Auld, F., Jr. Influence of social class on personality test responses. Psychol. Bull., 1952, 49, 318–332.
Bross, I. D. J. Design for Decision. New York: Macmillan, 1953.
Churchman, C. W. Prediction and Optimal Decision: Philosophical Issues of a Science of Values. Englewood Cliffs, N.J.: Prentice-Hall, 1961.

Cole, J. K., & Magnussen, M. G. Where the action is. *J. Consult. Psychol.*, 1966, *30*, 539–543.

Cowan, T. A. Decision theory in law, science, and technology. *Science*, 1963, *140*, 1065–1075.

Cronbach, L. J., & Gleser, G. C. *Psychological Tests and Personnel Decisions.* Urbana, Ill.: University of Illinois Press, 1965.

Edwards, W. The theory of decision making. *Psychol. Bull.*, 1954, *51*, 380–417.

Edwards, W., Lindman, H., & Savage, L. J. Bayesian statistical inference for psychological research. *Psychol. Rev.*, 1963, *70*, 193–242.

Edwards, W. Personal communication, 1966.

Elias, G. Construction of a test of non-homeyness and related variables. Unpublished doctoral dissertation, Purdue University, 1949.

Girshick, M. A. An elementary survey of statistical decision theory. *Rev. Educ. Res.*, 1954, *24*, 448–466.

Gross, M. L. *The Brain Watchers.* New York: The New American Library of World Literature, Inc., 1962.

Hoch, E. L., & Darley, J. G. A case at law. *Am. Psychol.*, 1962, *17*, 623–654.

Hoffman, B. *The Tyranny of Testing.* Riverside, N.J.: Macmillan, 1962.

Holzberg, J. D. The role of the internship in the research training of the clinical psychologist. *J. Consult. Psychol.*, 1961, *25*, 185–191.

Janis, I. L. *Pyschological Stress.* New York: Wiley, 1958.

Jeffery, R. The psychologist as an expert witness on the issue of insanity. *Am. Psychol.*, 1964, *19*, 838–843.

Leifer, R. The psychiatrist and tests of criminal responsibility. *Am. Psychol.*, 1964, *19*, 825–830.

Levitt, E. E. Results of psychotherapy with children: an evaluation. *J. Consult. Psychol.*, 1957, *21*, 189–196.

Levitt, E. E. Psychotherapy with children: a further evaluation. *Behav. Res. Ther.*, 1963, *1*, 45–51.

Levy, L. H. *Psychological Interpretation.* Chicago: Holt, Rinehart, Winston, 1963.

Lindzey, G. Seer versus sign. *J. Experim. Res. Pers.*, 1965, *1*, 17–26.

Meehl, P. E. *Clinical Versus Statistical Prediction: A Theoretical Analysis and a Review of the Evidence.* Minneapolis: University of Minnesota Press, 1954.

Meehl, P. E. The cognitive activity of the clinician. *Am. Psychol*, 1960, *15*, 19–27.

Meehl, P. E. Seer over sign: the first good example. *J. Experim. Res. Pers.*, 1965, *1*, 27–33.

Motorola's Employment Test Procedure, 1964.

Northrop, F. S. C. *The Complexity of Legal and Ethical Experience.* Toronto: Little, Brown, 1959.

Oppenheimer, R. Analogy in science. *Am. Psychol.*, 1956, *11*, 127–135.

Society for the Psychological Study of Social Issues Council statement dated

January 31, 1960, on the New York City Youth Board Report: An experiment in predicting juvenile delinquency. SPSSI Newsletter, April, 1960.

Spickler, M. W. Psychological services in a child development center: a guide for teachers and teacher-aides. Project Head Start 382-8544, mimeographed final draft, January 28, 1966.

Sundberg, N. D., & Tyler, Leona E. *Clinical Psychology*. New York: Appleton-Century-Crofts, 1962.

Szasz, T. *Law, Liberty, and Psychiatry*. New York: Macmillan, 1963.

Testimony Before House Special Subcommittee on Invasion of Privacy of the Committee on Government Operations. *Am. Psychol.*, 1965, *20*, 955–988.

Towbin, A. P. When are cookbooks useful? *Am. Psychol.*, 1960, 15, 119–123.

Tukey, J. W. Conclusions versus decisions. *Technometrics*, 1960, *2*, 423–433.

Tyler, E. A., Truumaa, A., & Henshaw, Patricia. Family group intake by a child guidance team. *Arch. Gen. Psychiat.*, 1962, 6, 214–218.

Wasserstrom, R. A. *The Judicial Decision*. Stanford: Stanford University Press, 1961.

10

Research Applications of Projective Methods

Jerome L. Singer

In addressing oneself to a review of the research applications of the projective methods one must confront a curious dilemma of cultural lag and the sociology of professional practice. The widespread practical application of projective techniques continues almost unabated in mental hospitals and clinics. Indeed Sundberg's (1961) survey indicated that the Rorschach, Thematic Apperception Test, Draw-a-Person and Bender Visual-Motor Gestalt Test (often used projectively) head the list of frequently used assessment techniques in 185 hospitals, counseling centers, and clinics. Even today the situation seems relatively unchanged despite increasing doubts about the validity and practical utility of many of these procedures (Zubin, et al., 1965). If the research literature on projective techniques tells us anything (and I think it tells a great deal) it clearly suggests that the current clinical uses of those war-horses like the Rorschach, TAT, and Figure-Drawing are old-fashioned and unsophisticated either psychometrically or in relation to personality theory. Indeed, the literature on research with the projective methods provides ample evidence that many ingenious modifications and variations of these methods exist and could be better applied in dealing with specific questions such as the prediction of aggressive behavior. Nevertheless, faced with a live patient across the desk, we clinicians cling to our

Some of the research and bibliographical work described in this paper was supported by the United States Public Health Service Grant NH M-10956.

battered original set of inkblots like a three-year-old to his tattered old blanket. Did not Rorschach himself claim he had alternate series of blots? Are we oblivious still to the existence of alternate forms such as the Behn or Holtzman or Harrower series and of the many experimental uses of alternate series for special purposes such as Siipola and Taylor's (1952) or Barron's (1955) blots, to mention just a few? The present chapter represents an effort by one who has long loved his fingerprint-bedecked, somewhat battered old "bat" blots and that pathetic "boy with the violin" picture (will he or won't he pick it up and practice?) to urge upon the reader a serious reexamination of the projective tools. I hope to encourage more imaginative directions in the clinical as well as research applications of these fascinating instruments. Our highest allegiance is to psychology, which can best be served not by rash rejection of the projective techniques when the literature is replete with fascinating results or on the other hand by a loyal but naïve faith in any given instrument, but by a serious examination of the ways in which a variety of difficult practical and research problems can be solved. An attitude of enlightened curiosity may well lead to experimentation with a host of "projective" or "non-projective" assessment techniques yielding rewards in research knowledge or human welfare.

AN OVERVIEW OF RESEARCH USES
OF PROJECTIVE TECHNIQUES

If we remember that Rorschach (1942) himself stressed the tentative and experimental nature of his investigations and that Murray (1937) was clearly interested in studying personality generally rather than specifically in devising clinical tests, then we can see that the research history of projective methods is as old as the most popular of the projective methods. Indeed, Rorschach himself performed some crude experiments on empathy and form-color discrimination as an underpinning to his concepts of the roles of movement and color in relation to motor activity. And Murray's (1933) study of the projection of maliciousness by girls frightened by "murder" games at night, however crude by today's "sophisticated" standards, was an early and imaginative effort to use projective methods (pictures from *Time* magazine) in examining an intriguing aspect of personality theory.

A sampling of the thousands of references in the psychological and psychiatric literature which involve projective techniques suggests that most studies fall roughly into the following categories:

Research on the Projective Techniques Themselves

1. Reliability studies and other attempts to evaluate the consistency within subjects or within the test or the stability of response patterns under various conditions or across alternate forms.

2. Validity studies including attempts to support a specific underlying premise, to demonstrate comparability of two techniques presumably measuring the same construct (e.g., Rorschach and TAT measures of aggression or imagination), diagnostic accuracy or predictive power, and matching of known external characteristics to "blind" personality evaluations.

3. Normative and quasi-parametric studies such as the establishment of response patterns at various age levels, preparation of tables for adequate scoring of certain variables, development of forms for use with special clinical populations, e.g., blind subjects or various racial groups, comparison of various scoring or interpretive systems, etc.

4. Establishment of clinical group patterns on the particular method.

The Use of the Projective Techniques as Criteria for Evaluation of Disturbance or Intellectual or Personality Change

1. Studies of the effects of brain damage, neurological defect, mental retardation, old age, or severe emotional disturbance on performance on some projective tool.

2. Studies of the outcome of some particular treatment method on personality, e.g., effects of electroshock or special medication, changes associated with psychotherapy.

3. Studies of the effects of special experimental conditions upon perceptual-motor or fantasy responses, e.g., effects of severe hunger, anoxia, sensory-deprivation, or sexual arousal.

Testing of Personality or Perceptual-motor Theories through Applications of Projective Methods

1. Studies of the psychoanalytic hypotheses concerning the motivational or affective structure of a particular clinical group by their response of projective methods.

2. Studies of deductions from a specific theory of perceptual-motor response, e.g., Werner's, through reactions to projective methods.

3.   Testing of the effects of a particular theoretically relevant experimental variable on projective response, e.g., alterations in achievement motivation under different instructions or changes in projective expressions of aggression following certain experimental conditions.

4.   Stylistic differences in projective performance predicted from a theory or from some more specific experimental operation, e.g., projective responses associated with perceptual defense, field-dependence, etc.

A detailed examination of the varieties of research falling within the scope of these categories would require a work of several volumes. The reader is referred for specific instances of studies of reliability, validity, and research on psychopathology or special technique construction to Chapters 2, 3, 5 and 6 of the present volume. The present chapter will touch on some fundamental issues relating to these research applications and then move to some fairly detailed examples of specific problems which have been studied or engendered through the projective methods.

PROJECTIVE TECHNIQUES AS RESEARCH TOOLS

What are some of the special qualities of projective methods as techniques for research? Tentatively lumping these varied procedures under one rubric, we can say that their attractiveness lies in their ambiguity as stimuli, presumably lower susceptibility to conscious or even to unwittingly defensive falsification, disguised purposes, relationship to the types of fantasy or associative material elicited in the course of intensive psychotherapy, presumed ability to tap various "levels" of personality, and capacity to yield evidence on a variety of cognitive or personality dimensions simultaneously. Certainly no one ever advocated projective techniques because they were easy to score or obviously reliable! The challenge of projective techniques in the great upsurge of psychological interest in the 1940s lay in the fact that they seemed to provide cross-sectional behavioral samples of cognitive and personality material that were at once moderately well quantified or at least susceptible to some form of organized interpretive scheme and at the same time broad-banded and deep enough to permit personality descriptions that might take a psychiatrist hours to obtain in the course of standard psychotherapy or interviewing. For clinical purposes the possibility of integrating complex material into an ideographic description seemed especially attractive by comparison with the limitations of the paper and pencil personality inventories then available. And, no doubt, there was a certain aesthetic satisfaction in the elucidation of psychological data through quasi-artistic means such as responses to colors and ambiguous forms, storytelling, finger-painting, or organization of patterns from mosaic tiles.

From a formal standpoint, however, many critical problems soon emerged. One had to demonstrate, after all, that if responses to inkblots or stories were to be the basic data of a dependent or independent variable then these data should meet certain minimal standards of stability or internal consistency. If one is testing a psychiatric notion that two forms of schizophrenia differ systematically in their affective control or motivational hierarchies then one must be prepared to deal with a negative result. If on separate administrations the projective device doesn't yield comparable results with the same subjects, are negative findings a demonstration of the inadequacy of the original theory or an indication merely that the measuring device is too unstable to permit a suitable test of the theory? For example, Dawo (1952) reported finding a shift from introversion to extratensiveness in the Rorschach Experience-type of women during and prior to menstruation. To evaluate change when two Rorschach tests had to be given a few days apart she used the Behn Inkblots for the second testing. Since there is evidence that the latter series (while grossly suitable as an alternate form) differs specifically from the original series in its elicitation of a greater number of color responses which are used in scoring extratensiveness (Eichler, 1951; Singer, 1952), one can't know whether her positive results reflect an artifact of the techniques employed or an actual psychological change in her subjects.

Without belaboring the many obvious issues concerning the reliability of cumbersome techniques such as the Rorschach, TAT, MAPS, etc., as well as the difficulties in obtaining satisfactory scores from data provided by associations, stories, drawings, etc., it is clear that the serious investigator must take special precautions to make sure that the data to be obtained from projective methods meet some reasonable criteria of objectivity to insure replicability of his investigation. Without attempting coverage of all possibilities, here are some suggestive examples of precautions necessary in research with projective methods—cautions which are designed to insure at least reasonable objectivity of the data without seriously compromising some of the "projective" characteristics of the instruments.

Procedure for Obtaining Interjudge Agreement in Scoring Thematic Apperception Test or Related Techniques

If one desires to use projective data based on spontaneous productions to measure a recurrent pattern in responses to the TAT, a method such as the following has been successfully employed in research:

1.   The investigator decides that it is necessary to obtain a quantitative score for some need or motive or stylistic characteristic from thematic responses. For example, he may want to measure "means-end cognizance" or "achievement motivation" in samples of normals and schizophrenics or middle- and lower-class persons, otherwise equated on pertinent variables. He prepares a careful definition of the trait or need in question, specifically relating this definition to the type of material available, i.e., stories told to TAT cards.

2.   He delineates appropriate scorable units in the stories obtained, or, if he wishes a more global rating, sets up criteria for evaluating the importance of this variable in each card or for the whole test protocol along some quantitative scale.

3.   He prepares a manual of instructions for raters with sample scorings of the variable in question.

4.   Two or three raters *unfamiliar with the objectives of the study* are trained in scoring the variable from sample protocols not part of the study itself. When they can pass a test or meet a criterion of agreement satisfactory to the experimenter, they are assigned coded protocols which are part of the formal study.

5.   Following the blind ratings by the two judges, a percentage agreement or reliability coefficient is calculated. If agreement is high (meeting a prespecified criterion) the two sets of scores may be averaged or a third rater called in to rate, and the average of the three utilized for those items on which there is disagreement.

A general procedure of this type has proved effective in yielding reliable ratings of TAT data in a number of studies (e.g., Atkinson, 1958; Singer, 1954).

Global Matching of Projective Protocols

When it is desired to take into account as much as possible the clinician's skill in integrating various facets of a projective protocol, a matching technique may be more desirable than the type of rating described above. Here the sets of data that are to be compared are set up in coded form and clinicians match the projective test protocol with the data. A simple example is represented by the attempt to ascertain the comparability of the Behn and Rorschach protocols of various persons using clinicians who matched coded records (Singer, 1952). Using techniques based on the original concept of blind matching by Vernon (for use with expressive behavior samples), one can obtain a fairly definitive estimate of judges' agreement and also their accuracy in comparing two projective test protocols or in matching a protocol with a personality description or other relevant data. Cronbach (1949; 1956) has provided a variety of useful suggestions for statistical evaluation of matching techniques. The advantages of matching techniques have most recently been apparent in the recognition that dream reports from various stages of sleep must be subjected to a comparable procedure if we are to move beyond the anecdotal in the objective study of sleep mentation (Monroe, Rechtschaffen, Foulkes, & Jensen, 1965). By careful planning it is also possible to vary the amount of material available to judges for matching and hence, in effect, to "zero in" on the bases for decision in the interpretation of projective data.

Development of Specialized Scores or New Approaches to Evaluating Projective Technique Variables

That this area merits a volume in itself is an indication of the many clever and astute research approaches to dealing with the complexities of projective data. Some simple examples will be presented here with the hope that the reader interested in research with projective techniques will be encouraged to explore the relevant literature or to assess carefully the need for such a technique before blindly plunging into a large-scale investigation expecting to rely on the traditional scoring methods. The persons who originally devised techniques for evaluating projective protocols were generally insightful clinicians who, however, lacked the statistical sophistication which by today is a regular part of most professionals' repertory.

Consider, for example, Rorschach's notion of the Experience-type, the ratio of Human Movement to Color responses, which is considered one of the most original and fundamental features of the inkblot technique (Singer, 1960). By differentially weighting the color responses so that an FC received one-third the weight of a pure C and by setting up a ratio between color and movement, Rorschach in effect was proposing a quantitative approach to assessing this personality dimension. Yet, in addition to many, by now, obvious limitations of these weightings, e.g., the uneven distributions of color in the cards, it is clear that the ratio is meaningless if one does not take into account the number of responses in a given protocol. Palmer (1955; 1956; 1963) was able to deal with this problem by developing a score for the experience-balance which took into account the response total; he was then able to develop considerable normative data as well as satisfactory statistical comparisons between this Rorschach variable and objective personality scale measures.

Recognizing that there is no intrinsic magic in the original scoring scheme provided by Rorschach, other investigators have moved even further toward developing unique scores for Rorschach data. Fisher's concept of the body-image score (1958) represents one type of revision related to a theoretical construct which has engendered an intriguing series of investigations of correlates of projective test performance. Still another approach has been that developed by Holt, Klein, Lindzey, and their collaborators which involved attempts to rescore Rorschach protocols in relation to assumed stylistic dimensions such as tolerance for unreal experiences or primary and secondary process (Gardner, Holzman, Klein, Linton, & Spence, 1959; Holt & Havel, 1960). For example, Eiduson (1959) scored both Rorschach protocols and dream reports using a variant of the "tolerance for unreal experiences" score and was able to show consistency for subjects in these two differing media of experience. Other examples of variants of Rorschach scores will be presented later in this chapter.

Still other approaches to new scorings of the Rorschach blots for specific research uses may be cited briefly. Zubin, Eron, and Schumer (1965) have pursued with great care an approach to scoring Rorschach responses along scaled dimensions originally advocated 30 years ago by Zubin. These scales attempt to classify response content such as dominance, mood, definiteness, dehumanization, self-references, etc., and have particular advantages in studies comparing normal and pathological groups before and after different types of treatment. Other approaches involving both content and structural scoring are those of Levine and Spivack (1964; discussed below) for measuring "repressive style," or De Vos (1952) and Elizur (1949) for measuring aggressive or hostile manifestations. For research purposes a variety of studies have indicated the decided utility of these last two scoring approaches (Buss, 1961).

While the emphasis so far has been on the Rorschach, comparable indications of the desirability of specialized methods to deal with special problems apply to other types of projective techniques as well. The development of reliable scoring criteria for measuring achievement motivation, affiliation, or other general motives from responses to TAT-type stimuli are amply documented in Atkinson (1958). Particular mention may be made of the approach of using quasi-multiple choice techniques in obtaining responses from picture story material. Suppose an investigator wishes to test a hypothesis that a certain group of subjects will manifest more indication of maternal attachment than some other group in their reactions to fantasy stimuli. Subjects may be shown pictures varying systematically in their ambiguity in relation to parent–child interaction. The subject (in addition to being asked for a spontaneous response) may be asked to indicate which of a series of statements seems best to apply to the picture in terms of her or his own imaginative inclination. These statements can be preselected on the basis of judge's ratings for maternal dependence on other relevant hypotheses and the subject may be asked to choose one of a group of statements as most relevant or to rank-order a series of statements. Quite suitable quantitative data can thus be obtained without seriously interfering with the relative "projective" quality of the subject's reaction (Lane & Singer, 1959).

Specialized Modifications of Projective Techniques for Research Use

It seems more and more clear that any really serious approach to research study which seeks to take advantage of the relatively disguised or ambiguous quality of projective methods necessitates a careful examination of those characteristics of the method especially relevant to the study in question. Thus, Barron (1955), especially interested in examining the imaginative characteristics of groups being assessed on a variety of personality dimensions, developed a series of inkblots which could yield a threshold score for human movement. These blots have been applied with varying success in a number of studies. While it is not clear that the threshold measure itself is satisfactory, the essential notion of pinpointing more specifically the characteristic one wishes to study and eliminating the "noise" produced by a variety of other scores or stimuli has some morit in rcsearcli.

The Holtzman inkblots (Holtzman, et al., 1961) represent an extension of this notion and a series of parallel forms with special value for research. Holtzman and his collaborators have provided reasonably satisfactory reliability data for the two forms of the test as well as a much more statistically workable instrument. They have also taken advantage of the developments in research in incorporating scoring systems developed for special purposes, such the Fisher Body Image technique or scores for hostility and bizarre verbalization. As a result, research use of the method is decidedly enhanced. A more recent example is Lerner's (1966) study, which indicated that "dream-deprived" subjects produced more Movement responses than controls. Here Lerner used the Holtzman blots and could employ 22 even- and 22 odd-numbered cards from Form A to provide her with sufficient data to make reasonable comparisons of before and after scores. It is likely that the next decade will witness an increasing reliance on forms such as the Holtzman blots in research studies.

Another example relating to the Thematic Apperception Test has been the increased realization that for picture story material, ambiguity *per se* is not quite as desirable as was thought. If anything, the weight of current evidence in the measurement of motives such as aggression suggests that special pictures depicting some aggression are more useful than the traditional set of cards (Buss, 1961).

It should be clear from the few examples cited above that the trend of evidence and a thoughtful examination of the issues may well lead the reader to anticipate a much more flexible and varied use of projective instruments in future research. Rather than citing a host of specific studies in varieties of fields, I shall move now to present some fairly detailed examples, one might almost say case histories, of the research applications of projective techniques to special problems in the psychology of personality. My hope is to stimulate the reader to examine the research in a variety of fields from a similar point of view before he or she plunges into a use of traditional projective methods in his or her own pet research project. Here, then, is an example of how projective methods have been applied to the study of imagination and fantasy processes.

Projective Techniques in the Study of Imagination: Their Values and Limitations

It may seem curious indeed to raise some questions about the use of projective techniques in the study of imagination. After all, the whole exciting development of those colorful and sometimes poetic personality-assessment devices we call projective methods grew out of our

increasing awareness that man's imagination possessed lawful characteristics related to many layers of experience and overt behavior.
Binet's, and later Whipple's, use of inkblots, Stern's Cloud Pictures,
even the composer Scriabin's experimentation with the color-organ,
represented early 20th-century efforts utilizing loosely structured
materials to tap cognitive and affective associations. The important
advance from a scientific standpoint came, however, with Hermann
Rorschach's recognition that not merely the association to the material but the structure of those associations and their relation to the
characteristics of the stimulus material were the link between overt
response, imagination, and personality style or psychopathology.

Undoubtedly, Rorschach reflected the important influences of
Freud, Jung, and Bleuler, all of whom had been especially alert to the
necessity of categorizing psychic functioning along structural dimensions that were more related to personality, instinct, and social experience than were the more static conceptions of Wundt and his
school. Rorschach suggested that by classifying a series of associations to a set of inkblots whose stimulus-evoking characteristics were
established through normative data, we could obtain specific sets of
scores which reflected corresponding patterns of overt behavior, dis-
positions toward action, or characteristic cognitive and affective tendencies. More specifically, he indicated that all associations to inkblots were not reflections of the "imagination" of the respondent.
Rather, some classifications yielded information concerning emotional reactivity; others, information concerning relative emphasis on
concrete or generalized thought; and still others, information on the
relative flexibility of imagination. In effect he suggested that imaginativeness was one of a number of dimensions of thought or action
tapped by associations. This conception has been extremely influential in the further development of projective methods. Common sense
today clearly tells us that *quantity* or *content* of associations to inkblots or ambiguous pictures must reflect some aspects of the ongoing
imaginative life of an individual. Still, the information yield from
those sources seems far less than that which we get from some system
of classification of associations along dimensions that coordinate
more precisely with a theoretically consistent classification of man's
"psychic structure." In the framework of the Rorschach method the
category of scoring that seems closest to tapping man's imagination is
the movement response, especially Human Movement. Despite the
great proliferation of projective techniques since Rorschach's day
(except for some specific approaches used with the Thematic

Apperception Test), surprisingly little effort has been made to de-velop categories within the later techniques to measure the imagina-tive dimension. Probably most devisers of projective techniques were so impressed with Rorschach's achievement in developing the move-ment determinant that they looked for other personality dimensions to study and left the field of imagination to Rorschach. Let me there-fore summarize some of the work on imagination growing out of the inkblot method.

RORSCHACH'S HUMAN MOVEMENT RESPONSE

In experimenting with individual patterns of reaction to various ink-blots, Rorschach (1942) made an interesting observation. Persons who tended to respond frequently to inkblots by reporting they might represent human beings in action ("Two men bowing, two girls danc-ing, a woman with arms upraised doing a Spanish dance," etc.) seemed to show a contradictory pattern in their behavior. They were relatively less active overtly, more controlled in their motility, or perhaps somewhat awkward physically. They were also likely to be persons with considerable imagination, much given to inner living or attention to their own thoughts or daydreams. Although much struck by this observation and feeling it was perhaps the single most impor-tant outcome of his inkblot studies, Rorschach made no attempt to develop a theoretical formulation about this triadic relationship of Human Movement perception in inkblots, inhibited overt motility, and imaginative tendencies.

Formalized into the M determinant as part of the scoring system for the Rorschach technique, the Human Movement response became an important feature of the interpretation of Rorschach protocols in clinical work. The chief teachers and Rorschach theoreticians, e.g., Beck, Klopfer, Schachtel, Hertz, and Piotrowski in the United States, all were in general agreement that the frequency and quality of M responses were related to overt motility and inhibition and to im-agination in much the manner suggested by Rorschach. They differed somewhat in their relative interpretative emphasis on the content of the perceived human movement as a reflection of personality style or role and also on the importance of the relationship of movement to color responses which Rorschach felt was so important.

Despite the general clinical agreement about the inverse relation of M to overt motility on the one hand, and its direct relation to imagination on the other, no formal experimental work was carried out to test this observation until well into the 1940s. At that time, the late Heinz Werner, the distinguished investigator in developmental psychology, observed that Rorschach's linkage of perceived motion (in the inkblots) and inhibited overt motion could serve as an exemplification of a perceptual theory which he had developed. Werner (1945) had proposed a sensory-tonic theory of perception, an organismic conception which stressed that the body's tonicity was the dynamic link between muscular activity and perception. He showed in various experiments that alteration in body position altered perceptual response and went on to demonstrate that retarded children who differed characteristically in their overt motility also differed in their perception of motion or in producing movement responses to Rorschach inkblots. The endogenous mentally retarded who were generally more controlled or phlegmatic in motility showed significantly more Rorschach movement responses and lower thresholds for stroboscopic or tachistoscopically presented motion than did the hyperkinetic exogenous mentally retarded.

Meltzoff, Singer, and Korchin (1953) carried this formal experimental approach a step further with a study which demonstrated that persons who were required to inhibit motility by means of a slow-writing task showed a subsequent increase in their perception of Human Movement responses in the Rorschach. Persons who showed numerous M responses also were better able to inhibit writing speed. Singer, Meltzoff, and Goldman (1952) found that Rorschach M responses increased after Ss were required to "freeze in place" for a period of time. Subsequently, a series of studies (Singer, 1960) provided considerable support to the notion that persons who showed more M responses were likely to be able to inhibit motility, showed more deliberation in problem-solving, Porteus Maze performance, and time estimation, were less active during solitary enforced waiting periods, were less likely to use gestures in defining verbs, or, in the case of mental patients, were less likely to be described by nurses or attendants as overactive on the wards.

These findings thus afford considerable support to Rorschach's original observation of the inverse relationship of overt motility and perception of movement on the inkblots. Somewhat less directly they support Werner's sensory-tonic theory, although Werner's formulations apply chiefly to perception and have not been extended to the study of imagination in their more definitive statement (Werner & Wapner, 1952).

What of the relationship of the M response to imaginative behavior, daydreaming, or "creative intelligence," as Rorschach also put it? One approach to measuring imaginative tendencies has been to score stories told to Thematic Apperception Test pictures for degree of creativity or for what Weisskopf termed "transcendance," the ability to include elements in a story that go beyond mere description of the immediate content of the picture. Thus, a story told to Card I of the TAT (a boy gazing at a violin) which merely described in detail the boy's appearance and the shading of the card, would receive a minimal score for transcendance. A story like "This boy is trying to decide whether to practice or not. Outside he hears the other kids playing ball and envies them. Then he thinks of his mother and how much it would mean to her if he could learn to play. He remembers how often she's spoken of how great a violinist his dead father was. He determines he'll play, sets out practicing day after day . . . and at last appears in Lincoln Center before a cheering audience." This story obviously introduces characters, time dimension, and locations not actually represented on the card and seems clearly a more imaginative response (even if it is not, in terms of TAT responses, an unusually original one) than the card-descriptive reaction.

Employing such criteria of imagination, a number of investigators have indeed found considerable support for some degree of relationship between Rorschach's M response and TAT measures of imagination (Singer, 1960). Other studies have shown that persons rated as imaginative or having considerable inner life also show tendencies to produce more M responses (Singer, 1960). King (1960) found that persons with more frequent M responses showed greater interpersonal awareness and sensitivity. Brenner in an unpublished experiment found that persons encouraged to adopt a creative attitude were more likely to give Rorschach M responses, and Bruel, in another unpublished study, found a greater number of M responses in the Rorschach records of students of writing than in those of ballet students. Teltscher (1964) reported that extremely active college athletes gave far fewer Rorschach M responses than did sedentary, literary-minded, but otherwise intellectually comparable, college students. Goldberger and Holt (1961) found that persons in a sensory-deprivation situation who showed the capacity for extended thought devoted to topics other than the immediate experimental situation also gave considerably more Rorschach Movement responses.

More recently some rather striking experimental findings have led to additional intriguing evidence that in a rather general way supports Rorschach's linkage of Movement and imaginative trends and, indeed, dreaming and fantasy inclinations. Loveland and Singer (1959) found that M (taken as a percentage of R) increased significantly in Ss who had incurred 100 hours of sleep deprivation. Palmer (1963), using his measure of experience-balance cited above, found a similar result, a shift toward introversion, in Ss who had been sleep-deprived for 120 hours. An important control involved the fact that Palmer also studied *food*-deprived Ss and found that they *did not* show the increase in the M but rather a shift toward an increase in color responses and extratensiveness. Bendick and Klopfer (1964) were led to a conclusion that M was related to kinesthetic symbolism in their study of sensory deprivation and motoric inhibition. Finally, Lerner (1966), relying on the Holtzman blots as her measure, carried out a careful study of deprivation of the rapid-eye movement phase of sleep (REM) that is generally thought to be most associated with vivid dreaming. Lerner interfered with the normal "dreaming" cycles by administration of a combination of amphetamines and pentobarbitols which tend to minimize occurrence of REM cycles in sleep. Experimental Ss showed a clearly significant increase in production of Movement responses compared with a nondeprived group and also with a group who received placebo drugs and were tested under comparable circumstances. In other words, the interference with normal eye-movement and presumably dreaming cycle of an individual led to an increased projection of Movement on to inkblots shown upon awakening.

Some methodological features ought to be pointed out in keeping with the spirit of this chapter. Lerner assigned weights to responses for evidence of unequivocal human movement as kinesthetically experienced in a special effort to adhere to Rorschach's notion of the empathy in "kinesthesias." She also used several raters to evaluate the increase in total responses as well as her weighted M score and was able to show that the increase in M was the major factor in the change in experimental protocols and not a general increase in responsiveness. A similar significant result, although slightly less dramatic, was obtained when more conventional Rorschach scoring was used, with

Human Movement alone accounting for the major increase in the scores of the experimental Ss rather than animal or abstract movement.

It seems likely therefore that the Rorschach Movement response does indeed relate to tendencies to manifest imaginative or dreamlike responses at least when such activity is apparently interfered with by artificial deprivation techniques. Still another link in the chain of relating M to fantasy processes and daydreaming came in a study by Page (1957). Employing a questionnaire-listing of daydreams quite similar to the type of questionnaire developed somewhat later by Singer and McCraven (1961), Page compared frequency of reported daydreaming to a number of Rorschach variables. Only the number of M responses proved to be significantly associated with daydream frequency. A link between the Rorschach (in this case the Barron Movement threshold score) and *recall* of dreams was found in a study by Schonbar (1965). She studied persons who kept a log of their dreams for several weeks and found that those recalling dreams on more nights during that period were also more likely to show M responses earlier on the Barron series and were likely, too, to do better on the embedded figures test from Witkin's series. An earlier study (Singer & Schonbar, 1961) had already indicated that frequency of reported daydreaming as measured by a scale similar to Page's was also significantly associated with frequency of recall of night dreams. A really critical study linking Rorschach M to perceptual responses, daydreaming, TAT measures, measures of delay, and inhibition still remains to be done, although Singer, Wilensky, and McCraven (1955) in a factor analytic study using schizophrenic patients did take some steps in that direction with positive results.

Pending such a comprehensive study, the evidence linking Rorschach M responses to motor inhibition or delaying capacity and to measures of imaginativeness seems moderately convincing. Is there any systematic theoretical position that bears on this linkage of perception of motion, delaying ability, and imagination or acceptance of inner life? An examination of a number of strains of thought from the period of the turn of the century does indeed suggest that there was a kind of *zeitgeist* which pervaded the thought of persons otherwise as different as Dewey, Freud, Washburn, and Holt, concerning the inverse relationship between thought and action (Singer, 1955). Perhaps the most elaborated statement of a position came from Freud, however, since it was more clearly an integral part of a general theory of thought and action.

THE PSYCHOANALYTIC THEORY OF THOUGHT AND DELAYED GRATIFICATION

Freud's linkage of imagination with deferred gratification and motor control grew out of his attempt to explain the relationship between the illogicality and drive-subordinated thought of the dream with its condensation and displacement and the organized processes of mature thought in which relationships to primitive drives were less obvious or almost absent.

As elaborated by Rapaport (1951), Freud hypothesized that the transition from primary to secondary process thought, or, in effect, from an id-dominated psychic topography to one in which the ego could be differentiated, came through the medium of the hallucinatory imagery of the child. A hungry child, in the absence of immediate gratification or the presence of Mama, automatically hallucinates the image of the bottle or of his mother, since what is wished for occurs at once in primary process thought. The occurrence of the image has a temporarily satisfying value, however, and gradually the child learns that he need not thrash around or spill over into violent crying or fruitless motor activity, but that thinking about the gratification is at least releasing enough so that he can stall until mother's appearance.

In terms of energy concepts, then, Freud postulated that thought and fantasy discharged small quantities of energy and permitted delay and experimental action in this fashion. This partially drive-reducing character of thought decreased the pressure on the child and opened the way for planning, organization of behavior, and the synthetic and defensive capacities which were conceptualized as the ego.

Neither Freud nor Rapaport has dealt in detail with the manner in which the hallucinated image occurs in the first place nor with the way in which the "hallucination" is internalized as daydreaming or fantasy thought. One might speculate that Werner's sensory-tonic theory may serve as a link—the checked motor impulses of the child making him more susceptible to motion in the environment, or lacking that, to the re-creation of movement through memory of the previously satisfying movements associated with gratification. Another important link in psychoanalytic theory has been the role of identification with the mother in internalization of thought. Indeed, if the mother is reasonably regular and affectionate in providing gratification, one might guess that in her absence the child might be more likely to attempt to imitate her movements or to reconstruct her image. The implication growing from this notion is that an early experience with a benign, consistent figure, who provides affection or nurturance, is a crucial element in the degree to which the child can internalize fantasy and use it at least to some extent as a means of reducing drive during an enforced delay.

After so long a detour let us return now to the relationship between the psychoanalytic theory and the empirical findings with the M response of the Rorschach. It seems likely that the Freudian conception of an association between delay and thought or imaginative development can serve as a theoretical basis for comprehending the Rorschach findings about motor inhibition, perception of humans in motion, and imagination (Singer, 1955; 1960). Even the notion of the relationship between identification with the mother and fantasy has been supported in relation to Rorschach M responses (Singer & Sugarman, 1955; Singer & Opler, 1956; Shatin, 1953). Sharaf (1959) found that young men who report a close, confidante relationship with their mothers are also more inclined toward introspection or imaginative thought. The findings using questionnaire measures on the relationships between maternal identification and frequency of reported daydreaming (Singer & McCraven, 1961; 1962; Singer & Schonbar, 1961) are also in accord with the concept, although they did not specifically involve the M response.

If we examine the relationship of the Rorschach M response and the psychoanalytic theory more closely, however, the connection of theory and empirical results is less clear-cut. What the Rorschach results suggest is that some long-term, crystallized cognitive style, linking controlled motility and imagination, does appear to exist, but it is less certain that the drive-reducing characteristics of thought or fantasy can be a sufficient explanation for such a crystallized pattern. The increase in M after inhibition of motion, while supportive of Werner's theory, cannot be used to support Freud's concept unless it were shown that after producing the M responses Ss were less inclined toward motility than they were prior to inhibition. Such data have not yet been reported for the Rorschach. In view of the relatively large number of studies supporting the tie between inhibition or delaying capacity, motion perception, and imagination, as well as more positive maternal identification, and the findings of Page that M and reported daydream frequency are positively associated, an intriguing avenue for further study is opened. We need more evidence that M and daydream characteristics are linked; we need to be able to specify whether it is human movement alone or all types of movement responses to the blots that are associated with fantasy, although Lerner's (1966) data emphasize Human Movement. Recall that the Singer and Antrobus (1963) factor analytic study found two poles of a general day-dreaming factor at the second order level, one personally oriented, one impersonal. Roe (1952) in her studies of scientists found that physicists, undeniably persons with considerable inner living, also showed more abstract movement responses, while psychologists showed more human movement. This apparent parallel with the Singer and Antrobus results is intriguing but no systematic link has yet been formed. Indeed, Schechter, Schmeidler, and Staal (1965) found that art students recalled more dreams and showed more "imaginativeness" in their dreams than did students of science. The possibility exists that other explanations, such as the linkage of verbal habit patterns to motor activity, can more succinctly explain the findings for the Rorschach M than the drive theory of Freud. A great deal clearly remains to be done.

THE THEMATIC APPERCEPTION TEST AND THE STUDY OF IMAGINATION

In the realm of the projective techniques, the TAT is the great companion of the Rorschach in clinical usage. The associations or stories produced to ambiguous pictures or related techniques essentially involving storytelling have proved invaluable tools for clinical practice and, indeed, even more for research, particularly with emphasis upon the motive patterns of the respondent. Our concern here is with what the TAT can tell us about the dimension of imagination. Most of the workers with the TAT have assumed that the stories told to pictures are relatively accurate reflections of ongoing or unconscious fantasies. TAT's have been scored in three ways that appear relevant to tapping the *degree* or *pattern of imagination* rather than its *content*. Originally, Morgan and Murray indicated that need *introception* could be scored from among the themas of a protocol. A recent use of this has been by Sharaf (1959), who related introception to maternal identification in young college men. Tomkins has extended this technique in his clinical scoring scheme by paying careful attention to the frequency and configuration of the characters' resort to thought or action in the respondent's stories.

A third approach to studying the imaginative dimension in TAT productions involves attention to the degree to which the narrator's material transcends the stimulus characteristics of the picture or introduces dramatis personae, emotions, vividness of feeling, novel arrangements, and space-time alterations not directly derived from the pictures. Some of the work relating these transcendance measures from the TAT to the Rorschach M score hs been cited already. It seems clear that techniques of this type, whether relying on specific counts or more global ratings of "imagination in storytelling," such as those used in work with children by Singer (1961) and Singer and Streiner (1966), are useful approaches to obtaining evidence of imagination from the TAT. Indeed, an intriguing study by Pytkowicz (1963) reported evidence that persons revealing considerable predisposition to imagination on a daydream questionnaire also responded differently to an opportunity for TAT fantasy following insult than did persons low in imagination by these criteria.

In general, however, work with the TAT has been more concerned with the issue of whether material expressed therein is a direct reflection of behavioral predispositions or an alternative channel whose expression on the TAT subsequently precludes direct expression in behavior. This issue, dealt with at length elsewhere (Buss, 1961; Epstein, 1962; Singer, 1966), is not directly related to the study of the imaginative dimension. It does seem clear, however, that to the extent that material describing aggression or antisocial behavior is expressed in unqualified form in TAT content it is likely to be associated with comparable behavioral expression. Where qualification or verbal elaboration and conflict are involved in the fantasy production, the likelihood is that such aggression will not be expressed in direct action. This finding suggests that the more elaborated TAT response pattern represents some aspect of an elaborated imagination or a whole series of differentiated cognitive structures or verbal discriminations, which, in effect, lead to a more subtle analysis of a given situation and hence to less direct "primitive" action.

Work such as that of Epley and Ricks (1963) has carried the relation of Thematic Apperception content to imagination further by delineating important differences in reliance on prospective and retrospective time span. These results open the way for further studies of the distinction between future-oriented rehearsal fantasies, more obviously adaptive, and reveries which recreate past events.

WHAT THE RESULTS OF PROJECTIVES
TELL ABOUT IMAGINATION

What do the many clinical and research findings with the Rorschach and TAT tell us about man's imaginative realm? Perhaps most exciting is the recurrent evidence that important stylistic differences do exist in the general tendency to produce varied and flexible imagery and that these differences are also associated with special patterns of overt motor and interpersonal behavior. The fairly sizable body of data from studies with the M response, for example, suggests that the tendency to report percents of humans in action on inkblots is linked to a number of other measures suggesting imagination, such as greater richness of storytelling, reported acceptance of inner thoughts, adaptation through fantasy under conditions of sensory deprivation, greater interpersonal awareness, planfulness, self-reports of frequent daydreaming, generally greater associational fluency during psychotherapy, and, in the case of schizophrenic adults, emphasis on elaborated paranoid delusion rather than somatic preoccupation in the pattern of symptomatology.

At the opposite pole, ample data from both Rorschach and TAT measures of imagination suggest that absence of elaborated fantasy responses are often associated with tendencies toward impulsive or often antisocial and aggressive action, less capacity to defer gratification, more direct expression of emotion, greater use of motor gesturing or physical movements during adaptive behavior, etc. If we add to the Rorschach M or TAT transcendence score additional data based on scoring systems which are somewhat broader, e.g., Holt and Havel's Primary-Secondary Process Scoring (1960), the genetic scoring scheme based on Werner's work, Klein, Gardner, and Schlesinger's (1962) Tolerance for Unrealistic Experiences, Levine and Spivack's (1965) Rorschach Index of Repressive Style, results generally extend the above instances. This is not surprising, since most of these other measures place considerable weight on well-delineated Human Movement responses as components of scoring, or apply criteria to Rorschach blots similar to those used in scoring imagination in TAT stories, e.g., transcendence of the concrete stimulus properties of the blots with the constraint that some control, e.g., "adaptive regression," be involved.

Let us take a closer look at one of these systems and what more it tells us about imagination. Levine and Spivack (1965), in their *Rorschach Index of Repressive Style*, have carefully standardized a system for scoring Rorschach protocols according to the language used. They use Specificity, Elaboration, Impulse Responses, Primary Process Thinking, Self-References, Movement, and Organization to build up a score which should measure freedom from repressive tendencies. They have obtained satisfactory scorer and retest reliabilities, which suggests that they are dealing with a reasonably consistent response-style. The Rorschach M response scored either from the original blots or by the scoring system in the newer Holtzman inkblots was most highly correlated of all scores with RIRS. Levine and Spivack found evidence that Ss in the interesting Holt and Goldberger (1960) sensory-deprivation studies who produced considerable imagery, but were coping adaptively with the situation of deprivation, were those with highest RIRS scores, i.e., least repression. Similarly, greater spontaneous imagery was associated with high RIRS. "The more an S responded to the Rorschach situation with rich and full ideation the more able he was to accept the sensory isolation situation ..." (Levine & Spivack, 1965, p. 92). Similarly, there were indications that RIRS was somewhat associated with Field Independence in Witkin's experimental situation, with sharpening tendency rather than leveling in the scoring system of Gardner and co-workers (1959). Striking differences in the patterns of fantasy and obsessional rumination also emerged for normal and neurotic individuals who differed in the RIRS, corresponding in general to the difference in degree of elaboration of imagination. The authors write,

> The high RIRS [subject] will act but his action is more likely to be a deliberate, a focused and a partial response, rather than a diffuse, impulsive, unthinking reflex-like response. It is more likely that interposed between stimulus and response are a chain of thoughts, or means-end considerations" [Levine & Spivack, 1965, p. 145].

Considerable support for this position also emerged in another study by these authors (Spivack & Levine, 1964) comparing middle-class adolescents who differed in the degree of antisocial "acting-out" behavior they manifested.

In summary, then, the projective test results suggest that there does indeed exist a dimension of imagination or a capacity or skill in producing spontaneous cognitive responses, images, plans, verbal elaborations, or internal monologues. While this may be an adaptive capacity in many instances, it need not be sufficient to avoid pathology, since within pathological individuals this capacity may merely lead to different symptomatology. The evidence from the projectives leads us inescapably to the conclusion that some characteristic such as introversion, in the sense used by Rorschach, is a major feature of the taxonomy of personality. In this respect, therefore, the projective test data are similar to those reported from factor analyses of questionnaire data, except that the behavioral referents of the projective material seem more extensive than those from most questionnaire studies of introversion–extroversion (Carrigan, 1960). Differences in activity preferences along motor and ideational lines (Stein & Craik, 1965) or in patterns of curiosity along personal or interpersonal lines (Singer & Antrobus, 1963; Schonbar, 1965) may also represent comparable manifestations of an important stylistic component of personality related to the type of material elicited from projectives.

BEYOND THE PROJECTIVE TECHNIQUES

A closer scrutiny of the subject of the nature of man's imagination and of individual differences in the realm of fantasy style leaves one wondering what more projective techniques can offer. Some of the questions one can raise about the nature of man's inner stream of thought seems to call for a far more direct approach than what the projectives can provide. I am not going to discuss the limitations of the Rorschach or TAT as psychometric instruments. These are well-known, and, for research purposes, newer developments such as the extensive use of well-defined ratings or scales or new standardized blots like Holtzman's make for quite satisfactory data. The issue is rather how many steps of inference are necessary to get at a phenomenon as pervasive but elusive as the stream of thought.

Consider the relation of the human movement response to fantasy. Most people report some degree of daydreaming every day, and since Galton's Inquiries into the Human Faculty and Its Development, we have been aware of striking individual differences in vividness and modality of imagery. Yet we still know little of the pattern of daydreaming, its relationship to internal or external sources of stimulation, the relationship of types of daydreaming to actual behavioral patterns, or the relationships between daydreaming or other spontaneous cognitive processes and affects or the general arousal or activation patterns of the organism. The insight of Rorschach in sensing that M of all the types of associations to inkblots was related to both Ideation and motor patterns in a specific way was remarkable.

Yet he relied only on human movement. Why should animal movement or abstract movement responses be different from human movement? Does this difference reflect a difference in interest pattern only, as Roe's data (1952) suggest? The limited number of stimuli evoking abstract movement on inkblots may make it impossible to ascertain whether such nonhuman motion perception does indeed represent an alternative form of "inner living," less personal and less psychologically oriented but of as much value for thought and planning along more objective lines. If we rely on the Rorschach or related scores and on responses to inkblots or ambiguous stimuli, we are introducing a new set of intermediary steps, the characteristics of the physical stimuli themselves, which may alter the response pattern in unknown ways.

An additional problem is raised by the heavy involvement of language in the production of Rorschach responses. Movement responses generally involve somewhat more elaboration verbally, and Levine and Spivack's work (1965) indicates that the verbal elaboration of all Rorschach responses is more significant than the movement alone. I do not wish to belabor the many technical questions that can be raised about distinctions between human and animal responses versus human and animal *movement*, as well as questions of the form-level, originality, or location of these responses and their relation to the actual ongoing experience.

SOME ALTERNATIVE APPROACHES TO STUDYING THE STREAM OF THOUGHT

A number of possibilities for more direct study of man's ongoing thought stream may be cited briefly. One way is to ask people directly to describe the frequency or vividness or content of their daydreams or other spontaneous cognitive processes. Once one has established a reasonable definition and established a suitable rapport, considerable frank material is obtainable. The use of daydreaming questionnaires has also been very effective, although care must be taken to account for the effects of response styles or acquiescence sets. Page (1957), for example, developed such a questionnaire, a listing of daydreams, with Ss subscribing to their frequency of occurrence. Only M, of all the Rorschach factors, was significantly associated with daydream frequency. A series of studies using similar daydream questionnaires and some structured interviewing (Singer & McCraven, 1961; 1962;

Singer & Schonbar, 1961; Singer & Antrobus, 1963) have also been carried out. They open up the possibility of studying personality correlates of daydream frequency, the factorial structure of a series of daydream scales in relation to cognitive variables, and sociocultural variations in content and frequency of daydreaming. I do not mean to suggest that such interview or questionnaire methods are necessarily superior to the projective approach. Questionnaires generate their own problems, despite the greater ease of statistical analysis. The whole literature on response sets begins to develop a superstructure of complex hierarchies of response-significance far removed from the original function that one sought to tap through the questions of the scale.

It would seem desirable, therefore, to view projective and more direct inquiry methods of studying man's ongoing stream of thought as alternative approaches. Future work might include both projective and questionnaire responses, so as to carry out appropriate taxonomic or classifactory analyses (if we can get past the obstacle that questionnaire responses if any type go together better than they do with a behavioral sample of projective measures). One kind of issue that has emerged from the Singer–Antrobus factor analysis is the following: There is evidence that a variety of scales defining a number of daydreaming factors correlate at the second-order level in a bipolar fashion. At one pole we have scales or tests suggesting a more "fanciful" pattern of daydreaming, with links to measures of Interpersonal Curiosity. At the other pole, there are measures of controlled, objective thought, philosophical-mindedness, and somewhat "masculine" orientation, associated also with Curiosity of an Impersonal Type. These two poles, rather resembling C. P. Snow's distinction between the two humanist-scientific cultures, are both introversive orientations, quite distinct from a rather clear-cut extroversion pattern also obtained. We need to replicate this type of finding on different samples and with a variety of types of stimulus materials. What would the Rorschach and the TAT tell us about persons who represent extremes along the dimensions I have described? It seems likely that the capacity for dwelling at length and with some positive satisfaction in an inner realm of experience may take a number of forms, all quite different in content but nevertheless involving a moderately controlled withdrawal of attention from the external stimulus sources which are ordinarily most demanding. Relationships to affective experience, such as Tomkins' distinction of left- and right-wing ideology (Tomkins, 1963), can also be explored, using both affective arousal techniques and questionnaire or TAT-type instruments. The possibilities are exciting. First, I believe we must free ourselves from too rigid a view of the projective methods. If we avoid reifying the given responses, M or C or need introception, but remain constantly aware of their operational properties, we can begin to design better integrative studies using a variety of modalities and stimulus sources.

It may be useful to contrast the approaches via projectives to some recent experimental work which suggests possibilities of more direct approaches to daydreaming and the stream of thought (Antrobus & Singer, 1964; Singer, 1966).

In one experiment, the subject is in a small dark chamber room, monitoring a flickering light. He is detecting signals, pressing a button when a light just a bit brighter than the standard illumination flashes. In one condition, he is required to free associate aloud throughout the course of an hour-and-a-half period of signal detections. White noise fed in by earphones prevents auditory feedback, making the situation more analogous to varied associative thought. A contrasting condition limits S's continuous talk to simple repetitive counting from 1 to 9 throughout the 90-minute watch. Results from two experiments indicate that varied internal cognitive activity maintains arousal during such a long repetitive task when other external stimulation is eliminated. The subjects under the counting condition tended to fall asleep at the switch. When arousal was maintained by piping in band music periodically, however, the attention to one's varied internal environment occasioned by free association led to a greater number of errors of signal detection than did the routine counting task. What these studies suggest is that a varied stream of internal associations can provide a lively environment for a person and maintain arousal with some cost in attention to a routine. The person with little variety of internal activity may become too dependent on external cares to maintain arousal, and lacking those, may drift off into sleep. Those Ss who reported that they managed to sneak some daydreaming in while counting actually showed greater accuracy in signal detection and greater arousal! Of special interest here is the fact that these Ss did provide a great deal of spontaneous material in their free associations; they kept talking on a whole variety of topics and revealed much about themselves and many personal concerns. While we did not attempt to analyze the tapes of their verbalization for content, such an analysis could be done and would, I suspect, come fairly close to the ordinary interior monologue that many people carry on in themselves when not heavily engaged in social intercourse.

Another approach, somewhat similar to the one above, requires the subject to monitor randomly presented auditory signals, again in a relatively stimulation-deprived environment. The task is a simple one—pressing a button when a tone is higher-pitched than the one preceding it, or whenever the lower of two experimental tones is presented. By increasing or decreasing the rate of signals or by increasing the demand on S for short-term memory storage, it is possible to vary the demand for attention to external channels. Ss are regularly interrupted and required to report on the degree, vividness, and content of task-irrelevant thought in the preceding brief intervals. These task-irrelevant thoughts are the subject's spontaneous cognitive processes, and they range the full spectrum of imagery and fancifulness. By frequent interruptions it has proven possible to get quite reliable evaluations of the degree of daydreaming under various conditions and to study what rate of task demand is necessary before daydream reports disappear almost completely. It turns out that there is a remarkably high degree of such spontaneous cognitive activity, even at very high rates of signal presentation. Interesting individual differences also emerge. For example, a young engineering student showed a pattern of very great control over spontaneous cognitive processes. When being paid only for correct detections, he missed no signals at high rates of presentation and had no spontaneous imagery. When no detections were required, considerable imagery emerged. On being questioned at length, he described a fantasy-life of the impersonal, controlled, objective type we had found in the Factor Analytic Studies. For example, he would plan a weekend date, but if he found himself thinking too much and too warmly about a specific girl, he would stop dating her for a while since he didn't want to get "too involved" until he finished school.

Still a third approach to studying ongoing fantasy involves the study of eye movements and EEG patterns while a person is engaging in spontaneous daydreams or in transitional stages of consciousness. Results from some of these investigations indicate that an extended conscious fantasy is accompanied by relatively little eye-movement, while the attempt at suppressing a fantasy evokes considerable eye-movement. The degree to which consistent patterns of ocular motility, the ability to entertain or suppress vivid fantasies either on demand or spontaneously, and longstanding fantasy tendencies measured by either questionnaire or projective methods are interrelated also beckons as an avenue for research. These three types of studies are cited not by any means as clinical substitutes for projective tech-

niques, but as indications that considerable opportunity for systematic study of imaginative phenomena exists outside of the realm of the
traditional projective techniques. Of special interest is the possibility
that by carefully considering the relative contributions of the various
approaches, their stimulus-evoking character, the degree to which
they make demands on internal or external responsiveness, we can
begin to tie together some of the loose ends in this field. For example,
one would expect that persons chosen because they showed numerous Rorschach M responses and high RIRS scores as well as high
transcendence or introception on the TAT should also reveal more
extensive imaginative reports in some of the kinds of experimental
situations described. We might also test the limits of these individual
differences by experimental manipulation, e.g., we might find that
high fantasy Ss stay awake longer under conditions of reduced external stimulation during a signal detection task or can, by making a
fantasy game of such a task, prolong their stay despite the routine
nature of the operations involved. Under conditions of considerable
alertness, however, low fantasy individuals might prove more effective in performing the routine signal detections or might report considerably less distraction from their own spontaneous cognitive processes. One might make a beginning at studying conditions conducive
to either increasing or suppressing fantasy capacities in persons
whose predispositions are strongly indicated by their performance on
projective or questionnaire measures of fantasy. And, indeed, we may
begin to test some of the relationships between Rorschach M, the
degree of spontaneous fantasy reports in relaxed conditions, and then
(using EEG measures) the speed of onset of imagery and dream content in the transition to sleep. The point is that we must constantly
look for the main chance, rather than reify M or Need Introception or
some category peculiar to a specific projective method and assume
that these scores *are* imagination. Let us accept the testimony of our
phenomenal experience—we do produce spontaneous images and
hold internal conversations and engage in a variety of manifestations
of an ongoing stream of thought. *That* is what we are out eventually to
study—not man's response to inkblots, pictures, or inventory statements, but the spontaneous ongoing experience. Anything we can do
to zero in on that target is worth trying. Projective techniques, systematic interviews, questionnaires, and experimental apparatus are
all means that we can and ought to use to pin down the elusive
"castles in Spain" or "images in our mind's eye," which intrigue us
while they bedevil our scientific efforts to study them.

SOME NEW DIRECTIONS IN THE RESEARCH USE OF PROJECTIVE METHODS

It should be clear to the reader from the various examples presented that what is needed is a much more flexible and *problem-centered* approach to the employment of projective techniques in formal research. Rather than ask, "What will schizophrenics and neurotics do on my new 'Draw-a-Nose test'?" the investigator ought better to consider what underlying psychological process needs measurement and then *choose or devise* his instruments accordingly. Psychologists can lead themselves into an endless morass if they devote themselves only to studying indefinitely the properties of a specific tool. To some extent this has already happened with both the Rorschach as a projective device and the MMPI as an objective test. It seems more important to decide on important human interaction issues that need to be studied and then carefully examine what measuring devices are most applicable.

An example may be drawn from research on acting-out or impulsivity in adolescents. Merely using global projective devices has not proven satisfactory in discriminating these groups. There is, however, ample evidence (Buss, 1961; Spivack & Levine, 1964) that when special instruments specifically geared to tap presumed behavioral or imaginative differences are employed, results can be quite meaningful. Indeed, as we regard the problem in this light, the gross distinction between projective and nonprojective techniques begins to blur and we are again confronted with the responsibility of thinking through a research problem in relation to what needs to be studied.

Investigators in the fields of social psychology and children's attitudes and values have shown increasing ingenuity in the development of specialized techniques, many of which could be used quite effectively in clinical situations. A modified combination of thematic technique, doll play, and role-playing was developed by Chein and Evans (1948) for tapping interracial attitudes. Subsequently, Stanton, Back, and Litwak (1956) showed that a similar approach could be employed in survey research methods to good effect. In a study of interracial attitudes of Negro and white children attending integrated and segregated schools, Singer (1966) used a modified Bogardus Social Distance Scale and a specially developed quasi-projective technique to elicit attitudes along various dimensions. A picture of a bus with alternate Negro and white children's faces peeping out was presented to fifth grade children. The pictured Negro and white

children were given names and the respondents were then presented
with a series of statements such as:

.........never likes to study.
.........likes to hit other children at the bus stop.
.........is always quiet and neat.

The respondents had merely to fill in appropriate names from those
supplied in the bus picture. It was thus possible in a fairly specific
fashion to obtain scores for assignment of various traits or behavioral
tendencies to Negro or white, boy or girl, etc., from the children's
responses to this simple technique. Yet for younger children the
purpose remains moderately disguised and involves the element of
choice so often sought in projective techniques.

There is indeed a proliferation of devices of this sort available to
the investigator who examines the research literature in a specific
field. Obviously one does not wish to abandon the advantages of more
complex personality studies. It remains a question, however, as to
whether the mere use of measuring techniques whose properties are
themselves obscure can deal with the problem of subtlety. An interesting recent development in research studies has been the examination of family interaction patterns. More and more, both clinically and in formal study, the relatedness of family members is of
significance. While it is clear that some interesting results have
emerged from use of standard projectives with family members
(Handel, 1962), it seems increasingly clear that more subtle and
specialized techniques may have special advantages in this field.
Thus, Strodtbeck's (1954) "revealed difference" technique actually
generates an interaction sequence between family members and can
lead to a host of intriguing situations, e.g., comparing parents interact-
ing with a normal and then later with a schizophrenic child, or
comparing relative degree of maternal or paternal domination in
different cultural groups. Techniques such as the "It" test or game
choices have also proved to be of considerable value in studies of sex
role preferences or sex typing in children (Kagan, 1964) and these,
too, open interesting approaches for quasi-projective devices to deal
with specific research or clinical problems. Indeed, when one considers how hard clinicians stretch to come up with a notion of sex-role
conflict from the few available bits of information usually obtainable
from a Rorschach or a TAT, the failure to employ more specific tools
of the kind increasingly available in the research literature seems
almost like sheer negligence.

The gap between clinical practice and research applications of
projective techniques remains wide indeed. To this writer the failure

of clinicians to reexamine their tools in the light of increasingly ingenious research developments of specific devices for measuring mood and affect, values, aggression, dependency, achievement, motivation, etc., represents a tragic failure in modern psychology. As society increasingly demands that the psychologist and psychiatrist attend to the largely neglected urban masses, the culturally disadvantaged, the disorganized family, psychology will have to accept the challenge of more ingenious and appropriate measurement techniques for research or practice. Perhaps then the gap will be narrowed, but it would be an embarrassment indeed for the profession if the initiative is not seized by the practitioners and investigators before such an ultimate confrontation. The number of studies employing intriguing tools for special purposes is staggering and perhaps many psychologists are put off by the immensity of the task. But useful aids are available in the form of many helpful summary articles in special areas of child, social, and clinical psychology, which point the way to the appropriate segments of the literature. The research application of the projective techniques has been an exciting and fruitful development in psychology. Psychologists should not let such ripeness wither on the vine.

REFERENCES

Antrobus, J. S., & Singer, J. L. Visual signal detection as a function of sequential variability of simultaneous speech. *J. Experim. Psychol.*, 1964, *68*, 603–610.

Atkinson, J. W. (Ed.). *Motives in Fantasy, Action and Society.* Princeton, N.J.: Van Nostrand, 1958.

Barron, F. Threshold for the perception of human movement in inkblots. *J. Consult. Psychol.*, 1955, *19*, 33–38.

Bendick, M. R., & Klopfer, W. G. The effect of sensory-deprivation and motor inhibition on Rorschach movement responses. *J. Proj. Tech.*, 1964, *28*, 261–264.

Buss, A. *The Psychology of Aggression.* New York: Wiley, 1961.

Carrigan, P. Extraversion-introversion as a dimension of personality: a reappraisal. *Psychol. Bull.*, 1960, *57*, 329–360.

Chein, I., & Evans, M. The movie study game: a projective test of interracial attitudes for use with Negro and white children. *Am. Psychol.*, 1948, *3*, 268.

Cronbach, L. J. Statistical methods applied to Rorschach scores. *Psychol. Bull.*, 1949, *46*, 393–429.

Cronbach, L. J. Assessment of individual differences. *Ann. Rev. Psychol.*, 1956, *7*, 173–196.

Dawo, D. Nachweis psychischer Veränderungen gesunder Frauen während de Menstruation mittels des Rorschach Versuches. *Rorschachiana*, 1952, 1, 238–249.

De Vos, G. A. A quantitative approach to affective symbolism in Rorschach responses. *J. Proj. Tech.*, 1952, 16, 133–150.

Eichler, R. A comparison of the Rorschach and Behn ink-blot tests. *J. Consult. Psychol.*, 1951, 15, 186–189.

Eiduson, B. T. Structural analysis of dreams: clues to perceptual style. *J. Abn. Soc. Psychol.*, 1959, 58, 335–339.

Elizur, A. Content analysis of the Rorschach with regard to anxiety and hostility. *J. Proj. Tech.*, 1949, 13, 247–284.

Epley, D., & Ricks, D. Foresight and hindsight in TAT. *J. Proj. Tech.*, 1963, 27, 51–69.

Epstein, S. The measurement of drive and conflict in humans: theory and experiment. In M. R. Jones (Ed.). *Nebraska Symposium on Motivation.* Lincoln, Nebraska: University of Nebraska Press, 1962.

Fisher, S., & Cleveland, S. E. *Body Images and Personality.* Princeton, N.J.: Van Nostrand, 1958.

Gardner, R. W., Holzman, P. S., Klein, G. S., Linton, H. B., & Spence, D. P. Cognitive control: a study of individual consistencies in cognitive behavior. *Psychol. Iss.*, 1959, 1, No. 4.

Goldberger, L., & Holt, R. R. A comparison of isolation effects and their personality correlates in two divergent samples. *WADD Technical Report*, Wright Air Development Division, Wright-Patterson Air Force Base, Ohio, March 1961.

Handel, G. A study of family and personality. Unpublished doctoral dissertation, University of Chicago, 1962.

Holt, R. R., & Goldberger, L. Research on the effects of isolation on cognitive functioning. *WADD Technical Report 60-260*, Wright Air Development Division, Wright-Patterson Air Force Base, Ohio, March 1960.

Holt, R. R., & Havel, J. Primary-secondary process scoring. In M. R. Rickers-Ovsiankina (Ed.). *Rorschach Psychology.* New York: Wiley, 1960.

Holtzman, W., Thorpe, J. W., Swartz, J. D., & Herron, W. *Inkblot Perception and Personality.* Austin, Texas: University of Texas Press, 1961.

Kagan, J. Acquisition and significance of sex-typing and sex role identity. In M. L. Hoffman & L. W. Hoffman (Eds.). *Review of Child Development Research.* New York: Russell Sage Foundation, 1964.

King, G. F. An interpersonal conception of Rorschach human movement and delusional content. *J. Proj. Tech.*, 1960, 24, 161–163.

Klein, G. S., Gardner, R. W., & Schlesinger, H. J. Tolerance for unrealistic experiences: a generality study. *Brit. J. Psychol.*, 1962, 53, 41–55.

Lane, R., & Singer, J. L. Familial attitudes on paranoid schizophrenics and normals from two socioeconomic classes. *J. Abn. Soc. Psychol.*, 1959, 58, 328–339.

Lerner, B. Rorschach movement and dreams. *J. Abn. Psychol.*, 1966, *71*, 75–86.

Levine, M., & Spivack, G. *Rorschach Index of Repressive Style*. Springfield, Ill.: Charles C. Thomas, 1965.

Loveland, N. T., & Singer, M. T. Projective test assessment of the effects of sleep deprivation. *J. Proj. Tech.*, 1959, *23*, 323–354.

Meltzoff, J., Singer, J. L., & Korchin, S. J. Motor inhibition and Rorschach movement responses: a test of sensory-tonic theory. *J. Pers.*, 1953, *21*, 400–410.

Monroe, L. J., Rechtschaffen, A., Foulkes, D., & Jensen, J. Discriminability of REM and NREM reports. *J. Pers. Soc. Psychol.*, 1965, *2*, 456–460.

Murray, H. A. The effect of fear upon estimates of the maliciousness in other personalities. *J. Soc. Psychol.*, 1933, *4*, 310–329.

Murray, H. A. Techniques for a systematic investigation of fantasy. *J. Psychol.*, 1937, *3*, 115–143.

Page, H. A. Studies in fantasy-daydreaming frequency and Rorschach scoring categories. *J. Consult. Psychol.*, 1957, *21*, 111–114.

Palmer, J. O. Rorschach's experience-balance: the concept, general population characteristics, and intellectual correlates. *J. Proj. Tech.*, 1955, *19*, 138–145.

Palmer, J. O. Attitudinal correlates of Rorschach's experience-balance. *J. Proj. Tech.*, 1956, *20*, 208–211.

Palmer, J. O. Alterations in Rorschach's experience-balance under conditions of food and sleep deprivation. *J. Proj. Tech.*, 1963, *27*, 208–213.

Pytkowicz, A. R. An experimental study of the reduction of hostility through phantasy. Unpublished doctoral dissertation, University of Washington, 1963.

Rapaport, D. *Organization and Pathology of Thought*. New York: Columbia University Press, 1951.

Roe, A. *The Making of a Scientist*. New York: Dodd, Mead, 1952.

Rorschach, H. *Psychodiagnostics*. Berne: Hans Huber, 1942.

Schechter, N., Schmeidler, G., & Staal, M. Dream reports and creative tendencies in students of the arts, sciences and engineering. *J. Consult. Psychol.*, 1965, *29*, 415–421.

Schonbar, R. Differential dream recall frequency as a component of "life style." *J. Consult. Psychol.*, 1965, *29*, 468–474.

Sharaf, M. R. An approach to the theory and measurement of introception. Unpublished doctoral dissertation, Harvard University, 1959.

Shatin, L. Rorschach adjustment and the Thematic Apperception Test. *J. Proj. Tech.*, 1953, *17*, 92–101.

Siipola, Elsa, & Taylor, Vivian. Reactions to ink blots under free and pressure conditions. *J. Pers.*, 1952, *21*, 22–47.

Singer, D. G. Interracial attitudes of Negro and white fifth grade children in segregated and unsegregated schools. Unpublished doctoral dissertation, Teachers College, Columbia University, 1966.

Singer, J. L. The Behn-Rorschach inkblots: a preliminary comparison with the original Rorschach series. *J. Proj. Tech.*, 1952, *16*, 238–245.

Singer, J. L. Projected familial attitudes as a function of socioeconomic status and psychopathology. *J. Consult. Psychol.*, 1954, *18*, 325–331.

Singer, J. L. Delayed gratification and ego-development: implications for clinical and experimental research. *J. Consult. Psychol.*, 1955, *19*, 259–266.

Singer, J. L. The experience-type: some behavioral correlates and theoretical implications. In M. R. Rickers-Ovsiankina (Ed.). *Rorschach Psychology*. New York: Wiley, 1960.

Singer, J. L. Imagination and waiting ability in young children. *J. Pers.*, 1961, *29*, 396–413.

Singer, J. L. *Daydreaming*. New York: Random House, 1966.

Singer, J. L., & Antrobus, J. S. A factor-analytic study of daydreaming and conceptually-related cognitive and personality variables. *Percept. Mot. Skills*. Monograph Supplement 3–17, 1963.

Singer, J. L., & McCraven, V. Some characteristics of adult daydreaming. *J. Psychol.*, 1961, *51*, 151–164.

Singer, J. L., & McCraven, V. Patterns of daydreaming in American subcultural groups. *Internat. J. Soc. Psychiat.*, 1962, *8*, 272–282.

Singer, J. L., Meltzoff, J., & Goldman, G. D. Rorschach movement responses following motor inhibition and hyperactivity. *J. Consult. Psychol.*, 1952, *16*, 359–364.

Singer, J. L., & Opler, M. K. Contrasting patterns of fantasy and motility in Irish and Italian schizophrenics. *J. Abn. Soc. Psychol.*, 1956, *53*, 42–47.

Singer, J. L., & Schonbar, R. Correlates of daydreaming: a dimension of self-awareness. *J. Consult. Psychol.*, 1961, *25*, 1–6.

Singer, J. L., & Streiner, B. Imaginative content in the dreams and fantasy play of blind and sighted children. *Percept. Mot. Skills*, 1966, *22*, 475–482.

Singer, J. L., & Sugarman, D. Some Thematic Apperception Test correlates of Rorschach human movement responses. *J. Consult. Psychol.*, 1955, *19*, 117–119.

Singer, J. L., Wilensky, H., & McCraven, V. Delaying capacity, fantasy, and planning ability: a factorial study of some basic ego functions. *J. Consult. Psychol.*, 1956, *20*, 375–383.

Spivack, G., & Levine, M. Self-regulation and acting-out in normal adolescents. Progress Report for National Institutes of Mental Health, Grant M-4531. Devon, Penn.: Devereux Foundation, 1964.

Stanton, H., Back, K., & Litwak, E. Role playing in survey research. *Am. J. Soc.*, 1956, *62*, 172–176.

Stein, K. B., & Craik, K. H. Relationship between motoric and ideational activity preference and time perspective in neurotics and schizophrenics. *J. Consult. Psychol.*, 1965, *26*, 460–467.

Strodtbeck, F. L. The family as a three-person group. *Am. Soc. Rev.*, 1954, *19*, 23–29.

Sundberg, N. D. The practice of psychological testing in clinical services in the United States. *Am. Psychol.*, 1961, *16*, 79–83.

Teltscher, H. O. A study of the relationship between the perception of movement on the Rorschach and motoric expression. Unpublished doctoral dissertation, Yeshiva University, 1964.

Tomkins, S. S. Left and right: a basic dimension of ideology and personality. In R. W. White (Ed.). *The Study of Lives.* New York: Atherton Press, 1963.

Werner, H. Motion and motion perception: a study on vicarious perception. *J. Psychol.*, 1945, *19*, 317–327.

Werner, H., & Wapner, S. Toward a general theory of perception. *Psychol. Rev.*, 1952, *59*, 324–333.

Zubin, J., Eron, D., & Schumer, F. *An Experimental Approach to Projective Techniques.* New York: Wiley, 1965.

Subject Index

Author Index

337